Good Housekeeping™

BEST RECIPES

2000

Good Housekeeping™

BEST RECIPES

2000

Time Inc.
HOME ENTERTAINMENT

Hearst Communications, Inc.

Good Housekeeping™ BEST RECIPES 2000

GOOD HOUSEKEEPING

Editor in Chief:	Ellen Levine
Food Director:	Susan Westmoreland
Associate Food Director:	Susan Deborah Goldsmith
Food Associates:	Lori Perlmutter, Mary Ann Svec, Lisa Troland
Nutrition Director:	Delia Hammock
Food Appliances Director:	Sharon Franke
Hearst Brand Development:	Carrie Bloom

TIME INC. HOME ENTERTAINMENT

President:	Stuart Hotchkiss
Director, Continuities and Single Sales:	David Arfine
Director, Continuities and Retention:	Michael Barrett
Director, New Products:	Alicia Longobardo
Director, Licensing:	Risa Turken
Group Product Manager:	Jennifer McLyman
Product Managers:	Roberta Harris, Carlos Jimenez, Kenneth Maehlum, Andre Okolowitz
Manager, Retail and New Markets:	Thomas Mifsud
Associate Product Managers:	Daria Raehse, Dennis Sheehan, Meredith Shelley, Bill Totten, Niki Viswanathan, Lauren Zaslansky, Cheryl Zukowski
Assistant Product Managers:	Victoria Alfonso, Jennifer Dowell, Ann Gillespie
Editorial Operations Manager:	John Calvano
Book Production Manager:	Jessica McGrath
Assistant Book Production Manager:	Jonathan Polsky
Book Production Coordinator:	Kristen Lizzi
Fulfillment Manager:	Richard Perez
Financial Director:	Tricia Griffin
Financial Manager:	Robert Dente
Assistant Financial Manager:	Stephen Sandonato

GOOD HOUSEKEEPING BEST RECIPES 2000
Produced by Rebus, Inc.
New York, NY

First Edition
Printed in the United States of America
ISBN# 0-883013-81-X
ISSN# 1096-2697

We welcome your comments and suggestions about Good Housekeeping Books.
Please write us at: Good Housekeeping Books, Attention: Book Editors, P.O. Box 11016. Des Moines, IA 50336-1016

If you would like to order any of our Hard Cover Collector Edition books, please call us at 1-800-327-6388
(Monday through Friday, 7 a.m.–8 p.m. or Saturday, 7 a.m. Central Time).

Contents

Welcome TO GOOD HOUSEKEEPING'S newest edition of *Best Recipes*, our annual anthology of great cooking. With so much hoopla surrounding the dawn of the new century, it's reassuring to turn our attention to the timeless topic of good food. And the twelve months' worth of recipes collected here encompass both a healthy helping of the past and an intriguing taste of things to come. Hungry for traditional home cooking? Serve up Country Hash or Turkey Gumbo, Classic Lasagna with Meat Sauce or Stuffed Cabbage. Stir sweet memories with old-fashioned desserts like Lazy-Daisy Cake, Hermit Bars, and Down-Home Peach Ice Cream. If it's something new and novel you crave, try Mushroom-Barley Miso Soup, Moroccan-Style Steaks, Baby Broccoli with Garlic, or Lemongrass Tabbouleh. Our Ice-Cream Pyramid, Cappuccino Cream with Warm Chocolate Sauce, or Lemon-Thyme Sorbet are suitably innovative desserts.

True to *Good Housekeeping* tradition, we've kept a close eye on noteworthy products and foods, tasting and testing to help you select the best. This time around, our News & Notes chapter features a lightning-quick electric kettle, a super-powerful blender, and an ingenious poultry baster that practically skims the fat for you. We've comparison-tested gas grills, knives, baking pans, mandolines (food-slicing gadgets)—even cooking spoons. We also bring you delectable data on old-fashioned peaches, farm-raised game, and the many forms of ginger.

As always, each of our recipes is triple-tested. And complementing the recipes are sidebars spotlighting, among other things, the subtleties of savory Japanese miso, the benefits of beta carotene, the varieties of vanilla extract, and the fun of baking your own fortune cookies. Whatever your cookie-fortune foretells, you can depend on *Best Recipes 2000* to keep your meals bright and inviting throughout the year.

A SALTSHAKER THAT SPRINKLES AND POURS

Sometimes you'd like just a dash of salt on a baked potato; other times, you want a teaspoonful to season a pot of soup. Now you can always get what you want with one convenient new tool—the OXO saltshaker (pictured below, left). Turn the dial on top

to choose from 4 settings: light sprinkle, heavy sprinkle, pour, or closed, which prevents spills and keeps salt clean and dry. Also available: a companion pepper mill (above, right) that's simple to fill and has a window so you can see how many peppercorns are left inside. It evenly dispenses pepper as fine as dust or coarse and cracked. Look for this salt-and-pepper pair where kitchenware is sold, or call 800-545-4411 for a store near you.

ODE TO AN OLD-TIME PEACH

The ultimate peach is soft, amber-gold, sweet, juicy, and most likely a Sun Crest. Third-generation Del Rey, CA, farmer David Mas Masumoto writes about this exquisite variety in *Epitaph for a Peach: Four Seasons on My Family Farm* (HarperSan-Francisco). His father first planted 15 acres of Sun Crests more than 20 years ago, when they were considered marketable. But now grocery chains want firm, bright-red fruit that has a long shelf life and is hardy enough to ship long distances. Although the Sun Crests that Masumoto and a handful of other farmers grow don't meet these criteria, the beauties are worth tracking down if you live in central California or the Bay Area. They taste like a little bit of heaven. Otherwise, talk to local farmers to find out where you can get heirloom peaches for your family's fruit bowl.

A HEALTH FOOD TURNS DANGEROUS

You may want to think twice before adding alfalfa sprouts to a salad or sandwich. Since 1995, they've been linked to outbreaks of food-borne disease caused by salmonella and potentially deadly

Escherichia coli O157:H7; symptoms range from vomiting to fever, cramping, and diarrhea. Incidents have been traced to sprouts that may have been contaminated by dirty water, improperly composted manure, or even bird and rodent droppings. The moderate temperatures and high moisture needed to germinate alfalfa seeds also allow rapid bacterial growth. Refrigeration will limit it but won't kill existing pathogens. And a thorough rinse won't remove germs in seed crevices. Sprout growers are working on ways to keep seeds clean (such as chemical treatment, irradiation, or pasteurization). But for now, the FDA does caution that children, the elderly, and people with weakened immune systems should pass on raw alfalfa sprouts. Stick to varieties that taste good cooked (such as white mung bean sprouts).

LOSE THE FAT

Traditional basters don't give you a chance to let the fat float to the top; they start dripping almost as soon as you fill them up. But the Artex Dripless Baster (pictured at right) holds steady until the juices separate, so you get a lighter drizzle for the bird. At specialty stores, or call 800-521-0505.

continued on page 10

New Kitchen Helpers From a recent crop of cooking tools, the GH Institute experts singled out 4 that really measure up.

RUSSELL HOBBS MILLENNIUM ELECTRIC KETTLE: Does the 2 minutes it takes to boil water in the microwave seem like an eternity when you want tea? To the rescue: This kettle brings a cup to a boil in under a minute. An entire pot (about 1¾ quarts) boils in just 6 minutes as opposed to 10 on the stove. There are windows on both sides, so you can easily tell how much water is inside. The kettle itself is cordless (it sits on a plug-in base), so you can carry it to the table. And no need to worry that it will boil dry—it shuts off once the water is piping hot. Take advantage of the kettle's speed for preparing couscous, instant soups, and oatmeal. 800-669-7434

REVEL WET 'N DRY GRINDER: A coffee grinder is the best tool for pulverizing coffee beans and dried spices. But most aren't immersible, so they can't be washed thoroughly. With this one, you don't run the risk of having your morning brew taste like the cumin seeds you ground up the night before, because the bowl comes off for cleaning in the dishwasher. It's handy for grinding small amounts of onion, garlic, and fresh herbs as well. 888-MY-REVEL (888-697-3835)

KRUPS POWER EXTREME PREMIUM BLENDER: This blender combines top performance with innovative features and doesn't make a racket. It has a base that sits sturdily without "walking," touch-pad controls, and a large-capacity (50-ounce) glass jar. It pulses automatically when it chops, to cut up—not mash—as evenly as a food processor. To clean, fill halfway with warm water and a drop of dishwashing liquid, blend, remove from base, and rinse. Also available in white. 800-526-5377

T-FAL MULTI-GRILL EXCELIO INDOOR BBQ & GRIDDLE: Yes, you can barbecue indoors. This countertop model sears steaks with deep-brown, picture-perfect grill marks and delivers the flavor of backyard cooking. And unlike outdoor grills, this one keeps smoke and spatter to a minimum because fats drip into a water-filled tray. Another plus: It comes with a griddle to replace the grill surface for cooking pancakes, eggs, or French toast. Both surfaces are easy to care for—they have nonstick coatings and are dishwasher safe. 800-395-8325

continued from page 8

SPICE THINGS UP.

To get the freshest flavor from dried spices and herbs, grind them as you need them. The Gemco Spice Grinder Set (pictured below) includes 3 small glass jars and a top with a ceramic grinding mechanism that also fits onto McCormick spice containers. Turn the container upside down and you can quickly grind whole dried sage leaves right into your turkey stuffing, or sprinkle a bit of bay leaf into holiday soups and stews instead of using a whole one and fishing it out later. This is a real convenience for aromatic spices like cumin and cardamom that you'd put in a coffee grinder otherwise. At mass-merchandise and specialty stores, or call 800-735-4362.

KEEP FOODS HOT THROUGH DINNER

Nobody wants a second helping of candied yams if they're cold. Pyrex Bake and Serve Warmables from Corning Consumer Prod-ucts (pictured above) keep dishes toasty with a microwavable hot pack that slips between the 13" by 9" glass baking dish and a sturdy wood serving basket. There's a plastic lid, too, for storing leftovers in the fridge. At department stores, or call 800-999-3436.

3-INGREDIENT MEALS

If you don't count the bare basics (like grilled cheese sandwiches or burgers on buns with ketchup), there isn't much you can make for dinner with just 3 ingredients. But award-winning chef Rozanne Gold has whittled down her lists to just that for every dish and dessert in her new book—and that includes entrées and sides for holidays. Her 3 big tips for simple cooking from the *Recipes 1-2-3 Menu Cookbook* (Little, Brown & Company):

• Reduce sauces, juices, or stocks until most of the water evaporates and you're left with a fragrant essence. For Almond Water Ice with Fresh Cherry Salad, for instance, Gold heats plump cherries to make a sweet syrup to drizzle over the ice.
• Use richly seasoned ingredients. Case in point: Smoky Pink Beans and Rice, which calls for hickory-smoked bacon. Or Chocolate Biscotti Terrine, made with anisette toasts.

• Select only high-quality groceries at the peak of freshness: no "over-the-hill or inferior" cheese for Gold's Gorgonzola-Grappa Rib Steak; only sweet, yielding cantaloupe for Tequila Melon.

CUT ABOVE: TOOLS THAT LET YOU SLICE LIKE A PRO

The fish in your favorite bistro comes wrapped in translucent slices of potato; the golden-brown tart shell is lined with slivers of a Granny Smith apple. How does the chef make such slender cuts? The secret is a mandoline, a hand-operated machine that comes with various blades that can be adjusted for thin to thick slicing. It can make julienne strips, french fries, even delicate waffled rounds for potato chips. Once you get the knack of using a mandoline (it is an art you have to learn), you can cut faster and more precisely than with a food processor or knife. The best mandolines are pricey, but if you're serious about how a dish looks, this once-in-a-lifetime purchase is worthwhile.

The GH Institute's Food Appliance testers sliced potatoes, carrots, cucumbers, lemons, and other foods on 4 models. Here's what we found:

• The German-made V-Slicer Mandoline from Boerner (pictured opposite page, left) slices and juliennes but only in 2 thicknesses. We found it worked well for cutting the 5 pounds of cucumbers in our Simple Cucumber Salad for a Crowd (page 156) and like the way the safety holder provides a good grip.

• The top performer (and the one our *Good Housekeeping* dining-room chef uses): The handsome French stainless-steel Bron Mandoline (opposite page, right), which cut the thinnest, most perfect slices, and can make rippled carrots or waffled potato chips. All the blades are stored in the instrument, so there are no small attachments to lose track of.

• A close second: The Matfer Mandolin (below, left), which is also made in France and has a fiberglass frame and stainless-steel blade. Although it doesn't cut quite as precisely as the Bron, it's easier to adjust, comes with a helpful video, and can be popped in the dishwasher. It, too, can produce ripple or waffle chips.

• The Japanese Joyce Chen Asian Mandoline Plus from Benriner (below, right), a plastic box topped with a lid that contains the stainless-steel blade, is the neatest to use. As you work, slices fall into the box. You can count

on it for paper-thin slices but not waffles or fries. The finger guard offers less protection than the expensive models so it needs to be handled with extra care. For the store nearest you, call 800-333-0208.

Although the Bron, Joyce Chen, and V-Slicer models need to be hand-washed, they rinse off easily. Just beware of the sharp blades.

STEAM ROOM: BEST NEW RICE COOKER
If your family eats a lot of rice—and you can spare the counter space—a rice cooker may be a good investment. But don't say we didn't warn you: We tried out 9 electric rice cookers and found that they are slow (you need about 45 minutes for long-grain white rice instead of 20 on the stovetop) and aren't failproof. Some batches came out mushy, others undercooked. One standout: The Krups OptiSteam (pictured above) steamed up to 6 cups of rice to fluffy perfection every time. Its oblong shape is versatile enough to hold asparagus spears, corn on the cob, a whole fish, or cut-up vegetables. The cook-and-serve bowl is dishwasher-safe. At department stores. For information, call 800-526-5377.

TEA TIME: SIP TO YOUR HEALTH
Not since pre-Revolutionary Boston has America seen such a tea party: The amount of money we spend on tea has more than doubled since 1990. Could it be that the grandé-double-decaf-skim-latté coffee culture is finally getting on everybody's nerves? Or is it the mounting evidence showing that tea is steeped in health benefits? Here's what's new, what's true—and what's just hype.

• What's the difference between black, green, and herbal teas? Strictly speaking, the only true teas are those derived from the plant *camellia sinensis*: black (such as English Breakfast and Earl Grey), green, and a less-common brew called oolong. Black tea—the choice of 94 percent of American tea drinkers—is air-cured before it's heated, giving it a different tint and flavor than green tea. And, herbal teas aren't really teas at all—they're made from a different class of edible plants.

• Which brew is healthiest? Both black and green teas contain high levels of antioxidants, substances that many scientists believe prevent or delay damage to your body's cells and tissues. In fact, these teas pack in more antioxidants than most vegetables, according to a study conducted by the government's Human Nutrition Research Center on Aging. Two cups contain about the same amount of antioxidants as a full serving of fruits or vegetables. Research has also linked black tea to lowered cholesterol levels and a reduced risk of urinary and digestive-tract cancers for older women; green tea

continued on page 14

Kitchen Knives

You're in the store, confronted with a wall of knives—everything from tiny 3-inch parers to 10-piece sets that go for hundreds of dollars. How many do you need? Does it matter which you choose? It does. With a great knife in hand, you'll realize how easy food preparation can be. And you can manage with just one: an all-purpose 8-inch chef's model. The workhorse of the kitchen, a *chef's knife* has a wide blade—designed for slicing, chopping, and mincing—that's rounded so that you can use a rocking motion for chopping. The tip of the blade is thin and flexible enough to work around bones; the hefty rear of the blade (the heel) can chop through a chicken back. Even the flat of the blade is useful—for crushing garlic or pounding cutlets. Chef's knives come with blades measuring from 6 to 12 inches long. An 8-inch size is ideal for home use, as it can chop a bunch of parsley or slice through a large roast without feeling unwieldy.

The best knives are high-carbon stainless steel—so they're easy to sharpen and clean—and are either forged from molded and hammered steel or stamped, which means they're cut out of a sheet of metal. Forged knives, heavier and more expensive (ranging from $75 to $100) than stamped ones ($40 to $50), have a bolster or shoulder between the handle and the blade, which makes them feel easier to control. It's how the knife rests in your hand that's most important: The handle should be easy to grasp and seem in balance with the blade. Though you want to avoid an uncomfortably heavy knife, some weight is necessary for chopping, crushing, and pounding, so don't choose one that's excessively light. Trust your first instincts on whether the knife "works" for you: Our testers returned to their initial favorites at the final count.

ASK THE EXPERT

Q I cook a lot. What other knives do you recommend?
A We'd pass on a paring knife and choose the 1½-inch-longer utility knife (1) that's small enough to peel fruit, but handy for cutting cheese or mincing garlic. A serrated bread knife (3) is the best way to slice a loaf because it cuts through the crust without crushing the inside. It slices tomatoes easily too. You need a boning knife (2) only if you often butcher large cuts of meat or

whole poultry, or fillet fish. For smaller items, like a chicken breast, use your utility knife or the tip of your chef's knife. When it's time to slice the turkey, a carving knife (4) is the best tool.
Q Is it true that serrated knives never need to be sharpened? Do you recommend them?
A Yes, and we suggest them if you don't want to sharpen knives. Serrated blades don't slice as smoothly as fine-edge blades, but cut better than dull ones. We tested ten 8-inch serrated chef's knives and 2 stood out: Classic Chef from Chicago Cutlery and EverSharp from J. A. Henckels International.
Q How do I keep my knife sharp?
A Nothing's more important than keeping your knife sharp. How does the blade become dull? Every time you use your knife, a microscopic portion of the edge is bent. By passing it over a sharpening steel before each use, you unbend the edge and won't need to sharpen (actually grind away metal) more than once a year. Pull your knife

lightly across the steel at a 20-degree angle, covering the entire blade and alternating sides. When your knife no longer feels sharp after "steeling," bring it to a professional sharpener. Your butcher can recommend one. If you don't steel your knife, it will dull quickly. You can use just about any sharpening tool, except for the sharpeners on electric can openers (which get so hot, they can detemper and ruin the blade). Chef'sChoice sharpeners hold your knife at the proper angle to create a new edge; ($20–30 for manual; $60–130 for electric).
Q Can I put knives in the dishwasher?
A Though knives won't be destroyed by cleaning them in the dishwasher, it's not a good practice. As they rattle around, they can nick dishes, glasses, and the plastic racks, and can become dull from contact with these surfaces. Plastic handles may be discolored by detergents; wooden ones are damaged by soaking.

BEST ALL-AROUND
WÜSTHOF-TRIDENT OF AMERICA CLASSIC SERIES
All but a lone tester ranked this among their top 3 choices. Moderately heavy, it "feels just right in the hand" and was deemed "perfect" at performing task after task, from cutting ribbons of basil to cubing beef for stew. Phone: 800-289-9878

BANTAMWEIGHT WINNER
LAMSON & GOODNOW LAMSONSHARP
The lightest of all the forged knives (7 ounces), this is the one for cooks who want the control of a fully forged knife but feel more comfortable with a lighter weight. Has an attractive rosewood handle. Phone: 800-872-6564

COMFORTABLE GRIP
EDGECRAFT CHEF'SCHOICE
With its contoured plastic handle, this knife was singled out for comfort, providing a good grip even when wet. Thanks to its weight (almost 10 ounces) and a slightly longer blade, the knife made quick work of mincing parsley. And it was sharp enough to cut paper-thin slices of tomato. Phone: 800-342-3255

TEST-KITCHEN FAVORITE
FRIEDR. DICK TRADITIONAL SERIES
Judged the "must buy" by our recipe testers, who put all the knives to heavy use and found this one stayed sharp longest. It cut acorn squash "like butter"; the long blade chops more food at once. Phone: 800-554-3425 Note: Also sold as Calphalon Professional Cutlery by Internet at http://www.calphalon.com.

Seven that made the final cut in our tests

HIGH-TECH HANDLE
ZWILLING J. A. HENCKELS FIVE STAR $106
Features an ergonomic plastic handle that most of our testers loved although a few felt it was too thick. But everyone found its blade supersharp from the tip to the heel. It minced garlic in seconds, sliced flank steak extrathin for stir-fries, and cut green onion clean through. Phone: 914-749-3425

HEAVY WEIGHT CHAMP
CHICAGO CUTLERY LEGACY FORGED
Razor-sharp and heaviest of all our contenders, at 10½ ounces (average weight is 8 ounces), it was equally great at mincing herbs and slicing hard vegetables, where weight is an asset. But some testers found it too hefty, noting that it squished rather than cleanly sliced ripe tomatoes. Its laminated wood handle is thick and durable—good for those with larger hands. Phone: 800-545-4411

BUDGET CHOICE
CHICAGO CUTLERY THE WALNUT TRADITION
The only one of our picks that's stamped out of a sheet of steel. Testers were surprised it did an excellent job, in spite of its light weight (only 5¾ ounces). They rated the blade extremely sharp, and the walnut handle felt secure when gripped. Phone: 800-545-4411

continued from page 11
may help prevent skin cancer. Scientists are so optimistic about tea's healthful properties that the M.D. Anderson Cancer Center in Houston and Memorial Sloan-Kettering Cancer Center in New York City are currently studying green-tea extract for its possible use in treatment.

Herbal teas don't contain the same cocktail of antioxidants, so their benefits aren't nearly as significant. But they may remedy some problems: Chamomile, lavender, or lemon-balm tea, for instance, can help you fall asleep, while mint teas may ease nasal congestion, according to James A. Duke, Ph.D., author of *The Green Pharmacy*.

THE PERFECTLY RIPE PEAR

Pears are one of the few fruits that don't ripen well on the tree. Picked, packed, shipped, and stored in a hard yet mature state, they soften from the inside out and can spoil very quickly if left at room temperature for too long.

• To get your money's worth, let fruit stand in a cool place for a few days or up to a week. This allows for the changes in sugar and juice content that signal ripening. (To speed things up, keep pears out of direct sunlight in a loosely closed paper bag; they will absorb the natural ethylene gas that ripening fruit produces. Putting a ripe banana in the bag with them steps things up even more.)

• Don't count on color changes alone to tell if a pear is ripe. A good rule of thumb is to gently press the stem end. If the flesh yields slightly, the fruit is ready to eat. (At this point, you can refrigerate pears for several days.)

• Pear Profile: A typical 6-ounce pear has 100 calories, 1 g protein, 25 g carbohydrate, 1 g fat, 0 mg sodium, 210 mg potassium, and 4 g fiber—that's about as much fiber as in 2 slices of whole wheat bread.

THE FAT AND SKINNY ON ORANGE JUICE

Ever wonder why something as basic as OJ can have a different calorie count from brand to brand? "The values on the Nutrition Facts label are really just an average," according to Bill Widmer, Ph.D., research scientist at the Florida Department of Citrus, which oversees the state's orange-juice producers. "The exact numbers vary, depending on the type of oranges or even the season." And values from 100 to 120 calories per 8 ounces may simply reflect the different methods used by juice producers to determine calorie content.

According to U.S. Department of Agriculture data, fresh orange juice averages 111 calories per cup—but many companies do their own analyses, which may push the count up or down a bit. Federal regulations require that the number be rounded off to the nearest ten-calorie increment, so 114 calories would read 110 calories on the label, and 116 calories would turn up as 120, although the difference is insignificant. Beyond that, the Food and Drug Administration (FDA) allows a 20 percent margin of error, so even a claim of 100 calories when the juice actually has 120 would not be considered mislabeling. The key factor for nutritional payoff is that you reach for 100 percent pure juice (fresh squeezed or from concentrate) without words like drink, beverage, or cocktail tagged on to the name—which mean the OJ has been diluted with water and/or sweetened.

PAN HANDLING

Does pan type affect a bar cookie's crumb and texture?
To find out, we took on the sweet task of baking batch after batch of brownies and blondies, plus lemon bars and shortbread, in 4 different 13" by 9" pans. We left each in the oven for the shortest time suggested in the recipes, then cooled, cut, and sampled the bars.

It turns out that pan choice made a big difference.

• The popular Ekco Baker's Secret steel nonstick pan gave us a batch that was cakey in the center, and dry around the pan edges. Our quick fix for softer squares: Reduce baking time by 5 minutes.

• WearEver CushionAire insulated aluminum pan took longer to bake our bars; we had to leave them in the oven for 5 extra minutes. The goodies also didn't brown as much—but were evenly cooked across the board. This is your choice if you want look-alike pieces but won't miss a moist middle and crusty corners.

• Our third contestant, a Pyrex glass baking dish from Corning, produced squares that were extracrisp on the bottom—a plus for lemon bars and other 2-layer cookies with a separate crust, but not our top choice for brownies.

• The blue-ribbon winner was a Nordic Ware shiny aluminum one (pictured above), the kind we've sworn by for years in our GH kitchens, passed the test with a perfect score. Bars consistently baked up moist in the center of the pan and cakelike at the edges. The pan comes with a handy blue snap-on metal cover for storage or traveling, and can do double duty for lasagna, macaroni and cheese, or baked chicken that you need to tote to a party. Note: Bar cookies should stay fresh (uncut) in this pan with the lid on for up to 3 days

RIPE & READY

Have an urge to bake banana bread but the supermarket has only young, green bunches? Or do your bananas turn black before you can eat them? Stores and catalogs sell hooks and hangers designed to let the fruit ripen without bruising. Dole and Chiquita recommend placing green bananas in a brown paper bag and adding an apple, which releases ethylene gas, to speed things up. But we wanted to see for ourselves what works best, so our Food Appliances Department tested 6 ripening methods, using tough green bananas.

We put 1 bunch each on a freestanding banana hanger; on a plastic hook under a cabinet; in a brown bag with an apple and without an apple; in a dome-covered large clear plastic bowl with breathing holes; and in the likely choice of most American families, a bowl on the counter. Results? After 3½ days, all the skins were yellow with green tinges near the stems—but the fruit was still not ready for baking. (Our cake and baked dessert recipes call for ripe bananas. Unripened ones are harder to mash and don't taste as sweet.) By the fifth day, all samples except those on the hanger were fully ripened. The bananas hanging under a cabinet were brown on the back, where they were near the wall. The bunch in the special plastic ripening bowl was no riper than the others but got moldy around the stems.

So an ordinary bowl on the counter is still top banana. But if you use only 1 piece of fruit a day and want to extend the life of the whole bunch, get a hanger. The lightweight plastic Natures Way Banana Keeper (pictured below) is $3.99 in supermarket produce sections and housewares stores.

THE POWER OF POTASSIUM

A banana gives you more than great taste: For a measly 100 fat-free calories, a medium banana (4 ounces without the peel) delivers about 450 milligrams (mg) of potassium. And according to the National Heart, Lung, and Blood Institute of the National Institutes of Health, a high intake of this mineral may stave off high blood pressure and improve blood pressure control in people who already have hypertension. Other foods that pack a hefty dose of potassium: cantaloupe (1 cup cubes, 494 mg), tomato juice (1 cup, 521 mg), potatoes (1 medium, 592 mg), yogurt (1 cup, 582 mg), and prune juice (1 cup, 707 mg). Scientists are still trying to determine exactly how the miner-
continued on page 18

Gas Grills

Ready to fire up the barbecue? Nowadays, grill lovers are choosing gas over charcoal because it opens up the possibilities for outdoor cooking. When we looked at 18 new models, priced from $159 to $2,900, we found features like rotisseries (for roasting meat) and extra burners (to heat up side dishes). Grills have become bigger, too, accommodating everything from at least 12 burgers to large pizzas to turkeys. (Consult our "burger count" to gauge the cooking-surface area of each pick.)

Though grills are getting easier to use, they can still be difficult to assemble: Our engineers clocked an average 2½ hours per model! Most stores will do it for you for a fee of $20 to $50. Here are this season's best grills, which delivered preheat times from 6 to 16 minutes, and heated evenly over the cooking grid.

HOT STUFF

FIESTA CLASSIC 300: Want a no-frills grill? This model was the least expensive of those tested, but it provides heat high enough to sear a sirloin (over 500° F.) or low enough to roast a turkey breast (at 300° F.). Food gets its barbecue flavor from smoke rising from lava rocks that line the bottom of the grill. Over time, the rocks become greasy and cause flare-ups; you'll need to replace them at the beginning of the season. Although the housing is made of thinner cast aluminum than our other picks, it won't rust. The tank is simple to install with minimal lifting (a full fuel tank weighs up to 38 pounds!).

Assembly time: 1 hour and 20 minutes
Burger count: 12 patties
Features: Right and left burners; temperature gauge; wooden side shelves; 2 warming racks; condiment basket; towel bar

BARGAIN BBQ

SUNBEAM GRILLMASTER 550EPB (pictured above): If you're cooking for a crowd, this big grill is a good buy—it even has a nifty side burner for extras like sauerkraut or a pot of barbecue sauce. Ceramic briquettes impart great barbecue flavor, but because they line the entire bottom of the grill, the grease

doesn't drip down; as a result, there are a lot of flare-ups. Another minus: It's hard to hook up the gas tank on this model, which can be annoying when you need to refuel.

Assembly time: 2½ hours
Burger count: 15 patties
Features: Right and left burners; temperature gauge; covered side burner; plastic side shelf; 2 warming racks; condiment basket

FIERY!

CHAR-BROIL PRECISION FLAME 4638975: This grill heats up to over 700° F.—a plus for cooking T-bones—and its wide grate bars produce picture-perfect grill marks. For flavor, it uses a layer of ceramic briquettes, and it's easy to start up because of its battery-operated electronic ignition. There's a built-in burner on the back for a rotisserie, but you'll pay extra ($30) for a motor and spit—worth the premium, because it turns out delectable chickens. We found it especially easy to position and remove the gas tank, tucked into one side of the front panel.

Assembly time: 3½ hours
Burger count: 18 patties
Features: Front and back burners; temperature gauge; side burner; plastic side shelf; warming rack; condiment basket

QUICK ON THE DRAW

KENMORE PRECISION FLAME 15697: If you like to grill at a moment's notice, this model heats up in only 6 minutes—faster than any of our other picks. Ceramic briquettes around the burner deliver barbecue taste. The warming racks allow plenty of room to heat up extras like garlic bread and baked potatoes, but they sit low, so it's hard to flip a steak underneath them. You can install the tank—or remove it for refueling—in a snap.

Assembly time: 3 hours
Burger count: 18 patties
Features: Front and back burners; electronic ignition; temperature gauge; side burner; plastic side shelf; 2 warming racks; condiment basket; utensil hooks

SMALL BUT MIGHTY

WEBER SPIRIT 500: Like all Weber grills, this model offers sturdy construction, top-notch cooking performance, and user-friendly features (pull-out drip pan, cooking chart, and fuel gauge). And because it's more compact, it's more affordable than other Webers, which run from $479 to $3,300. It heats very evenly and doesn't get superhot, so it browns without charring—depend on it for chicken with a crispy, golden skin and a juicy interior. Another plus: Instead of lava rocks or briquettes, it uses triangular bars, so grease runs off them into a drip pan for easy cleanup. The tank isn't difficult to install, but it requires a bit of lifting.

Assembly time: 1 hour (many parts come partially assembled, so the grill is simple to fit together)
Burger count: 15 patties
Features: Front and back stainless-steel burners; fuel gauge; thermometer that measures temperature of grill and/or food; side shelf with plastic insert that comes off for cleaning; warming rack; available in red or black; recipe booklet with detailed grilling instructions

CHEF'S SPECIAL

SUNBEAM GRILLMASTER 850CPB9: This is a large, well-made grill with a huge cooking area. Grates are porcelain-coated cast iron, so they're good for searing (but won't rust), and the peaked bars don't absorb grease, which greatly reduces flare-ups. With 3 burners, you can roast a turkey breast by placing it on the center of the grate and heating just the side burners. The warming racks are large and high enough to make it easy to flip food on the main grill. The tank is a cinch to hook up—just place it in the stand.

Assembly time: 4 hours
Burger count: 28 patties
Features: Right, center, and left stainless-steel burners; temperature gauge; covered side burner; flip-down plastic side shelf with utensil hooks and cup holder; 2 warming racks

TRENDSETTER

KENMORE DIAMOND FLAME 15780: If you're into the latest look, you'll love the stainless-steel hood. Using briquettes and an aluminum lining that reflects the heat, this grill imparts a smoky flavor to everything from fish to veggies. Cast-iron grates brown foods quickly, but after washing, they need to be dried and oiled to prevent rusting. We loved how the spacious warming rack is positioned out of the way. It takes some maneuvering to position the tank.

Assembly time: 1 hour and 50 minutes
Burger count: 18 patties
Features: Right and left stainless-steel burners; temperature gauge; 2 cast-aluminum side shelves; warming rack; towel bar and utensil hooks

Status Symbol BBQs

We looked at the Weber Summit 425LP, $2,900 (below), to see what you get for megabucks. The key difference is the heavy all-stainless-steel construction of the trim, burners, and grates, which will last a lifetime. But even with extras like a smoker basket (you'll never buy smoked turkey again) and a brand-new cookbook, *Weber's Art of the Grill*, the price is astronomical. (At least, the cost includes assembly.)

Two well-built grills with stainless-steel burners that won't set you back quite as much: The Broilmaster P3CP, $1,120, has a cast-aluminum base, a stainless-steel cart, porcelain-coated cast-iron grids, 1 fold-down front shelf, 2 side shelves, and a foldaway warming rack. For information, call 800-255-0403. The Napoleon Prestige 450RB ($1,005) has 4 burners, stainless-steel grates, 2 side shelves with removable Corian inserts, a warming rack, and a rotisserie. Questions? Call 888-726-2220.

HERE'S A LIST OF FEATURES TO CHECK FOR BEFORE YOU BUY:

✔ **Examine the tank.** Every time you grill, you need to turn the tank on and off, so be sure you can reach the valve and see the open/close arrow easily—attributes of all of our picks.

✔ **Weigh the pros and cons of a side burner.** If you'll be using your grill far away from the kitchen, a side burner is handy. But it may not be able to bear the weight of a huge pot of corn—and it jacks up the price. Plus, unless the burner is covered, you sacrifice work space on the side.

✔ **Don't be wowed by Btus.** The British thermal unit rating is an indication of the amount of heat a burner emits. Though more Btus should generate higher temperatures, size and design also affect how hot a grill gets. We looked at cheaper models with Btu ratings as high as 45,000, but that didn't grill as well as ones with lower ratings.

✔ **Reach under the racks.** We love the convenience of warming racks, but be sure they don't hang too low and/or extend too far over the cooking surface, making it awkward to slide your spatula under them to flip the burgers.

✔ **Ask about the burners.** Do they power the left and right sides or the front and back? When you need to use only half the grill, the left or right side is less awkward to use than the front or back.

✔ **Inspect the wheels.** Models with casters on 1 side and 2 wheels on the other are easier to maneuver. Hard rubber wheels are the most durable.

✔ **Don't run out of gas.** Purchase a Gas Level Indicator ($7), a magnetized card that sticks onto the bottom half of your tank and shows a color change when gas runs low. For information, call 888-257-2464. To estimate how much gas is left, use a bathroom scale to weigh the tank. An empty one weighs about 18 pounds; a full tank, about 38.

continued from page 15
al helps regulate blood pressure, but while research continues, why not go bananas now?

THE DATING GAME: WHAT FOOD EXPIRATION STAMPS MEAN

It's not always easy to know if a packaged food is fresh. The Federal government requires that baby-formula cans be stamped with an expiration date, but all other freshness regulations are established by individual states. Although more than 20 stipulate that at least some products be dated, manufacturers aren't always consistent. Still, time lines can be helpful—if you know how to interpret them:

• A "sell by" date is a marker for stores, so they know how long to keep a product on the shelf. If the food is handled properly, you should be able to eat it several days or even weeks later. (Eggs can generally be used three to five weeks past the date you purchase them.)

• "Best if used by," on staples like cereal, refers to the period in which a product is at its peak. It doesn't relate to food safety and isn't a mandate to throw something away.

• A "use by" date is a sterner warning that applies to perishable items; you'll often see it on fresh meat and poultry. Toss any such food once its time has passed. Groceries with "use or freeze by" guidelines can be frozen indefinitely, although obviously they may dry out after a while and develop off flavors.

Regardless of dates, what matters most is careful handling: Always cook and store foods properly.

SOME LIKE IT HOT

If you entertain a lot (or a little, but want everything just right), you need a warming tray for foods like scalloped potatoes, fresh-baked biscuits, and especially gravy. Besides, who wants to run back and forth to the kitchen to zap things in the microwave? The electric Maxim Warming Tray (pictured below) with black tempered-glass surface and stay-cool handles, introduced some 20 years ago, is still a great investment. It keeps foods piping hot for more than 2 hours, has 3 temperature settings (use the lowest for breads and rolls), and looks sleek and contemporary. Measuring 28½" by 11¾", it can hold a

china platter, a vegetable dish, a basket of garlic bread, and a gravy boat all at once. (A red circle marks the hottest area on the surface, good for sauces.)

LEAN MEAT FROM THE HEART OF TEXAS

Want something a little different for dinner? Something that will please the meat eaters at your table but stay within reasonable fat guidelines? Maybe it's time to dial the mother-daughter ranchers in Texas hill country who supply GoodHeart Brand Specialty Meats to restaurants nationwide.

Amalia Palmaz and her daughter, Florencia are known for their care packages of Argentine beef, venison (from their own deer farm), ostrich, quail, and delicacies like seasoned bison sausage. Most of their products are leaner and lower in saturated fat than supermarket meats, so they're heart-healthy too. So now you can splurge guiltlessly on ground ostrich burgers ($6 per pound plus shipping and handling) and venison porterhouse steaks (2 for $14), which are trimmer than their beefy counterparts but still grill up nicely. To get a copy of the company's new retail catalog, Haute @ Home Cuisine, call 888-466-3992 or visit its Web site at www.goodheart.com.

CUTTING-EDGE BAGEL SLICERS

No matter how you slice it, cutting a bagel is tricky business. You can make the job safer by trading your bread knife for a bagel slicer. Good Housekeeping Institute's Food Appliances Director, Sharon Franke, found that there's a gadget for every personality.

• The Neat Freak: Craving a perfectly halved bagel? The supersharp Bagel Biter makes the cleanest cut of the bunch. Stick the bagel in the box, and as you push down on top, the V-Shaped knife inside plunges through.

• The Faint of Heart: Your hands never come close to the blade of the Bagel Wizard, a plastic box with built-in knife. But this slicer is no wizard at cutting. You have to wiggle the blade through the bagel by lowering the side handles.

• The Decorator: The attractive wooden Bagel Holder from Mountain Woods holds your bagel snugly, but you still have to wield a knife and keep the holder steady.

• The Minimalist: The Bagel Halves—a small blade encased by plastic "arms"—fits in a drawer. It's clumsier than a knife, but safer.

• The Traditionalists: If only a knife will do for you, protect your bagel-holding hand with the cut-resistant K-Steel Fillet Glove.

Manual cutting is the fastest method: Lay the bagel flat, hold it down with your palm, then slice across the middle.

BLUE-RIBBON COOKING UTENSILS

In a search for the best kitchen tools, our GH equipment experts examined 27 trios (each included a slotted spoon, ladle, and spatula) to get their hands on the ones that really make cooking easy—and as mess-proof as possible. They served peas from a saucepan, ladled out vegetable soup, and flipped burgers to find their favorites. The winners:

• Chantal Kitchen Tools. New from Chantal cookware, these are durable stainless steel and made to last a lifetime. The handles rest nicely in the curve of your hand, and the spoon (pictured, left) has a beautiful classic oval shape. At $25 to $35 per tool, they're pricey but worth it. In department stores, or call 800-365-4354.

• T-Fal Traditional Tools. In black, blue, or green plastic, these beauties work wonders with traditional and non-stick cookware. The angled spatula (at left) was the clear-cut winner at turning burgers. At Kmart, or call 800-395-8325 for a store near you.

• Rubbermaid Chef utensils. They come in sturdy black or white plastic, and are safe for nonstick pots and pans as well as classic stainless steel or cast iron. Testers found the extralarge ladle (at left)—with 2 pouring spouts and a comfortable handle—perfectly angled for dishing out soup. These helpers are at mass-merchandise stores and supermarkets. For information, call 800-643-3490.

IN PRAISE OF HERBS

Who better to salute parsley, sage, rosemary, and thyme than Monique Jamet Hooker, the French-born chef and cooking teacher whose recipes are sprinkled liberally with sun-dappled greens? Hooker, who grew up with 3 brothers and 6 sisters on a farm, stresses the importance of using what's fresh in *Cooking with the Seasons: A Year in My Kitchen* (Henry Holt and Company), coauthored with Tracie Richardson.

As a girl in Brittany, Hooker acquired her love of produce plucked straight from the garden. You can't go wrong with her Herb Ravioli with Shrimp and Fennel, and Sweet Corn Soup with Dill. Basil is at the top of her list: "August's vegetable garden wouldn't be complete without it," she says. "Basil enhances the flavors of all vine vegetables." She freezes it, dries it, and steeps it in vinegar. For more seasonal ideas, check out her Web site at www.floatpoint.com/food.

ALL ABOUT GINGER

Ginger adds inimitable zest and flavor to everything from salads to deep, dark gingerbread. The knobby, gnarled, and fibrous spice grows in Jamaica (the United States imports most of its supply from there), Africa, Australia, and China, and has been integral to Indian, Pakistani, and South Asian cooking for centuries. A look at the common forms, and how to use them:

• Crystallized ginger: Also known as candied ginger, this is cooked in a sweet syrup, then tossed with coarse sugar to coat. It is generally nibbled on as a confection or added to desserts from biscotti to crème brûlée. For a summer splurge, stir it into homemade (or store-bought) vanilla or peach ice cream.

• Ground ginger: This has a completely different flavor from fresh ginger—it's not as heady and strong—and is not meant to be used as a substitute. It's good for gingerbread, spice cakes, and that cookie-jar staple, gingersnaps.

• Pickled ginger: Thin slices of ginger are cured in a salt, vinegar, and sugar solution and served as a tangy garnish for Asian dishes. When young pink ginger is pickled, it is known as *gari*, the popular sushi condiment.

• Preserved ginger: Cooked and packed in a heavy sugar syrup, this delicacy can be used in baking and is delectable spooned over cool honeydew or cantaloupe wedges or watermelon chunks.

• Traditional (mature) ginger: This is the kind sold most often in produce aisles; perfect for grating or pickling, it has smooth skin that is tan to light brown, flesh that is ivory to pale gold, a crunchy texture, and pungent scent. If ginger looks wrinkled, skip it; that's a tip-off that it's old and dried out.

To store fresh ginger: Wrap, unpeeled, first in a paper towel, then tightly in plastic wrap. It will keep in the refrigera-tor up to 2 weeks. Or peel and slice or cut into chunks, and preserve in a jar of dry sherry or mirin (Japanese rice wine) in the fridge for several months.

To peel and prepare it: Use a vegetable peeler and be careful to remove only the very top layer of skin because the flesh directly beneath is the most delicate. Then, chop, slice, or shred with a sharp knife or box grater. A ginger grater (a relatively inexpensive tool) works best for fine grating because it yields plenty of juice with a minimum of fibers.

MAKE FANCY GARNISHES FAST

Decorate hors d'oeuvre trays, cheese platters, sandwich set-ups, and other party plates with pretty veggie accents. Joyce Chen's Spiral Slicer (pictured at left) turns carrots, daikon radishes, and zucchini into strands or ribbons you can mound up for a special effect. Just turn the crank and it does the job. At specialty cookware stores, or call 800-688-3003.

TAKE IT WITH YOU

A new insulated food carrier from Ovations (pictured above) by Anchor Hocking keeps food warm for up to 2 hours. The vinyl carrier has a cozy plaid fleece lining and straps for toting without spills. Designed to hold the new glass Ovations baking dishes, which have convenient plastic grips on the handles. The snap-on lids even have steam vents for microwaving. At specialty stores, or call 800-688-3003.

Appetizers &
Soups

Tomatoes, Goat Cheese & Arugula

PREP: 10 MINUTES

2 tablespoons plus ¼ teaspoon coarsely ground
  black pepper
3 logs (3.5 ounces each) goat cheese
2 tablespoons red wine vinegar
1 tablespoon extravirgin olive oil
½ teaspoon dried basil
¼ teaspoon sugar
1 bunch arugula (4 ounces) or watercress
1 recipe Home-Dried Tomatoes (below) or 24 oil-
  marinated dried tomato halves, well drained

1 Sprinkle 2 tablespoons pepper on waxed paper. Roll cheese logs in pepper; slice each into 6 pieces.

2 In bowl, with whisk or fork, mix red wine vinegar, olive oil, basil, sugar, and ¼ teaspoon pepper.

3 Arrange arugula on plates with goat cheese and dried tomatoes. Serve with red wine vinaigrette. Makes 6 first-course servings.

Each serving: About 235 calories, 10 g protein, 13 g carbohydrate, 18 g total fat (8 g saturated), 4 g fiber, 26 mg cholesterol, 390 mg sodium.

Home-Dried Tomatoes

PREP: 20 MINUTES • BAKE: 5 HOURS 30 MINUTES

12 plum tomatoes (3 pounds), peeled, each cut
  lengthwise in half, and seeded
2 tablespoons extravirgin olive oil
½ teaspoon dried basil
½ teaspoon dried thyme
½ teaspoon salt
¼ teaspoon coarsely ground black pepper

1 Preheat oven to 250°F. In large bowl, toss tomatoes with oil, basil, thyme, salt, and pepper.

2 Arrange tomatoes cut-side down on wire rack on cookie sheet. Bake tomatoes 5½ hours or until tomatoes are shriveled and partially dried. Cool complete-

ly. Store in zip-tight plastic bag in refrigerator up to 2 months or in freezer up to 6 months. Makes 24 tomato halves.

Each tomato half: About 20 calories, 0 g protein, 2 g carbohydrate, 1 g total fat (0 g saturated), o.5 g fiber, 0 g cholesterol, 540 g sodium.

Bruschetta with Tomatoes, Basil & Olives

PREP: 20 MINUTES • BROIL: 2 MINUTES

A classic Mediterranean mix of herbs, tomatoes, and olives on toasted French or Italian bread makes a nice nibble when you serve cocktails.

1 loaf (8 ounces) French or Italian bread
1 garlic clove, peeled and cut in half
8 ripe small tomatoes (about 1½ pounds)
  chopped
¼ cup Kalamata olives, pitted and chopped
¼ cup loosely packed fresh basil leaves,
  chopped
¼ cup loosely packed fresh parsley leaves,
  chopped
3 tablespoons extravirgin olive oil
¼ teaspoon salt
⅛ teaspoon coarsely ground black pepper

1 Preheat broiler. Cut off ends from loaf of bread; reserve for making bread crumbs another day. Slice loaf diagonally into ½-inch-thick slices.

2 Place bread slices in 15½" by 10½" jelly-roll pan. Place pan in broiler at closest position to source of heat, and broil bread about 1 minute on each side or until lightly toasted. Rub 1 side of each toast slice with cut sides of garlic.

3 In medium bowl, combine tomatoes with remaining ingredients. Spoon tomato mixture on top of toast slices. Serve immediately. Makes about 16 bruschetta or 8 appetizer servings.

Each bruschetta: About 70 calories, 1 g protein, 9 g carbohydrate, 4 g total fat (1 g saturated), 1 g fiber, 0 mg cholesterol, 145 mg sodium.

Tomatoes, Goat Cheese & Arugula ➤

Pimiento-Studded Deviled Eggs

PREP: 40 MINUTES

These appetizers are festive and colorful, and can easily be made the day ahead. Simply spoon the yolk mixture into the whites, or for a more formal look, use a decorating bag with a large star tube.

12 large eggs, hard-cooked and shelled
¼ cup sliced pimientos, chopped
¼ cup low-fat mayonnaise dressing
1 tablespoon plus 1 teaspoon Dijon mustard
½ teaspoon ground red pepper (cayenne)
¼ teaspoon salt

1 Slice each egg lengthwise in half. Gently remove yolks and place in small bowl; with fork, finely mash yolks. Stir in pimientos, mayonnaise dressing, mustard, ground red pepper, and salt until well mixed.

2 Place egg-white halves in 15½" by 10½" jelly-roll pan lined with paper towels (to prevent eggs from rolling). Spoon yolk mixture into egg-white halves. Cover and refrigerate until ready to serve. Makes 24 stuffed-egg halves.

Each stuffed-egg half: About 45 calories, 3 g protein, 1 g carbohydrate, 3 g total fat (1 g saturated), 0 g fiber, 106 mg cholesterol, 100 mg sodium.

Spiced Nut & Pretzel Mix

PREP: 5 MINUTES PLUS COOLING • BAKE: 30 MINUTES

Prepare this party nosh up to a week ahead and store in an airtight container. It makes a great gift, too, packed in a decorative tin or airtight jar tied with ribbon.

1 large egg white
2 tablespoons sugar
2 teaspoons ground cumin
1½ teaspoons salt
¾ teaspoon ground red pepper (cayenne)
1 pound unsalted natural almonds
½ pound unsalted cashews
1 package (9 to 10¼ ounces) pretzel sticks

1 Preheat oven to 350°F. Spray 15½" by 10½" jelly-roll pan with nonstick cooking spray.

2 In large bowl, with wire whisk or fork, beat egg white, sugar, cumin, salt, and ground red pepper. Add almonds and cashews; toss to coat with egg-white mixture.

3 Spread nut mixture in jelly-roll pan. Bake nuts 30 minutes, lifting and stirring them with a metal spatula every 5 minutes.

4 Spread hot nut mixture on large cookie sheet; place cookie sheet on wire rack to cool nuts completely. (Nuts will be crisp when cool.) When cool, toss nuts with pretzels. Store nut mixture in tightly covered container. Makes about 9 cups.

Each ¼ cup: About 145 calories, 4 g protein, 11 g carbohydrate, 10 g total fat (1 g saturated), 2 g fiber, 0 mg cholesterol, 230 mg sodium.

Shrimp & Avocado in Roasted Red-Pepper Sauce

PREP: 45 MINUTES • COOK: 20 MINUTES

Make the roasted red-pepper sauce and clean the shrimp a day ahead. Store both in separate airtight containers in the refrigerator.

3 medium red peppers
30 large shrimp (about 1½ pounds)
1½ teaspoons salt
½ cup chicken broth
3 tablespoons olive oil
1 small shallot, cut up
1 tablespoon balsamic vinegar
1 teaspoon sugar
2 ripe medium avocados, thinly sliced
2 large lemons, each cut into wedges

1 Preheat broiler. Cut each pepper lengthwise in half; discard stem and seeds. Arrange peppers, cut-side down, in 15½" by 10½" jelly-roll pan. Place jelly-roll pan in broiler at closest position to source of heat and broil peppers 15 minutes or until charred and blistered. Turn peppers and broil 5 minutes longer.

2 Meanwhile, shell and devein shrimp, leaving tail part of shell on if you like. Rinse shrimp with running cold water. In 4-quart saucepan over high heat, heat *8 cups water* to boiling. Add shrimp and 1 teaspoon salt; heat to boiling. Cook 1 to 2 minutes until shrimp turn opaque throughout. Drain shrimp well.

3 Transfer peppers to brown paper bag; fold top of bag over to seal it and let stand at room temperature 15 minutes (keeping peppers in bag to steam makes them easier to peel). Remove peppers from bag and peel off skin.

4 Place peppers in blender; add chicken broth, olive oil, shallot, vinegar, sugar, and remaining ½ teaspoon salt and blend until smooth.

5 Spoon pepper sauce onto 10 small plates. Arrange shrimp and avocado slices over sauce. Serve with lemon wedges. Makes 10 first-course servings.

Each serving: About 170 calories, 12 g protein, 6 g carbohydrate, 11 g total fat (2 g saturated), 1 g fiber, 85 mg cholesterol, 270 mg sodium.

Braised Baby Artichokes with Olives

Braised Baby Artichokes with Olives

PREP: 20 MINUTES • COOK: 15 MINUTES

Baby artichokes are not a special variety. They grow on the same plant as do regular artichokes, but lower on the stalk, where they are shielded from the sun and its growth-producing rays.

16 baby artichokes (about 2 pounds)
¼ cup olive oil
3 medium garlic cloves, sliced
½ teaspoon salt
½ teaspoon coarsely ground black pepper
⅓ cup oil-cured or Kalamata olives, pitted and
     coarsely chopped
Lemon wedges for garnish

1 Trim baby artichokes: Bend back the outer green leaves and snap them off at the base until leaves are half green (at the top) and half yellow (at the bottom). Cut off stems and across top of each artichoke at point where yellow meets green. Cut each artichoke lengthwise in half.

2 In 12-inch skillet, heat *1 inch water* to boiling over high heat. Add artichokes and cook 5 minutes; drain.

3 Dry skillet. In same skillet, heat olive oil over medium-high heat. Add garlic and cook until lightly browned. Add artichokes; brown 2 minutes. Stir in salt, pepper, and *1 cup water*; cook, covered, until artichokes are tender, about 5 minutes longer or until knife inserted in bottom of artichoke goes through easily. Stir in olives; heat through. To serve, spoon into bowl; garnish with lemon wedges. Makes 8 first-course servings.

Each serving: About 100 calories, 2 g protein, 6 g carbohydrate, 8 g total fat (1 g saturated), 2 g fiber, 0 mg cholesterol, 290 mg sodium.

Chinese Dumplings

PREP: 40 MINUTES • COOK: 10 MINUTES

FILLING:
2 cups packed, sliced Napa cabbage
½ pound ground pork
2 tablespoons soy sauce
1 tablespoon dry sherry
2 teaspoons cornstarch
1½ teaspoons minced, peeled fresh ginger
1 green onion, minced
36 (3½" by 3¼" each) wonton wrappers (about
   three-fourths 12-ounce package)
1 large egg white, beaten

SOY DIPPING SAUCE:
¼ cup soy sauce
¼ cup seasoned rice vinegar or white wine
   vinegar
2 tablespoons angel hair-thin strips fresh ginger

Green onions for garnish

1 Prepare Filling: In 2-quart saucepan, bring *1 inch water* to boiling over high heat. Add cabbage and return to boiling. Cook 1 minute; drain. Immediately run cold water over cabbage to cool. With hands, squeeze as much water out of cabbage as possible.

2 Finely chop cabbage and squeeze out excess liquid; place in medium bowl. Stir in pork, soy sauce, sherry, cornstarch, ginger, and minced green onion.

3 Arrange half of wonton wrappers on large sheet of waxed paper. With pastry brush, brush each wonton wrapper lightly with egg white. Spoon 1 rounded teaspoon filling onto center of each wonton wrapper. Bring opposite corners of wonton wrapper up over filling; pinch and pleat edges together to seal in filling. Repeat with remaining wonton wrappers, egg white, and filling.

4 In deep 12-inch skillet, heat *½ inch water* to boiling over high heat. Place all dumplings, pleated edges up, in one layer in skillet. Stir gently with spoon to prevent dumplings from sticking to bottom of skillet. Heat dumplings to boiling. Reduce heat to low; cover and simmer 5 minutes or until dumplings are cooked through.

5 Meanwhile, prepare Soy Dipping Sauce: In small serving bowl, combine soy sauce, vinegar, and ginger. Makes about ½ cup sauce.

6 With slotted spoon, remove dumplings to platter; garnish with green onions. Serve with dipping sauce. Makes 12 appetizer or 6 first-course servings.

Each appetizer serving: About 130 calories, 6 g protein, 15 g carbohydrate, 4 g total fat (2 g saturated), 1 g fiber, 16 g cholesterol, 540 g sodium.

Smoked Trout Pâté

PREP: 30 MINUTES

This tasty spread is easy to make in a food processor and can be prepared up to two days in advance. Serve with assorted crackers and cucumber slices.

3 whole smoked trout (about 1¼ pounds)
1 package (8 ounces) whipped cream cheese
¼ cup low-fat mayonnaise dressing
3 tablespoons fresh lemon juice
⅛ teaspoon coarsely ground black pepper
1 tablespoon minced chives or green onion

1 Cut head and tail from each trout; remove skin and bones and discard. In food processor with knife blade attached, blend trout, cream cheese, mayonnaise dressing, lemon juice, and black pepper until smooth.

2 Spoon trout mixture into medium bowl; stir in minced chives. Cover and refrigerate if not serving right away. Allow refrigerated pâté to stand at room temperature 15 minutes to soften before serving. Makes about 3 cups.

Each tablespoon pâté: About 30 calories, 2 g protein, 1 g carbohydrate, 2 g total fat, (1 g saturated) 0 g fiber, 7 mg cholesterol, 100 mg sodium.

◄ *Chinese Dumplings*

Green-Onion Purses with Yogurt Sauce

PREP: 20 MINUTES • COOK: 4 TO 5 MINUTES PER BATCH

Impressive, yet surprisingly easy.

2 tablespoons margarine or butter
3 bunches green onions, chopped
⅛ teaspoon coarsely ground black pepper
2½ teaspoons salt
1 container (8 ounces) plain low-fat yogurt
1 garlic clove, crushed with garlic press
1 tablespoon minced fresh mint or cilantro leaves
24 (3½" by 3¼" each) wonton wrappers (about half 12-ounce package)

1 In 12-inch skillet, melt margarine or butter over medium heat. Add green onions, pepper, and ¼ teaspoon salt. Cook green onions 8 to 10 minutes, until soft but not browned, stirring occasionally. Cool mixture 10 minutes.

2 Meanwhile, in 5-quart saucepot, heat 3 *quarts water* and 2 teaspoons salt to boiling over high heat. Prepare yogurt sauce: In small bowl, with spoon, mix yogurt, garlic, mint, and remaining ¼ teaspoon salt until blended; set aside.

3 Arrange 8 wonton wrappers on work surface. Place 1 rounded teaspoon green-onion filling in center of each wonton wrapper. Run finger, dipped in water, over edges of each wonton wrapper to moisten, rewetting finger as necessary. Diagonally fold each wonton wrapper over filling, forming a triangle. Pinch and pleat edges of dumpling to seal in filling.

4 Place dumplings on flour-dusted 15½" by 10½" jelly-roll pan. Cover dumplings with damp (not wet) paper towels to prevent drying out.

5 Repeat steps 3 and 4 to make a total of 24 dumplings. Cook dumplings, 12 at a time, in *boiling salted water*, 4 to 5 minutes, until cooked through. With slotted spoon, remove dumplings; drain (still held in slotted spoon) on paper towels. Transfer to plate. Serve with yogurt sauce. Makes 2 dozen dumplings.

Each dumpling with sauce: About 45 calories, 2 g protein, 6 g carbohydrate, 1 g total fat (0 g saturated), 1 g fiber, 1 mg cholesterol, 110 mg sodium.

Leek Consommé with Herbs

PREP: 30 MINUTES • COOK: 25 MINUTES

A simple yet elegant clear soup for a light start to the big meal.

6 medium leeks (about 2 pounds)
2 medium celery stalks
4 medium carrots
1 lemon
3 cans (14½ ounces each) chicken or vegetable broth
⅛ teaspoon coarsely ground black pepper
¼ cup loosely packed fresh parsley leaves, chopped
1 tablespoon coarsely chopped fresh dill
Lemon slices for garnish

1 Cut root ends from leeks. Cut each leek crosswise to separate green tops from white bottoms, removing any tough outer leaves. Cut green tops crosswise into 1-inch pieces; place in large bowl of cold water. Use hands to swish leeks around to remove any grit or sand; repeat process, changing water several times. Drain well and place in 4-quart saucepan. Slice leek bottoms crosswise into thin slices; rinse thoroughly as with green tops and reserve separately.

2 Cut celery and 2 carrots crosswise into 1-inch chunks; thinly slice remaining 2 carrots crosswise on the diagonal. From lemon, with vegetable peeler, remove four 3" by 1" strips of peel; squeeze 1 tablespoon juice.

3 To saucepan with leek tops, add celery and carrot chunks, 2 strips lemon peel, broth, and 3 *cups water*; heat to boiling over high heat. Reduce heat to low; cover and simmer 15 minutes.

4 Strain broth into 8-cup glass measuring cup or large bowl, pressing down on vegetables in strainer to extract as much broth as possible; discard vegetables. Return broth to saucepan.

5 Prepare consommé Add pepper, lemon juice, leek bottoms, carrot slices, and remaining lemon peel to broth in saucepan; heat to boiling over high heat.

Reduce heat to low; cover and simmer 10 minutes or just until vegetables are tender. Remove saucepan from heat; discard lemon peel. Stir in parsley and dill. Garnish each serving with a lemon slice. Makes about 10 cups or 10 first-course servings.

Each serving: About 45 calories, 3 g protein, 6 g carbohydrate, 1 g total fat (0 g saturated), 1 g fiber, 1 mg cholesterol, 405 mg sodium.

Mushroom-Barley Miso Soup

PREP: 20 MINUTES • COOK: ABOUT 1 HOUR

Simmer meaty shiitake mushrooms, creamy barley, and vegetables in a broth made with miso.

1 package (1 ounce) dried shiitake mushrooms
1 tablespoon olive oil
3 medium carrots, cut into ¼-inch dice
1 medium onion, chopped
2 garlic cloves, minced
1 tablespoon grated, peeled fresh ginger
½ cup pearl barley
½ teaspoon salt
¼ teaspoon coarsely ground black pepper
1½ pounds bok choy, trimmed and chopped
6 tablespoons dark red miso
1 tablespoon brown sugar

1 In 2-quart saucepan, heat *4 cups water* to boiling over high heat. Remove saucepan from heat; add dried shiitake mushrooms. Allow mushrooms to soak until softened, about 15 minutes. With slotted spoon, remove mushrooms from soaking liquid. Strain liquid through sieve lined with paper towel into 4-cup glass measuring cup. Add enough *water* to liquid in cup to equal 4 cups and set aside. Rinse mushrooms under cold running water to remove any sand or grit; drain on paper towels. Cut stems from mushrooms and discard. Thinly slice mushroom caps.

2 In nonstick 5-quart Dutch oven, heat oil over medium heat until hot. Add carrots, onion, and mushrooms, and cook until vegetables are tender, about 15 minutes. Add garlic and ginger, and cook 1 minute longer.

3 Add barley, salt, pepper, reserved mushroom liquid, and an additional *4 cups water*, and heat to boil-ing over medium-high heat. Reduce heat to low; cover and simmer 40 minutes or until barley is tender.

4 Add bok choy; heat to boiling over medium-high heat. Reduce heat to low and simmer, uncovered, 5 to 7 minutes longer or until bok choy wilts and is tender-crisp, stirring occasionally.

5 With ladle, remove ½ cup broth from soup to small bowl. Add miso and brown sugar to broth in bowl, and stir until smooth paste forms.

6 Remove Dutch oven from heat; stir in miso mixture. (Never boil miso—its delicate flavor and nutrients will be destroyed by high heat.) Makes about 10 cups or 6 main-dish servings.

Each serving: About 170 calories, 7 g protein, 29 g carbohydrate, 4 g total fat (0 g saturated), 7 g fiber, 0 mg cholesterol, 985 mg sodium.

MISO

Miso, the intense Japanese soybean paste that punches up soups and dressings, is coming into its own in American kitchens. A little goes a long way toward adding a wonderful depth of flavor to foods (try our Miso-Glazed Salmon, page 41, or Mushroom-Barley Miso Soup, at left).

Sold in small tubs or jars at health-food stores and Asian markets, this high-protein, peanut butterlike paste is made from cooked soybeans, salt, water, and *koji* (a mold cultivated in a barley, rice, or soybean base) and fermented for 6 months to 3 years. The type of grain base, amount of *koji*, and length of fermentation affect the color (from pale golden to dark brown) and flavor—sweet, mild, salty, earthy, or meaty. Textures range from smooth to chunky.

High heat and boiling change miso's flavor, so incorporate it into a dish near the end of the cooking process. To avoid undissolved clumps, blend a few tablespoons into hot water or broth first. After stirring the diluted miso into a soup or stew, heat just to a simmer; serve immediately.

Store miso in the refrigerator in an airtight container for up to 1 year.

Escarole & Bean Soup

PREP: 15 MINUTES • COOK: 15 MINUTES

This soup is perfect when you need to get a homey dinner on the table in a hurry. Our secret ingredient is store-bought refrigerated pesto, which adds delectable flavor. Serve the soup with freshly grated Parmesan cheese or additional pesto.

½ cup small elbow macaroni
1 can (15 to 19 ounces) white kidney beans (cannellini), rinsed and drained
2 cans (14½ ounces each) chicken broth
1 large head escarole (10 ounces), coarsely chopped
2 tablespoons prepared pesto

1 In 2-quart saucepan, prepare pasta in *boiling water* as label directs, omitting salt.

2 Meanwhile, in small bowl, mash ½ cup beans until almost smooth. In 4-quart saucepan, heat chicken broth and 3 *cups water* to boiling over high heat.

3 Drain pasta. Add pasta, mashed and whole beans, and escarole to broth mixture; heat to boiling. Reduce heat to low; simmer 5 minutes or until escarole is tender, stirring occasionally. Stir in pesto. Makes about 9 cups or 4 main-dish servings.

Each serving: About 225 calories, 13 g protein, 31 g carbohydrate, 6 g total fat (1 g saturated), 8 g fiber, 2 mg cholesterol, 960 mg sodium.

Tomato & Rice Soup

PREP: 20 MINUTES • COOK: ABOUT 50 MINUTES

Serve this old-fashioned comfort food with crusty bread and a tossed salad for a satisfying winter meal. If you can't find either Wehani (an aromatic, reddish-brown rice that splits slightly when cooked and has a chewy texture) or black Japonica (a dark rice that tastes like a cross between basmati and wild rice), you can use long-grain brown rice.

½ cup Wehani, black Japonica, or long-grain brown rice
1 tablespoon margarine or butter
1 medium onion, finely chopped
1 medium celery stalk, finely chopped
1 medium carrot, peeled and diced
1 garlic clove, crushed with garlic press
¼ teaspoon dried thyme
1 can (28 ounces) plum tomatoes in juice
1 can (14½ ounces) chicken broth
½ teaspoon salt
¼ teaspoon coarsely ground black pepper
1 bay leaf
½ cup loosely packed fresh parsley leaves, chopped

1 Prepare rice as label directs but do not add salt, margarine, or butter; set rice aside.

2 Meanwhile, in 4-quart saucepan, melt margarine or butter over medium heat. Add onion, celery, and carrot, and cook 10 minutes or until tender, stirring occasionally. Stir in garlic and thyme; cook 1 minute.

3 Add tomatoes with their juice, chicken broth, salt, pepper, bay leaf, and *1 cup water*; heat to boiling over high heat, breaking up tomatoes with side of spoon. Reduce heat to medium-low and cook, covered, 30 minutes. Discard bay leaf.

4 In blender, with center part of cover removed to allow steam to escape, blend tomato mixture in small batches until almost smooth. Pour each batch of blended soup into large bowl. Return soup to saucepan; heat over high heat until hot. Remove pan from heat; add cooked rice and chopped parsley. Makes about 7½ cups or 8 first-course or 4 main-dish servings.

Each first-course serving: About 95 calories, 3 g protein, 16 g carbohydrate, 2 g total fat (1 g saturated), 2g fiber, 0 mg cholesterol, 485 mg sodium.

Tomato & Rice Soup ➤

Russian Red-Lentil Soup

PREP: 20 MINUTES • COOK: ABOUT 1 HOUR

We adapted this recipe from Anya von Bremzen, one of the foremost authorities on Russian cooking in the United States. This sweet-and-sour soup provides you with a good supply of vitamins, protein, and fiber. Serve as a hearty main dish with crusty whole-grain bread and a crisp salad.

1 tablespoon olive oil
1 large onion, chopped
3 garlic cloves, minced
⅓ cup dried apricots, chopped
1½ cups dried red lentils
½ teaspoon ground cumin
½ teaspoon dried thyme
1 can (14½ ounces) chicken broth
1 can (14½ ounces) diced tomatoes
1 tablespoon honey
¾ teaspoon salt
½ teaspoon coarsely ground black pepper
⅓ cup fresh lemon juice
2 tablespoons chopped fresh parsley or mint leaves for garnish
1½ cups plain nonfat yogurt

1 In nonstick 5-quart Dutch oven or saucepot, heat oil over medium heat until hot. Add onion, garlic, and apricots, and cook until onion is tender, about 10 minutes, stirring often.

2 While onion mixture is cooking, rinse lentils with cold running water and discard any stones or shriveled lentils.

3 Add cumin and thyme to onion mixture; cook 1 minute longer, stirring. Add lentils, chicken broth, and 3 *cups water*; heat to boiling over medium-high heat. Reduce heat to low; cover and simmer until lentils are tender, about 30 minutes.

4 Stir in tomatoes with their juice, honey, salt, and pepper, breaking up tomatoes with spoon; heat to boiling over high heat. Reduce heat to low; simmer, uncovered, 10 minutes longer, stirring occasionally.

5 Remove 4 cups lentil mixture to large bowl; set aside. In blender at low speed, with center part of cover removed to allow steam to escape, blend remaining lentil mixture in small batches until smooth. Pour pureed lentils into bowl with reserved lentil mixture after each batch.

6 Return soup to Dutch oven; heat through over medium-high heat, stirring occasionally. Stir in lemon juice and remove from heat. Top soup with parsley and yogurt. Makes about 8 cups or 6 main-dish servings.

Each serving: About 295 calories, 17 g protein, 51 g carbohydrate, 3 g total fat (1 g saturated), 9 g fiber, 1 mg cholesterol, 665 mg sodium.

Chilled Buttermilk & Corn Soup

PREP: 20 MINUTES PLUS CHILLING

This refreshing refrigerator soup—with corn, tomatoes, cucumber, and basil—is low-fat and satisfying.

1 quart buttermilk
4 medium tomatoes, seeded and chopped (2 cups)
1 small cucumber, peeled, seeded, and chopped (1 cup)
2 cups fresh corn kernels (from 3 to 4 ears)
½ teaspoon salt
¼ teaspoon coarsely ground black pepper
12 large basil leaves
6 small basil sprigs

1 In large bowl, stir buttermilk, tomatoes, cucumber, corn, salt, and pepper. Cover and refrigerate at least 2 hours or until very cold.

2 To serve, thinly slice large basil leaves. Spoon soup into 6 soup bowls; garnish with sliced basil and small basil sprigs. Makes about 4½ cups or 6 first-course servings.

Each serving: About 135 calories, 8 g protein, 24 g carbohydrate, 2 g total fat (1 g saturated), 3 g fiber, 6 mg cholesterol, 365 mg sodium.

◀ *Chilled Buttermilk & Corn Soup*

Basic Chicken Soup

PREP: 25 MINUTES • COOK: 25 MINUTES

1 tablespoon olive oil
1 small onion, finely chopped
2 medium carrots, cut into ¼-inch-thick slices
2 medium celery stalks, cut into ¼-inch-thick slices
2 cans (14½ ounces each) chicken broth,
   skimmed of fat
⅛ teaspoon coarsely ground black pepper
10 ounces skinless, boneless chicken breast

1 In 4-quart saucepan, heat oil over medium heat. Add onion and cook until tender and lightly browned, about 5 minutes, stirring occasionally.

2 Add carrots, celery, chicken broth, pepper, and 3 *cups water*; heat to boiling over high heat. Add chicken to saucepan and reduce heat to low. Cover saucepan and simmer 8 to 10 minutes, until chicken just loses its pink color throughout and carrots and celery are tender. Remove saucepan from heat.

3 Using slotted spoon or tongs, remove chicken from saucepan to plate; cool slightly until easy to handle. With fingers, pull chicken into shreds.

4 Return chicken to soup; heat through. Makes about 8½ cups or 4 main-dish servings.

Each serving: About 150 calories, 20 g protein, 7 g carbohydrate, 4 g total fat (1 g saturated), 2 g fiber, 41 mg cholesterol, 635 mg sodium.

Chicken Noodle Soup

PREP: 25 MINUTES • COOK: 25 MINUTES

Basic Chicken Soup (above)
2 cups medium egg noodles (about 3 ounces)
1 cup frozen peas
Grated Parmesan cheese (optional)

Prepare Basic Chicken Soup as in steps 1 through 3. Meanwhile, prepare noodles in *boiling water* as label directs. Complete soup as in step 4, adding cooked noodles and peas to soup with shredded chicken. Serve with Parmesan cheese if you like. Makes about 9½ cups or 4 main-dish servings.

Each serving: About 290 calories, 26 g protein, 33 g carbohydrate, 6 g total fat (1 g saturated), 4 g fiber, 68 mg cholesterol, 675 mg sodium.

Mexican Chicken Soup

PREP: 25 MINUTES • COOK: 25 MINUTES

Basic Chicken Soup (at left)
½ lime
1 cup fresh or frozen corn kernels
½ cup loosely packed fresh cilantro leaves,
   chopped
Lime wedges, coarsely crushed tortilla chips, hot
   pepper sauce (optional)

Prepare Basic Chicken Soup as in steps 1 through 3, adding lime half to saucepan with chicken broth. Complete soup as in step 4, adding corn and cilantro to soup with shredded chicken. With slotted spoon, remove lime from soup and squeeze juice into saucepan; discard lime. Serve with lime wedges, crushed tortilla chips, and hot pepper sauce if you like. Makes about 9½ cups or 4 main-dish servings.

Each serving: About 185 calories, 22 g protein, 16 g carbohydrate, 4 g total fat (1 g saturated), 2 g fiber, 41 mg cholesterol, 640 mg sodium.

Asian Chicken Soup

PREP: 25 MINUTES • COOK: 25 MINUTES

Basic Chicken Soup (at left)
2 slices (⅛-inch-thick each) fresh ginger
½ cup regular long-grain rice
1 bunch (about 6 ounces) watercress, thick stems
   removed
2 medium green onions, sliced
1 tablespoon soy sauce
½ teaspoon Asian sesame oil

Prepare Basic Chicken Soup as in steps 1 through 3, adding ginger slices to saucepan with chicken broth. Meanwhile, prepare rice as label directs. With slotted spoon, remove ginger slices from soup and discard. Complete soup as in step 4, adding cooked rice, watercress, green onions, soy sauce, and sesame oil to soup with shredded chicken. Makes about 9½ cups or 4 main-dish servings.

Each serving: About 245 calories, 22 g protein, 26 g carbohydrate, 5 g total fat (1 g saturated), 2 g fiber, 41 mg cholesterol, 900 mg sodium.

FISH & SHELLFISH

Kedgeree

A spiced East Indian dish made with flaked smoked haddock (known as finnan haddie), hard-cooked eggs, and rice, Kedgeree makes a delicious brunch or supper main dish that can be prepared a day ahead.

1 tablespoon margarine or butter
1 small onion, finely chopped
¾ teaspoon curry powder
1½ cups long-grain white rice
1 teaspoon salt
¼ teaspoon coarsely ground black pepper
1 pound smoked haddock fillets (finnan haddie)
   or 12 ounces smoked trout fillets*
2 lemons
4 large eggs, hard-cooked and coarsely
   chopped
½ cup loosely packed fresh parsley leaves,
   chopped
½ cup half-and-half or light cream

1 In 2-quart saucepan, melt margarine or butter over medium heat. Add onion and cook until tender, about 5 minutes, stirring occasionally. Stir in curry powder, then rice; cook 1 minute. Add salt, pepper, and 3 *cups water*; heat to boiling over high heat. Reduce heat to low; cover and simmer 15 to 18 minutes, until rice is tender and water is absorbed. Transfer rice to large bowl.

2 Meanwhile, in 10-inch skillet, place smoked haddock or trout fillets with enough *water* to cover; heat to boiling over high heat. Reduce heat to low; simmer, uncovered, 5 minutes. Drain.

3 Preheat oven to 350°F. From 1 lemon, grate ½ teaspoon peel and squeeze 1 tablespoon juice; add to cooked rice, fluffing with fork. Flake haddock or trout, discarding any skin and bones. Add fish, eggs, and all but 1 tablespoon parsley to rice, toss gently.

4 Spoon rice mixture evenly into 13" by 9" glass baking dish; drizzle half-and-half evenly over top. Cover with foil and bake 15 minutes or until hot. (If making ahead and refrigerating, heat about 30 minutes or until hot.) Cut remaining lemon into 6 wedges. Spoon Kedgeree into serving bowl if you like; sprinkle with remaining 1 tablespoon parsley. Serve with lemon wedges. Makes 6 main-dish servings.

*If smoked haddock or trout fillets are unavailable, you can substitute smoked white fish.

Each serving: About 355 calories, 27 g protein, 40 g carbohydrate, 9 g total fat (3 g saturated), 1 g fiber, 206 mg cholesterol, 1010 mg sodium.

Cod with Mayo & Mustard

If you like a lot of topping, or are cooking for 8, the recipes double easily.

¼ cup light mayonnaise
½ teaspoon Dijon mustard
⅛ teaspoon salt
⅛ teaspoon coarsely ground black pepper
4 small cod steaks, ¾ inch thick (6 ounces each)

1 Preheat broiler. Lightly spray rack in broiling pan with nonstick cooking spray.

2 In small bowl, mix mayonnaise, mustard, salt, and pepper; set aside.

3 Place cod steaks on rack in broiling pan. With broiling pan at closest position to source of heat, broil cod 7 minutes. Remove pan from broiler; do not turn cod over. Spread mayonnaise mixture on top of cod. Return pan to broiler and broil cod 1 to 2 minutes longer, until mayonnaise mixture is lightly browned and bubbly and cod flakes easily when tested with a fork. Makes 4 main-dish servings.

Each serving: About 165 calories, 30 g protein, 4 g carbohydrate, 5 g total fat (2 g saturated), 0 g fiber, 73 mg cholesterol, 325 mg sodium.

Kedgeree ➤

Lime & Jalapeño Cod

If you like a lot of topping, or are cooking for 8, the recipes double easily.

Cod with Mayo & Mustard (page 36)
½ teaspoon freshly grated lime peel
1 small jalapeño chile, seeded and minced

Prepare Cod with Mayo & Mustard, but in step 2, stir lime peel and jalapeño into mayonnaise mixture. Makes 4 main-dish servings.

Each serving: About 165 calories, 30 g protein, 4 g carbohydrate, 5 g total fat (2 g saturated), 0 g fiber, 73 mg cholesterol, 325 mg sodium.

Cod with Horseradish & Dill

If you like a lot of topping, or are cooking for 8, the recipes double easily.

Cod with Mayo & Mustard (page 36)
2 tablespoons chopped fresh dill
1 teaspoon prepared white horseradish

Prepare Cod with Mayo & Mustard, but in step 2, stir dill and horseradish into mayonnaise mixture. Makes 4 main-dish servings.

Each serving: About 165 calories, 30 g protein, 4 g carbohydrate, 5 g total fat (2 g saturated), 0 g fiber, 73 mg cholesterol, 340 mg sodium.

Flounder with Asian Glaze

The zesty glaze was inspired by our good friend cookbook author Barbara Tropp, an expert in Chinese cuisine.

¼ cup light mayonnaise
1 tablespoon reduced-sodium soy sauce
2 teaspoons grated, peeled fresh ginger
1 jalapeño chile, seeded and minced
4 flounder fillets (6 ounces each)

1 Preheat broiler. Spray rack in broiling pan with nonstick cooking spray.

2 In small bowl, mix mayonnaise, soy sauce, ginger, and jalapeño.

3 Place flounder fillets, flat side down, on rack in broiling pan. Spread mayonnaise mixture on top of fillets; broil 4 minutes or until mayonnaise mixture is lightly browned and bubbly, and fish flakes easily when tested with a fork (do not turn fish over). Makes 4 main-dish servings.

Each serving: About 185 calories, 33 g protein, 5 g carbohydrate, 3 g total fat (1 g saturated), 0 g fiber, 91 mg cholesterol, 435 mg sodium.

FISHING FOR FLOUNDER

Many seafood recipes call for flounder by name—it's quick-cooking, has a light, subtle flavor, and is low in fat (try our Flounder with Asian Glaze, above). But if you can't find it, other flatfish will work equally well—especially sole, which is actually a species of flounder. (We like lemon sole and gray sole.) Turbot, red snapper, and grouper fillets can also be substituted, though their texture is firmer than flounder's and they usually cost more (up to $15 per pound compared to flounder's usual selling price of about $8 to $10 per pound).

Teriyaki Salmon Burgers

PREP: 15 MINUTES • COOK: 10 MINUTES

5 sesame-seed hamburger buns
1 salmon fillet (1 pound), skin removed*
2 tablespoons teriyaki sauce
2 medium green onions, chopped
1½ teaspoons grated, peeled fresh ginger

1 Coarsely grate 1 hamburger bun to make bread crumbs. Measure ⅓ cup bread crumbs; set aside. Reserve remaining crumbs to coat patties.

2 With tweezers, remove any bones from salmon. Finely chop salmon and place in medium bowl. Add teriyaki sauce, green onions, ginger, and reserved ⅓ cup bread crumbs.

3 On waxed paper, shape salmon mixture into four 3-inch round patties. Coat patties with remaining bread crumbs.

4 In nonstick 10-inch skillet, cook patties 10 minutes over medium heat, turning once, until golden and cooked through. Serve patties on hamburger buns.

*If you don't want to buy fresh salmon, substitute 14¾-ounce can of salmon, drained, and add 1 large egg to mixture. Makes 4 main-dish servings.

Each serving: About 280 calories, 20 g protein, 23 g carbohydrate, 11 g total fat (2 g saturated), 1 g fiber, 47 mg cholesterol, 565 mg sodium.

Lemon-Caper Salmon

PREP: 10 MINUTES • COOK: 10 MINUTES

Swirl the lemony sauce right in the skillet—natural juices from the fish will add a delectable richness. Serve with steamed asparagus spears and buttered red potatoes.

4 pieces salmon fillet (6 ounces each)
¼ teaspoon salt
⅛ teaspoon coarsely ground black pepper
2 lemons
4 teaspoons capers, drained
2 garlic cloves, crushed with garlic press
⅓ cup chicken broth

1 Heat nonstick 12-inch skillet over medium-high heat until hot. Add salmon fillets to skillet; sprinkle with salt and pepper. Cook salmon 10 minutes or until fish flakes easily when tested with fork, turning once halfway through cooking. Transfer salmon to platter; keep warm.

2 Meanwhile, from 1 lemon, grate ½ teaspoon peel and squeeze 1 tablespoon juice. Slice remaining lemon for garnish; set aside.

3 Reduce heat to medium; add capers to skillet and cook 1 minute, stirring. Add garlic and cook 30 seconds longer. Add broth, lemon peel, and lemon juice, and heat through, stirring occasionally.

4 To serve, spoon sauce over salmon and garnish with lemon slices. Makes 4 main-dish servings.

Each serving: About 315 calories, 34 g protein, 1 g carbohydrate, 19 g total fat (4 g saturated), 0 g fiber, 101 mg cholesterol, 405 mg sodium.

Toasted-Sesame Salmon

PREP: 10 MINUTES • COOK: 8 TO 10 MINUTES

1 egg white
3 tablespoons sesame seeds, lightly toasted
½ teaspoon salt
¼ teaspoon coarsely ground black pepper
4 pieces center-cut salmon fillet with skin (4 ounces each)
Lemon slices (optional)

1 In small bowl, lightly beat egg white with *1 tablespoon water*. On waxed paper, mix sesame seeds, salt, and pepper. Dip flesh side of each piece of salmon fillet in egg-white mixture, then dip same side in sesame-seed mixture to coat.

2 Heat nonstick 10-inch skillet over medium-high heat until hot. Add salmon fillets, sesame-seed side down, and cook 3 minutes. With metal spatula, turn salmon over and cook 5 to 7 minutes longer, until fish flakes easily when tested with a fork. Serve salmon with lemon slices if you like. Makes 4 main-dish servings.

Each serving: About 225 calories, 22 g protein, 2 g carbohydrate, 14 g total fat (3 g saturated), 1 g fiber, 59 mg cholesterol, 365 mg sodium.

Grilled Tuna with Tuscan White Beans

PREP: 35 MINUTES • GRILL/BROIL: 3 TO 4 MINUTES

Serve tuna slices on a bed of warm cannellini beans seasoned with lemon, garlic, and sage. With 2 cans of beans, a pound of tuna stretches nicely to 6 servings.

1 lemon
1 tablespoon plus 3 teaspoons extravirgin olive oil
1 medium onion, chopped
1 medium celery stalk, finely chopped
2 garlic cloves, crushed with garlic press
1 tablespoon fresh sage leaves (about 6 large), thinly sliced
2 cans (15 to 19 ounces each) white kidney beans (cannellini), rinsed and drained
1 teaspoon salt
½ teaspoon coarsely ground black pepper
1 tuna steak, 1 inch thick (1 pound), cut into ½-inch-thick slices
2 medium plum tomatoes, cut into ¼-inch dice
1 tablespoon chopped fresh parsley leaves for garnish

1 Grate ½ teaspoon peel and squeeze 2 tablespoons juice from lemon.

2 In 3-quart saucepan, heat 1 tablespoon plus 1 teaspoon oil over medium heat. Add onion and celery, and cook about 12 minutes or until tender, stirring occasionally. Add garlic, sage, and lemon peel, and cook 1 minute, stirring. Add beans, lemon juice, ½ teaspoon salt, and ¼ teaspoon pepper, and cook 2 minutes or until heated through, stirring gently.

3 Meanwhile, brush both sides of tuna with remaining 2 teaspoons oil and sprinkle with remaining ½ teaspoon salt and ¼ teaspoon pepper.

4 Heat grill pan over medium-high heat until hot. Add tuna and cook 3 to 4 minutes, until it just loses its pink color throughout, turning once. (Or, preheat broiler. Place tuna on rack in broiling pan; with pan at closest position to source of heat, broil tuna 3 to 4 minutes.)

5 Place warm bean mixture on platter and top with tuna. Sprinkle with diced tomatoes and chopped parsley. Makes 6 main-dish servings.

Each serving: About 275 calories, 27 g protein, 30 g carbohydrate, 6 g total fat (1 g saturated), 10 g fiber, 33 mg cholesterol, 745 mg sodium.

Miso-Glazed Salmon

PREP: 10 MINUTES • BROIL: ABOUT 10 MINUTES

Brian Hagiwara, one of *Good Housekeeping*'s favorite food photographers, shared this special recipe. We love the taste of the rich salmon with the sweet and savory glaze. Serve with a side of steamed aromatic rice.

¼ cup white miso
5 teaspoons sugar
4 teaspoons seasoned rice vinegar
2 teaspoons minced, peeled fresh ginger
4 salmon steaks, 1 inch thick (6 ounces each)
1 green onion, thinly sliced diagonally

1 Preheat broiler. Lightly spray rack in broiling pan with nonstick cooking spray.

2 In small bowl, mix miso, sugar, vinegar, ginger, and *1 tablespoon water*; set aside.

3 Place salmon steaks on rack in broiling pan. With broiling pan at closest position to source of heat, broil salmon 5 minutes. Remove pan from broiler and spread half of miso mixture on salmon; broil 1 minute longer.

4 Remove pan from broiler; turn salmon over and top with remaining miso mixture. Broil salmon 3 to 4 minutes longer, until miso mixture is bubbly and salmon flakes easily when tested with a fork. Sprinkle with green onion before serving. Makes 4 main-dish servings.

Each serving: About 260 calories, 35 g protein, 13 g carbohydrate, 7 g total fat (1 g saturated), 1 g fiber, 86 mg cholesterol, 870 mg sodium.

◄ *Miso-Glazed Salmon*

Homemade Sushi

PREP: 1½ HOURS PLUS CHILLING • COOK: 25 MINUTES

All of our suggestions for homemade sushi use cooked fish, such as shrimp or smoked salmon, and/or vegetables. You can make the sushi rolls up to 6 hours before serving.

FILLINGS:
4 ounces cooked, shelled, and deveined shrimp, thinly sliced lengthwise
4 ounces imitation crab sticks (surimi), cut lengthwise into pencil-thin sticks
4 ounces thinly sliced smoked salmon
1 ripe medium avocado, cut lengthwise in half, then thinly sliced lengthwise
1 medium carrot, cut crosswise in half, then lengthwise into pencil-thin sticks
1 small cucumber, cut lengthwise into matchsticks

GARNISHES:
Black sesame seeds
White sesame seeds, toasted
Minced chives

ACCOMPANIMENTS:
Pickled ginger
Soy sauce
Wasabi (Japanese horseradish)

SUSHI RICE:
2 cups Japanese short-grain rice
2 tablespoons sugar

1 teaspoon salt
½ cup seasoned rice vinegar
1 package (ten 8" by 7" sheets) roasted seaweed for sushi (nori)

1 Assemble Fillings: Place each Filling in a small bowl. Cover bowls with plastic wrap and place in 15½" by 10½" jelly-roll pan for easy handling. Refrigerate Fillings until ready to use.

2 Assemble Garnishes and Accompaniments: Place each Garnish in a small bowl. Place each Accompaniment in a small serving dish; cover. If not serving right away, refrigerate pickled ginger and wasabi.

3 Prepare Sushi Rice: In 3-quart saucepan, heat rice, sugar, salt, and 2½ cups water to boiling over high heat. Reduce heat to low; cover and simmer 25 minutes or until rice is tender and liquid is absorbed (rice will be sticky). Remove saucepan from heat; stir in vinegar. Cover and keep warm.

4 Make sushi rolls: Place 12-inch-long piece of plastic wrap on work surface. Place small bowl of water within reach of work area; it's easiest to handle sticky sushi rice with damp hands.

5 Place 1 nori sheet, shiny (smooth) side down, with a short side facing you, on plastic wrap; top with generous ½ cup Sushi Rice. With small metal spatula and damp hands, spread and pat rice down to make an even layer over nori, leaving ¼-inch border all around sheet. (To make an inside-out roll, flip rice-covered nori sheet over so that nori is on top.)

6 On top of rice (or nori), starting about 2 inches away from side facing you (see photo at left), arrange desired fillings crosswise in 1½-inch-wide strip.

7 Using end of plastic wrap closest to you, lift edge of sushi, then firmly roll, jelly-roll fashion, away from you. Seal end of nori with water-dampened finger. (If making inside-out roll, coat outside of roll with 1 of the Garnishes.) Place sushi roll on tray or platter.

8 Repeat steps 5 through 7 to make 10 sushi rolls in all, changing plastic wrap when necessary. Cover and refrigerate sushi rolls 30 minutes or up to 6 hours.

9 To serve, with serrated knife, slice off and discard ends from each roll. Slice each roll crosswise into ten ½-inch-thick slices. Arrange sliced rolls on platter. Serve with Accompaniments. Makes about 100 pieces.

Each piece: About 25 calories, 1 g protein, 4 g carbohydrate, 0 g total fat, 0 g fiber, 3 mg cholesterol, 70 mg sodium.

Use plastic wrap to lift edge of rice-topped nori and firmly roll up away from you.

Homemade Sushi ▶

Tuna-Melt Casserole

If you enjoy diner tuna-melt sandwiches, you'll love the flavor of this!

1 package (16 ounces) corkscrew or medium
  shell pasta
Salt
3 cups broccoli flowerets
2 tablespoons margarine or butter
2 tablespoons all-purpose flour
¼ teaspoon coarsely ground black pepper
4 cups reduced-fat (2%) milk
4 ounces Swiss cheese, shredded (1 cup)
1 can (12 ounces) chunk light tuna in water,
  drained and flaked
2 medium tomatoes, cut into ¼-inch-thick slices

1 Preheat oven to 400°F. In large saucepot, cook pasta in *boiling salted water* 5 minutes; add broccoli to pasta and cook another 5 minutes or until broccoli is tender and pasta is al dente. Drain well and return to saucepot; set aside.

2 Meanwhile, in 3-quart saucepan, melt margarine or butter over low heat. Stir in flour, ¾ teaspoon salt, and pepper until blended and cook, stirring, 1 minute. Gradually stir in milk; increase heat to medium-high and cook, stirring occasionally, until mix-ture thickens and boils. Boil 1 minute, stirring fre-quently. Remove saucepan from heat and stir in ½ cup cheese until blended.

3 Add cheese sauce and tuna to pasta and broccoli in saucepot; toss until evenly mixed. Transfer mixture to shallow 3½-quart casserole or 13" by 9" glass baking dish. Arrange tomato slices on top, overlapping if nec-essary. Sprinkle with remaining ½ cup cheese.

4 Cover baking dish with foil and bake 20 minutes or until hot and bubbly. Makes 6 main-dish servings.

Each serving: About 570 calories, 39 g protein, 71 g carbohydrate, 14 g total fat (6 g saturated), 5 g fiber, 29 mg cholesterol, 755 mg sodium.

Seafood-Stuffed Shells

30 jumbo pasta shells
Salt
1 tablespoon olive oil
1 small onion, chopped
2 garlic cloves, minced
1 bottle (8 ounces) clam juice
1 can (28 ounces) whole tomatoes in puree
2 tablespoons tomato paste
1 teaspoon sugar
¼ teaspoon crushed red pepper
⅓ cup heavy or whipping cream
1 pound medium shrimp, shelled, deveined, and
  coarsely chopped
1 pound scrod fillet, coarsely chopped
1 package (10 ounces) frozen peas

BREAD-CRUMB TOPPING:
1 tablespoon olive oil
1 garlic clove, crushed with side of chef's knife
2 slices firm white bread, torn into ¼-inch pieces

1 Prepare pasta shells in *boiling salted water* as label directs. Drain shells and rinse with cold running water to stop cooking; drain again. Arrange shells in single layer on waxed paper and set aside.

2 Meanwhile, in 4-quart saucepan, heat olive oil over medium heat until hot. Add onion and cook until tender, about 5 minutes. Add garlic and cook 1 minute longer, stirring frequently. Add clam juice and cook 7 minutes over high heat until reduced to ½ cup. Stir in tomatoes with their puree, breaking up tomatoes with side of spoon. Add tomato paste, sugar,

Seafood-Stuffed Shells

and crushed red pepper; heat to boiling. Reduce heat to low; partially cover and simmer about 20 minutes, stirring occasionally. Stir in cream and cook 2 minutes longer; remove saucepan from heat.

3 Transfer 1 cup tomato sauce to 3-quart saucepan. Add shrimp and scrod, and cook over medium-high heat until seafood just turns opaque throughout, about 5 minutes, gently stirring occasionally. Remove saucepan from heat; stir equal amounts of frozen peas into both saucepans.

4 Preheat oven to 400°F. Fill each pasta shell with 2 heaping tablespoons seafood mixture and place in 13" by 9" glass baking dish. Pour tomato sauce over stuffed shells.

5 Prepare Bread-Crumb Topping: In nonstick 10-inch skillet, heat olive oil and garlic over medium heat. Add bread and cook until golden, about 5 minutes, stirring often. Discard garlic.

6 Spoon bread crumbs over stuffed shells. Bake 20 minutes or until hot and bubbly. Makes 10 main-dish servings.

Each serving: About 325 calories, 23 g protein, 38 g carbohydrate, 9 g total fat (3 g saturated), 5 g fiber, 87 mg cholesterol, 450 mg sodium.

Shrimp with Mint Orzo

PREP: 25 MINUTES • COOK: 20 MINUTES

The no-cook sauce, laced with delicate dill and fresh mint, is perfect with shrimp and feta cheese.

1½ cups orzo (rice-shaped pasta)
Salt
1 bay leaf
2 tablespoons olive oil
1 pound medium shrimp, shelled and deveined, each cut crosswise into 3 pieces
1 ripe large tomato, chopped
1 medium red onion, finely chopped
¾ cup crumbled feta cheese (3 ounces)
½ cup loosely packed fresh parsley leaves, chopped
1 tablespoon plus 2 teaspoons fresh lemon juice
2 tablespoons chopped fresh mint leaves
1 tablespoon chopped fresh dill
⅛ teaspoon ground red pepper (cayenne)

1 Prepare orzo in *boiling salted water* as label directs, but add bay leaf.

2 Meanwhile, in nonstick 12-inch skillet, heat 1 tablespoon olive oil over medium-high heat until hot. Add shrimp and ¼ teaspoon salt, and cook 2 to 3 minutes, until shrimp turn opaque throughout. Spoon shrimp into large bowl.

3 Drain orzo; discard bay leaf. Add to bowl with shrimp; gently stir in tomato, onion, feta, parsley, lemon juice, mint, dill, ground red pepper, remaining 1 tablespoon olive oil, and ¼ teaspoon salt. Serve at room temperature. Makes 4 main-dish servings.

Each serving: About 475 calories, 31 g protein, 55 g carbohydrate, 14 g total fat (5 g saturated), 3 g fiber, 161 mg cholesterol, 720 mg sodium.

Shrimp Creole

PREP: 45 MINUTES • BAKE: 30 MINUTES

1 tablespoon olive oil
1 large onion, diced
1 medium green pepper, coarsely chopped
1 medium red pepper, coarsely chopped
½ pound ready-to-eat chorizo sausage or pepperoni, cut into ¼-inch-thick slices
2 garlic cloves, minced
1½ cups parboiled rice
1 can (14½ ounces) stewed tomatoes
1 bottle (8 ounces) clam juice
1 package (10 ounces) frozen whole okra, thawed
1 pound medium shrimp, shelled and deveined

1 Preheat oven to 350°F. In 3- to 3½-quart Dutch oven, heat oil over medium heat until hot. Add onion and peppers and cook 10 minutes or until tender and lightly browned. Add chorizo and garlic and cook 5 minutes longer until chorizo is lightly browned.

2 Stir in rice, stewed tomatoes, clam juice, and 1¼ *cups water*; heat to boiling over high heat. Cover Dutch oven, place in oven, and bake 20 minutes. Stir okra and shrimp into rice mixture; cover and bake 10 minutes longer or until rice and shrimp are tender. Makes 6 main-dish servings.

Each serving: About 405 calories, 26 g protein, 34 g carbohydrate, 18 g total fat (6 g saturated), 4 g fiber, 127 mg cholesterol, 800 mg sodium.

Orzo Paella

PREP: 20 MINUTES • COOK: 1 HOUR 10 MINUTES

This is primarily a seafood paella. For one that includes chicken, see the recipe on page 56.

1 dozen medium mussels
1 dozen littleneck clams
1¾ cups orzo (rice-shaped pasta)
1 tablespoon olive oil
1 large onion, chopped
1 large green pepper, cut into ¾-inch pieces
1 pound hot Italian-sausage links
1 can (14½ to 16 ounces) tomatoes
1 jar or can (12 to 15 ounces) white clam sauce
   for pasta
1 package (9 ounces) frozen cut green beans,
   thawed

1 With stiff brush, scrub mussels and clams in running cold water to remove any sand. Remove beards from mussels; set aside.

2 In saucepot, prepare orzo as label directs but do not use salt in water. Drain orzo and set aside.

3 Meanwhile, in 3½-quart Dutch oven, heat oil over medium heat until hot. Add onion and pepper and cook 10 to 15 minutes until tender and lightly browned; transfer to small bowl. In same Dutch oven, heat sausages and ¼ *cup water* to boiling over medium-high heat. Cover and cook 5 minutes. Remove cover; reduce heat to medium and continue cooking, turning sausages frequently, until water evaporates and sausages are well browned, about 15 minutes. Transfer sausages to plate. Cut each sausage diagonally in half. Discard any fat in Dutch oven.

4 In same Dutch oven, heat tomatoes with their liquid to boiling over high heat, breaking up tomatoes with side of spoon. Add mussels and clams. Reduce heat to medium-low, cover, and simmer 5 to 10 minutes until shells open. Transfer mussels and clams to medium bowl; discard any that do not open.

5 Add clam sauce, green beans, orzo, and onion mixture to Dutch oven. Heat over medium-high heat until mixture is hot. Add mussels, clams, and sausage, and heat through. Makes 6 main-dish servings.

Each serving: About 565 calories, 30 g protein, 58 g carbohydrate, 24 g total fat (6 g saturated), 4 g fiber, 66 mg cholesterol, 960 mg sodium.

Paella Pronto

PREP: 10 MINUTES • COOK: 25 MINUTES

And here's a version of paella that has been streamlined for busy cooks.

2 hot Italian-sausage links (about 6 ounces),
   casings removed
1 cup regular long-grain rice
½ teaspoon salt
1 can (14½ to 16 ounces) stewed tomatoes
1 pound large shrimp, shelled and deveined
1 cup frozen peas, thawed

1 Heat nonstick 10-inch skillet over medium-high heat until hot. Add sausages and cook, breaking up sausages with spoon, until browned. With slotted spoon, transfer sausage meat to bowl.

2 Reduce heat to medium. Add rice to drippings in skillet and cook 2 minutes, stirring occasionally. Add salt and 2½ *cups water*; heat to boiling. Reduce heat to low; cover and simmer 12 to 15 minutes.

3 Add stewed tomatoes and sausage meat; heat to boiling over high heat. Add shrimp; heat to boiling. Reduce heat to medium; cover and cook 4 minutes. Stir in peas; cover and cook until shrimp turn opaque throughout and peas are heated through. Makes 4 main-dish servings.

Each serving: About 470 calories, 31 g protein, 50 g carbohydrate, 16 g total fat (5 g saturated), 3 g fiber, 172 mg cholesterol, 1020 mg sodium.

POULTRY

Island-Spiced Roast Chicken

PREP: 15 MINUTES • ROAST: 50 TO 60 MINUTES

As the chicken roasts, the savory juices drip into the pan and help flavor the sweet-potato chunks. Serve with a squeeze of fresh lime juice.

1 whole chicken (3½ to 4 pounds)
2 tablespoons chipotle chiles in adobo,* finely
    chopped
1 tablespoon dark brown sugar
½ teaspoon freshly grated lime peel
½ teaspoon salt
¼ teaspoon coarsely ground black pepper
4 medium sweet potatoes (about 2¼ pounds),
    peeled and each cut lengthwise into 6 wedges

1 Preheat oven to 450°F. Remove giblets and neck from chicken; refrigerate for use another day.

2 In cup, stir chipotle chiles, brown sugar, lime peel, salt, and black pepper until blended.

3 With fingertips, gently separate skin from meat on chicken breast and thighs. Spread chipotle mixture under skin.

4 With breast side up, lift wings up toward neck, then fold wing tips under back of chicken so wings stay in place. With string, tie legs together.

5 Place chicken, breast side up, on small rack in medium roasting pan (15½" by 10½"). Place sweet-potato wedges around rack in pan. Roast chicken and potatoes 50 to 60 minutes, tilting chicken to drain juices from cavity and stirring potatoes halfway through cooking. (Cover chicken loosely with foil if skin browns too quickly.) Chicken is done when temperature on meat thermometer inserted in thickest part of thigh next to body reaches 175° to 180°F.

6 Place chicken on warm platter. Toss sweet potatoes with any juices in pan; transfer to platter. Let chicken stand 10 minutes to allow juices to set for easier carving. Remove skin from chicken before eating if you like. Makes 4 main-dish servings.

*Canned chipotle chiles in adobo (a vinegary marinade) are available in Hispanic markets.

Each serving without skin: About 450 calories, 41 g protein, 31 g carbohydrate, 17 g total fat (5 g saturated), 3 g fiber, 127 mg cholesterol, 425 mg sodium.

Roast Chicken with Squash

PREP: 25 MINUTES • ROAST: 50 MINUTES

Sweet prunes and savory rosemary flavor this luscious low-maintenance meal. And it's packed with protein and fiber.

1 cup long-grain brown rice
1 chicken (3½ pounds), cut into 8 pieces,
    skin removed
2 large red onions, each cut into 8 wedges
1 acorn squash (about 2 pounds), seeded and
    cut into 8 wedges
2 tablespoons olive oil
2 tablespoons chopped fresh rosemary leaves or
    1 teaspoon dried rosemary, crushed
1 tablespoon freshly grated lemon peel
1½ teaspoons salt
½ teaspoon coarsely ground black pepper
1 cup pitted prunes, each cut in half
Rosemary sprigs for garnish

1 Prepare rice as label directs; keep warm.

2 Meanwhile, preheat oven to 450°F. In large roasting pan (17" by 11½"), toss chicken, onions, and squash with olive oil; sprinkle with rosemary, lemon peel, salt, and pepper.

3 Roast chicken and vegetables 20 minutes, stirring twice, until juices run clear when chicken breasts are pierced with tip of knife. Transfer chicken breasts to platter; cover and keep warm.

4 Add prunes to roasting pan and continue roasting 15 minutes longer or until juices run clear when remaining chicken pieces are pierced with tip of knife and vegetables are tender. Transfer remaining chicken pieces and vegetables to platter with breasts. Garnish with rosemary sprigs. Serve chicken and vegetables with brown rice. Makes 4 main-dish servings.

Each serving: About 650 calories, 48 g protein, 81 g carbohydrate, 14 g total fat (3 g saturated), 9 g fiber, 131 mg cholesterol, 960 mg sodium.

Roast Chicken with Squash ➤

Roast Chicken Pieces

Here's a basic recipe that can serve as a jumping-off point for such dishes as Roast Chicken with Fennel & Carrots (below). If you remove the skin before eating, you'll save about 7 grams of fat per serving.

1 chicken (about 3½ pounds), cut into 8 pieces
1 tablespoon olive oil
1 teaspoon salt
½ teaspoon coarsely ground black pepper

1 Preheat oven to 450°F. In 17" by 11½" roasting pan or 15½" by 10½" jelly-roll pan, toss chicken pieces with oil, salt, and pepper.

2 Roast chicken 35 to 40 minutes, until juices run clear when thickest parts of chicken pieces are pierced with tip of knife. Transfer chicken to platter; cover and keep warm.

3 If you like, skim fat from drippings in pan, then add ¼ *cup hot water*, stirring to loosen brown bits. Spoon drippings over chicken. Makes 4 main-dish servings.

Each serving without drippings: About 360 calories, 38 g protein, 1 g carbohydrate, 22 g total fat (6 g saturated), 0 g fiber, 152 mg cholesterol, 645 mg sodium.

Roast Chicken with Fennel & Carrots

Roast Chicken Pieces (above)
8 ounces peeled baby carrots
8 ounces shallots (7 large), peeled
1 large fennel bulb (about 1 pound), trimmed
    and cut into 12 wedges
2 tablespoons fennel seeds, crushed

Prepare Roast Chicken Pieces as in steps 1 through 3, but add carrots, shallots, fennel wedges, and fennel seeds to pan with chicken before roasting. Makes 4 main-dish servings.

Each serving: About 520 calories, 42 g protein, 26 g carbohydrate, 28 g total fat (7 g saturated), 2 g fiber, 156 mg cholesterol, 745 mg sodium.

Coq au Vin

If you're planning to make our streamlined Shortcut Cassoulet (page 97), be sure to put aside 2 cups cooking liquid (veggies included) and half of 1 chicken from the finished recipe.

2 slices bacon (about 2 ounces), chopped
2 tablespoons olive oil
3 medium carrots, cut into ¼-inch dice
2 medium celery stalks, cut into ¼-inch dice
1 bag (16 ounces) frozen pearl onions, thawed

FOOD EDITOR'S TIP

Q What's the difference between fennel and anise? I thought they were just 2 names for the same vegetable that tastes like licorice, but apparently I'm wrong.

A You're not the only one who's confused—some groceries and markets continue to mislabel fennel as anise, even though they are 2 distinct plants. Both are herbs of the carrot family, but anise has a sweeter, stronger licoricelike flavor. Its tiny seeds and leaves are used mostly to flavor and perfume other foods—from cookies to drinks such as French pastis or Greek ouzo.

Fennel is cultivated for its foliage and its seeds. The fennel often found in the produce section—sometimes referred to by its Italian name, *finocchio*—has a thick, bulb-shaped base of overlapping broad layers, celerylike stalks, and feathery green leaves or fronds similar to dill. All parts of the vegetable, with its mild aniselike flavor, get even mellower when cooked. The stalks are delicious in fish soups and meat stews; use the delicate leaves as you would fresh dill in salads and garnishes, and serve the crisp bulb sliced raw in salads, braised in a little oil or butter, or roasted (see Roast Chicken with Fennel & Carrots, at left).

Look for pearly white fennel bulbs with no cracks or browning; you want them to be heavy for their size. The stalks should still be attached and have pale-green leaves. "Common" or "wild" fennel (grown primarily in Europe) is bulbless, but its longer seeds are used frequently in Italian sausage and make an aromatic addition to meat or cabbage dishes.

10 ounces large mushrooms, each cut into
   quarters
2 garlic cloves, minced
2 chickens (about 4 pounds each), each cut into
   8 pieces, skin removed
3 tablespoons tomato paste
2 strips (3" by 1" each) fresh orange peel
3 tablespoons brandy
1¾ cups dry red wine
1 cup chicken broth
¾ teaspoon salt
¼ teaspoon coarsely ground black pepper
¼ teaspoon dried thyme
1 bay leaf
2 tablespoons all-purpose flour

1 In 8-quart Dutch oven, cook bacon over medium heat until browned. With slotted spoon, transfer bacon to paper towels to drain. Pour off bacon fat from Dutch oven; reserve.

2 In same Dutch oven, heat 1 teaspoon bacon fat and 2 teaspoons oil until hot. Add carrots, celery, and pearl onions, and cook 20 minutes or until vegetables are tender and golden, stirring occasionally. Transfer vegetables to medium bowl.

3 In same Dutch oven, heat 2 teaspoons bacon fat and 1 teaspoon oil over medium-high heat until hot. Add mushrooms and cook 8 minutes or until tender and browned. Add garlic and cook 1 minute, stirring. Transfer mushrooms to bowl with other vegetables.

4 Add remaining 1 tablespoon oil to Dutch oven; add half of chicken pieces and cook over medium-high heat until browned; transfer to large bowl. Repeat with remaining chicken pieces.

5 Reduce heat to medium; add tomato paste and orange peel, and cook 30 seconds, stirring. (Tomato paste will stick to bottom of pan and darken, helping to intensify the flavor of the broth.) Add brandy and cook 30 seconds, stirring.

6 Return chicken pieces and vegetables to Dutch oven. Add wine, chicken broth, salt, pepper, thyme, and bay leaf; heat to boiling over high heat. Reduce heat to low; cover and simmer 30 minutes or until juices run clear when thickest part of chicken is pierced with tip of knife.

7 Meanwhile, in cup, with fork, mix flour with 3 *tablespoons cold water* until blended; set aside.

8 Transfer chicken to warm serving bowl. With slotted spoon, transfer vegetables to same bowl; cover and keep warm.

9 Slowly whisk flour mixture into broth in Dutch oven; heat until mixture boils and thickens slightly, stirring frequently. Spoon broth over chicken and vegetables in bowl. Discard bay leaf. Sprinkle with bacon before serving. Makes 8 main-dish servings.

Each serving: About 325 calories, 40 g protein, 12 g carbohydrate, 12 g total fat (3 g saturated), 2 g fiber, 122 mg cholesterol, 485 mg sodium.

Roast Chicken with Potatoes & Garlic

· ·
PREP: 15 MINUTES • ROAST: 35 TO 40 MINUTES

Roast Chicken Pieces (opposite page)
1 pound small red potatoes, each cut into
   quarters
1 small red pepper, cut into 1-inch pieces
1 small yellow pepper, cut into 1-inch pieces
1 whole head garlic, cloves separated and
   unpeeled
1 tablespoon dried rosemary, crushed

Prepare Roast Chicken Pieces as in steps 1 through 3, but add potatoes, peppers, garlic cloves, and rosemary to pan with chicken before roasting. After roasting, squeeze garlic from peels, if you like. Makes 4 main-dish servings.

Each serving: About 520 calories, 42 g protein, 26 g carbohydrate, 27 g total fat (7 g saturated), 2 g fiber, 156 mg cholesterol, 655 mg sodium.

Lemony Roast Chicken with Artichokes

PREP: 30 MINUTES • ROAST: ABOUT 40 MINUTES

Cook plump thighs and drumsticks with spring artichokes and baby red potatoes for a delectable dinner. Make sure to use a large roasting pan; otherwise ingredients will steam, not brown.

2 large lemons
3 garlic cloves, crushed with garlic press
3 tablespoons olive oil
1½ teaspoons salt
1 teaspoon dried oregano
½ teaspoon coarsely ground black pepper
6 medium chicken thighs (about 1¾ pounds with bones), skin removed
6 medium chicken drumsticks (about 1½ pounds with bones), skin removed
2 pounds baby red potatoes, each cut in half
4 medium or 16 baby artichokes*
Lemon-peel slivers for garnish

1 Preheat oven to 450°F. From lemons, grate 2 teaspoons peel and squeeze ½ cup juice.

2 In cup, mix lemon peel with garlic, oil, salt, oregano, and pepper. In large roasting pan (17" by 11½"), toss chicken thighs, drumsticks, and potatoes with oil mixture. Roast 20 minutes.

3 While chicken is roasting, prepare artichokes: With serrated knife, cut 1 inch straight across top of medium artichoke. Cut off stem; peel. Pull dark outer leaves from artichoke bottom. With kitchen shears, trim thorny tips of remaining leaves. Cut artichoke lengthwise into quarters. Scrape out choke, removing center petals and fuzzy center portion; discard. Repeat with remaining artichokes. Rinse artichokes well.

4 In 5-quart saucepot, heat 1 tablespoon lemon juice and *1 inch water* to boiling over medium-high heat. Add artichokes and stems, and cook, covered, 10 minutes or until fork-tender. Drain well on paper towels.

5 Add artichokes to roasting pan with chicken, and roast 20 minutes longer or until juices run clear when thickest part of chicken is pierced with tip of knife and potatoes are tender.

6 Pour remaining lemon juice over chicken and vegetables; toss before serving. Transfer chicken and vegetables to serving bowl. Sprinkle with lemon-peel slivers. Makes 6 main-dish servings.

*To prepare baby artichokes: Bend back green outer leaves and snap them off at base until remaining leaves are half green (at the top) and half yellow (at the bottom). Cut off stems and top of each artichoke at point where yellow meets green. Cut each artichoke lengthwise in half. Do not discard center portion; baby artichokes are completely edible.

Each serving: About 385 calories, 34 g protein, 36 g carbohydrate, 12 g total fat (2 g saturated), 5 g fiber, 111 mg cholesterol, 740 mg sodium.

Roast Chicken with Mushrooms & Peas

PREP: 15 MINUTES • ROAST: 35 TO 40 MINUTES

Roast Chicken Pieces (page 50)
8 ounces cremini or white mushrooms, each cut into quarters
2 small onions, each cut into 6 wedges
1 teaspoon dried thyme
1 cup frozen peas, thawed

Prepare Roast Chicken Pieces as in steps 1 through 3, but add mushrooms, onion wedges, and thyme to pan with chicken pieces before roasting. Roast chicken and vegetables 35 to 40 minutes; add peas and heat through. Makes 4 main-dish servings.

Each serving: About 465 calories, 42 g protein, 12 g carbohydrate, 27 g total fat (7 g saturated), 3 g fiber, 156 mg cholesterol, 685 mg sodium.

◄ *Lemony Roast Chicken with Artichokes*

Caribbean Roast Chicken

Our new take on basic roast chicken calls for flavorful spices, citrus juices, brown sugar, and pineapple to turn mealtime into a tropical feast.

2 limes
1 orange
2 tablespoons light brown sugar
1 tablespoon vegetable oil
1 teaspoon salt
½ teaspoon dried thyme
¼ teaspoon ground red pepper (cayenne)
¼ teaspoon ground allspice
2 garlic cloves, crushed with garlic press
1 chicken (about 3½ pounds), cut into 8 pieces, skin removed
2 small onions, each cut into 6 wedges
1 medium pineapple, cored and cut into 8 wedges

1 Preheat oven to 450°F. From limes, grate ½ teaspoon peel and squeeze 2 tablespoons juice. From orange, grate ½ teaspoon peel and squeeze ¼ cup juice.

2 In cup, with fork, mix brown sugar, oil, salt, thyme, ground red pepper, allspice, garlic, 2 tablespoons orange juice, 1 tablespoon lime juice, orange peel, and lime peel until blended.

3 In large roasting pan (17" by 11½"), toss chicken, onions, and pineapple with juice mixture until evenly coated. Roast 35 to 40 minutes, tossing mixture once during cooking, until juices run clear when thickest parts of chicken pieces are pierced with tip of knife. Transfer chicken, onions, and pineapple to platter; cover and keep warm.

4 Add remaining 2 tablespoons orange juice and remaining 1 tablespoon lime juice to drippings in roasting pan, stirring to loosen brown bits. Spoon drippings over chicken, onions, and pineapple. Makes 4 main-dish servings.

Each serving: About 325 calories, 34 g protein, 28 g carbohydrate, 9 g total fat (2 g saturated), 2 g fiber, 109 mg cholesterol, 660 mg sodium.

Chicken & Sweet-Potato Stew

Coat chicken thighs with an exotic mix of cumin and cinnamon, then simmer with beta-carotene-rich sweet potatoes in a creamy peanut-butter sauce. Delectable over brown rice.

4 medium chicken thighs (about 1½ pounds with bones), skin removed
1 teaspoon ground cumin
¼ teaspoon ground cinnamon
1 tablespoon olive oil
3 medium sweet potatoes (about 1½ pounds), peeled and cut into ½-inch chunks
1 medium onion, sliced
1 can (28 ounces) whole tomatoes in juice
3 tablespoons natural peanut butter
½ teaspoon salt
¼ teaspoon crushed red pepper
2 garlic cloves, peeled
¼ cup packed fresh cilantro leaves plus 2 tablespoons chopped cilantro leaves

1 Rub chicken thighs with cumin and cinnamon; set aside.

2 In nonstick 12-inch skillet, heat oil over medium heat. Add sweet potatoes and onion, and cook until onion is tender, 12 to 15 minutes, stirring occasionally. Transfer sweet-potato mixture to plate.

3 Increase heat to medium-high. Add seasoned chicken, and cook 5 minutes or until chicken is lightly browned on both sides.

4 Meanwhile, drain tomatoes, reserving juice. Coarsely chop tomatoes and set aside. In blender at high speed or in food processor with knife blade attached, blend tomato juice, peanut butter, salt, crushed red pepper, garlic, and ¼ cup cilantro leaves until smooth.

5 Add sweet-potato mixture, peanut-butter sauce, and chopped tomatoes to skillet with chicken; heat to boiling over high heat. Reduce heat to low; cover and simmer 25 minutes or until juices run clear when chicken is pierced with tip of knife. To serve, sprinkle with chopped cilantro. Makes 4 main-dish servings.

Each serving: About 410 calories, 26 g protein, 50 g carbohydrate, 12 g total fat (2 g saturated), 8 g fiber, 76 mg cholesterol, 725 mg sodium.

Spicy Moroccan Stew

PREP: 30 MINUTES • COOK: 40 MINUTES

This dish is delicious alone, or served the way we like it best, with piping hot couscous.

8 ounces peeled baby carrots (half 16-ounce package)
2 tablespoons all-purpose flour
1 teaspoon ground cumin
½ teaspoon ground coriander
¼ teaspoon ground red pepper (cayenne)
¼ teaspoon coarsely ground black pepper
⅛ teaspoon ground cinnamon
¾ teaspoon salt
8 medium chicken thighs (about 2 pounds with bones), skin removed
1 tablespoon vegetable oil

1 medium onion, sliced
2 medium zucchini (8 ounces each), each cut lengthwise in half, then crosswise into ¼-inch-thick slices
1 can (28 ounces) tomatoes in puree
1 can (15 to 19 ounces) garbanzo beans, rinsed and drained
1 package (10 ounces) couscous (Moroccan pasta)
1 cup packed fresh cilantro leaves, chopped

1 In 10-inch skillet, heat *1 inch water* to boiling over high heat. Add carrots; heat to boiling. Reduce heat to low; cover and simmer 5 minutes or until carrots are just tender-crisp. Drain carrots; set aside.

2 Meanwhile, in large self-sealing plastic bag, combine flour, cumin, coriander, ground red pepper, black pepper, cinnamon, and ½ teaspoon salt. Add chicken and toss with flour mixture until coated.

3 In nonstick 12-inch skillet, heat oil over medium-high heat until hot. Add chicken and cook 10 minutes or until browned all over, turning once. With tongs, transfer chicken to large bowl.

4 Reduce heat to medium. Add onion, zucchini, and remaining ¼ teaspoon salt, and cook 8 to 10 minutes, until onion is lightly browned, stirring occasionally. Add carrots and ¼ *cup water*, and cook 5 minutes longer.

5 To vegetables in skillet, add tomatoes with puree, garbanzo beans, and chicken; heat to boiling over medium-high heat, stirring and breaking up tomatoes with side of spoon. Reduce heat to medium-low; cover and simmer 10 minutes or until juices run clear when thickest part of chicken is pierced with knife.

6 Meanwhile, prepare couscous as label directs.

7 To serve, spoon couscous onto large platter; top with chicken mixture. Sprinkle with cilantro leaves. Makes 4 main-dish servings.

Each serving: About 465 calories, 38 g protein, 53 g carbohydrate, 12 g total fat (2 g saturated), 16 g fiber, 110 mg cholesterol, 1540 mg sodium.

YELLOW-ORANGE VEGETABLES: WHY YOU NEED THEM

Sweet potatoes, butternut and acorn squash, carrots, and pumpkin get their color from beta-carotene, a yellowish-orange carotenoid pigment that the body converts into vitamin A. Beta-carotene made news more than a decade ago when research showed that populations that ate more fruits and veggies and had high blood levels of the pigment had relatively low risks of heart disease and cancer. Beta-carotene is also an antioxidant (defending the body against unstable oxygen molecules thought to damage cell structure and contribute to chronic diseases). Beyond that, yellow-orange veggies also provide a lot of fiber, vitamins, minerals, and phytochemicals. While you're buying the bright stuff, pick up tomatoes too. They contain the carotenoid lycopene, a red pigment that may be an even more powerful cancer fighter than beta-carotene.

Chicken Breasts with Vegetable Ribbons

PREP: 15 MINUTES • COOK: ABOUT 25 MINUTES

A quick sprinkle of lemon peel, garlic, and parsley adds a burst of flavor and an elegant touch.

4 medium skinless, boneless chicken-breast
   halves (about 1¼ pounds)
¼ teaspoon coarsely ground black pepper
½ teaspoon salt
2 garlic cloves, minced
2 teaspoons freshly grated lemon peel
1 tablespoon olive oil
3 medium carrots, peeled
2 medium zucchini (about 8 ounces each)
¾ cup chicken broth
1 cup loosely packed fresh parsley leaves,
   chopped

1 Sprinkle chicken with pepper and ¼ teaspoon salt. In cup, mix garlic, lemon peel, and remaining ¼ teaspoon salt; set aside.

2 In 12-inch skillet, heat oil over medium-high heat until hot. Add chicken and cook 6 minutes. Reduce heat to medium; turn chicken over and cook 6 to 8 minutes longer, until juices run clear when thickest part of breast is pierced with tip of knife.

3 Meanwhile, with sharp vegetable peeler, peel carrots lengthwise into wide, thin strips. Repeat with zucchini (see photo at right).

4 Transfer chicken to plate; sprinkle with garlic mixture and keep warm. In same skillet, heat chicken broth and ¼ *cup water* to boiling over high heat. Reduce heat to medium-low; add carrots and cook, covered, 3 minutes. Add zucchini and cook, covered, 5 to 7 minutes longer, until vegetables are just tender. Stir in all but 1 tablespoon parsley.

5 To serve, spoon vegetable ribbons and broth onto 4 dinner plates; top with chicken. Sprinkle with remaining parsley. Makes 4 main-dish servings.

Each serving: About 240 calories, 36 g protein, 10 g carbohydrate, 6 g total fat (1 g saturated), 2 g fiber, 82 mg cholesterol, 530 mg sodium.

Paella

PREP: 1 HOUR • COOK: 50 MINUTES

The quintessential Spanish dish is traditionally cooked in a paella pan over an open fire of vine cuttings, and may include a range of ingredients, from seafood to rabbit. But the crucial part—in the classic pan or in a skillet—is rice, preferably short-grain white. (Just for a change of pace, you might like to try our orzo-based paella on page 46, although it does not include any chicken.)

1½ pounds skinless, boneless chicken thighs, cut
   into 2-inch pieces
1 package (3½ ounces) cooked chorizo sausage,
   thinly sliced
1 medium onion, finely chopped
1 medium red pepper, finely chopped
2 garlic cloves, minced
¼ teaspoon ground red pepper (cayenne)
½ cup dry white wine
1 can (14½ ounces) chicken broth

MAKING VEGETABLE RIBBONS

These pretty ribbons cook quickly in the skillet. Holding zucchini or carrot at an angle, make paper-thin slices with a sharp vegetable peeler, pressing harder than you would when scraping off just the skin.

2 cups short-grain white rice
¼ pound green beans, trimmed and cut into
    1-inch pieces
2 tablespoons tomato paste
1½ teaspoons salt
¼ teaspoon loosely packed saffron threads,
    crumbled
⅛ teaspoon dried thyme
1 bay leaf
1 pound mussels, scrubbed, with beards
    removed
¾ pound large shrimp, shelled and deveined
1 large plum tomato, chopped
½ cup loosely packed fresh parsley leaves,
    chopped
Lemon wedges (optional)

1 Heat deep nonstick 12-inch skillet over medium-high heat until hot. Add chicken and chorizo, and cook until browned all over, about 5 minutes, stirring frequently. Transfer chicken and chorizo to plate.

2 Reduce heat to medium; add onion and red pepper to skillet, and cook 5 minutes or until vegetables are tender. Stir in garlic and ground red pepper, and cook 30 seconds. Add wine; heat to boiling over medium-high heat. Continue cooking until mixture is very dry, stirring frequently.

3 Stir in chicken broth, rice, green beans, tomato paste, salt, saffron, thyme, bay leaf, chicken, chorizo, and *3 cups water*; heat to boiling over medium-high heat. Reduce heat to low; cover skillet and simmer 15 minutes.

4 Tuck mussels into rice mixture; cover and cook 5 minutes. Tuck in shrimp; cover and cook 8 minutes longer or just until mussels open and shrimp turn opaque. Remove skillet from heat and let paella stand 5 minutes.

5 Discard bay leaf. Sprinkle with chopped tomato and parsley. Serve with lemon wedges if you like. Makes 8 main-dish servings.

Each serving: About 410 calories, 36 g protein, 44 g carbohydrate, 9 g total fat (2 g saturated), 2 g fiber, 153 mg cholesterol, 1010 mg sodium.

Peachy Chicken with Basil

PREP: 20 MINUTES • COOK: ABOUT 15 MINUTES

Combine fragrant basil and juicy fruit slices in a perfect sauce for sautéed chicken breasts. Spoon over noodles or rice, so you get every drop.

3 tablespoons all-purpose flour
½ teaspoon salt
½ teaspoon coarsely ground black pepper
4 medium skinless, boneless chicken-breast
    halves (about 1¼ pounds)
2 tablespoons margarine or butter
¾ cup chicken broth
3 medium peaches (about 1 pound), peeled and
    sliced
1 small red onion, thinly sliced
¼ teaspoon freshly grated lemon peel
8 large basil leaves, thinly sliced

1 On waxed paper, mix flour, salt, and pepper. Coat chicken breasts with seasoned flour.

2 In nonstick 12-inch skillet, melt margarine or butter over medium heat. Add chicken and cook 10 to 12 minutes, until juices run clear when thickest part of chicken breast is pierced with tip of knife, turning once. Transfer chicken to platter; keep warm.

3 Add chicken broth to skillet; heat to boiling over high heat. Add peaches, red onion, and lemon peel. Cook, stirring frequently, about 3 minutes or until peaches are softened and sauce is slightly thickened. Stir sliced basil into skillet.

4 Spoon sauce over chicken to serve. Makes 4 main-dish servings.

Each serving: About 280 calories, 35 g protein, 16 g carbohydrate, 8 g total fat (2 g saturated), 2 g fiber, 82 mg cholesterol, 580 mg sodium.

Cutlets Romano with Arugula Salad

PREP: 25 MINUTES • COOK: ABOUT 8 MINUTES

A flavor-packed coating of bread crumbs and grated cheese quickly transforms ordinary chicken breasts.

ARUGULA SALAD:
2 tablespoons fresh lemon juice
1 tablespoon olive oil
½ teaspoon sugar
⅛ teaspoon salt
⅛ teaspoon coarsely ground black pepper
1 jar (7 ounces) roasted red peppers, drained and thinly sliced
2 bags (3 to 4 ounces each) arugula or 1 bag (about 6 ounces) baby spinach

CHICKEN CUTLETS:
½ cup plain dried bread crumbs
⅓ cup grated Romano cheese
¼ teaspoon salt
¼ teaspoon coarsely ground black pepper
1 large egg
4 small skinless, boneless chicken-breast halves (about 1 pound), pounded to ¼ inch thickness
1 tablespoon olive oil
Lemon wedges

1 Prepare Arugula Salad: In large bowl, with wire whisk or fork, mix lemon juice, oil, sugar, salt, and black pepper. Add red peppers and toss to coat; place arugula on top and set aside.

2 Prepare Chicken Cutlets: On waxed paper, combine bread crumbs, Romano cheese, salt, and pepper. In pie plate, beat egg with fork. Dip chicken cutlets into egg, then into crumb mixture to coat both sides.

3 In nonstick 12-inch skillet, heat 1½ teaspoons oil over medium-high heat until hot. Add half of cutlets and cook about 2 minutes per side or just until chicken loses its pink color inside and is golden brown outside. Repeat with remaining oil and cutlets.

4 To serve, toss Arugula Salad and spoon onto 4 dinner plates. Arrange cutlets on top of salad. Serve with lemon wedges. Makes 4 main-dish servings.

Each serving: About 320 calories, 34 g protein, 17 g carbohydrate, 13 g total fat (3 g saturated), 1 g fiber, 128 mg cholesterol, 665 mg sodium.

Warm Chicken & Spinach Salad

PREP: 15 MINUTES • COOK: 20 MINUTES

A perfect dinner on the lighter side—sauté chicken tenders and asparagus, and serve on a bed of baby spinach, drizzled with mustard vinaigrette.

1 bag (about 6 ounces) baby spinach
3 teaspoons plus 1 tablespoon olive oil
1 pound medium asparagus, trimmed and cut diagonally into 1½-inch pieces
1 large shallot, thinly sliced
1 pound chicken-breast tenders
½ teaspoon salt
¼ teaspoon coarsely ground black pepper
1 tablespoon balsamic vinegar
1 tablespoon fresh lemon juice
½ teaspoon Dijon mustard
¼ teaspoon sugar

1 Place spinach leaves on large platter; set aside.

2 In nonstick 12-inch skillet, heat 2 teaspoons olive oil over medium-high heat until hot. Add asparagus and shallot, and cook 5 minutes or until golden, stirring occasionally. Reduce heat to medium; add *2 tablespoons water* and cook, covered, 5 minutes longer or until asparagus is tender, stirring occasionally. Spoon asparagus mixture over spinach.

3 Increase heat to medium-high. In same skillet, in 1 teaspoon olive oil, cook chicken with ¼ teaspoon salt and ⅛ teaspoon pepper until it loses its pink color throughout, 5 minutes, turning once.

4 Meanwhile, prepare dressing: In cup, with wire whisk or fork, mix vinegar, lemon juice, mustard, sugar, remaining 1 tablespoon olive oil, remaining ¼ teaspoon salt, and remaining ⅛ teaspoon pepper until blended.

5 Spoon chicken onto platter with spinach and asparagus. Add dressing to hot skillet and cook 30 seconds, stirring. Drizzle mixture over chicken and vegetables. Makes 4 main-dish servings.

Each serving: About 225 calories, 30 g protein, 8 g carbohydrate, 9 g total fat (1 g saturated), 3 g fiber, 66 mg cholesterol, 395 mg sodium.

Cutlets Romano with Arugula Salad ➤

Stuffed Chicken Breasts with Leek Sauce

PREP: 30 MINUTES • COOK: 30 MINUTES

For a special company entrée, fill pockets in boneless chicken breasts with prosciutto and Fontina, sauté, then serve smothered with savory leeks.

1 small bunch leeks (about 1¼ pounds)
4 medium skinless, boneless chicken-breast
    halves (about 1¼ pounds)
4 slices prosciutto (about 2 ounces)
2 ounces Fontina cheese, sliced into 4 pieces
¼ teaspoon salt
¼ teaspoon coarsely ground black pepper
1 teaspoon olive oil
1 tablespoon margarine or butter
½ cup chicken broth

1 Trim off roots and leaf ends from leeks. Discard any tough outer leaves. Cut each leek lengthwise in half, then thinly slice crosswise. Place leeks in large bowl of cold water; swish leeks around to remove any sand. With hand, transfer leeks to colander. Repeat process, changing water several times, until all sand is removed. Drain well.

2 With knife, cut each chicken-breast half parallel to its surface to form a deep pocket with a small opening. Place equal portions of prosciutto and Fontina cheese in each pocket, cutting to fit if necessary; press chicken to seal in filling. Sprinkle chicken with salt and pepper.

3 In nonstick 12-inch skillet, heat oil over medium-high heat until hot. Add chicken and cook 6 minutes, turning once. Reduce heat to medium-low; cover and cook 6 to 8 minutes longer, until juices run clear when thickest part of breast is pierced with tip of knife. Transfer chicken to platter; keep warm.

4 In same skillet, melt margarine or butter over medium heat. Add leeks and cook, stirring frequently, 10 to 12 minutes, until tender and golden. Add chicken broth and ¼ *cup water*; heat to boiling over medium-high heat. Boil 2 minutes or until slightly reduced.

5 To serve, pour sauce over chicken. Makes 4 main-dish servings.

Each serving: About 325 calories, 42 g protein, 10 g carbohydrate, 13 g total fat (5 g saturated), 1 g fiber, 108 mg cholesterol, 830 mg sodium.

Thai Chicken with Asparagus

PREP: 25 MINUTES • COOK: 30 MINUTES

Ginger, chiles, and Asian fish sauce turn up the heat in this weeknight dish. If you prefer, use fresh green beans instead of the asparagus.

1 teaspoon salt
1 pound thin asparagus, trimmed and cut
    diagonally into 3-inch pieces
1 tablespoon sugar
3 tablespoons Asian fish sauce*
2 tablespoons fresh lime juice

Thai Chicken with Asparagus

1 tablespoon plus 1 teaspoon soy sauce
4 medium skinless, boneless chicken-breast halves (about 1¼ pounds), thinly sliced
3 teaspoons vegetable oil
1 jumbo onion (about 1 pound), thinly sliced
1 piece fresh ginger (about 2" by 1"), peeled and cut into matchstick-thin strips
2 jalapeño chiles, seeded and cut into matchstick-thin strips
2 cups packed fresh basil leaves
1 cup packed fresh cilantro leaves

1 In 10-inch skillet, heat *1 inch water* and salt to boiling over high heat. Add asparagus; heat to boiling. Reduce heat to low; simmer, uncovered, 3 to 5 minutes, until asparagus are just tender-crisp. Drain asparagus; set aside.

2 In medium bowl, mix sugar, fish sauce, lime juice, and soy sauce. Stir in chicken until evenly coated. (Coat chicken just before cooking, because the lime juice will change its texture.)

3 In nonstick 12-inch skillet, heat 2 teaspoons oil over medium-high heat until hot. Add chicken and cook 5 minutes or just until it loses its pink color throughout, stirring occasionally. With tongs or slotted spoon, transfer chicken to bowl, leaving any cooking liquid in skillet.

4 Add onion, ginger, and jalapeños to skillet, and cook until onion is tender, about 8 minutes. Transfer onion mixture to bowl with chicken.

5 In same skillet, heat remaining 1 teaspoon oil over medium heat until hot. Add asparagus to skillet and cook until it begins to brown, about 5 minutes, stirring occasionally. Return onion mixture and chicken to skillet; heat through.

6 Toss basil and cilantro leaves with chicken mixture just before serving. Makes 4 main-dish servings.

*Asian fish sauce (nuoc nam or nam pla) is available in specialty sections of some supermarkets or in Asian groceries.

Each serving: About 290 calories, 38 g protein, 21 g carbohydrate, 6 g total fat (1 g saturated), 4 g fiber, 82 mg cholesterol, 1555 mg sodium.

Skillet Arroz con Pollo

PREP: 15 MINUTES • COOK: ABOUT 40 MINUTES

This dish, popular in Spain and Mexico, literally means "rice with chicken." We call for chicken-breast tenders instead of bone-in pieces to shorten cooking time.

1 tablespoon olive oil
1 medium onion, finely chopped
1 medium red pepper, cut into ½-inch pieces
1 cup long-grain white rice
1 garlic clove, minced
⅛ teaspoon ground red pepper (cayenne)
1 strip (3" by ½") fresh lemon peel
¼ teaspoon salt
1 can (14½ ounces) chicken broth
¼ cup dry sherry or water
1 pound chicken-breast tenders, cut into 2-inch pieces
1 cup frozen peas
¼ cup drained salad olives (chopped pimiento-stuffed olives)
½ cup loosely packed fresh cilantro leaves or parsley leaves, chopped
Lemon wedges

1 In nonstick 12-inch skillet, heat oil over medium heat until hot. Add onion and red pepper, and cook until tender, about 12 minutes, stirring occasionally. Stir in rice, garlic, and ground red pepper; cook 2 minutes. Stir in lemon peel, salt, chicken broth, and sherry; heat to boiling over medium-high heat. Reduce heat to low; cover and simmer 13 minutes.

2 Stir in chicken tenders; cover and simmer 13 minutes longer or until juices run clear when chicken is pierced with tip of knife and rice is tender, stirring once halfway through cooking time. Stir in frozen peas; cover and heat through. Remove skillet from heat; let stand 5 minutes.

3 To serve, stir in olives and sprinkle with cilantro. Pass lemon wedges to squeeze over each serving. Makes 4 main-dish servings.

Each serving: About 410 calories, 34 g protein, 49 g carbohydrate, 7 g total fat (2 g saturated), 3 g fiber, 66 mg cholesterol, 925 mg sodium.

Asian Stir-Fry with Spring Peas

PREP: 20 MINUTES • COOK: 20 MINUTES

Serve over fluffy white rice for a simple any-day supper.

1 pound chicken-breast tenders
½ teaspoon Chinese five-spice powder
¼ teaspoon salt
3 teaspoons vegetable oil
8 ounces snow peas and/or sugar snap peas, strings removed
1 medium red pepper, thinly sliced
1 cup chicken broth
1 tablespoon dark brown sugar

1 tablespoon soy sauce
2 teaspoons cornstarch
2 green onions, trimmed and cut into ½-inch pieces
1 tablespoon grated, peeled fresh ginger
2 garlic cloves, crushed with garlic press

1 On waxed paper, sprinkle chicken with Chinese five-spice powder and salt. In nonstick 12-inch skillet, heat 1 teaspoon oil over medium-high heat until hot. Add chicken and cook just until it loses its pink color throughout, about 5 minutes, turning once. Transfer to plate; set aside.

2 To same skillet, add remaining 2 teaspoons oil, and cook peas and red pepper until golden, about 5 minutes, stirring occasionally. Add *2 tablespoons water* and cook, covered, 3 minutes or until vegetables are tender-crisp, stirring occasionally.

Curried Chicken-Mango Salad

3 Meanwhile, in 2-cup glass measuring cup, mix broth, brown sugar, soy sauce, and cornstarch.

4 Add green onions, ginger, and garlic to skillet; cook 1 minute, stirring. Stir broth mixture, then add to skillet; heat to boiling. Boil 30 seconds. Add chicken and heat through. Makes 4 main-dish servings.

Each serving: About 220 calories, 30 g protein, 12 g carbohydrate, 5 g total fat (1 g saturated), 2 g fiber, 66 mg cholesterol, 665 mg sodium.

Curried Chicken-Mango Salad

PREP: 20 MINUTES

Precooked chicken from the deli or supermarket makes our salad a cinch. The recipe can easily be doubled if you need to feed a crowd.

1 store-bought rotisserie chicken (about
   2 pounds)
¼ cup plain low-fat yogurt
¼ cup light mayonnaise
2 tablespoons mango chutney, chopped
1 tablespoon fresh lime juice
1 teaspoon curry powder
1 ripe large mango, peeled and diced
1 medium celery stalk, diced
1 medium Granny Smith apple, cored and diced
½ cup loosely packed fresh cilantro leaves,
   chopped
1 head leaf lettuce, separated and rinsed
Cilantro leaves for garnish

1 Remove skin from chicken; discard. With fingers, pull chicken meat into 1-inch pieces (you should have about 3 cups, or about ¾ pound meat).

2 In large bowl, mix yogurt, mayonnaise, chutney, lime juice, and curry powder until combined. Stir in chicken, mango, celery, apple, and cilantro until well coated. Serve salad on bed of lettuce leaves. Garnish with cilantro leaves. Makes 4 main-dish servings.

Each serving: About 310 calories, 32 g protein, 25 g carbohydrate, 9 g total fat (2 g saturated), 3 g fiber, 95 mg cholesterol, 255 mg sodium.

Cajun Chicken Salad with Green Grapes

PREP: 25 MINUTES • COOK: ABOUT 20 MINUTES

A great combination of poached chicken, red pepper, juicy grapes, and onion slivers with a spicy lightened-up dressing.

1 lemon, thinly sliced
1 bay leaf
½ teaspoon whole black peppercorns
½ teaspoon dried thyme
6 medium skinless, boneless chicken-breast
   halves (1¾ pounds)
¾ teaspoon paprika
⅓ cup light mayonnaise
⅓ cup reduced-fat sour cream
¾ teaspoon salt
¼ teaspoon coarsely ground black pepper
⅛ teaspoon ground nutmeg
3 cups green grapes (about 12 ounces), each cut
   in half
1 large red pepper, cut into ½-inch dice
½ cup loosely packed fresh parsley leaves,
   chopped
¼ cup thinly sliced red onion
1 large pickled jalapeño chile, minced

1 In 12-inch skillet, heat *1 inch water* with lemon slices, bay leaf, peppercorns, and ¼ teaspoon thyme to boiling over high heat. Add chicken; reduce heat to low and simmer 12 to 14 minutes, turning chicken over halfway through cooking, until chicken just loses its pink color throughout. With slotted spoon or tongs, transfer chicken from skillet to cutting board; cool slightly until easy to handle. Cut chicken into ¾-inch pieces.

2 Discard poaching liquid and wipe skillet dry. Add paprika and remaining ¼ teaspoon thyme to skillet; toast over medium-low heat, stirring, 2 minutes.

3 Transfer paprika mixture to large bowl; stir in mayonnaise, sour cream, salt, pepper, and nutmeg until blended. Add chicken, grapes, red pepper, parsley, onion, and jalapeño; toss until evenly coated. Serve salad warm, or cover and refrigerate until ready to serve. Makes 8 main-dish servings.

Each serving: About 200 calories, 24 g protein, 16 g carbohydrate, 4 g total fat (1 g saturated), 1 g fiber, 64 mg cholesterol, 380 mg sodium.

Old-Time Roast Turkey

PREP: 45 MINUTES • ROAST: ABOUT 3¾ HOURS

No exotic seasonings, no fancy gravy—just plain, good cooking. We didn't stuff this turkey because we found that cooking the stuffing separately yields a juicier bird. If you want to stuff your turkey, extend roasting time by about 30 minutes and make sure that the stuffing temperature reaches 165°F. on a meat thermometer to be safe.

One 14-pound fresh or frozen (thawed) turkey
1½ teaspoons salt
½ teaspoon coarsely ground black pepper
Giblet Gravy (at right)
Fresh herbs and champagne grapes for garnish

1 Preheat oven to 325°F. Remove giblets and neck from turkey; reserve for making gravy.

2 Fasten neck skin to back with 1 or 2 skewers. With turkey breast side up, fold wings under back of turkey so they stay in place. Depending on brand of turkey, with string, tie legs and tail together, push drumsticks under band of skin, or use stuffing clamp.

3 Place turkey, breast side up, on rack in large roasting pan. Rub turkey all over with salt and pepper. Insert meat thermometer into thickest part of thigh next to body, being careful that pointed end of thermometer does not touch bone. Cover turkey with a loose tent of foil, letting top of thermometer poke through. Roast turkey about 3¾ hours; start checking for doneness during last hour of roasting.

4 While turkey is roasting, begin Giblet Gravy.

5 To brown turkey, remove foil during last 1 hour of roasting time and baste with pan drippings occasionally. Turkey is done when thigh temperature on meat thermometer reaches 175° to 180°F. and drumstick feels soft when pressed with fingers protected by paper towels; breast temperature should reach 165° to 170°F. (Upon standing, temperature of thigh will rise to 180° to 185°F.; breast, 170° to 175°F.)

6 When turkey is done, place on large platter; cover with foil to keep warm. Complete Giblet Gravy.

7 To serve, garnish platter with fresh herbs and champagne grapes. Serve with gravy. Remove skin from turkey before eating if you like. Makes 14 main-dish servings.

GIBLET GRAVY: In 3-quart saucepan, heat gizzard, heart, neck, and *4 cups water* to boiling over high heat. Reduce heat to low; cover and simmer 45 minutes. Add liver if you like, and cook 15 minutes longer. Strain, reserving meat and broth. Pull meat from neck; discard bones. Coarsely chop neck meat and giblets. Cover and refrigerate meat and broth separately.

To make gravy, remove rack from roasting pan. Pour pan drippings through sieve into 4-cup glass measuring cup or medium bowl. Add 1 cup giblet broth to roasting pan and stir until brown bits are loosened; pour through sieve into drippings in measuring cup. Let stand 1 minute, until the fat separates from drippings. Spoon 2 tablespoons fat from the drippings into 2-quart saucepan; skim and discard any remaining fat from drippings. Add remaining giblet broth and enough *water* to drippings in cup to equal 3 cups.

Into fat in saucepan, stir ¼ *cup all-purpose flour* and ½ *teaspoon salt*; cook over medium heat, stirring, until flour turns golden brown. Gradually stir in drippings mixture and cook, stirring, until gravy boils and thickens slightly. Stir in reserved giblets and neck meat; heat through. Pour gravy into gravy boat. Makes about 3½ cups.

Each ¼ cup gravy: About 70 calories, 7 g protein, 2 g carbohydrate, 3 g total fat (1 g saturated), 0 g fiber, 63 mg cholesterol, 140 mg sodium.

Each serving of turkey without skin or gravy: About 330 calories, 57 g protein, 0 g carbohydrate, 10 g total fat (3 g saturated), 0 g fiber, 149 mg cholesterol, 330 mg sodium.

Roast Turkey with Wild-Mushroom Gravy

PREP: 1 HOUR • ROAST: ABOUT 3¾ HOURS

White, shiitake, and dried porcini mushrooms add rich flavor to classic giblet gravy.

TURKEY:
Old-Time Roast Turkey (page 64)

WILD-MUSHROOM GRAVY:
1 package (⅓ ounce) dried porcini mushrooms (about ⅓ cup)
1 tablespoon margarine or butter
1 medium shallot, minced (¼ cup)
10 ounces white mushrooms, sliced
8 ounces shiitake mushrooms, stems discarded and caps sliced
¼ cup all-purpose flour
¼ teaspoon salt

1 Prepare Old-Time Roast Turkey as in steps 1, 2, 3, and 5.

2 While turkey is roasting, begin Wild-Mushroom Gravy: In 3-quart saucepan, heat turkey gizzard, heart, neck, and *4 cups water* to boiling over high heat. Reduce heat to low; cover and simmer 45 minutes. Strain, reserving broth; discard giblets and neck. Cover and refrigerate broth.

3 Meanwhile, in small bowl, soak dried porcini mushrooms in *1 cup boiling water* 30 minutes. With slotted spoon, remove porcini mushrooms from soaking liquid, reserving liquid. Rinse porcini mushrooms to remove sand; slice. Strain soaking liquid through sieve lined with paper towel. Set aside.

4 In nonstick 12-inch skillet, melt margarine or butter over medium-low heat. Add shallot and cook until tender, about 10 minutes, stirring occasionally. Increase heat to medium-high; add white, shiitake, and porcini mushrooms and cook 15 minutes, stirring occasionally, until tender and golden. Add porcini soaking liquid; heat to boiling and cook 1 minute. Transfer mixture to medium bowl.

TAKING A TURKEY'S TEMPERATURE

Despite repeated warnings linking undercooked meat and poultry to food-borne illnesses, 92 percent of American families do not use a thermometer to test doneness for roasts and turkeys, according to a study conducted last year by Audits International.

At *Good Housekeeping*, we stress the importance of getting a temperature reading on all large cuts of meat and poultry, including ham, rib roast, goose, turkey breast, and especially whole Thanksgiving turkeys, because they're so large and take hours to cook thoroughly.

There's really nothing complicated about using a meat thermometer. First, decide whether you want the instant-read kind (remove turkey from oven and insert point) or the traditional oven-safe variety, which is placed in the turkey before you roast it. (Pop-up thermometers, already in some birds when you buy them, are usually accurate, but there's a chance they won't spring up if, for example, you rubbed the skin with seasonings. And we recommend double-checking them with another thermometer anyway to be absolutely safe.)

No matter which type of thermometer you pick, insert it into the thickest part of the inner thigh, near the turkey breast, but not touching the bone. The bird is done, but still at its juiciest, when the internal temperature reaches 180° to 185°F. (or 170° to 175°F. in the thickest part of the breast). Be sure to clean the shaft on the instant-read kind thoroughly before reinserting it for the final doneness test. (If you inserted it once and the meat was uncooked, you don't want to transfer those juices back into the bird.)

To keep your thermometer on the mark, wash between uses in warm, soapy water, submerging only the metal shaft, not the whole instrument.

Two for good measure, pictured: The instant-read Professional Digital Pocket Thermometer is accurate and reliable. It comes with a storage case and an extra 1.5-volt watch battery. The oven-safe Classic Roast-Yeast Thermometer is a trusty standby. Both from Taylor, at mass-merchandise, hardware, and specialty stores; call 888-29-taylor (888-298-2956).

5 When turkey is done, place on large tray; cover with foil to keep warm.

6 Complete Wild-Mushroom Gravy: Remove rack from roasting pan. Pour pan drippings through sieve into 8-cup glass measuring cup or medium bowl. Add 1 cup giblet broth to roasting pan and stir until brown bits are loosened; pour through sieve into drippings in measuring cup. Let stand 1 minute, until fat separates from drippings. Spoon 2 tablespoons fat from drippings into 3-quart saucepan; skim and discard any remaining fat from drippings. Add mushroom mixture and enough broth (about 2 cups) to drippings in measuring cup to equal 5 cups.

7 Into fat in saucepan, stir flour and salt; cook over medium heat, stirring, until flour turns golden-brown. Gradually stir in mushroom mixture and cook, stirring, until gravy boils and thickens slightly. Pour gravy into gravy boat. Makes about 6 cups.

8 Serve turkey with gravy. Remove skin before eating if you like. Makes 14 main-dish servings.

Each serving of turkey without skin or gravy: About 330 calories, 57 g protein, 0 g carbohydrate, 10 g total fat (3 g saturated), 0 g fiber, 149 mg cholesterol, 330 mg sodium.

Each ¼ cup gravy: About 30 calories, 1 g protein, 3 g carbohydrate, 2 g total fat (1 g saturated), 0 g fiber, 1 mg cholesterol, 65 mg sodium.

Sausage & Apple Stuffing

PREP: 1 HOUR • BAKE: 45 MINUTES

This crowd-pleasing holiday accompaniment is chock-full of veggies and toasted bread chunks, with a classic diced-apple-and-sausage mixture. If you like, prepare the stuffing a day ahead and refrigerate, covered, overnight. If you plan to stuff your turkey, don't do it until just before the bird goes in the oven.

12 ounces pork-sausage meat
2 medium Granny Smith apples, peeled, cored, and diced
½ teaspoon coarsely ground black pepper
½ teaspoon dried thyme
6 tablespoons margarine or butter
2 celery stalks, diced
1 jumbo onion (12 ounces), diced
2 large carrots, shredded
1 can (14½ ounces) chicken broth
½ cup loosely packed fresh parsley leaves, chopped
1½ loaves (16 ounces each) firm white bread, sliced, cut into ¾-inch cubes, and lightly toasted*

1 Preheat oven to 325°F. In 12-inch skillet, cook sausage meat over medium-high heat 8 minutes or until lightly browned, stirring and breaking up sausage with side of spoon. Add apples, pepper, and thyme, and cook 5 minutes longer, stirring occasionally and scraping up browned bits. Spoon sausage mixture and any drippings into large bowl; set aside.

2 In same skillet, melt margarine or butter over medium-high heat. Add celery and onion, and cook 10 minutes or until lightly browned, stirring occasionally. Add carrots and cook 5 minutes longer. Stir in chicken broth, parsley, and *¼ cup water*; heat to boiling. Spoon vegetable mixture and bread cubes into bowl with sausage mixture; toss to mix well.

3 Spoon stuffing mixture into 13" by 9" glass baking dish; cover with foil and bake 45 minutes or until heated through. Makes about 12 cups.

*To toast bread cubes, bake in a preheated 400°F. oven for 10 minutes, stirring occasionally.

Each ½ cup: About 180 calories, 5 g protein, 18 g carbohydrate, 10 g total fat (3 g saturated), 1 g fiber, 10 mg cholesterol, 340 mg sodium.

Wheatberry Stuffing with Apricots

PREP: 1 HOUR 15 MINUTES • BAKE: 20 MINUTES

Our new version of stuffing—made with grains, veggies, and dried fruit—will quickly become a family favorite. It's a good choice to make ahead. Just allow more time to bake if cold.

1½ cups wheatberries*
1 cup regular long-grain rice
1 tablespoon olive oil
3 carrots, cut in ¼-inch dice
3 celery stalks, cut in ¼-inch dice
2 red onions, cut in ¼-inch dice
2 strips (3" by 1" each) fresh orange peel
⅛ teaspoon ground allspice

¾ cup dried apricots, sliced
¾ cup pitted prunes, coarsely chopped
1 can (14½ ounces) chicken or vegetable broth
1½ teaspoons salt
½ teaspoon coarsely ground black pepper
½ cup loosely packed fresh parsley leaves, chopped

1 Preheat oven to 350°F. In 4-quart saucepan, heat wheatberries and 6 *cups water* to boiling over high heat. Reduce heat to low; cover and simmer 1 hour or until wheatberries are firm to the bite but tender enough to eat; drain and set aside.

2 Meanwhile, prepare rice in 5- to 6-quart saucepot as label directs. Spoon cooked rice into medium bowl; cover and set aside. Wash and dry saucepot.

3 In same saucepot, heat olive oil over medium heat until hot. Add carrots, celery, and red onions, and cook 15 minutes or until tender and lightly browned,

STUFFING SANDWICHES

These make a surprisingly hearty meal– you can try them on onion or poppy-seed rolls too.

PREP: 10 MINUTES • COOK: 10 TO 12 MINUTES

3 cups leftover Sausage & Apple Stuffing (page 67) or Wheatberry Stuffing with Apricots (above)
1 large egg
¾ cup plain dried bread crumbs (only for wheatberry patties)
Olive oil
4 Kaiser rolls or sandwich buns

1 To prepare sausage-stuffing patties: In large bowl, with hand, mix stuffing and egg until combined. To prepare wheatberry-stuffing patties: In large bowl, with hand, mix stuffing, egg, and ½ cup bread crumbs until combined.

2 On waxed paper, divide either stuffing mixture into 4 equal portions. With damp hands, shape each portion into a 3-inch round patty. For wheatberry patties only, use remaining ¼ cup bread crumbs to coat patties.

3 In nonstick 12-inch skillet, heat 1 tablespoon olive oil over medium heat. Cook patties 10 to 12 minutes, until golden on both sides. Turn patties over halfway through cooking time, adding 1 more tablespoon olive oil to skillet if making wheatberry patties. Serve on rolls. Each recipe makes 4 patties.

Each sausage-stuffing patty without roll: About 315 calories, 9 g protein, 27 g carbohydrate, 19 g total fat (5 g saturated), 2 g fiber, 68 mg cholesterol, 525 mg sodium.

Each wheatberry-stuffing patty without roll: About 350 calories, 10 g protein, 55 g carbohydrate, 11 g total fat (2 g saturated), 3 g fiber, 53 mg cholesterol, 545 mg sodium.

stirring often. Add orange peel and allspice, and cook 2 minutes longer. Add apricots, prunes, broth, salt, pepper, and ½ cup water; heat to boiling over high heat. Reduce heat to low; simmer, uncovered, 5 minutes to blend flavors. Discard orange peel.

4 Add wheatberries, rice, and parsley to vegetable mixture, stirring to combine. Spoon wheatberry mixture into 13" by 9" glass baking dish. Cover with foil and bake 20 minutes or until heated through. Makes about 10 cups.

*Wheatberries are unmilled whole wheat kernels that have a delicious nutty, toasty flavor. Look for them in health-food stores or some supermarkets.

Each ½ cup: About 125 calories, 4 g protein, 27 g carbohydrate, 1 g total fat (0 g saturated), 2 g fiber, 0 mg cholesterol, 235 mg sodium.

Turkey Breast with Roasted Vegetables

PREP: 40 MINUTES • ROAST: ABOUT 2½ HOURS

Crisp bacon, caramelized onions, and garlic are roasted under the turkey skin for extra flavor. Save 2 cups of leftover turkey meat if you want to make our Mexican-style soup, Turkey Posole (page 74).

4 slices bacon, chopped
1 medium red onion, chopped
2 large garlic cloves, thinly sliced
1 teaspoon dried thyme
¾ teaspoon salt
½ teaspoon coarsely ground black pepper
1 bone-in turkey breast (about 6½ pounds)
2 pounds Yukon Gold potatoes, each cut into
   quarters
1 pound carrots, cut into 2-inch pieces
1 large onion, cut into 8 wedges
1 tablespoon vegetable oil
¼ cup dry white wine
1 cup chicken broth
1 tablespoon cornstarch

1 In 10-inch skillet, cook bacon over medium heat until browned. With slotted spoon, transfer bacon to paper towels to drain. Discard all but 1 tablespoon fat from skillet; add red onion and cook until golden and tender, about 10 minutes, stirring often. Add garlic, ½ teaspoon thyme, ½ teaspoon salt, and ¼ teaspoon

pepper; cook 3 minutes longer, stirring. Add 2 *tablespoons water*, stirring to loosen brown bits; cook 1 minute. Transfer onion mixture to small bowl; stir in bacon and let cool until easy to handle.

2 Preheat oven to 325°F. With fingertips, gently separate skin from meat on turkey breast. Spread cooled onion mixture on meat under skin.

3 Place turkey breast, skin side up, on small rack in large roasting pan (17" by 11½"). Insert meat thermometer into center of breast being careful that pointed end of thermometer does not touch bone.

4 In large bowl, toss potatoes with carrots, onion wedges, oil, remaining ½ teaspoon thyme, ¼ teaspoon salt, and ¼ teaspoon pepper. Arrange vegetables in roasting pan around turkey breast. Cover turkey breast (not vegetables) with a loose tent of foil. Roast turkey about 2 hours 30 minutes or until temperature on meat thermometer reaches 165°F. Internal temperature of meat will rise to 170°F. upon standing. Start checking for doneness during last 30 minutes of roasting.

5 Transfer turkey to carving board. Cover with foil to keep warm. Let turkey stand 15 minutes to set juices for easier slicing. Meanwhile, transfer vegetables to bowl. Remove rack from roasting pan. Pour pan drippings into cup; skim and discard fat. Reserve pan drippings. Turn oven control to 450°F.

6 Return roasting pan with vegetables to oven and roast 15 minutes longer to brown and crisp vegetables. Transfer vegetables to serving platter; keep warm.

7 Prepare gravy: Pour wine into roasting pan; cook 2 minutes over medium heat, stirring and scraping pan to loosen brown bits. Pour wine mixture into 1-quart saucepan; stir in chicken broth and reserved pan drippings. In cup, with small wire whisk or fork, mix cornstarch with ⅓ cup water until blended. Slowly whisk cornstarch mixture into wine mixture; heat over high heat until gravy boils and thickens slightly, whisking constantly. Boil 1 minute.

8 Serve gravy with sliced turkey breast and vegetables. Makes 10 main-dish servings.

Each serving: About 355 calories, 39 g protein, 23 g carbohydrate, 11 g total fat (3 g saturated), 3 g fiber, 76 mg cholesterol, 930 mg sodium.

Turkey Marsala

PREP: 10 MINUTES • COOK: ABOUT 25 MINUTES

Turkey cutlets are time-savers—pound to an even thickness, and sauté just until they lose their pink color.

1 package (10 ounces) mushrooms, sliced
⅛ teaspoon salt
⅛ teaspoon coarsely ground black pepper
4 turkey cutlets (about 1 pound), pounded to ¼-inch thickness
⅓ cup dry or sweet Marsala wine
½ cup chicken broth
1 package (10 ounces) frozen peas in butter sauce

1 Heat nonstick 12-inch skillet over medium-high heat until hot. Add mushrooms to skillet; sprinkle with salt and pepper. Cook mushrooms 8 minutes or until lightly browned, stirring occasionally. Transfer mushrooms to small bowl.

2 In same skillet, cook turkey cutlets 6 minutes, turning once, until cutlets are lightly browned on the outside and just lose their pink color throughout. Transfer cutlets to platter; keep warm.

3 Add Marsala to skillet; boil 30 seconds. Add chicken broth, peas with their sauce, and mushrooms; heat to boiling. Reduce heat to medium and cook, covered, 7 minutes or until heated through, stirring occasionally. Spoon mixture over cutlets. Makes 4 main-dish servings.

Each serving: About 210 calories, 32 g protein, 13 g carbohydrate, 4 g total fat (1 g saturated), 3 g fiber, 71 mg cholesterol, 495 mg sodium.

Lemon Turkey

PREP: 15 MINUTES • COOK: ABOUT 5 MINUTES

4 large turkey cutlets (about 1 pound)
¼ teaspoon salt
¼ teaspoon coarsely ground black pepper
1 tablespoon olive oil
2 medium lemons
1½ teaspoons cornstarch
¾ cup chicken broth
1 garlic clove, crushed with garlic press
2 tablespoons chopped fresh parsley leaves
Lemon-peel strips for garnish

COLD TURKEY: TOP SANDWICHES

Go beyond the basics with these new ways to jazz up sliced white meat. Stack with:

• Sautéed onions and cranberry sauce on toasted walnut-raisin bread

• Coleslaw and tomato slices on multigrain bread

• Thinly sliced ham, American cheese, and mustard on white bread; brown in buttered skillet

• Jarred roasted red peppers and prepared pesto on Italian bread

• Mango chutney and Brie on a French baguette or sourdough roll

• Potato salad and horseradish on pumpernickel

• Sliced cucumber, baby spinach, and garlicky yogurt in a pita pocket

• Cheddar cheese and pickles on a sesame-seed bun

• Sliced avocado, lettuce, and cilantro leaves with a mix of mayo and chopped canned chipotle chile in adobo in a flour tortilla

• Thousand Island dressing, sauerkraut, and Swiss cheese on rye; cook in a lightly oiled skillet until hot and golden

• Sliced green onion and watercress rolled in a flour tortilla brushed lightly inside with hoisin sauce

• Blue cheese dressing and apple slices on toasted pecan bread

• Tomato slices plus mayonnaise mixed with jarred olive paste on country white bread

• Jalapeño-pepper Monterey Jack and salsa between flour tortillas; panfry (quesadilla-style) in a nonstick skillet until cheese melts

1 Rub cutlets with salt and pepper. In nonstick 12-inch skillet, heat oil over medium-high heat until hot. Add cutlets and cook about 4 minutes or until golden, turning once. Transfer cutlets to platter; cover with foil to keep warm.

2 Thinly slice 1 lemon; reserve half of lemon slices for garnish. From other lemon, grate ½ teaspoon peel and squeeze 2 tablespoons juice. In cup, whisk cornstarch with chicken broth. To same skillet, add garlic, lemon peel, lemon juice, and half of the lemon slices, and cook 30 seconds. Add chicken-broth mixture, and boil 1 minute. Stir in parsley.

3 To serve, pour sauce over turkey cutlets. Garnish with lemon slices and lemon peel. Makes 4 main-dish servings.

Each serving: About 175 calories, 28 g protein, 2 g carbohydrate, 5 g total fat (1 g saturated), 0 g fiber, 68 mg cholesterol, 350 mg sodium.

Curried Turkey with Apricot-Raisin Sauce

PREP: 15 MINUTES • COOK: ABOUT 5 MINUTES

1 teaspoon curry powder
½ teaspoon ground cumin
¼ teaspoon salt
¼ teaspoon coarsely ground black pepper
4 large turkey cutlets (about 1 pound)
1 tablespoon olive oil
1 teaspoon cornstarch
¾ cup chicken broth
¼ cup apricot preserves
¼ cup golden raisins
1 teaspoon distilled white vinegar
Parsley sprigs for garnish

1 In small bowl or cup, combine curry powder, cumin, salt, and pepper. Rub 1 side of each cutlet with the curry mixture. In nonstick 12-inch skillet, heat oil over medium-high heat until hot. Add cutlets and cook about 4 minutes or until golden, turning once. Transfer cutlets to platter; cover with foil to keep warm.

2 In cup, whisk cornstarch with chicken broth. To same skillet, add apricot preserves, raisins, vinegar, and broth mixture; boil 2 minutes.

3 To serve, spoon apricot sauce over turkey cutlets. Garnish with parsley. Makes 4 main-dish servings.

Each serving: About 260 calories, 28 g protein, 23 g carbohydrate, 6 g total fat (1 g saturated), 1 g fiber, 68 mg cholesterol, 355 mg sodium.

Turkey Stir-Fry

PREP: 20 MINUTES • COOK: ABOUT 12 MINUTES

Toss bite-size pieces of turkey meat with broccoli, red pepper, mushrooms, and a tasty ginger-and-garlic sauce. Serve with rice or curly egg noodles.

2 tablespoons seasoned rice vinegar
2 tablespoons soy sauce
1 tablespoon grated, peeled fresh ginger
1 teaspoon sugar
¼ teaspoon crushed red pepper
2 garlic cloves, crushed with garlic press
1 teaspoon cornstarch
¾ cup chicken broth
1 tablespoon olive oil
4 cups broccoli flowerets
1 medium red pepper, thinly sliced
8 ounces white mushrooms, thinly sliced
2 cups bite-size pieces leftover cooked turkey meat (about 8 ounces)

1 In small bowl, combine vinegar, soy sauce, ginger, sugar, crushed red pepper, and garlic. In 1-cup glass measuring cup, mix cornstarch and chicken broth.

2 In nonstick 12-inch skillet, heat oil over medium-high heat until very hot. Add broccoli, red pepper, and mushrooms, and cook 5 minutes, stirring often. Stir in soy-sauce mixture, and cook 3 to 5 minutes longer, until vegetables are lightly browned and tender-crisp.

3 Add turkey meat and chicken-broth mixture to vegetables in skillet; heat to boiling, stirring. Boil 1 minute. Makes 4 main-dish servings.

Each serving: About 210 calories, 22 g protein, 16 g carbohydrate, 7 g total fat (2 g saturated), 4 g fiber, 44 mg cholesterol, 930 mg sodium.

Turkey Chili

PREP: 20 MINUTES • COOK: 20 MINUTES

This spicy potful is made with limas and white beans—it's just right for a simple Sunday-evening supper. Serve with tortilla chips or corn bread.

1 tablespoon olive oil
1 medium onion, chopped
3 garlic cloves, minced
1½ teaspoons chili powder
1 teaspoon ground cumin
1 teaspoon ground coriander
¼ teaspoon salt
¼ teaspoon coarsely ground black pepper
1 can (15 to 16 ounces) Great Northern or small white beans, rinsed and drained
1 can (14½ ounces) reduced-sodium chicken broth
1 package (10 ounces) frozen lima beans
1 can (4 to 4½ ounces) chopped mild green chiles
2 cups bite-size pieces leftover cooked turkey meat (about 8 ounces)
1 cup loosely packed fresh cilantro leaves, chopped
2 tablespoons fresh lime juice
Lime wedges (optional)

1 In 5-quart Dutch oven, heat olive oil over medium heat until hot. Add onion and cook until tender, about 5 minutes, stirring often. Add garlic and cook 30 seconds. Stir in chili powder, cumin, coriander, salt, and pepper; cook 1 minute longer.

2 Meanwhile, in small bowl, mash half of Great Northern beans.

3 Add mashed beans and unmashed beans, chicken broth, frozen lima beans, green chiles, and turkey meat to mixture in Dutch oven. Heat to boiling over medium-high heat. Reduce heat to low; cover and simmer 5 minutes to blend flavors. Remove Dutch oven from heat; stir in cilantro and lime juice. Serve with lime wedges if you like. Makes about 6 cups or 4 main-dish servings.

Each serving: About 380 calories, 33 g protein, 45 g carbohydrate, 8 g total fat (2 g saturated), 7 g fiber, 44 mg cholesterol, 995 mg sodium

Turkey with Warm Arugula Salad

PREP: 15 MINUTES • COOK: ABOUT 5 MINUTES

TURKEY CUTLETS:
4 large turkey cutlets (about 1 pound)
¼ teaspoon salt
¼ teaspoon coarsely ground black pepper
1 tablespoon olive oil

TOMATO-ARUGULA SALAD:
4 large plum tomatoes (12 ounces), cut into ½-inch pieces
1 green onion, thinly sliced
2 tablespoons grated Parmesan cheese
1 tablespoon red wine vinegar
1 tablespoon olive oil
¼ teaspoon salt
¼ teaspoon coarsely ground black pepper
2 bunches arugula (about 8 ounces), coarsely chopped

1 Rub cutlets with salt and pepper. In nonstick 12-inch skillet, heat oil over medium-high heat until hot. Add cutlets and cook about 4 minutes or until golden, turning once. Transfer cutlets to platter; cover with foil to keep warm.

2 Prepare Tomato-Arugula Salad: To same skillet, add tomatoes and cook 1 minute. Remove skillet from heat; set aside. In medium bowl, with fork, mix green onion, Parmesan, vinegar, oil, salt, and pepper. Add arugula, and gently toss to mix well. To serve, top turkey cutlets with arugula mixture; spoon warm tomatoes over greens. Makes 4 main-dish servings.

Each serving: About 330 calories, 30 g protein, 6 g carbohydrate, 10 g total fat (2 g saturated), 1 g fiber, 70 mg cholesterol, 420 mg sodium.

◄ *Turkey Chili*

Turkey Posole

PREP: 20 MINUTES • COOK: 20 MINUTES

A delicious south-of-the-border dinner. Serve with warm flour tortillas and a crisp lettuce salad.

1 tablespoon olive oil
1 large onion, chopped
1 medium red pepper, cut into ½-inch pieces
4 jalapeño chiles, seeded and minced
3 garlic cloves, minced
1 teaspoon chili powder
1 teaspoon ground cumin
1 teaspoon ground coriander
¼ teaspoon salt
⅛ teaspoon ground red pepper (cayenne)
1 can (30 ounces) hominy (posole), rinsed and drained
1 can (14½ ounces) chicken broth
2 cups chopped leftover cooked turkey meat (about 8 ounces)
1 cup loosely packed fresh cilantro leaves, chopped
2 tablespoons fresh lime juice

1 In 5-quart Dutch oven or saucepot, heat oil over medium heat until hot. Add onion and red pepper; cook until vegetables are tender, about 10 minutes, stirring often.

2 Add jalapeños and garlic, and cook 1 minute longer. Add chili powder, cumin, coriander, salt, and ground red pepper; cook 30 seconds, stirring constantly.

3 Add hominy, chicken broth, and turkey to mixture in Dutch oven; heat to boiling over high heat. Reduce heat to low; cover and simmer 5 minutes to blend flavors and heat through. Remove Dutch oven from heat; stir in cilantro and lime juice. Makes 4 main-dish servings.

Each serving: About 300 calories, 27 g protein, 30g carbohydrate, 8 g total fat (2 g saturated), 3 g fiber, 49 mg cholesterol, 825 mg sodium.

SAFELY STORING LEFTOVERS

Dessert has been served, the table is cleared, the dishes await. If you're tempted to curl up in front of a good movie and leave cleanup for later, at least put the turkey away first. "Store it within two hours of serving. Bacteria grow rapidly at room temperature, and refrigeration will not eliminate microorganisms that have already grown," says Sandy Kuzmich, Ph.D., the GH Institute's Chemistry Director.

More pointers for safe stowaways

• Take all meat off the carcass and store in serving-size packets or shallow containers. The smaller the portion, the faster you can thoroughly defrost and reheat it. (To refrigerate in packets, wrap meat in plastic wrap or foil and place in self-sealing plastic bags. To freeze, use same procedure but with freezer-weight bags.)

• To thaw leftover turkey, place it in the refrigerator overnight. To warm, stir into hot gravy just to heat through. Or stir frozen turkey shreds or small pieces directly into soups at the last minute; cook just until hot.

"Shelf life" for leftover turkey

IN THE FRIDGE:	3 to 4 days
IN THE FREEZER:	4 months (plain)
	6 months (in broth or gravy)

Country Hash

PREP: 20 MINUTES • COOK: 35 MINUTES

This is like chunky, golden hash browns with delectable extras stirred in.

3 large all-purpose potatoes (1¾ pounds), peeled and cut into ¾-inch chunks
2 medium carrots, cut into ¾-inch pieces
1 tablespoon margarine or butter
1 tablespoon vegetable oil
1 medium onion, coarsely chopped
1 large celery stalk, cut into ¾-inch pieces
½ teaspoon salt
¼ teaspoon coarsely ground black pepper
2 cups bite-size pieces leftover cooked turkey meat (about 8 ounces)
2 ounces Fontina or Swiss cheese, shredded (½ cup)
1 tablespoon chopped fresh parsley leaves

1 In 2-quart saucepan, place potatoes and enough *water* to cover; heat to boiling over high heat. Add carrots to saucepan. Reduce heat to low; cover and simmer 5 minutes or until vegetables are almost fork-tender. Drain.

2 Meanwhile, in nonstick 12-inch skillet, heat margarine or butter with oil over medium heat. Add onion and celery, and cook, stirring occasionally, 15 minutes or until lightly browned and tender.

3 Increase heat to medium-high; add potatoes, carrots, salt, and pepper, and cook, stirring occasionally, 10 to 15 minutes, until browned.

4 Stir in turkey and cook 1 minute. Sprinkle top with cheese; cover skillet and cook 1 minute or until cheese melts. Sprinkle with parsley to serve. Makes 4 main-dish servings.

Each serving: About 370 calories, 25 g protein, 38 g carbohydrate, 14 g total fat (5 g saturated), 4 g fiber, 60 mg cholesterol, 490 mg sodium.

Turkey Gumbo

PREP: 20 MINUTES • COOK: 2 HOURS 15 MINUTES

A delicious stew you would never guess is made with leftovers. Use the turkey carcass to make a flavorful broth—for the gumbo and tender rice. Serve with a dash of hot pepper sauce if you like.

1 turkey carcass plus about 8 ounces leftover
   cooked turkey meat
1 medium carrot
2 large celery stalks
2 medium onions
2 garlic cloves
¼ cup all-purpose flour
1 tablespoon vegetable oil
4 ounces kielbasa (smoked Polish sausage),
   diced (about 1 cup)
1 can (14½ ounces) diced tomatoes
¼ cup tomato paste
1 medium red pepper, chopped
1 bay leaf
½ teaspoon salt
¼ teaspoon dried thyme
¼ teaspoon ground red pepper (cayenne)
¼ teaspoon ground allspice
1 package (10 ounces) frozen cut okra
1 cup regular long-grain rice

1 Prepare turkey broth: With kitchen shears or cleaver, cut carcass into several pieces. Cut leftover turkey meat into ¾-inch pieces; cover and refrigerate. (You should have about 2 cups.) Cut carrot and 1 celery stalk into 2-inch pieces; cut 1 onion into 4 wedges. Reserve remaining celery and onion for making gumbo later.

2 In 6-quart saucepot, place turkey-carcass pieces, cut-up carrot, celery, and onion wedges, and 1 garlic clove. Add *2 quarts water*; heat to boiling over high heat. Reduce heat to low and simmer, uncovered, 1 hour.

3 Drain broth through colander into 8-cup glass measuring cup or bowl. Discard solids and return broth to saucepot. Heat broth to boiling over high heat; boil uncovered, 5 minutes or until broth is reduced to 5 cups. Set broth aside.

4 Meanwhile, prepare gumbo: In 4-quart saucepan, cook flour over low heat until golden, about 10 minutes, stirring frequently. Transfer flour to cup; set aside.

5 While flour is cooking, thinly slice reserved celery and onion, and mince remaining garlic clove.

6 In same saucepan, heat oil over medium-high heat. Add kielbasa and cook 2 minutes or until lightly browned, stirring. With slotted spoon, transfer kielbasa to plate. Stir ¼ cup turkey broth into flour in cup until paste forms. Reduce heat to medium; add paste to saucepan and cook 1 minute, stirring. Gradually stir in 2¾ cups turkey broth.

7 Return kielbasa to saucepan. Stir in onion, celery, garlic, tomatoes with their juice, tomato paste, red pepper, bay leaf, salt, thyme, ground red pepper, and allspice; heat to boiling over high heat. Add frozen okra; reduce heat to low and simmer, covered, 45 minutes or until vegetables are tender. Stir in turkey meat; cook 1 minute.

8 Meanwhile, prepare rice: In 2-quart saucepan, heat remaining 2 cups turkey broth to boiling over high heat. Add rice; heat to boiling. Reduce heat to low; cover and simmer 18 to 20 minutes, until rice is tender.

9 To serve, discard bay leaf from gumbo. Spoon gumbo over rice in bowls. Makes about 8 cups gumbo or 4 main-dish servings.

Each serving with rice: About 525 calories, 31 g protein, 63 g carbohydrate, 16 g total fat (5 g saturated), 3 g fiber, 67 mg cholesterol, 1020 mg sodium.

Turkey Shepherd's Pies

PREP: 30 MINUTES • BAKE: 30 MINUTES

Here's a good way to use up some of the Thanksgiving leftovers: A turkey-meat filling is topped with leftover mashed potatoes. We think our Mashed Potatoes with Horseradish Cream (page 150) make an especially good topping for these individual shepherd's pies. Although the canned chicken broth called for here works well, we recommend using the turkey carcass to make a flavorful homemade turkey broth.

1 tablespoon olive oil
2 medium carrots, cut into ½-inch dice
1 medium onion, cut into ½-inch dice
1 medium celery stalk, cut into ½-inch dice
2 cups leftover mashed potatoes
¾ cup milk
2 tablespoons all-purpose flour
1 cup chicken broth or turkey broth
2 cups bite-size pieces leftover cooked turkey
    meat (about 8 ounces)
1 cup frozen peas
¼ teaspoon salt
⅛ teaspoon coarsely ground black pepper
Pinch dried thyme
Thyme sprigs for garnish

1 In 5- to 6-quart Dutch oven, heat olive oil over medium heat until hot. Add carrots, onion, and celery, and cook until vegetables are tender and lightly browned, about 15 minutes.

2 Meanwhile, in small bowl, stir mashed potatoes with ¼ cup milk until combined.

3 Preheat oven to 450°F. In 2-cup glass measuring cup, mix flour with broth and remaining ½ cup milk until blended. Pour broth mixture into Dutch oven with vegetables; heat over high heat until mixture boils and thickens slightly, stirring often. Boil 1 minute. Reduce heat to medium; add turkey, frozen peas, salt, pepper, and thyme, and heat through.

Turkey Shepherd's Pies

4 Place four 1½-cup ramekins or soufflé dishes on 15½" by 10½" jelly-roll pan for easier handling. Spoon warm turkey mixture into ramekins; top with potato mixture. Bake 30 minutes or until hot and bubbly and potatoes are lightly browned. Garnish with thyme sprigs. Makes 4 main-dish servings.

Each serving: About 320 calories, 25 g protein, 33 g carbohydrate, 10 g total fat (3 g saturated), 4 g fiber, 54 mg cholesterol, 615 mg sodium.

MEAT

Raspberry-Balsamic Steaks

PREP: 10 MINUTES • COOK: 15 MINUTES

SKILLET STEAKS:
4 beef cubed steaks (about 4 ounces each)
¼ teaspoon salt
¼ teaspoon coarsely ground black pepper
2 teaspoons vegetable oil

RASPBERRY-BALSAMIC SAUCE:
1 teaspoon vegetable oil
1 small red onion, finely chopped
2 tablespoons balsamic vinegar
3 tablespoons seedless red raspberry jam
2 tablespoons chopped fresh parsley leaves
⅛ teaspoon coarsely ground black pepper

1 Prepare Skillet Steaks: Pat steaks dry with paper towels. Sprinkle steaks with salt and pepper.

2 In nonstick 12-inch skillet, heat oil over medium-high heat until hot. Add steaks, and cook 5 to 6 minutes for medium, turning steaks over once. When steaks are done, transfer to platter with any juice; cover with foil.

3 Prepare Raspberry-Balsamic Sauce: In same skillet, heat oil over medium heat until hot. Add red onion and ¼ *cup water*, and cook about 5 minutes or until onion is tender, stirring occasionally. Stir in balsamic vinegar and another ¼ *cup water*; heat to boiling over medium-high heat. Boil 1 minute or until slightly reduced. Remove skillet from heat; stir in jam, parsley, and pepper until blended. Return steaks with their juice to skillet; heat through. Makes 4 main-dish servings.

Each serving: About 320 calories, 23 g protein, 14 g carbohydrate, 19 g total fat (6 g saturated), 0 g fiber, 72 mg cholesterol, 200 mg sodium.

Moroccan-Style Steaks

PREP: 10 MINUTES • COOK: 15 MINUTES

Cubed steak, a convenient cut tenderized by a machine, is ready in a matter of minutes—and the sauce cooks up right in the same skillet. Serve with couscous, rice, or noodles to soak up the juice.

SKILLET STEAKS:
4 beef cubed steaks (about 4 ounces each)
¼ teaspoon salt
¼ teaspoon coarsely ground black pepper
2 teaspoons vegetable oil

MOROCCAN-STYLE SAUCE:
1 teaspoon vegetable oil
1 small yellow or red pepper, thinly sliced
½ teaspoon ground cumin
¼ teaspoon ground cinnamon
1 cup bottled salsa
1 tablespoon brown sugar
2 tablespoons chopped fresh cilantro leaves
Cilantro sprigs for garnish

1 Prepare Skillet Steaks: Pat steaks dry with paper towels. Sprinkle steaks with salt and pepper.

2 In nonstick 12-inch skillet, heat oil over medium-high heat until hot. Add steaks, and cook 5 to 6 minutes for medium, turning steaks over once. When steaks are done, transfer to platter with any juice; cover with foil.

3 Prepare Moroccan-style Sauce: In same skillet, heat oil over medium heat until hot. Add yellow or red pepper, cumin, cinnamon, and ¼ *cup water*, and cook about 5 minutes or until pepper is tender, stirring occasionally. Stir in salsa, brown sugar, and another ¼ *cup water*; heat to boiling over medium-high heat. Boil 1 minute or until slightly reduced. Remove skillet from heat; stir in chopped cilantro. Return steaks with their juice to skillet and heat through. Garnish with cilantro sprigs. Makes 4 main-dish servings.

Each serving: About 305 calories, 24 g protein, 9 g carbohydrate, 19 g total fat (6 g saturated), 0 g fiber, 72 mg cholesterol, 465 mg sodium.

Moroccan-Style Steaks ➤

Pepper-Crusted Beef Tenderloin with Red-Wine Gravy

PREP: 30 MINUTES PLUS STANDING • ROAST: 50 MINUTES

A simple black-pepper crust highlights this elegant piece of meat. When shopping for a whole tenderloin, don't be surprised that it weighs up to 6 pounds before it's trimmed down to its roasting weight of 4½ pounds. If possible, ask the butcher to do it for you. If tying the roast yourself, make sure to tuck the thin, narrow end under so the tenderloin is uniformly thick.

TENDERLOIN ROAST:
3 tablespoons cracked black pepper
1 tablespoon olive oil
1 teaspoon salt
1 whole beef tenderloin, trimmed and tied (4½ pounds)

RED-WINE GRAVY:
2 tablespoons margarine or butter
4 medium shallots (6 ounces), minced (½ cup)
1 can (14½ ounces) chicken broth
1 cup dry red wine
½ cup loosely packed fresh parsley leaves, chopped
Parsley sprigs for garnish

1 Prepare Tenderloin Roast: Preheat oven to 425°F. In cup, mix pepper, olive oil, and salt; rub mixture all over meat. Place tenderloin on rack in large roasting pan (17" by 11½'). Roast tenderloin 50 minutes or until meat thermometer reaches 140°F. Internal temperature of meat will rise to 145°F. (medium-rare) upon standing. Or, roast to desired doneness.

2 About 20 minutes before tenderloin is done, prepare Red-Wine Gravy: In 2-quart saucepan, melt margarine or butter over medium heat. Add shallots and cook 10 minutes or until tender and golden, stirring often. Add chicken broth and wine; heat to boiling over high heat. Boil 10 minutes or until sauce is reduced to about 2⅓ cups. Remove saucepan from heat.

KITCHEN WINE LIST

What makes the fruit sauce served with our roast pork loin (page 89) so delectable? A cup of Madeira, a fortified wine. Unlike fortified milk and cereal, which get their oomph from vitamins and minerals, fortified wines are enriched with a neutral grape brandy—either before or after fermentation—to sweeten the flavor and increase the alcohol content. But what you've heard before is true—most alcohol does evaporate during cooking, so the wine's main job is to impart aromatic flavor notes. When using wines in recipes, stick to the type recommended; the wrong choice can affect the outcome dramatically.

A Short Glossary
Madeira Named for the Portuguese island where it's made, this rich, slightly nutty, brownish-gold wine is unique because it's heated during production. The 4 types—dry, medium-dry, medium-sweet, and sweet —are often distinguished by the grapes used. We chose dry Madeira for the sauce served with our pork because it blended so well with the sweet apricots and cranberries.

Marsala Italy's most famous fortified wine, golden in color, is better known for cooking than drinking (think veal Marsala). It comes in dry, semidry, and sweet versions, and is a key ingredient in the Italian dessert zabaglione.

Port This full-bodied, typically sweet wine takes its name from the Portuguese city of Oporto. Whether a young ruby port or a wood-aged tawny one, this wine works wonders in fruit compotes as well as in sweet and savory sauces.

Sherry Many Americans automatically think of the sweet, syrupy, cream type that their grandmas and great-aunts sipped, but it's dry sherry (from Spain, the United States, or Australia) that is often used in seafood dishes and stir-fries. Although cooking sherry is sold in supermarkets, we don't recommend it— like other so-called cooking wines, it usually contains a lot of salt and other additives.

3 When tenderloin is done, transfer to large platter; let stand 10 minutes for easier slicing. Meanwhile, remove rack from roasting pan. Skim any fat from drippings in roasting pan and discard.

4 To serve, add drippings from roasting pan and any meat juice on platter to gravy; heat through. Stir in chopped parsley. Remove string from tenderloin and cut meat into thin slices. Garnish platter with parsley sprigs. Serve tenderloin with gravy. Makes 10 main-dish servings.

Each serving of tenderloin: About 360 calories, 43 g protein, 1 g carbohydrate, 19 g total fat (7 g saturated), 1 g fiber, 127 mg cholesterol, 310 mg sodium.

Each ¼ cup gravy: About 40 calories, 1 g protein, 2 g carbohydrate, 3 g total fat (1 g saturated), 0 g fiber, 0 mg cholesterol, 165 mg sodium.

Stroganoff Steaks

PREP: 10 MINUTES • COOK: 15 MINUTES

SKILLET STEAKS:
4 beef cubed steaks (about 4 ounces each)
¼ teaspoon salt
¼ teaspoon coarsely ground black pepper
2 teaspoons vegetable oil

STROGANOFF SAUCE:
1 teaspoon vegetable oil
10 ounces sliced white mushrooms
1 small onion, finely chopped
½ cup chicken broth
¼ cup reduced-fat sour cream
½ teaspoon Dijon mustard
⅛ teaspoon coarsely ground black pepper
1 tablespoon chopped fresh dill

1 Prepare Skillet Steaks: Pat steaks dry with paper towels. Sprinkle steaks with salt and pepper.

2 In nonstick 12-inch skillet, heat oil over medium-high heat until hot. Add steaks, and cook 5 to 6 minutes for medium, turning steaks over once. When steaks are done, transfer to platter with any juice; cover with foil.

3 Prepare Stroganoff Sauce: In same skillet, heat oil over medium-high heat until hot. Add mushrooms and onion, and cook about 8 minutes or until onion is tender and all liquid evaporates, stirring occasion-ally. Add chicken broth; heat to boiling. Boil 1 minute or until slightly reduced. Remove skillet from heat; stir in sour cream, mustard, pepper, and dill. Return steaks with their juice to skillet; heat through. Makes 4 main-dish servings.

Each serving: About 315 calories, 26 g protein, 6 g carbohydrate, 20 g total fat (6 g saturated), 1 g fiber, 77 mg cholesterol, 320 mg sodium.

Orange Beef

PREP: 10 MINUTES • COOK: ABOUT 12 MINUTES

A quick take on the classic Chinese restaurant dish—add steamed rice and veggies for a complete meal. If you like your beef hot and spicy, substitute crushed red pepper for the black pepper.

2 boneless beef top loin steaks, ¾ inch thick
    (10 ounces each), trimmed
¼ teaspoon salt
2 medium oranges
1 tablespoon dark brown sugar
4 tablespoons soy sauce
1¼ teaspoons cornstarch
¼ teaspoon coarsely ground black pepper

1 Heat nonstick 12-inch skillet over medium-high heat until hot. Sprinkle steaks with salt. Add steaks to skillet and cook 4 minutes; turn steaks over and cook 4 to 5 minutes longer for medium-rare or until of desired doneness.

2 Meanwhile, from oranges, remove 6 strips of peel (3" by 1" each) and squeeze ½ cup juice. Stir brown sugar, soy sauce, cornstarch, and ¼ *cup cold water* into orange juice until blended.

3 Transfer cooked steaks to platter and keep warm. Reduce heat to medium; add orange peel and pepper to skillet and cook 1 minute, stirring. Add orange-juice mixture to skillet and heat to boiling; boil 1 minute.

4 To serve, cut each steak crosswise in half; pour sauce over steaks. Makes 4 main-dish servings.

Each serving: About 225 calories, 28 g protein, 8 g carbohydrate, 8 g total fat (3 g saturated), 0 g fiber, 75 mg cholesterol, 555 mg sodium.

Corned Beef with Cabbage & Potatoes

••
PREP: 30 MINUTES • COOK: 3 HOURS 25 MINUTES

Boil lean corned beef with carrots, parsnips, potatoes, and cabbage, and serve with a mustard sauce accented with horseradish and maple syrup. Reserve 4 cups cooked potatoes and 1½ cups bite-size pieces corned beef if you want to turn them into our Red Flannel Hash (opposite page).

CORNED BEEF & VEGETABLES:
1 corned-beef brisket (about 4½ pounds), trimmed of excess fat
20 whole black peppercorns
5 whole allspice
5 garlic cloves, unpeeled
2 bay leaves
4 pounds all-purpose potatoes, peeled and each cut into quarters

1 pound carrots, peeled
1 pound parsnips, peeled
1 medium head green cabbage (about 3 pounds), cut into 8 wedges, with core attached

HORSERADISH-MUSTARD SAUCE:
½ cup Dijon mustard with seeds
2 tablespoons pure maple syrup
1 tablespoon prepared white horseradish
Chopped parsley for garnish

1 Prepare Corned Beef & Vegetables: In 8-quart Dutch oven or saucepot, place brisket, peppercorns, allspice, garlic, bay leaves, and enough *water* to cover; heat to boiling over high heat. Reduce heat to low; cover and simmer 2 hours 30 minutes.

2 Add quartered potatoes, whole carrots, and whole parsnips to Dutch oven; heat to boiling over high heat. Reduce heat to low; cover and simmer 30 minutes or until meat and vegetables are tender. With tongs and slotted spoon, transfer meat and vegetables to platter; cover and keep warm.

Corned Beef with Cabbage & Potatoes (above) with Soda Bread (page 169)

3 Add cabbage to liquid in Dutch oven; heat to boiling over high heat. Reduce heat to low; cover and simmer 5 minutes or until cabbage is tender.

4 Meanwhile, prepare Horseradish-Mustard Sauce: In small bowl, with fork, mix mustard, maple syrup, and horseradish until smooth; set sauce aside.

5 Drain cabbage and add to platter with meat. Thinly slice meat and serve with vegetables and mustard sauce. Garnish with chopped parsley. Makes 8 main-dish servings.

Each serving: About 520 calories, 41 g protein, 64 g carbohydrate, 12 g total fat (4 g saturated), 10 g fiber, 105 mg cholesterol, 1450 mg sodium.

Red Flannel Hash

PREP: 15 MINUTES • COOK: 30 MINUTES

Sauté the ingredients until golden and crisp. Serve by the plateful with a cucumber-and-dill salad.

1 tablespoon margarine or butter
1 tablespoon vegetable oil
1 jumbo onion (about 1 pound), chopped
2 large celery stalks, cut into ½-inch pieces
1 can (14½ ounces) whole beets, drained and cut into ½-inch pieces
4 cups bite-size pieces cooked potatoes (reserved from Corned Beef with Cabbage & Potatoes, at left)
1½ cups bite-size pieces cooked corned beef (reserved from Corned Beef with Cabbage & Potatoes, at left), about 6 ounces
½ teaspoon salt
¼ teaspoon coarsely ground black pepper
1 tablespoon chopped fresh parsley leaves

1 In nonstick 12-inch skillet, heat margarine or butter with oil over medium heat. Add onion and celery, and cook 15 minutes or until lightly browned and tender, stirring occasionally.

2 Increase heat to medium-high; add beets, potatoes, corned beef, salt, and pepper, and cook 15 minutes or until browned, stirring occasionally. Sprinkle with parsley to serve. Makes 4 main-dish servings.

Each serving: About 415 calories, 19 g protein, 62 g carbohydrate, 11 g total fat (3 g saturated), 7 g fiber, 40 mg cholesterol, 1065 mg sodium.

Traditi_
_L_

PREP: 30 MINUT_

A great family-frie_
turkey. Try the b_
ethnically inspir_
(page 85), Italia_
Swedish Meat Loaves (pa_

1 pound ground turkey
1 pound lean ground beef
2 large eggs, beaten
1 small zucchini (8 ounces), grated
1 cup fresh bread crumbs (about 2 slices firm white bread)
1½ teaspoons salt
½ teaspoon coarsely ground black pepper
1 tablespoon margarine or butter
1 medium onion, coarsely chopped
2 garlic cloves, crushed with garlic press

1 Preheat oven to 400°F. Line 15½" by 10½" jelly-roll pan with foil.

2 In large bowl, with hands, mix ground turkey, ground beef, eggs, zucchini, bread crumbs, salt, and pepper; set aside.

3 In nonstick 12-inch skillet, heat margarine or butter over medium heat. Add onion and cook until tender, about 5 minutes, stirring occasionally. Add garlic, and cook 1 minute longer. With hands, combine onion mixture with meat mixture in bowl.

4 On foil-lined pan, shape ground-meat mixture into eight 4½" by 2½" loaves.

5 Bake loaves 25 to 30 minutes, until browned on the outside and internal temperature of loaves is 160°F. (temperature will rise to 165°F. upon standing). Slice to serve if you like. Makes 8 main-dish servings.

Each serving: About 260 calories, 23 g protein, 5 g carbohydrate, 15 g total fat (4 g saturated), 1 g fiber, 117 mg cholesterol, 535 mg sodium.

Porcupine Meatballs

PREP: 30 MINUTES • COOK: 40 MINUTES

As these meatballs poach in chicken broth, the rice cooks and expands, so that the meatballs resemble porcupines.

1 tablespoon vegetable oil
½ small red pepper, finely chopped (½ cup)
3 green onions, finely chopped
2 garlic cloves, crushed with garlic press
1 tablespoon minced, peeled fresh ginger plus
    four ¼-inch-thick slices
1 pound ground pork
½ cup long-grain white rice
1 tablespoon soy sauce
⅛ teaspoon ground red pepper (cayenne)
1 large egg
1 can (14½ ounces) chicken broth
¼ teaspoon Asian sesame oil
Julienne strips green onion and red pepper for
    garnish

1 In deep 10-inch skillet, heat oil over medium-high heat until hot. Add red pepper and cook 5 minutes or just until tender and golden, stirring occasionally. Add green onions, garlic, and minced ginger, and cook 1 minute longer, stirring.

2 Transfer vegetable mixture to medium bowl. Stir in ground pork, uncooked rice, soy sauce, ground red pepper, and egg until blended.

3 Line 15½" by 10½" jelly-roll pan with waxed paper. With damp hands, shape meat mixture by rounded tablespoons to form about thirty-two 1½-inch meatballs (mixture will be soft); place on jelly-roll pan.

4 In same skillet, heat broth, sesame oil, ginger slices, and 1½ *cups water* to boiling over high heat.

5 Carefully arrange meatballs in simmering broth mixture (skillet will be very full); heat to boiling. Reduce heat to low; cover and simmer 30 minutes.

6 Serve meatballs with broth in shallow bowls; top with green-onion and red-pepper strips. Makes 4 main-dish or 8 first-course servings.

Each main-dish serving: About 475 calories, 25 g protein, 22 g carbohydrate, 31 g total fat (10 g saturated), 1 g fiber, 126 mg cholesterol, 680 mg sodium.

Asian Meat Loaves with Cabbage & Ginger

PREP: 30 MINUTES • BAKE: 25 TO 30 MINUTES

You can also shape the meat into 24 balls. Place on 2 foil-lined jelly-roll pans, brush with choice of glaze, and bake for 20 minutes at 400°F.

Traditional Meat Loaves (page 83)
8 ounces Napa cabbage, chopped (4 cups
    loosely packed)
2 tablespoons grated, peeled fresh ginger
¼ teaspoon ground red pepper (cayenne)
3 tablespoons hoisin sauce
¼ cup ketchup

Prepare Traditional Meat Loaves as in steps 1 through 4, but in step 3, add cabbage, ginger, and ground red pepper to skillet with cooked onion mixture; increase heat to medium-high and cook 5 minutes longer, stirring occasionally. Combine cabbage mixture, 2 tablespoons hoisin sauce, and ¼ cup water with meat mixture in bowl. Before baking loaves in step 5, in cup, stir ketchup with remaining 1 tablespoon hoisin sauce; spread glaze over tops of loaves. Bake as directed. Makes 8 main-dish servings.

Each serving: About 285 calories, 23 g protein, 10 g carbohydrate, 16 g total fat (4 g saturated), 1 g fiber, 117 mg cholesterol, 730 mg sodium.

◄ *Porcupine Meatballs*

Keema
with Spiced Rice

The richly seasoned Indian entrée of ground lamb and peas is the perfect topper for a fluffy mound of rice flavored with cloves and pepper.

KEEMA:
1 tablespoon olive oil
1 medium onion, finely chopped
1 tablespoon minced, peeled fresh ginger
2 garlic cloves, minced
1 cinnamon stick (3 inches long)
1 tablespoon ground coriander
2 teaspoons ground cumin
¼ teaspoon ground red pepper (cayenne)
1 pound lean ground beef or lamb
2 tablespoons tomato paste
1 tablespoon fresh lemon juice
¾ teaspoon salt

SPICED RICE:
1 tablespoon olive oil
1 cinnamon stick (3 inches long)
10 whole black peppercorns
6 whole cardamom pods
4 whole cloves
1 cup long-grain white rice
½ teaspoon salt
1½ cups frozen peas
½ cup packed cilantro leaves, chopped

1 Prepare Keema: In nonstick 12-inch skillet, heat oil over medium heat until hot. Add onion and cook until tender, about 5 minutes. Add ginger and garlic; cook 1 minute, stirring constantly. Add cinnamon, coriander, cumin, and ground red pepper; cook 1 minute longer, stirring.

2 Stir in ground meat, tomato paste, lemon juice, and salt, and cook over medium-high heat until meat is browned, stirring often. Reduce heat to low; cover and simmer 20 minutes.

3 Meanwhile, prepare Spiced Rice: In 2-quart saucepan, heat oil over medium heat. Add cinnamon, peppercorns, cardamom, and cloves; cover and cook just until spices begin to pop, about 2 minutes, swirling pan occasionally. (If you like, transfer heated

spices to a piece of cheesecloth to make a spice bag; tie with string and return to saucepan. This will make it easier to remove spices after cooking.)

4 Add rice to spice mixture and cook 1 minute, stirring. Add salt and *2 cups water*; heat to boiling over high heat. Reduce heat to low; cover and simmer 15 to 18 minutes, until rice is tender and liquid is absorbed.

5 To serve, stir frozen peas and cilantro into meat mixture; heat through. Spoon Keema over spiced rice. Makes 4 main-dish servings.

Each serving: About 520 calories, 31 g protein, 53 g carbohydrate, 20 g total fat (7 g saturated), 4 g fiber, 81 mg cholesterol, 805 mg sodium.

Italian Meat
Loaves with Spinach
& Fennel

You can also shape the meat into 24 balls. Place on 2 foil-lined jelly-roll pans, brush with choice of glaze, and bake for 20 minutes at 400°F.

Traditional Meat Loaves (page 83)
1 package (10 ounces) frozen chopped spinach, thawed and squeezed dry
1 teaspoon fennel seeds, crushed
1 can (8 ounces) tomato sauce
1 tablespoon Worcestershire sauce

Prepare Traditional Meat Loaves as in steps 1 through 4, but in step 3, stir spinach, fennel seeds, and ½ cup tomato sauce into skillet with cooked onion mixture. Before baking loaves in step 5, in cup, stir Worcestershire with remaining tomato sauce; spread glaze over tops of loaves. Makes 8 main-dish servings.

Each serving: About 285 calories, 24 g protein, 10 g carbohydrate, 16 g total fat (4 g saturated), 2 mg fiber, 117 mg cholesterol, 755 mg sodium.

THE WORLD'S BEST CHEESEBURGERS
...AND MORE

Right after steak, hamburgers are America's favorite choice for the grill, smoking out hot dogs, chicken, and ribs. (We ate 3.2 billion burgers at home last year.) Who can resist one cooked in the Great Outdoors? It's the perfect fit for a soft roll, and an instant meal-maker. Here, tips for mouthwatering results.

Ingredients: Use ground chuck, which is 81 to 85 percent lean. The leanest ground beef, such as sirloin or round (90 to 95 percent lean), is fine for slimming down chili and meatballs, but won't give you a plump, juicy burger. If you don't want to switch to chuck, mix in a tablespoon or 2 of water, wine, broth, or milk per pound, to make trimmer meat moister. And salt patties *after* cooking. Salt draws out juices, leaving meat cardboardlike.

Forming patties: Use a light touch. Handle ground beef gently when shaping it, so you don't end up with a dense, compact burger. Start with a mound (about 4 to 5 ounces), flatten it slightly, and smooth edge all around.

Keep it safe: Whether you're traveling to a picnic with raw patties or storing them in the fridge until dinner, don't let the uncooked beef or juices come in contact with other foods; the spread of deadly E. coli and other bacteria is a real risk. Stack burgers with waxed paper or plastic wrap in between. Place in an airtight container; transport in a cooler, surrounded by ice packs.

Cooking: Preheat grill. A hot grill sears hamburgers, so they don't stick. But be patient: Flattening patties with the spatula—which most of us do—doesn't speed up cook time. It just squeezes out the flavorful juices.

Even if you love them, stop serving burgers rare. According to the U.S. Department of Agriculture, they should be cooked at least to medium doneness in the center, 160°F. on an instant-read thermometer (for the most accurate reading, insert instant-read dial thermometer horizontally). A chilled burger that is ¾ inch thick should be ready to roll after about 10 minutes over the fire.

Basic Burgers
Shape 1¼ pounds ground beef chuck into 4 patties, each ¾ inch thick. Place patties on grill over medium heat; cook about 10 minutes for medium doneness, turning once. Makes 4 quarter-pound burgers.

The Ultimate Cheeseburger
So you want to blanket that charbroiled beauty with your favorite cheese, but it ends up melting all over the grill slats? Speed is of the essence. Place cheese on meat, close grill, and check when a minute is up.

Quick Changes
Jazz up a basic burger with tempting fixings and different breads:
- Prepared pesto mixed with mayonnaise to taste, roasted red peppers, sliced Italian bread
- Melted Swiss or Jarlsberg cheese, sautéed mushrooms and onions, toasted rye bread
- Melted Cheddar cheese, sliced pickles, sourdough roll
- Store-bought BBQ sauce,* soft roll, corn relish and coleslaw on the side
- Teriyaki sauce,* horseradish, sliced green onion, toasted sourdough English muffin
- Melted Monterey Jack cheese, sliced pickled jalapeños, tomato, avocado, cilantro, flour tortilla
- Melted American cheese, bacon, toasted English muffin
- Fresh mozzarella, tomato, a few basil leaves, focaccia bread
- Ketchup; a pinch of grated, peeled fresh ginger; sliced green onion; sesame-seed roll
- Honey mustard,* grilled pineapple rings, whole wheat bread
- Sliced beets and onions, dilled sour cream, pumpernickel bread
- Mango chutney, fresh apple slices, plain yogurt, pita pocket
- Worcestershire sauce,* salad greens, blue cheese, French bread

Roast Pork Loin with Apricot-Cranberry Pan Sauce

PREP: 30 MINUTES PLUS STANDING • ROAST: 1½ TO 2 HOURS

This succulent roast is served with a special "do-ahead" sauce made with dried fruits. A 5½- to 6-pound roast should have 10 ribs—check to make sure you have at least 1 per person.

PORK ROAST:
2 large lemons
2 garlic cloves, crushed with garlic press
1 tablespoon olive oil
2 teaspoons coarsely ground black pepper
1 teaspoon salt
1 pork loin roast (5½ to 6 pounds), trimmed and backbone cracked

FRUIT SAUCE:
2 tablespoons margarine or butter
1 small onion, finely chopped
1 can (14½ ounces) chicken broth
1 cup dry Madeira wine
½ cup dried cranberries
½ cup dried apricots, chopped
½ cup loosely packed fresh parsley leaves, chopped

Thyme sprigs for garnish

1 Prepare Pork Roast: Preheat oven to 350°F. From lemons, grate 2½ teaspoons peel and squeeze 1 tablespoon juice. In cup, mix lemon peel and juice, garlic, oil, pepper, and salt.

2 Pat pork loin dry with paper towels. Place pork in medium roasting pan (15½" by 10½"); rub lemon mixture all over pork. Insert meat thermometer into thickest part of pork, being careful that pointed end does not touch bone. Roast 1½ to 2 hours, depending on weight of loin, until thermometer reaches 155°F. Internal temperature of meat will rise to 160°F. upon standing.

3 While pork is roasting, prepare Fruit Sauce: In 2-quart saucepan, melt margarine or butter over medium heat. Add onion and cook 10 minutes or until tender and golden. Add chicken broth, Madeira, cranberries, and apricots; heat to boiling over high heat. Boil 8 minutes, stirring occasionally, until sauce is reduced to about 2⅔ cups. Remove saucepan from heat.

4 When pork is done, transfer to warm large platter. Let stand 15 minutes for easier carving; keep warm.

5 Meanwhile, skim fat from drippings in roasting pan and discard. Add Fruit Sauce to pan and cook over medium heat 1 minute, stirring to loosen brown bits from bottom of pan. Stir in parsley.

6 To serve, add any meat juice on platter to sauce. Garnish platter with thyme sprigs. Serve roast with Fruit Sauce. Makes 10 main-dish servings.

Each serving of roast: About 300 calories, 34 g protein, 1 g carbohydrate, 17 g total fat (6 g saturated), 0 g fiber, 77 mg cholesterol, 300 mg sodium.

Each ¼ cup Fruit Sauce: About 70 calories, 2 g protein, 10 g carbohydrate, 3 g total fat (1 g saturated), 1 g fiber, 0 mg cholesterol, 190 mg sodium.

Swedish Meat Loaves with Mushrooms & Dill

PREP: 30 MINUTES • BAKE: 25 TO 30 MINUTES

You can also shape the meat into 24 balls. Place on 2 foil-lined jelly-roll pans, brush with choice of glaze, and bake for 20 minutes at 400°F.

Traditional Meat Loaves (page 83)
10 ounces mushrooms, finely chopped
¼ cup milk
⅛ teaspoon ground nutmeg
½ cup plus 2 tablespoons chopped fresh dill
¼ cup light mayonnaise
1 tablespoon Dijon mustard

Prepare Traditional Meat Loaves as in steps 1 through 4, but in step 3, add mushrooms to skillet with cooked onion mixture; increase heat to medium-high and cook 8 minutes longer, stirring occasionally. Combine onion mixture, milk, nutmeg, and ½ cup dill with meat mixture in bowl. Before baking loaves in step 5, in cup, stir mayonnaise, mustard, and remaining 2 tablespoons dill; spread glaze over tops of loaves. Makes 8 main-dish servings.

Each serving: About 290 calories, 24 g protein, 9 g carbohydrate, 17 g total fat (5 g saturated), 1 g fiber, 118 mg cholesterol, 655 mg sodium.

◀ *Roast Pork Loin with Apricot-Cranberry Pan Sauce*

Red-Cooked Pork

PREP: 45 MINUTES • BAKE: 2 HOURS 30 MINUTES

This Chinese method of slow cooking turns a rich piece of meat into flavorful morsels that simply fall off the bone. "Red-cooked" refers to the dark, burnished color of the meat after it's braised in the aromatic cooking broth. If you'd like to make our Mu Shu Pork recipe (at right) reserve 3 cups shredded pork and ½ cup cooking broth.

1 whole bone-in pork shoulder roast (7 pounds), trimmed of skin and excess fat
1 piece (2 inches long) fresh ginger, peeled and thinly sliced
3 garlic cloves, crushed with flat side of chef's knife
2 strips (3" by 1" each) fresh orange peel
1 cinnamon stick (3 inches long)
1 whole star anise
¼ teaspoon crushed red pepper
½ cup plus 1 tablespoon packed brown sugar
¼ cup dry sherry or water
⅓ cup soy sauce
⅓ cup seasoned rice vinegar
Cornstarch

1 Heat 8-quart Dutch oven over medium-high heat until hot. Add pork and cook until browned on all sides, about 15 minutes. Transfer pork to plate.

2 Reduce heat to medium. Add ginger slices, garlic, orange peel, cinnamon stick, star anise, and crushed red pepper, and cook 5 minutes, stirring. Add ½ cup brown sugar and cook 10 minutes longer, stirring frequently. Add sherry or water, stirring to loosen brown bits; cook 2 minutes.

3 Preheat oven to 375°F. Stir in soy sauce, rice vinegar, and 4½ *cups water* into mixture in Dutch oven. Add pork and heat to boiling over high heat. Cover Dutch oven; place in preheated oven and bake 2 hours 30 minutes, turning meat over once during cooking, until meat is fork-tender.

4 Remove Dutch oven from oven. Transfer meat to platter; cover and keep warm.

5 Meanwhile, skim fat from cooking broth. Strain broth through fine-mesh sieve into large glass measuring cup to measure yield of broth. Pour broth back into Dutch oven.

6 In cup, with small wire whisk or fork, mix cornstarch (use 1½ teaspoons cornstarch for each 1 cup cooking broth) with ½ *cup cold water* until blended.

Slowly whisk cornstarch mixture into broth in Dutch oven. Heat broth over medium high heat until mixture boils and thickens slightly, stirring occasionally. Boil 1 minute.

7 Ladle 1 cup broth into 1-quart saucepan; stir in remaining 1 tablespoon brown sugar. Heat to boiling over medium-high heat; boil 15 minutes or until broth is thick and syrupy. With pastry brush, brush syrup over pork.

8 To serve, pour broth into gravy boat. Slice pork or, with 2 forks, shred pork coarsely. Makes 10 main-dish servings.

Each serving: About 400 calories, 43 g protein, 18 g carbohydrate, 16 g total fat (6 g saturated), 0 g fiber, 103 mg cholesterol, 790 mg sodium.

Mu Shu Pork

PREP: 30 MINUTES • COOK: 25 MINUTES

No need to order Chinese take-out when you have this recipe. Serve with a side salad of orange segments drizzled with rice vinegar.

3 teaspoons vegetable oil
2 large eggs, lightly beaten
1 package (10 ounces) mushrooms, sliced
2 cups shredded carrots (4 ounces)
1 pound Napa cabbage (½ small head), thinly sliced
2 garlic cloves, crushed with garlic press
1 tablespoon grated, peeled fresh ginger
8 ounces pork reserved from Red-Cooked Pork (at left), pulled into shreds (2 cups)
½ cup cooking broth reserved from Red-Cooked Pork (at left)
2 cups fresh bean sprouts (4 ounces)
2 green onions, thinly sliced diagonally
Hoisin sauce (optional)
8 (8-inch) flour tortillas, warmed

1 In 12-inch skillet, heat 1 teaspoon oil over medium heat until hot. Add eggs and cook, stirring, 1 to 2 minutes, until eggs are set and scrambled; transfer to medium bowl.

2 Increase heat to medium-high; in same skillet, in 1 teaspoon oil, cook mushrooms until liquid evaporates and mushrooms are browned, about 8 minutes, stirring occasionally. Add carrots and cook 2 minutes longer, stirring. Transfer vegetables to bowl with eggs.

3 In remaining 1 teaspoon oil, cook cabbage 5 to 7 minutes, until cabbage is tender and golden, stirring occasionally. Add garlic and ginger; cook 1 minute longer, stirring.

4 Return vegetable mixture to skillet. Add pork and pork cooking broth; heat through, stirring to loosen brown bits from bottom of skillet. Remove skillet from heat; stir in bean sprouts and sprinkle with green onions.

5 To serve, spread thin coating of hoisin sauce on warm tortillas if you like, then top with pork mixture. Roll up tortillas with filling, jelly-roll fashion. Makes 4 main-dish servings.

Each serving: About 530 calories, 35 g protein, 52 g carbohydrate, 20 g total fat (5 g saturated), 3 g fiber, 156 mg cholesterol, 565 mg sodium.

Pork Medallions with Shallot & Red-Wine Sauce

PREP: 15 MINUTES • COOK: ABOUT 20 MINUTES

Sauté pork tenderloin rounds, then pour on the flavorful pan sauce.

2 whole pork tenderloins (about 12 ounces each)
¼ teaspoon salt
¼ teaspoon coarsely ground black pepper
2 tablespoons margarine or butter
1 large shallot, minced (about ¼ cup)
⅓ cup dry red wine
⅓ cup chicken broth

1 Cut tenderloins crosswise into ½-inch-thick slices. Place pork slices between 2 sheets of waxed paper or plastic wrap and pound with meat mallet or rolling pin to ¼-inch thickness. Sprinkle pork medallions with salt and pepper.

2 In nonstick 12-inch skillet, heat 1 tablespoon margarine or butter over medium-high heat until melted and hot. Add half the pork and cook 2 minutes; turn pork over and cook 2 to 3 minutes longer, until browned on the outside and still slightly pink on the inside. Transfer to platter; keep warm. Repeat with remaining pork, but do not add additional margarine.

3 In same skillet, melt remaining 1 tablespoon margarine or butter over medium-low heat. Add shallot and 1 tablespoon water, and cook 5 minutes or until tender and golden, stirring constantly. Add red wine and chicken broth; heat to boiling over medium-high heat. Boil 3 minutes. Pour sauce over pork to serve. Makes 6 main-dish servings.

Each serving: About 195 calories, 26 g protein, 1 g carbohydrate, 8 g total fat (2 g saturated), 0 g fiber, 60 mg cholesterol, 265 mg sodium.

CRANBERRY-PEAR RELISH

Turkey isn't the only roasted meat that benefits from a pairing with a sweet and savory fruit sauce. Pork is also a perfect candidate. Try this relish with Roast Pork Loin (page 89) in place of the Apricot-Cranberry Pan Sauce. Of course if you're a purist, this relish will go quite nicely with the Thanksgiving bird, or even as part of a next-day sandwich (see Stuffing Sandwiches, page 68).

PREP: 10 MINUTES PLUS CHILLING
COOK: 30 MINUTES

2 teaspoons margarine or butter
2 small shallots (about 2 ounces), *thinly sliced*
¾ cup packed dark brown sugar
1 tablespoon balsamic vinegar
1 bag (12 ounces) cranberries (3 cups)
1 medium Bosc pear, peeled, cored, and diced
¼ teaspoon crushed red pepper
Pinch salt

1 In nonstick 10-inch skillet, melt margarine or butter over medium heat; add shallots and cook 8 minutes, stirring occasionally. Add ¼ cup brown sugar and cook 5 minutes, then add vinegar and cook 2 minutes longer, stirring. Add cranberries, remaining ½ cup brown sugar, and ¾ *cup water*; heat to boiling over medium-high heat. Reduce heat to low and cook, covered, 10 minutes.

2 Add pear, red pepper, and salt, and cook, covered, 5 minutes longer or until most cranberries pop and mixture thickens slightly. Spoon relish into bowl; cover and refrigerate until well chilled, about 3 hours or up to 3 days. Makes about 3 cups.

Each ¼ cup: About 85 calories, 0 g protein, 20 g carbohydrate, 1 g total fat (0 g saturated), 1 g fiber, 0 mg cholesterol, 25 mg sodium.

Breaded Pork Chops

PREP: 25 MINUTES • BROIL: ABOUT 10 MINUTES

These chops are broiled but taste like they've been deep-fried! Use this recipe as a template for one of our three variations: Chili-Crust Pork Chops (below), Herb-Coated Pork Chops (at right), or Parmesan-Coated Pork Chops (page 95).

⅓ cup plain dried bread crumbs
¼ teaspoon dried thyme
¼ teaspoon salt
¼ teaspoon coarsely ground black pepper
1 large egg
4 bone-in pork loin chops, ¾ inch thick
  (6 ounces each), well trimmed
Olive oil nonstick cooking spray

1 Preheat broiler. On waxed paper, mix bread crumbs, thyme, salt, and pepper. In pie plate, with fork, lightly beat egg. Dip each pork chop into beaten egg, then coat with crumb mixture. Spray both sides of chops generously with nonstick cooking spray.

2 Place pork chops on rack in broiling pan. With broiling pan 7 to 9 inches from source of heat, broil chops 8 to 10 minutes, until golden on the outside and still slightly pink on the inside, turning chops over once. Makes 4 main-dish servings.

Each serving: About 240 calories, 20 g protein, 12 g carbohydrate, 14 g total fat (4 g saturated), 1 g fiber, 110 mg cholesterol, 280 mg sodium.

Chili-Crust Pork Chops with Zucchini & Corn Sauté

PREP: 25 MINUTES • BROIL: ABOUT 10 MINUTES

Breaded Pork Chops (above)
4 teaspoons chili powder
1 tablespoon light brown sugar
2 teaspoons olive oil
2 small zucchini (8 ounces each), cut into 1-inch
  chunks
1 cup fresh or frozen corn kernels
½ teaspoon ground cumin
¼ teaspoon salt

¼ teaspoon coarsely ground black pepper
2 tablespoons chopped fresh cilantro leaves

Prepare Breaded Pork Chops as in steps 1 and 2, adding chili powder and brown sugar to crumb mixture. Meanwhile, in nonstick 10-inch skillet, heat oil over medium-high heat until hot. Add zucchini and cook, stirring frequently, 5 minutes or until golden. Add corn, cumin, salt, and pepper, and cook 2 minutes. Stir in chopped cilantro. Spoon sauté over chops. Makes 4 main-dish servings.

Each serving: About 305 calories, 23 g protein, 23 g carbohydrate, 15 g total fat (4 g saturated), 3 g fiber, 110 mg cholesterol, 445 mg sodium.

Herb-Coated Pork Chops with Apple & Onion Sauté

PREP: 25 MINUTES • BROIL: ABOUT 10 MINUTES

Breaded Pork Chops (at left)
2 teaspoons olive oil
2 medium onions, sliced
2 Granny Smith apples, cored and cut into
  ¼-inch-thick wedges
2 teaspoons light brown sugar
¼ teaspoon dried thyme
¼ teaspoon salt
¼ teaspoon ground black pepper
2 teaspoons cider vinegar

Prepare Breaded Pork Chops as in steps 1 and 2. Meanwhile, in nonstick 10-inch skillet, heat oil over medium-high heat until hot. Add onions and cook, stirring frequently, 5 minutes or until lightly browned. Add apples, brown sugar, thyme, salt, and pepper, and cook, stirring occasionally, 8 to 10 minutes longer, until onions and apple are tender. Stir in vinegar and ¼ *cup water*; heat through. Spoon sauté over pork chops. Makes 4 main-dish servings.

Each serving: About 325 calories, 21 g protein, 29 g carbohydrate, 14 g total fat (4 g saturated), 3 g fiber, 110 mg cholesterol, 415 mg sodium.

Chili-Crust Pork Chops with Zucchini & Corn Sauté ➤

Brazilian Pork Chops

PREP: 10 MINUTES • COOK: 45 MINUTES

Here's a dish that's ready with minimal fuss. We call for a packaged rice-and-bean mix so you get lots of flavor from only 5 ingredients.

2 medium oranges
4 bone-in pork loin chops, ¾ inch thick
   (6 ounces each)
⅛ teaspoon coarsely ground black pepper
1 large onion, sliced
¼ teaspoon salt
1 package (8 ounces) red beans and rice mix
1 cup loosely packed fresh cilantro leaves,
   chopped

1 From 1 orange, grate ¾ teaspoon peel and squeeze juice (you should have between ⅓ and ½ cup juice); cut remaining orange into wedges for garnish.

2 Heat nonstick 12-inch skillet over medium-high heat until hot. Add pork chops and sprinkle with pepper. Cook chops 6 minutes or until lightly browned on both sides, turning once. Transfer chops to plate; keep warm.

3 Reduce heat to medium. To same skillet, add onion, ¼ cup water, and salt. Cook onion 10 minutes or until tender and golden, stirring occasionally. Add orange peel and cook 30 seconds. Add bean-and-rice mix and prepare according to package directions, using orange juice plus enough water to equal amount of liquid called for in directions. Heat to boiling over medium-high heat. Reduce heat to low; cover and simmer 15 minutes.

BACON, CHEDDAR & PEA FRITTATA

PREP: 15 MINUTES • BAKE: 10 TO 12 MINUTES

Frittata Mixture:
6 large eggs
¼ cup milk
¼ teaspoon coarsely ground black pepper

Bacon, Cheddar & Pea Filling:
4 slices bacon, cut into ¼-inch pieces
1 cup frozen peas, thawed
2 ounces sharp Cheddar cheese, shredded (½ cup)

1 Preheat oven to 350°F. Use a nonstick 10-inch skillet with oven-safe handle or cover handle with heavy-duty foil for baking in oven later.

2 Prepare Frittata Mixture: In large bowl, with wire whisk or fork, beat eggs with milk and pepper until blended. Set Frittata Mixture aside.

3 Prepare Bacon, Cheddar & Pea Filling: In the skillet, cook bacon over medium heat until browned, about 5 minutes, stirring frequently. Pour off drippings from skillet, leaving bacon. Stir in peas and cook 1 minute.

4 Reduce heat to medium-low. Pour Frittata Mixture over filling in skillet; sprinkle top evenly with cheese. Cook 3 minutes, without stirring, or until egg mixture begins to set around edge. Place

skillet in oven and bake 10 to 12 minutes, until frittata is set.

5 To serve, gently slide frittata out of skillet and onto cutting board or platter. Cut into wedges. Makes 4 main-dish servings.

Each serving: About 305 calories, 22 g protein, 8 g carbohydrate, 21 g total fat (10 g saturated), 2 g fiber, 357 mg cholesterol, 415 mg sodium.

4 Tuck pork chops into rice mixture in skillet and cook, covered, 10 minutes longer or until rice is tender and chops just lose their pink color inside.

5 To serve, garnish with orange wedges and sprinkle with chopped cilantro. Makes 4 main-dish servings.

Each serving: About 590 calories, 31 g protein, 51 g carbohydrate, 29 g total fat (10 g saturated), 5 g fiber, 71 mg cholesterol, 670 mg sodium.

Parmesan-Coated Pork Chops with Tomato & Basil Sauté

PREP: 25 MINUTES • BROIL: ABOUT 10 MINUTES

Breaded Pork Chops (page 92)
3 tablespoons grated Parmesan cheese
Pinch ground red pepper (cayenne)
2 teaspoons olive oil
2 medium onions, sliced
6 large plum tomatoes (1 pound), cut into
   ¾-inch dice
2 teaspoons balsamic vinegar
¼ teaspoon salt
¼ teaspoon coarsely ground black pepper
2 tablespoons chopped fresh basil leaves

Prepare Breaded Pork Chops as in steps 1 and 2, adding Parmesan and ground red pepper to crumb mixture. Meanwhile, in nonstick 10-inch skillet, heat oil over medium heat until hot. Add onions and cook, stirring occasionally, 10 minutes or until tender and golden. Add tomatoes, vinegar, salt, and pepper, and cook 1 minute. Stir in basil. Spoon sauté over broiled chops. Makes 4 main-dish servings.

Each serving: About 305 calories, 24 g protein, 18 g carbohydrate, 16 g total fat (5 g saturated), 3 g fiber, 114 mg cholesterol, 515 mg sodium.

Chinese [

PREP: 20 M
COOK: 20 MINUTES PLUS

Just as tasty but much less gre
take-out. Stir-fry cooled, cooke
the night before) in a skillet wit
of ham, eggs, and Asian flavors.

3 teaspoons vegetable oil
2 large eggs, lightly beaten
8 ounces mushrooms, thinly sliced
1 medium red pepper, finely chopped
1 tablespoon grated, peeled fresh ginger
2 garlic cloves, minced
4½ cups cooked medium-grain white rice,
   cooled (from 1½ cups uncooked rice)
1 cup frozen peas, thawed
4 ounces sliced cooked ham, cut into 1" by ¼"
   strips
2 green onions, thinly sliced
½ cup chicken broth
2 tablespoons soy sauce
1 teaspoon Asian sesame oil
½ cup loosely packed fresh cilantro leaves,
   chopped

1 In nonstick 12-inch skillet, heat 1 teaspoon vegetable oil over medium heat until hot. Add eggs and cook about 2 minutes, stirring with wooden spoon until eggs are scrambled. Transfer eggs to plate; set aside.

2 In same skillet, heat remaining 2 teaspoons vegetable oil over medium-high heat. Add mushrooms and red pepper, and cook until tender and lightly golden, about 10 minutes, stirring occasionally. Add ginger and garlic, and cook, stirring, 1 minute.

3 Add rice, peas, ham, green onions, chicken broth, soy sauce, sesame oil, and scrambled eggs, and cook about 3 minutes or until heated through, stirring and separating rice with spoon. Toss with cilantro just before serving. Makes about 8 cups or 4 main-dish servings.

Each serving: About 470 calories, 18 g protein, 73 g carbohydrate, 11 g total fat (3 g saturated), 3 g fiber, 123 mg cholesterol, 1055 mg sodium.

Grilled Polenta with Sausage Sauce

PREP: 15 MINUTES • COOK: 30 MINUTES

Just slice packaged polenta, heat, and top with our hearty homemade sauce. Dust with grated Parmesan if you like.

1 pound hot and/or sweet Italian-sausage links, casings removed
1 large onion, chopped
1 package (24 ounces) precooked polenta, cut into 12 slices
¼ teaspoon coarsely ground black pepper
1 can (28 ounces) crushed tomatoes in puree
1 package (12 ounces) frozen Italian-style green beans

1 Heat nonstick 12-inch skillet over medium-high heat until hot. Add sausage and cook until browned, about 8 minutes, stirring frequently to break up sausage. With slotted spoon, transfer sausage to bowl. Discard all but 2 teaspoons sausage drippings.

2 Reduce heat to medium. To drippings in skillet, add onion and cook until soft and golden, about 15 minutes, stirring occasionally.

3 Meanwhile, preheat broiler. Place polenta slices on rack in broiling pan; sprinkle with pepper. With pan at closest position to source of heat, broil polenta slices 5 minutes. With wide metal spatula, turn polenta over and broil 5 minutes longer or until lightly golden.

4 To onion in skillet, add tomatoes with their puree, frozen beans, and sausage; heat to boiling over medium-high heat. Reduce heat to low; cover and simmer 8 minutes.

5 Serve polenta with sausage sauce. Makes 4 main-dish servings.

Each serving: About 490 calories, 24 g protein, 45 g carbohydrate, 24 g total fat (8 g saturated), 9 g fiber, 67 mg cholesterol, 1960 mg sodium.

Shortcut Cassoulet

PREP: 30 MINUTES • COOK: 30 MINUTES

Serve this flavorful winter entrée with a simple spinach salad to make a complete, delicious meal.

8 ounces garlic pork sausage or kielbasa, sliced
2 teaspoons olive oil
3 celery stalks, cut into ¼-inch dice
8 ounces baby carrots, each cut crosswise in half
1 garlic clove, minced
4 pieces chicken (1 breast, 1 thigh, 1 drumstick, 1 wing) reserved from Coq au Vin (page 50), bones discarded and meat pulled into shreds (about 2 cups)
1½ cups cooking broth (with vegetables) reserved from Coq au Vin (page 50)
1 can (14½ ounces) chicken broth
2 cans (15 to 19 ounces each) white kidney beans (cannellini), rinsed and drained
2 cups croutons reserved from Baby Greens with Herbed Croutons (page 158), coarsely broken
½ cup packed fresh parsley leaves, chopped

1 In 5- to 6-quart saucepot or Dutch oven or 12-inch skillet, cook sausage or kielbasa over medium-high heat 5 minutes or until browned, stirring occasionally. Transfer sausage to small bowl.

2 In same saucepot, heat oil over medium heat until hot. Add celery and carrots, and cook 10 minutes or until vegetables are golden, stirring occasionally. Add garlic and cook 1 minute longer, stirring.

3 Stir in chicken, cooking broth with vegetables, chicken broth, and sausage or kielbasa. Heat to boiling over high heat. Reduce heat to medium; cover and cook 15 minutes. Add white kidney beans and heat through. Sprinkle with crumbs and parsley to serve. Makes about 8 cups or 6 main-dish servings.

Each serving: About 575 calories, 45 g protein, 46 g carbohydrate, 23 g total fat (7 g saturated), 12 g fiber, 109 mg cholesterol, 1410 mg sodium.

◀ Grilled Polenta with Sausage Sauce

Muffuletta

PREP: 30 MINUTES PLUS CHILLING

This sandwich is a classic in the French Quarter of New Orleans, but with our recipe you won't have to travel to get it. It tastes even better made a day ahead.

4 medium celery stalks, finely chopped (about 1¼ cups)
1 cup drained giardiniera (Italian mixed pickled vegetables), finely chopped
1 cup loosely packed fresh parsley leaves, chopped
¾ cup pitted green olives, finely chopped
¼ cup olive oil
¼ teaspoon coarsely ground black pepper
1 garlic clove, minced
1 round (10-inch diameter) loaf soft French or Italian bread (1 pound), cut horizontally in half
6 ounces thinly sliced smoked ham
6 ounces thinly sliced provolone cheese
6 ounces thinly sliced Genoa salami

1 In medium bowl, combine celery, giardiniera, parsley, olives, oil, pepper, and garlic; set aside.

2 Remove a 1-inch layer of soft center of bread from both halves to make room for filling. On bottom half of bread, spread half of olive mixture; top with ham, cheese, salami, and remaining olive mixture. Replace top half of bread; press halves together.

3 Wrap sandwich tightly in plastic wrap, then foil, and refrigerate at least 2 hours or up to 24 hours. Cut into 8 wedges to serve. Makes 8 main-dish servings.

Each serving: About 390 calories, 19 g protein, 26 g carbohydrate, 24 g total fat (8 g saturated), 1 g fiber, 44 mg cholesterol, 1515 mg sodium.

Mediterranean Lamb Steaks

PREP: 10 MINUTES PLUS STANDING
COOK: 8 TO 10 MINUTES

Panfried steaks cut from the leg taste rich seasoned with red wine vinegar, oregano, and garlic. Great with couscous and broiled tomato halves.

2 tablespoons red wine vinegar
1 tablespoon olive oil
1 tablespoon minced fresh oregano leaves
¾ teaspoon salt
½ teaspoon coarsely ground black pepper
2 garlic cloves, crushed with garlic press
2 center-cut lamb leg steaks, ¾ inch thick (about 12 ounces each)

1 In large zip-tight plastic bag, mix vinegar, olive oil, oregano, salt, pepper, and garlic; add lamb steaks, turning to coat well. Seal bag, pressing out excess air; let stand 15 minutes.

2 Heat nonstick 12-inch skillet over medium-high heat until hot. Add lamb and cook 8 to 10 minutes for medium-rare or until of desired doneness, turning steaks once. Makes 4 main-dish servings.

Each serving: About 320 calories, 31 g protein, 1 g carbohydrate, 19 g total fat (8 g saturated), 0 g fiber, 122 mg cholesterol, 405 mg sodium.

WHAT'S IN A NAME?

Muffuletta: The word comes from the Italian *muffuliette*, which refers to soft Sicilian rolls. The famous New Orleans muffuletta is a savory meat-and-cheese sandwich with olive salad, stacked on a big round bread loaf that is cut into many servings. Central Grocery Company on the city's Decatur Street claims to have been the first to hit upon the idea in the early 1900's—and serious sandwich fans claim it still serves the best. Our version (above) is a picnic classic, and can be assembled and wrapped up to a day ahead.

PASTA

Corkscrews with Spring Veggies

PREP: 15 MINUTES • COOK: ABOUT 15 MINUTES

Toss sautéed asparagus and leeks with pasta and creamy goat cheese. Yum!

1 bunch leeks (about 1 pound)
1 package (16 ounces) corkscrew or bow-tie pasta
Salt
1 tablespoon margarine or butter
1 pound asparagus, trimmed and cut diagonally into 2-inch pieces
Coarsely ground black pepper
1 package (4 ounces) soft goat cheese, cut into small pieces

1 Cut off roots and leaf ends from leeks. Discard any tough outer leaves. Cut each leek lengthwise in half, then crosswise into ¼-inch-wide slices. Place leeks in large bowl of cold water; with hand, swish leeks around to remove any sand. Transfer leeks to colander. Repeat process, changing water several times, until all sand is removed. Drain well.

2 In large saucepot, prepare pasta in *boiling salted water* as label directs.

3 Meanwhile, in nonstick 12-inch skillet, melt margarine or butter over medium heat. Add leeks and cook until almost tender, about 5 minutes, stirring often. Stir in asparagus, ¾ teaspoon salt, and ¼ teaspoon pepper; cook 5 minutes longer, stirring often. Add ⅓ *cup water*; cover and cook 3 to 5 minutes, until asparagus is tender-crisp.

4 Drain pasta, reserving ¾ *cup pasta cooking water*. Return pasta to saucepot. Add asparagus mixture and pasta cooking water; toss well. Spoon into large serving bowl; sprinkle with goat cheese and black pepper. Makes 4 main-dish servings.

Each serving: About 580 calories, 23 g protein, 96 g carbohydrate, 11 g total fat (5 g saturated), 6 g fiber, 13 mg cholesterol, 705 mg sodium.

Rice Noodles with Many Herbs

PREP: 20 MINUTES • COOK: ABOUT 10 MINUTES

Whip up this light summer main dish or accompaniment with fast-cooking noodles, cucumber, carrots, herbs, and our delicious Asian dressing.

3 small carrots, cut into matchstick-thin strips (1⅓ cups)
⅓ cup seasoned rice vinegar
1 package (1 pound) ½-inch-wide flat rice noodles
⅓ English (seedless) cucumber, unpeeled and cut into matchstick-thin strips (1 cup)
1 cup loosely packed fresh cilantro leaves
½ cup loosely packed fresh mint leaves
⅓ cup loosely packed small fresh basil leaves
⅓ cup snipped fresh chives
2 teaspoons Asian sesame oil

1 In small bowl, stir carrots with rice vinegar. Let stand at room temperature while preparing noodles.

2 In 8-quart saucepot, heat 5 *quarts water* to boiling over high heat. Add noodles and cook 3 minutes or just until cooked through. Drain noodles; rinse under cold running water and drain again.

3 Transfer noodles to large shallow serving bowl. Add carrots with their liquid, cucumber, herbs, and sesame oil; toss to mix well. Makes 4 main-dish or 8 accompaniment servings.

Each main-dish serving: About 470 calories, 7 g protein, 105 g carbohydrate, 3 g total fat (0 g saturated), 3 g fiber, 0 mg cholesterol, 550 mg sodium.

Rice Noodles with Many Herbs ➤

Pasta Toss with Summer Basil

PREP: 45 MINUTES • COOK: ABOUT 35 MINUTES

Use any short pasta for this delicious dish chock-full of garden eggplant, zucchini, tomatoes, and peppers. If you like, you can substitute yellow summer squash for the zucchini.

3 medium red peppers
2 medium yellow peppers
1 package (16 ounces) penne, radiatore, or fusilli pasta
Salt

4 tablespoons olive oil
1 medium red onion, chopped
3 medium zucchini (6 ounces each), each cut lengthwise in half then thinly sliced crosswise
1 medium eggplant (1¼ pounds), cut into ½-inch chunks
3 ripe medium tomatoes (1 pound), chopped
1 cup loosely packed fresh basil leaves, chopped
2 tablespoons capers, drained

1 Preheat broiler. Line broiling pan (without rack) with foil. Cut each pepper lengthwise in half; discard stems and seeds. With hand, flatten each pepper half. Place peppers (half the amount at a time, if broiling pan is small), cut side down, in broiling pan. Place pan in broiler 5 to 6 inches from source of heat and

---

PESTO PERFECT: OUR FOOLPROOF RECIPE

If you're a pesto lover, try this GH-approved recipe, fine-tuned by our food editors so it's bursting with delectable flavor but not too oily.

Use it on everything from a plate of hot penne to a grilled turkey or veggie burger. All you need to make it is a blender or food processor. Hints from our pesto pros: Thoroughly pat basil dry after rinsing so you don't dilute the sauce. And be sure to use freshly grated Parmesan. The kind from a shaker won't add the same tasty tang. (If you want to thin pesto to sauce a pound of pasta, add up to ½ cup pasta cooking water or chicken broth, or a splash more oil to bowl when tossing.) If not using right away, refrigerate for up to 1 week. To use, leave at room temperature 15 minutes.

PREP: 10 MINUTES

2 cups firmly packed fresh basil leaves
¼ cup extravirgin olive oil
2 tablespoons pine nuts (pignoli), toasted
1 teaspoon salt
¼ teaspoon coarsely ground black pepper
½ cup freshly grated Parmesan cheese (about 2 ounces)
1 garlic clove, crushed with side of chef's knife

In blender or food processor with knife blade attached, blend basil, olive oil, pine nuts, salt, and pepper until smooth. Add Parmesan and garlic, and blend until thoroughly combined. Makes about ¾ cup, enough to sauce 1 pound pasta.

Per tablespoon: About 65 calories, 2 g protein, 1 g carbohydrate, 6 g total fat (2 g saturated), 0 g fiber, 3 mg cholesterol, 255 mg sodium.

To make things more interesting, whip up a new pesto, with different herbs, nuts, and cheeses. Add a spoonful or more to soups and sauces; serve as a condiment for charbroiled chicken, shrimp, or lamb; or thin slightly and drizzle over a platter of grilled vegetables. Try fresh cilantro, parsley, mint, and/or arugula with walnuts or pecans, and different hard cheeses such as Romano or dry Monterey Jack (with the texture of Parmesan). Whirl jalapeño chile, fresh lemon or lime juice, or sun-dried tomatoes into the mix to add a spark of new flavor. Our favorite variations on the basic recipe:

Asian: Replace basil with fresh cilantro leaves and stems; omit cheese and nuts; blend in 1 teaspoon Asian sesame oil. Drizzle over grilled chicken breasts or cool cucumber slices.

Country Garden: Use a combination of fresh mint, parsley, and basil leaves (2 cups total) instead of just basil. Toss with linguine or fettuccine.

Mediterranean: Replace basil with parsley; omit cheese; add 3 tablespoons drained capers. Excellent with beef or steamed cauliflower or broccoli.

Southwestern: Omit cheese; add 1 fresh jalapeño chile, seeded and minced, and 2 teaspoons freshly squeezed lime juice. Serve over sliced red and yellow tomatoes, steak, or hamburgers.

broil peppers until charred and blistered, 10 to 15 minutes. Wrap foil around peppers and allow to steam at room temperature 15 minutes or until cool enough to handle. (Repeat with remaining peppers.)

2 Meanwhile, prepare pasta in *boiling salted water* as label directs. Drain pasta; rinse with cold water, and drain again. Set aside.

3 Remove peppers from foil. Peel off skin and discard. Cut peppers into ½-inch pieces.

4 In nonstick 12-inch skillet, heat 1 tablespoon oil over medium heat until hot. Add onion and cook 6 minutes or until tender, stirring occasionally. Add zucchini and 1 tablespoon oil, and cook 7 minutes or until zucchini are tender-crisp, stirring frequently. Add eggplant, ¾ teaspoon salt, and remaining 2 tablespoons oil, and cook 8 minutes or until eggplant is tender, stirring frequently.

5 Transfer vegetables to large bowl; stir in tomatoes, basil, capers, and ½ teaspoon salt. Add pasta; toss well. Serve salad warm, or cover and refrigerate until ready to serve. Makes 12 accompaniment servings.

Each serving: About 225 calories, 7 g protein, 38 g carbohydrate, 6 g total fat (1 g saturated), 3 g fiber, 0 mg cholesterol, 285 mg sodium.

Creamy Rigatoni with Spinach

PREP: 10 MINUTES • COOK: 20 MINUTES

You'll love this simple toss of hot macaroni, creamy ricotta, Parmesan, spinach, and sun-dried tomatoes.

1 package (16 ounces) rigatoni or ziti pasta
Salt
1 package (10 ounces) frozen chopped spinach
1 container (15 ounces) part-skim ricotta cheese
¼ cup grated Parmesan cheese
10 oil-packed sun-dried tomatoes, drained and
    finely chopped (about ¼ cup)

1 In large saucepot, cook pasta in *boiling salted water* 5 minutes; add frozen spinach and cook 10 minutes longer or until spinach is tender and pasta is al dente. Drain well, reserving *½ cup pasta cooking water.*

2 Return pasta, spinach, and reserved cooking water to saucepot. Add ricotta, Parmesan, sun-dried tomatoes, and ¾ teaspoon salt. Heat over medium-low heat, tossing until pasta is evenly coated and heated through. Makes 6 main-dish servings.

Each serving: About 420 calories, 21 g protein, 64 g carbohydrate, 9 g total fat (5 g saturated), 4 g fiber, 25 mg cholesterol, 580 mg sodium.

Spaghetti with Marinara Sauce

PREP: 20 MINUTES • COOK: 30 MINUTES

Tired of using the same old jarred sauce? Cook a pound of your favorite pasta and toss with this homemade marinara. Or try one of these simple variations: Spaghetti with Garden Veggie Sauce (page 104), Spaghetti with Sausage & Pepper Sauce (page 109), or Spaghetti with Bacon & Hot Pepper Sauce (page 110).

1 tablespoon olive oil
1 small onion, cut into ½-inch pieces
2 garlic cloves, crushed with garlic press
1 can (28 ounces) whole tomatoes in juice
2 tablespoons tomato paste
Salt
¼ teaspoon coarsely ground black pepper
2 tablespoons chopped fresh basil or parsley
1 package (16 ounces) spaghetti or other
    favorite pasta

1 In 4-quart saucepan, heat oil over medium heat until hot. Add onion and cook until tender, stirring occasionally.

2 Stir in garlic, and cook 1 minute. Stir in tomatoes with their juice, tomato paste, ¾ teaspoon salt, and pepper; heat to boiling over high heat, stirring to break up tomatoes. Reduce heat to medium and cook, stirring occasionally, 15 minutes. Stir in basil.

3 While sauce is simmering, prepare pasta in *boiling salted water* as label directs. Drain.

4 To serve, in large bowl, toss hot pasta with sauce. Makes 4 main-dish servings.

Each serving: About 505 calories, 17 g protein, 97 g carbohydrate, 6 g total fat (0 g saturated), 2 g fiber, 0 mg cholesterol, 870 mg sodium.

Pasta with Eggplant Sauce

PREP: 5 MINUTES • COOK: 25 MINUTES

This recipe was designed to take advantage of leftovers from Eggplant Parmesan (page 134).

1 package (16 ounces) rigatoni or fusilli pasta
Salt
2 cups Tomato Sauce reserved from Eggplant Parmesan (page 134)
1 quarter (about 6" by 4" piece) reserved Eggplant Parmesan (page 134), cut into ¾-inch chunks (about 2½ cups)

1 In large saucepot, cook pasta in *boiling salted water* as label directs.

2 Meanwhile, in 2-quart saucepan, heat Tomato Sauce and cut-up Eggplant Parmesan over medium heat 15 minutes or until hot, stirring occasionally.

3 Drain pasta, reserving ¼ *cup pasta cooking water*. Return pasta to saucepot; add eggplant mixture and reserved pasta cooking water and toss well. Makes 4 main-dish servings.

Each serving: About 615 calories, 24 g protein, 107 g carbohydrate, 10 g total fat (3 g saturated), 9 g fiber, 15 mg cholesterol, 1280 mg sodium.

Spaghetti with Garden Veggie Sauce

PREP: 20 MINUTES • COOK: 30 MINUTES

Spaghetti with Marinara Sauce (page 103)
10 ounces white mushrooms, sliced (optional)
2 medium carrots, cut into 2" by ¼" sticks
1 medium zucchini, cut into 1-inch pieces
1 medium yellow summer squash, cut into 1-inch pieces
1 cup frozen peas, thawed

Prepare Spaghetti with Marinara Sauce, but in step 1, use 5-quart Dutch oven and heat oil over high heat until hot. Add mushrooms, carrots, zucchini, and yellow squash with onion, and cook until vegetables are

tender and liquid evaporates, about 10 minutes, stirring occasionally. Complete and serve as in steps 2 through 4, stirring in peas with basil. Makes 4 main-dish servings.

Each serving: About 590 calories, 22 g protein, 114 g carbohydrate, 6 g total fat (1 g saturated), 6 g fiber, 0 mg cholesterol, 790 mg sodium.

Thai Pasta with Shrimp

PREP: 15 MINUTES • COOK: 15 MINUTES

Delicate angel hair pasta absorbs sauce quickly, so put this on plates as soon as it's tossed. Serve with lime wedges if you like.

1 package (16 ounces) angel hair pasta
Salt
2 teaspoons curry powder
1 can (14 ounces) light coconut milk (not cream of coconut)
⅛ teaspoon coarsely ground black pepper
1 pound medium shrimp, shelled and deveined with tail part of shell left on
1 cup loosely packed fresh cilantro leaves

1 In large saucepot, prepare pasta in *boiling salted water* as label directs.

2 Meanwhile, in 10-inch skillet, cook curry powder over medium heat 2 minutes, stirring frequently. Stir in coconut milk, 1 teaspoon salt, and ⅛ teaspoon ground black pepper until blended; heat to boiling over high heat. Add shrimp; reduce heat to medium. Cover and cook 2 minutes or until shrimp just turn opaque throughout.

3 Drain pasta. In large bowl, toss pasta with shrimp mixture and cilantro. Makes 6 main-dish servings.

Each serving: About 410 calories, 23 g protein, 59 g carbohydrate, 8 g total fat (4 g saturated), 3 g fiber, 95 mg cholesterol, 550 mg sodium.

Pasta with Eggplant Sauce ➤

Linguine with Broccoli & Clams

PREP: 30 MINUTES • COOK: 20 MINUTES

Our lightened version of classic linguine with clam sauce includes healthy broccoli flowerets.

Salt
6 cups broccoli flowerets (15 ounces)
1 package (1 pound) linguine or spaghetti
½ cup dry white wine
2 dozen littleneck or small cherrystone clams, well scrubbed
1 tablespoon olive oil
2 garlic cloves, minced
¼ teaspoon coarsely ground black pepper
⅛ to ¼ teaspoon crushed red pepper
¼ cup loosely packed fresh parsley leaves, chopped

1 In large saucepot of *boiling salted water*, cook broccoli 4 to 6 minutes, until almost tender. With slotted spoon or metal strainer, transfer broccoli to bowl; do not discard cooking water. Rinse broccoli with cold running water to stop cooking.

2 In same saucepot of boiling water, prepare pasta as label directs.

3 Meanwhile, in deep 12-inch skillet, heat wine to boiling over high heat; add clams and cook 7 to 10 minutes, covered, removing clams to large bowl as they begin to open. Discard any unopened clams. Line large sieve with 2 layers of paper towels and set over medium bowl. Pour clam cooking broth from skillet into sieve; reserve strained broth. (You should have about 1 cup broth. Add enough *water* to equal 1½ cups.) Remove clams from shells (reserve a few in the shell for garnish if you like), adding any clam juices to reserved broth. Coarsely chop clams.

4 Clean skillet and wipe dry. Heat olive oil over medium heat until hot. Add garlic and cook 30 seconds, stirring. Add broccoli flowerets, black pepper, red pepper, clams, and reserved broth to skillet, and heat through, stirring gently.

5 Drain pasta. In large serving bowl, toss hot pasta with broccoli mixture. Add reserved clams in shells and sprinkle with parsley before serving. Makes 4 main-dish servings.

Each serving: About 520 calories, 24 g protein, 91 g carbohydrate, 6 g total fat (1 g saturated), 6 g fiber, 18 mg cholesterol, 360 mg sodium.

Chicken & Pasta Toss with Sautéed Green Onions

PREP: 20 MINUTES • COOK: ABOUT 20 MINUTES

This mouthwatering marriage of green onions and tender chicken arrives at the table sprinkled with crispy bacon.

12 ounces penne, ziti, or fusilli pasta
Salt
2 slices bacon, coarsely chopped
1 pound chicken cutlets, cut into 2-inch-wide strips
½ teaspoon coarsely ground black pepper
1 tablespoon margarine or butter
4 bunches green onions (about 1 pound), trimmed and cut into 2-inch pieces
¾ cup chicken broth

1 In large saucepot, prepare pasta in *boiling salted water* as label directs.

2 Meanwhile, in nonstick 12-inch skillet, cook bacon over medium heat until browned. With slotted spoon, transfer bacon to paper towels to drain.

3 To bacon drippings in skillet, add chicken, ¼ teaspoon pepper, and ¼ teaspoon salt, and cook over medium-high heat 4 minutes or just until chicken loses its pink color throughout, stirring frequently. Transfer chicken with any juices to plate; keep warm.

4 In same skillet, melt margarine or butter over medium heat. Add green onions, remaining ¼ teaspoon pepper, and ¼ teaspoon salt, and cook until green onions are tender, about 10 minutes, stirring often. Add chicken broth; heat to boiling over medium-high heat.

5 Drain pasta; return to saucepot. Add green-onion mixture and chicken with its juices; toss well. Sprinkle with bacon to serve. Makes 4 main-dish servings.

Each serving: About 555 calories, 40 g protein, 68 g carbohydrate, 13 g total fat (4 g saturated), 5 g fiber, 74 mg cholesterol, 715 mg sodium.

THE SHAPE OF THINGS TO COME

Just when you had a handle on the gazillion pasta shapes out there, here come more to shake up suppertime. Look for them in supermarkets, Italian specialty stores, and gourmet shops.

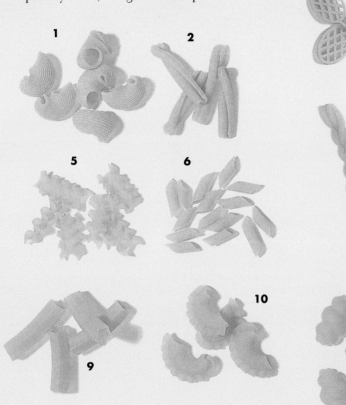
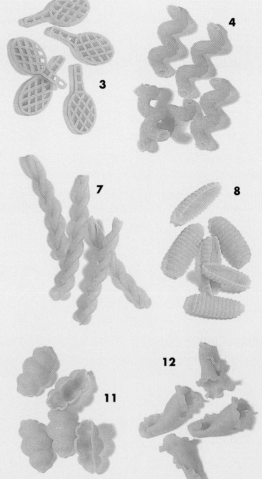

1 *Chiocciole:* small, curled tube (like elbow macaroni, but wider and ridged; the name means snails)

2 *Casareccia Molisana:* small rectangle with long sides folded in and slightly twisted

3 *Racchette:* small tennis-racket shape

4 *Cavatappi* (or *Cellentani* or *Succhietto*): short, ridged spiral

5 *Mafalda:* small rectangle with curly-edged sides (like a narrow lasagna noodle)

6 *Pennette:* tiny penne ("little quills")

7 *Gemelli:* 2 short strands of pasta twisted together (the word means twins)

8 *Gnocchi Sardi:* like gnocchi, but smaller with finer ridges

9 *Rizzone:* bite-size, 5-sided tube

10 *Creste di Galli:* small, tubular, curled, ridged noodle with ruffled edge; shaped like a rooster's comb

11 *Gnocchi:* little shell with wide ridges

12 *Campanelle:* short with curly sides folded around each other; resembles a lily

13 *Castellane:* medium-size, long, ridged shell

Bow Ties with Fennel & Leeks

The vegetables become sweet and tender when cooked in olive oil.

4 medium leeks (about 1½ pounds)
2 tablespoons olive oil
2 medium fennel bulbs (about 1 pound each)
2 garlic cloves, minced
1 tablespoon sugar
1 package (16 ounces) bow-tie (farfalle) or
  gemelli pasta
Salt
1 cup chicken broth
¼ cup heavy or whipping cream
¼ teaspoon coarsely ground black pepper
½ cup grated Parmesan cheese
1 ripe, medium tomato, cut into ¼-inch dice

1 Preheat oven to 400°F. Trim off roots and leaf ends from leeks. Discard any tough outer leaves. Cut each leek lengthwise in half, then crosswise into ¼-inch-wide slices. Place leeks in large bowl of cold water; with hand, swish leeks around to remove any sand. Remove leeks to colander. Repeat process, changing water several times until all sand is removed. Drain well.

2 In nonstick 12-inch skillet, heat 1 tablespoon olive oil over medium heat until hot. Add leeks and cook until tender and golden, about 15 minutes, stirring frequently.

3 While leeks are cooking, trim top and bottom from each fennel bulb; reserve fronds, if any, for garnish. Slice each bulb lengthwise in half; remove and discard core. Slice fennel-bulb halves crosswise into thin slices.

4 Add fennel, garlic, sugar, and remaining oil, and cook until fennel is tender and light golden, about 20 minutes, stirring frequently.

5 Meanwhile, prepare pasta in *boiling salted water* as label directs. Drain; return pasta to saucepot.

6 When leeks are tender, add broth, cream, pepper, ½ teaspoon salt, and all but 2 tablespoons Parmesan cheese; boil 1 minute.

7 Spoon pasta into deep 4-quart casserole. Add leek mixture and toss well. Sprinkle top with diced tomato and remaining 2 tablespoons Parmesan cheese. Bake, covered, 20 minutes or until hot and bubbly. Garnish with fennel fronds, if you like, to serve. Makes 6 main-dish servings.

Each serving: About 460 calories, 15 g protein, 77 g carbohydrate, 11 g total fat (4 g saturated), 2 g fiber, 17 mg cholesterol, 560 mg sodium.

Spaghetti with Sausage & Pepper Sauce

Spaghetti with Marinara Sauce (page 103)
8 ounces sweet Italian-sausage links, casings
  removed
2 small green, red, or yellow peppers, sliced
  ¼ inch thick

Prepare Spaghetti with Marinara Sauce, but in step 1, heat saucepan over medium-high heat until hot and do not use olive oil. Add sausage and peppers with onion, and cook until meat is browned and peppers are tender, about 10 minutes, stirring occasionally and breaking up sausage with side of spoon. Pour off drippings from saucepan, leaving sausage and vegetables. Complete and serve as in steps 2 through 4, reducing salt to ½ teaspoon. Makes 4 main-dish servings.

Each serving: About 640 calories, 26 g protein, 105 g carbohydrate, 13 g total fat (4 g saturated), 4 g fiber, 33 mg cholesterol, 990 mg sodium.

Spaghetti with Bacon & Hot Pepper Sauce

PREP: 20 MINUTES • COOK: 30 MINUTES

Spaghetti with Marinara Sauce (page 103)
4 slices bacon, cut into 1-inch pieces
⅛ to ¼ teaspoon crushed red pepper

Prepare Spaghetti with Marinara Sauce, but in step 1, add bacon with onion, and cook until bacon is browned and onion is tender, about 10 minutes, stirring occasionally. Pour off drippings from pan, leaving bacon and onion. Complete and serve as in steps 2 through 4, stirring in crushed red pepper with garlic and reducing salt to ¼ teaspoon. Makes 4 main-dish servings.

Each serving: About 515 calories, 19 g protein, 97 g carbohydrate, 6 g total fat (1 g saturated), 2 g fiber, 15 mg cholesterol, 570 mg sodium.

Bow Ties with Chicken & Wild Mushrooms

PREP: 20 MINUTES • COOK: ABOUT 25 MINUTES

A delicious medley of shiitake, oyster, and white mushrooms, tossed with boneless chicken thighs, a splash of cream, and brandy.

12 ounces bow-tie pasta
Salt
1 teaspoon olive oil
1 pound skinless, boneless chicken thighs, cut into 1-inch pieces
¼ teaspoon coarsely ground black pepper
1 tablespoon margarine or butter
8 ounces white mushrooms, thinly sliced
4 ounces shiitake mushrooms, stems removed and caps thinly sliced
4 ounces oyster mushrooms, tough stem ends removed and caps thinly sliced
1 medium onion, cut in half, then thinly sliced crosswise
1 garlic clove, crushed with garlic press
1 cup frozen peas
¼ cup heavy or whipping cream
2 tablespoons brandy

1 In large saucepot, prepare pasta in *boiling salted water* as label directs.

2 Meanwhile, in nonstick 12-inch skillet, heat oil over medium-high heat until hot. Add chicken, pepper, and ½ teaspoon salt, and cook 5 minutes or just until chicken loses its pink color inside, stirring frequently. Transfer chicken to plate; keep warm.

3 In same skillet, melt margarine or butter. Add mushrooms, onion, garlic, and ¼ teaspoon salt, and cook until vegetables are tender and golden, about 15 minutes, stirring often. Stir in peas, cream, and brandy; heat to boiling. Remove skillet from heat.

4 When pasta has cooked to desired doneness, remove ½ cup pasta cooking water. Drain pasta; return to saucepot. Add mushroom mixture, chicken, and reserved pasta cooking water; toss well. Makes 4 main-dish servings.

Each serving: About 625 calories, 39 g protein, 79 g carbohydrate, 16 g total fat (6 g saturated), 7 g fiber, 114 mg cholesterol, 720 mg sodium.

Ziti with Eggplant & Ricotta

PREP: 40 MINUTES • BAKE: 20 MINUTES

If preparing this dish ahead, roast eggplant and make sauce, and refrigerate separately. When ready to bake, cook pasta and assemble; add about 10 minutes to the baking time to compensate for the chilled ingredients.

1 medium eggplant (about 1½ pounds), cut into 1-inch pieces
3 tablespoons olive oil
Salt
1 small onion, finely chopped
2 garlic cloves, minced
1 can (28 ounces) plum tomatoes in juice
2 tablespoons tomato paste
¼ teaspoon coarsely ground black pepper
3 tablespoons chopped fresh basil leaves
1 package (16 ounces) ziti or penne pasta
¼ cup grated Parmesan cheese
1 cup ricotta cheese

1 Preheat oven to 450°F. In large bowl, toss eggplant, 2 tablespoons olive oil, and ¼ teaspoon salt until evenly coated. Arrange eggplant in single layer in two

PASTA POINTERS

Everyone can cook pasta, right? But not everyone knows how to keep noodles from clumping or the secret to using the leftover cooking water in sauces. Follow our tips:

Make room: Fill a large (6- to 8-quart) saucepot with cold water (use at least 4 quarts per pound). This prevents sticking and helps dilute the starch released during cooking so you don't end up with a gluey mess.

Put a lid on it: Cover the pot, and use high heat so water will reach the boiling point sooner (it still takes about 10 minutes).

Add salt: When water begins to boil, add about 2 teaspoons salt. This only slightly affects the sodium content of the finished dish but noticeably boosts the flavor.

Go slow: Add pasta gradually, stirring with a wooden spoon or fork to keep it from sticking together or to the bottom of the pot. If cooking long strands like spaghetti or linguine, use the spoon to bend them as they soften until completely submerged; stir well.

Boil again: Partially cover the pot until water bubbles once more, then uncover and adjust the heat so water is boiling, but not so fast that it will overflow.

Don't add oil: Your mother may have told you it keeps noodles from sticking, but so does frequent stirring. Besides, an oily coating makes it harder for sauce to cling.

Test it: Don't just go by the time on the package. Italians have been cooking their pasta al dente, literally, "to the tooth," for years, and with good reason: Pasta becomes gummy and absorbs too much sauce when overcooked. A noodle should offer some resistance—but never crunch—when you bite it. (Package guidelines for pastas that are generally baked, like lasagna, manicotti, and jumbo shells, usually take into account the additional oven time and reduce boiling time accordingly. But if you're making a casserole with a pasta that isn't usually baked—such as Tuna-Melt Casserole, page 44, which calls for corkscrews—reduce stovetop cooking time by one-third to compensate for baking time.)

Save the water: It helps to reserve ½ to 1 cup of the water before draining in case you need more sauce for your finished dish (often the case with angel-hair pasta, which seems to soak toppings right up). Gradually stir the water into tomato, veggie, or cream sauce.

Serve pronto: Drain pasta quickly and use immediately. Rinsing in cold water is unnecessary unless noodles will be served cold—the cool splash removes surface starch, which helps sauce hold on.

15½" by 10½" jelly-roll pans or 2 large cookie sheets. Place pans with eggplant on 2 oven racks in oven. Roast eggplant 30 minutes, rotating pans between upper and lower racks halfway through cooking and stirring twice, or until eggplant is tender and golden. Remove pans with eggplant from oven; set aside. Turn oven control to 400°F.

2 Meanwhile, in 3-quart saucepan, heat remaining 1 tablespoon olive oil over medium heat until hot. Add onion and cook until tender, about 5 minutes, stirring occasionally. Add garlic and cook 1 minute longer, stirring frequently.

3 Stir in tomatoes with their juice, tomato paste, pepper, and ½ teaspoon salt, breaking up tomatoes with side of spoon; heat to boiling over high heat. Reduce heat to low and simmer, uncovered, 10 minutes or until sauce thickens slightly. Stir in 2 tablespoons basil.

4 In large saucepot, prepare pasta in *boiling salted water* as label directs. Drain; return pasta to saucepot.

5 To pasta in saucepot, add roasted eggplant, tomato sauce, and Parmesan cheese; toss until evenly mixed. Spoon mixture into six 2-cup gratin dishes or shallow casseroles; top with dollops of ricotta cheese.

6 Cover casseroles with foil and bake 20 minutes or until hot and bubbly. To serve, sprinkle tops with remaining 1 tablespoon basil. Makes 6 main-dish servings.

Each serving: About 500 calories, 19 g protein, 73 g carbohydrate, 15 g total fat (5 g saturated), 2 g fiber, 24 mg cholesterol, 695 mg sodium.

Spaghetti Carbonara Pie

Spaghetti Carbonara Pie

PREP: 15 MINUTES • BAKE: 35 TO 40 MINUTES

Nothing's better on a chilly evening—and this takes just minutes to put together.

12 ounces spaghetti
Salt
4 ounces bacon (about 6 slices), cut into ¼-inch
    pieces
1 container (15 ounces) part-skim ricotta cheese
½ cup grated Romano cheese
2 large eggs plus 1 large egg yolk
½ teaspoon coarsely ground black pepper
Pinch nutmeg
2 cups milk

1 Preheat oven to 375°F. In large saucepot, prepare spaghetti in *boiling salted water* as label directs.

2 Meanwhile, in nonstick 10-inch skillet, cook bacon over medium heat until browned, about 12 minutes. With slotted spoon, transfer bacon to paper towels to drain; set aside.

3 In blender at low speed, blend ricotta, Romano, eggs, egg yolk, pepper, nutmeg, ½ cup milk, and ½ teaspoon salt until smooth.

4 Drain pasta and return to saucepot. Add ricotta mixture, bacon, and remaining 1½ cups milk, stirring to combine.

5 Transfer pasta mixture to 2½-quart baking dish (about 2 inches deep). Bake 35 to 40 minutes, until golden around edges and almost set but still slightly liquid in center. Let pie stand 10 minutes before serving (liquid will be absorbed during standing). Cut into wedges to serve. Makes 6 main-dish servings.

Each serving: About 470 calories, 25 g protein, 50 g carbohydrate, 18 g total fat (9 g saturated), 0 g fiber, 154 mg cholesterol, 595 mg sodium.

Macaroni & Cheese Deluxe

PREP: 30 MINUTES • BAKE: 25 MINUTES

This is filled with the sophisticated flavors of blue cheese, fragrant toasted nuts, and Parmesan-dusted tomatoes. It's perfect for a weekend dinner party.

1 package (16 ounces) campanelle or penne
    pasta
Salt
3 tablespoons margarine or butter
1 medium onion, diced
2 tablespoons all-purpose flour
¼ teaspoon coarsely ground black pepper
¼ teaspoon ground red pepper (cayenne)
¼ teaspoon ground nutmeg
4 cups low-fat (1%) milk
½ cup grated Parmesan cheese
1 cup frozen peas
4 ounces creamy blue cheese, such as
    Gorgonzola, cut up or crumbled into pieces
½ pint pear-shaped or round cherry tomatoes,
    each cut in half
½ cup walnuts, toasted

1 In large saucepot, prepare pasta in *boiling salted water* as label directs. Preheat oven to 400°F.

2 Meanwhile, in 3-quart saucepan, melt margarine or butter over medium heat; add onion and cook 8 to 10 minutes, until tender, stirring occasionally. With wire whisk, stir in flour, black pepper, ground red pepper, nutmeg, and ¼ teaspoon salt, and cook 1 minute, stirring constantly. Gradually whisk in milk and cook over medium-high heat, stirring frequently, until sauce boils and thickens slightly. Boil 1 minute, stirring. Stir in ¼ cup Parmesan cheese. Remove saucepan from heat.

3 Place frozen peas in colander; drain pasta over peas and return pasta mixture to saucepot. Stir in sauce and blue cheese. Transfer pasta mixture to deep 3-quart casserole.

4 In small bowl, toss tomato halves with remaining ¼ cup Parmesan cheese. Top casserole with tomato halves. Bake, uncovered, 20 minutes, or until hot and bubbly and top is lightly browned. Sprinkle with walnuts before serving. Makes 6 main-dish servings.

Each serving: About 610 calories, 26 g protein, 76 g carbohydrate, 23 g total fat (6 g saturated), 5 g fiber, 43 mg cholesterol, 965 mg sodium.

Family-Style Macaroni & Cheese

PREP: 20 MINUTES • BAKE: 20 MINUTES

We even tucked in some vegetables for good measure—a sneaky way to get them past little mac-and-cheese fans!

1 package (16 ounces) fusilli or rotini pasta
Salt
2 tablespoons margarine or butter
3 tablespoons all-purpose flour
¼ teaspoon coarsely ground black pepper
Pinch nutmeg
4 cups reduced-fat (2%) milk
1 package (8 ounces) pasteurized process
    cheese spread, cut up
¼ cup grated Parmesan cheese
6 ounces extrasharp Cheddar cheese, shredded
    (1½ cups)
1 package (10 ounces) frozen mixed vegetables

1 In large saucepot, prepare pasta in *boiling salted water* as label directs. Preheat oven to 400°F.

2 Meanwhile, in 3-quart saucepan, melt margarine or butter over medium heat. With wire whisk, stir in flour, pepper, nutmeg, and ½ teaspoon salt; cook 1 minute, stirring constantly. Gradually whisk in milk and cook over medium-high heat, stirring constantly, until sauce boils and thickens slightly. Boil 1 minute. Stir in cheese spread, Parmesan, and 1 cup Cheddar just until cheeses melt. Remove saucepan from heat.

3 Place frozen vegetables in colander; drain pasta over vegetables. Return pasta mixture to saucepot. Stir in cheese sauce. Transfer pasta mixture to 13" by 9" glass baking dish. Sprinkle with remaining ½ cup Cheddar. Bake, uncovered, 20 minutes or until hot and bubbly and top is lightly browned. Makes 8 main-dish servings.

Each serving: About 520 calories, 25 g protein, 58 g carbohydrate, 21 g total fat (12 g saturated), 3 g fiber, 52 mg cholesterol, 845 mg sodium.

Butternut Squash Lasagna

PREP: 1 HOUR 15 MINUTES • BAKE: 40 MINUTES

An elegant party entrée—serve with crusty bread and red wine.

12 lasagna noodles
Salt
1 large butternut squash (3 pounds), peeled, seeded, and cut into 1-inch chunks
2 tablespoons olive oil
1 jumbo onion (1 pound), cut in half and thinly sliced
1 large bunch Swiss chard (about 1½ pounds), coarsely chopped, with tough stems discarded

WHITE SAUCE:
2 tablespoons margarine or butter
⅓ cup all-purpose flour

¼ teaspoon coarsely ground black pepper
¼ teaspoon salt
¼ teaspoon ground nutmeg
¼ teaspoon dried thyme
4 cups low-fat (1%) milk
¾ cup grated Parmesan cheese

1 In saucepot, cook lasagna noodles in *boiling salted water* as label directs. Drain noodles and rinse with cold running water to stop cooking; drain again. Layer noodles between sheets of waxed paper.

2 Meanwhile, preheat oven to 450°F. In large bowl, toss butternut squash chunks with 1 tablespoon olive oil and ½ teaspoon salt. Place squash on 15½" by 10½" jelly-roll pan or large cookie sheet. Roast squash 30 minutes or until fork-tender, stirring halfway through cooking. Remove from oven and, with fork or potato masher, mash squash until almost smooth; set aside. Turn oven control to 375°F.

3 Meanwhile, in 5-quart Dutch oven or saucepot, heat remaining 1 tablespoon olive oil over medium heat until hot. Add onion and ¼ teaspoon salt, and

CAN LOWER-FAT CHEESE FOOL LASAGNA LOVERS?

Lasagna, with its layers of creamy ricotta and gooey mozzarella, has never been considered diet food. But wouldn't it be nice to save a few fat grams and calories without sacrificing texture or flavor? We gave it a try, inviting 7 hungry staffers from our Food and Nutrition departments to lunch so they could sample and compare 3 versions: one made with fat-free mozzarella and ricotta, one with part-skim cheeses, and one with whole-milk products.

The tasting was as blind as it could be, considering that most of our food pros could tell at a glance which was the fat-free version; they said the top layer of shredded mozzarella looked shiny, "plasticlike," and very white. Even for a savings of 8 fat grams and 64 calories per serving* compared to the full-fat lasagna (and 6.6 fat grams and 53 calories over part-skim), the lightest lasagna was not considered worth the effort. Comments ranged from "this is like chewing plastic" to "the ricotta leaves a bitter aftertaste." One die-hard lasagna fan said, "I'll eat any lasagna, but I wouldn't touch this one!"

The lasagna with part-skim cheeses was voted close enough to the real thing in taste and texture to mer-

it a switch, although the fat and calorie savings per serving (3 grams fat and 25 calories) were not as significant. Our panel said that although the mozzarella was a bit rubbery, it melted well and didn't make a major difference overall. No surprise: Many of the tasters use part-skim cheeses in the lasagnas they fix for their families.

The samples with whole-milk ricotta and mozzarella were, of course, the forks-down winner for "creamiest"—how could they miss? The mozzarella was soft and stretchy; it didn't melt into a solid sheet like the fat-free kind did.

In the end, the choice is yours. Your family may not be as picky as our experts, and the taste buds can get used to anything if you're really determined to trim calories—plus, regardless of their fat content, all of these cheeses, slimmed down or not, are good sources of calcium.

*We used a 32-ounce container of ricotta and 8 ounces mozzarella in each lasagna (baked in a 13" by 9" dish). If your recipe calls for more cheese, fat and calorie savings will be more significant.

cook about 25 minutes or until golden, stirring often. Add Swiss chard and cook until wilted and liquid evaporates, about 7 minutes. Remove Dutch oven from heat; set aside.

4 Prepare White Sauce: In 3-quart saucepan, melt margarine or butter over medium heat. With wire whisk, stir in flour, pepper, salt, nutmeg, and thyme, and cook 1 minute, stirring constantly. Gradually whisk in milk and cook over medium-high heat, stirring frequently, until sauce boils and thickens slightly. Boil 1 minute, stirring. Whisk in all but 2 tablespoons Parmesan. Remove saucepan from heat.

5 In 13" by 9" glass baking dish, evenly spoon about ½ cup white sauce to cover bottom of dish. Arrange 4 lasagna noodles over sauce, overlapping to fit. Evenly spread all Swiss chard mixture over noodles and top with about 1 cup white sauce. Arrange 4 lasagna noodles on top, then about 1 cup white sauce and all butternut squash. Top with remaining lasagna noodles and remaining white sauce. Sprinkle with reserved 2 tablespoons Parmesan cheese.

6 Cover lasagna with foil and bake 30 minutes; remove foil and bake 10 minutes longer or until hot and bubbly. Let lasagna stand 10 minutes for easier serving. Makes 10 main-dish servings.

Each serving: About 315 calories, 13 g protein, 47 g carbohydrate, 9 g total fat (3 g saturated), 3 g fiber, 10 mg cholesterol, 575 mg sodium.

Classic Lasagna with Meat Sauce

PREP: 1 HOUR • BAKE: 30 MINUTES

We call for no-boil noodles for this popular dish—they're a real time-saver. Layer them straight from the package with lots of sauce; as the lasagna bakes and absorbs the liquid, the pasta will soften and expand. If your package contains 15 noodles, use an extra noodle in the first 3 layers when assembling lasagna.

MEAT SAUCE:
8 ounces sweet Italian-sausage links, casings removed
8 ounces lean ground beef
1 small onion, diced
2 garlic cloves, minced

1 can (28 ounces) plus 1 can (14½ to 16 ounces) whole tomatoes in juice
2 tablespoons tomato paste
½ teaspoon salt
2 tablespoons chopped fresh basil leaves

CHEESE FILLING:
1 large egg
¼ teaspoon coarsely ground black pepper
1 container (15 ounces) part-skim ricotta cheese
4 ounces part-skim mozzarella cheese, shredded (1 cup)
¾ cup grated Parmesan cheese
1 package (8 ounces) no-boil lasagna noodles (12 noodles)

1 Prepare Meat Sauce: Heat 4-quart saucepan over medium-high heat until hot. Add sausage and ground beef, and cook, stirring, 1 minute. Add onion and cook until meat is browned and onion is tender, about 5 minutes, stirring occasionally and breaking up sausage with side of spoon. Pour off drippings from saucepan. Add garlic to meat mixture in saucepan and cook 1 minute.

2 Stir in tomatoes with their juice, tomato paste, and salt, breaking up tomatoes with spoon; heat to boiling. Reduce heat to medium and cook, uncovered, 20 minutes, stirring occasionally. Stir in basil. Makes about 6 cups sauce.

3 Meanwhile, in medium bowl, mix egg, pepper, ricotta, ½ cup mozzarella, and ½ cup Parmesan until blended.

4 Preheat oven to 350°F. Into 13" by 9" glass baking dish, evenly spoon 2 cups sauce. Arrange 3 noodles over sauce, making sure noodles do not touch sides of dish (they will expand). Top with 1¼ cups ricotta mixture, 3 noodles, and 2 cups sauce. Arrange 3 noodles on top; spread with remaining ricotta mixture. Top with remaining noodles and remaining sauce. Sprinkle with remaining ½ cup mozzarella and ¼ cup Parmesan. (If making a day ahead, cover and refrigerate.)

5 Cover lasagna with foil and bake 30 minutes (1 hour if refrigerated) or until hot and bubbly. Let lasagna stand 10 minutes for easier serving. Makes 10 main-dish servings.

Each serving: About 350 calories, 24 g protein, 27 g carbohydrate, 16 g total fat (8 g saturated), 2 g fiber, 78 mg cholesterol, 775 mg sodium.

Tuscan Lasagna Spirals

This is a terrific new twist on lasagna. If you don't have time on a weeknight to make it from start to finish, prepare and refrigerate the filling and sauce a day ahead. At dinnertime, fill, roll, and bake, but add 20 minutes to final baking time.

12 lasagna noodles
Salt
1 tablespoon olive oil
1 jumbo onion (about 1 pound), finely chopped
4 garlic cloves, crushed with garlic press
4 slices bacon (about 3 ounces), cut into ¼-inch pieces
1 pound white mushrooms, finely chopped
1 pound portobello mushrooms, stems removed and caps finely chopped
1 package (10 ounces) frozen chopped spinach, thawed and squeezed dry
4 ounces Fontina cheese, shredded (1 cup)
½ cup grated Parmesan cheese
¼ teaspoon coarsely ground black pepper
1 can (28 ounces) plus 1 can (14½ to 16 ounces) whole tomatoes in puree

1 In large saucepot, cook lasagna noodles in *boiling salted water* as label directs. Drain noodles and rinse with cold running water to stop cooking; drain again. Layer noodles between sheets of waxed paper.

2 Meanwhile, preheat oven to 450°F. In nonstick 12-inch skillet, heat olive oil over medium heat until hot. Add onion and cook 12 to 15 minutes, until tender and golden. Add garlic and cook 2 minutes longer, stirring frequently. Reserve ½ cup onion mixture for sauce; transfer remaining mixture to large bowl.

3 Add bacon to skillet and cook until browned, about 7 to 8 minutes, stirring occasionally. With slotted spoon, transfer bacon to bowl with onion mixture.

4 Into each of two 15½" by 10½" jelly-roll pans, spoon 2 teaspoons bacon fat from skillet. Discard any remaining fat; do not clean skillet. Place pans in oven to heat 3 minutes. Add white mushrooms to 1 hot pan and toss to coat. Add portobello mushrooms to other hot pan and toss to coat. Bake mushrooms on 2 racks in oven, uncovered, 25 minutes or until lightly browned, rotating pans between upper and lower racks halfway through cooking time. Transfer all mushrooms to bowl with onion mixture; stir in spinach, Fontina, Parmesan, pepper, and ½ teaspoon salt. Turn oven control to 350°F.

5 In same skillet, heat both cans of tomatoes with their puree, ⅓ *cup water*, and reserved ⅓ cup onion mixture to boiling over medium-high heat, stirring occasionally and breaking up tomatoes with side of spoon. Reduce heat to low; cover and simmer sauce 10 minutes. Stir ½ cup sauce into mushroom mixture in bowl. Spoon remaining sauce into 13" by 9" glass baking dish.

6 On work surface, place 6 lasagna noodles. Spoon scant ½ cup filling down center of each noodle. Roll each noodle, jelly-roll fashion; place rolled noodles, filling side up, in dish with sauce. Repeat with remaining noodles and filling.

7 Cover and bake 30 minutes or until heated through. Makes 6 main-dish servings.

Each serving: About 500 calories, 24 g protein, 66 g carbohydrate, 18 g total fat (8 g saturated), 9 g fiber, 35 mg cholesterol, 1360 mg sodium.

◄ *Tuscan Lasagna Spirals*

Pasta e Fagioli Bake

PREP: 35 MINUTES • BAKE: 15 MINUTES

We turned pasta e fagioli, the beloved Italian soup, into a casserole, topped it with bread crumbs and grated Romano cheese, and baked it until golden.

8 ounces ditalini pasta (1¾ cups)
Salt
2 slices bacon, cut into ½-inch pieces
1 medium onion, diced
2 teaspoons plus 1 tablespoon olive oil
3 garlic cloves, minced
2 cans (15½ to 19 ounces each) white kidney
    beans (cannellini), rinsed and drained
1 can (16 ounces) plum tomatoes in juice
¾ cup chicken broth
¼ teaspoon coarsely ground black pepper
¼ cup plus 2 tablespoons grated Romano cheese
2 slices firm white bread, torn into ¼-inch pieces
1 tablespoon chopped fresh parsley leaves

1 Preheat oven to 400°F. In large saucepot, cook pasta in *boiling salted water* as label directs. Drain well, reserving *½ cup pasta cooking water*. Return pasta to saucepot; set reserved cooking water aside.

2 Meanwhile, in 4-quart saucepan, cook bacon over medium heat until browned, stirring occasionally. Transfer bacon to paper towels to drain.

3 Pour off all but 1 teaspoon bacon fat from saucepan. Reduce heat to medium-low. Add onion and 2 teaspoons olive oil, and cook 5 minutes or until onion is tender, stirring occasionally. Stir in 1 teaspoon minced garlic, and cook 1 minute, stirring. Stir in beans, tomatoes with their juice, chicken broth, pepper, and cooked bacon, breaking up tomatoes with side of spoon; heat to boiling over high heat. Reduce heat to medium and simmer, uncovered, 5 minutes, stirring occasionally.

4 To pasta in saucepot, add bean mixture, ¼ cup Romano cheese, and reserved pasta cooking water; toss well. Transfer mixture to 3-quart casserole.

5 In small bowl, toss bread crumbs with parsley, remaining olive oil, remaining minced garlic, and remaining 2 tablespoons Romano cheese until evenly coated. Sprinkle crumb mixture over pasta. Bake pasta 15 minutes, uncovered, until hot and bubbly and top is golden. Makes 6 main-dish servings.

Each serving: About 405 calories, 19 g protein, 63 g carbohydrate, 9 g total fat (3 g saturated), 11 g fiber, 9 mg cholesterol, 815 mg sodium.

Pasta with Roasted Vegetables

PREP: 45 MINUTES • ROAST/BAKE: ABOUT 50 MINUTES

3 large red peppers, cut into 1-inch pieces
4 garlic cloves, peeled
2 tablespoons olive oil
Salt
1 large head cauliflower (about 2½ pounds),
    separated into 1-inch flowerets and larger
    pieces cut into 1-inch pieces
12 ounces cavatelli or bow-tie pasta
1 tablespoon cornstarch
1 can (14½ ounces) chicken broth
⅓ cup loosely packed fresh parsley leaves,
    chopped
3 tablespoons grated Parmesan cheese
¼ teaspoon ground red pepper (cayenne)
⅛ teaspoon dried thyme
4 ounces ricotta salata cheese, crumbled

1 Preheat oven to 450°F. In 15½" by 10½" jelly-roll pan, toss red-pepper pieces and garlic with 1 tablespoon olive oil and ¼ teaspoon salt. In another 15½" by 10½" jelly-roll pan or on a large cookie sheet, toss cauliflower pieces with 1 tablespoon olive oil and ¼ teaspoon salt.

2 Place pans with vegetables on 2 oven racks in oven. Roast vegetables 30 minutes or until browned, stirring halfway through roasting time and rotating pans between upper and lower racks after 15 minutes. Turn oven control to 400°F.

3 Meanwhile, in large saucepot, cook pasta in *boiling salted water* as label directs.

4 In 2-quart saucepan, with wire whisk, mix cornstarch with chicken broth and *½ cup cold water*; heat to boiling over medium-high heat. Boil 1 minute.

5 Drain pasta and return to saucepot. Toss pasta with roasted vegetables, broth mixture, parsley, Parmesan, ground red pepper, and thyme. Transfer pasta to deep 2½-quart baking pan or casserole.

6 Bake pasta 15 minutes. Remove from oven and top with crumbled ricotta salata cheese. Bake pasta, uncovered, 5 minutes longer or until hot. Makes 4 main-dish servings.

Each serving: About 560 calories, 23 g protein, 81 g carbohydrate, 17 g total fat (7 g saturated), 2 g fiber, 29 mg cholesterol, 1120 mg sodium.

MEATLESS

Curried Vegetable Stew

PREP: 30 MINUTES • COOK: 40 MINUTES

A fast, fragrant skillet dish flavored with rich Indian spices, raisins, and tomatoes. Serve over rice or with pita bread and plain yogurt.

1 tablespoon olive oil
1 medium onion, coarsely chopped
5 cups small cauliflower flowerets (about 1 small head cauliflower)
4 medium carrots, each cut lengthwise in half, then crosswise into ¼-inch-thick slices
1 tablespoon minced, peeled fresh ginger
3 garlic cloves, crushed with garlic press
1 tablespoon curry powder
1 teaspoon ground cumin
¾ teaspoon salt
⅛ to ¼ teaspoon ground red pepper (cayenne)
2 cans (15 to 19 ounces each) garbanzo beans, rinsed and drained
1 can (14½ ounces) diced tomatoes
¼ cup golden raisins
½ cup loosely packed fresh cilantro leaves, chopped

1 In nonstick 12-inch skillet, heat oil over medium heat. Add onion and cook 5 minutes, stirring occasionally. Increase heat to medium-high; add cauliflower and carrots, and cook 10 minutes or until vegetables are lightly browned, stirring occasionally. Add ginger, garlic, curry powder, cumin, salt, and ground red pepper; cook 1 minute, stirring.

2 Add garbanzo beans, tomatoes with their juice, raisins, and ½ *cup water*; heat to boiling over high heat. Reduce heat to low; cover and simmer 15 to 20 minutes, until vegetables are tender and sauce thickens slightly. Stir in cilantro. Makes about 10 cups or 5 main-dish servings.

Each serving: About 430 calories, 18 g protein, 74 g carbohydrate, 10 g total fat (1 g saturated), 17 g fiber, 0 mg cholesterol, 1430 mg sodium.

Vegetarian Chili

PREP: 30 MINUTES • COOK: 50 MINUTES

Black soybeans, sold in convenient cans, have a better texture and flavor than the usual beige variety, and add extra oomph to winter chili.

4 teaspoons olive oil
1 medium butternut squash (about 2 pounds), peeled and cut into ¾-inch cubes
3 medium carrots, cut into ¼-inch dice
1 large onion, chopped
2 tablespoons chili powder
2 garlic cloves, crushed with garlic press
1 can (28 ounces) plum tomatoes in juice
3 jalapeño chiles, seeded and minced
1 cup vegetable or chicken broth
1 tablespoon sugar
½ teaspoon salt
2 cans (15 ounces each) black soybeans, rinsed and drained
1 cup lightly packed fresh cilantro leaves, chopped
Plain nonfat yogurt (optional)

1 In nonstick 5-quart Dutch oven or saucepot, heat 2 teaspoons oil over medium-high heat until hot. Add squash, and cook 8 to 10 minutes, until golden, stirring occasionally. Transfer squash to bowl; set aside.

2 In same Dutch oven, heat remaining 2 teaspoons oil; add carrots and onion, and cook about 10 minutes or until golden, stirring occasionally. Stir in chili powder and garlic; cook 1 minute longer, stirring.

3 Add tomatoes with their juice, jalapeños, broth, sugar, and salt; heat to boiling over medium-high heat, stirring to break up tomatoes with side of spoon.

4 Stir in soybeans and squash; heat to boiling over medium-high heat. Reduce heat to low; cover and simmer 30 minutes or until squash is tender. Remove Dutch oven from heat; stir in cilantro. Serve chili with yogurt if you like. Makes about 10 cups or 6 main-dish servings.

Each serving: About 265 calories, 15 g protein, 40 g carbohydrate, 6 g total fat (1 g saturated), 12 g fiber, 0 mg cholesterol, 480 mg sodium.

Vegetarian Chili ➤

Corn Burritos with Tomatillo Salsa

Our mouthwatering burritos are stuffed with corn, tomatoes, and fresh fennel. Serve with a fork and knife—they're a bit messy!

TOMATILLO SALSA:
12 ounces fresh tomatillos, husked, rinsed, and
  each cut into quarters
1 medium onion, cut into eighths
1 garlic clove, peeled
1 cup loosely packed fresh cilantro leaves
1 tablespoon olive oil
1 teaspoon sugar
¼ teaspoon salt

CORN BURRITOS:
1 tablespoon olive oil
1 medium onion, chopped
½ small fennel bulb (about 1¼ pounds), trimmed
  and chopped
3 cups fresh corn kernels (from 5 to 6 ears)
1 jalapeño chile, seeded and minced
¼ teaspoon salt

SOY PRIMER

Why You Need It

Soybeans contain compounds called isoflavones, which are estrogenlike plant substances that may help reduce the risk of heart disease. Regular consumption of isoflavone-rich soy protein can cut harmful low-density lipoprotein (LDL) in the blood by nearly 13 percent on average. Preliminary research also hints that isoflavones help maintain strong bones in older women, while other studies suggest that soy may provide relief from hot flashes and other menopausal symptoms. Isoflavones may also be the good fairy behind dramatically lower rates of breast and prostate cancer in Asian countries, where soy foods are dietary staples; more research is needed before scientists will know for sure. But don't count on processed soy products like cheeses and burgers; many are not good sources of isoflavones.

Shopping for Soy

Now, you'll find plenty of good heart-helping soy-protein sources in health-food stores, specialty markets, and large grocery stores:

Soy drink: This milklike extraction is pressed from cooked soybeans, filtered, and usually lightly sweetened to make a nondairy beverage that's ideal for the lactose-intolerant. It has a nutty flavor and can be used in place of cow's milk in most recipes. You can buy soy beverages in whole, low-fat, and nonfat versions and in vanilla and chocolate flavors too.

Soy flour: Made from dried soybeans, this is denser and moister than grain-based flours—it's best com-

bined with other flours, not used solo. (It doesn't contain gluten, which gives baked goods their structure.) Look for full-fat, low-fat, and defatted kinds.

Soya powder: A more finely ground, more flavorful form of soy flour. (We used it along with all-purpose flour in Banana-Soy Muffins, page 166.)

Tempeh (TEHM-pay): A dense, chewy cake, this meat alternative is made from cooked, fermented soybeans. Like other soy products, tempeh absorbs the flavor of the ingredients it's cooked with, even though it has a smoky flavor of its own. Tempeh is sold refrigerated or frozen; try in soups or stir-fries.

Textured vegetable protein (TVP): Also known as textured soy protein, these dried granules made from defatted soy flakes have to be rehydrated in water before cooking (see Stuffed Cabbage, page 136). Commercially, TVP is used to make soy hot dogs and veggie burgers.

Tofu: This is soybean curd that is drained and pressed in a process similar to cheesemaking. The creamiest tofu (with the least liquid pressed out) is soft or silken. (Use it in shakes, dressings, and dips.) Extracting still more liquid produces regular tofu, then firm, and finally extrafirm (excellent grilled or in stir-fries). Look for nonfat, low-fat, and full-fat varieties. Avoid bulk tofu, unpackaged blocks sold in water; it can be contaminated with bacteria. Sealed water-packed tofu and the aseptically packaged kind (unrefrigerated) are much safer. To store tofu after opening, cover with cool water and refrigerate for up to 1 week; change water daily.

2 small tomatoes, chopped
6 (10-inch) flour tortillas, warmed
⅓ cup sour cream

1 Prepare Tomatillo Salsa: In food processor with knife blade attached, pulse all salsa ingredients until coarsely chopped. Set salsa aside at room temperature. Makes about 2 cups.

2 Prepare Corn Burritos: In nonstick 12-inch skillet, heat oil over medium heat until hot. Add onion and fennel, and cook 10 minutes, stirring occasionally. Stir in corn, jalapeño, and salt, and cook 5 minutes longer. Stir in tomatoes and 1 cup Tomatillo Salsa, and cook 1 minute to blend flavors.

3 To serve, spoon about 1 cup corn mixture onto center of each tortilla; fold up envelope-style. Serve with sour cream and remaining Tomatillo Salsa. Makes 6 main-dish servings.

Each serving: About 325 calories, 8 g protein, 55 g carbohydrate, 10 g total fat (2 g saturated), 4 g fiber, 4 mg cholesterol, 390 mg sodium.

Each tablespoon Tomatillo Salsa: About 10 calories, 0 g protein, 1 g carbohydrate, 1 g total fat (0 g saturated), 0 g fiber, 0 mg cholesterol, 15 mg sodium.

Tofu-Mushroom Stir-Fry

PREP: 20 MINUTES • COOK: ABOUT 10 MINUTES

3 tablespoons soy sauce
1 tablespoon grated, peeled fresh ginger
1 teaspoon sugar
1 teaspoon cornstarch
½ teaspoon Asian sesame oil (optional)
2 garlic cloves, crushed with garlic press
1 pound extra-firm tofu, well drained, patted dry, and cut into ½-inch cubes
3 teaspoons vegetable oil
12 ounces mushrooms, sliced
12 ounces bok choy, thinly sliced
¼ pound snow peas, strings removed
2 green onions, thinly sliced, for garnish

1 In 1-cup glass measuring cup, with fork, combine soy sauce, ginger, sugar, cornstarch, sesame oil, garlic, and ½ cup water. In medium bowl, toss tofu with 2 tablespoons sauce. Reserve remaining soy-ginger sauce to add to vegetables.

2 In nonstick 12-inch skillet, heat 2 teaspoons vegetable oil over medium-high heat until very hot. Add the tofu and cook until slightly golden, stirring frequently, about 5 to 8 minutes. Transfer to platter.

3 To same skillet, add remaining 1 teaspoon oil, and heat until hot. Add mushrooms, bok choy, and snow peas, and cook about 5 minutes, until vegetables are tender-crisp, stirring frequently and adding 2 *tablespoons water* if skillet is dry.

4 Pour remaining soy-ginger sauce over vegetables in skillet; boil 1 minute. Return tofu to skillet; heat through. Garnish with green onions. Makes 4 main-dish servings.

Each serving: About 165 calories, 14 g protein, 15 g carbohydrate, 7 g total fat (1 g saturated), 2 g fiber, 0 mg cholesterol, 865 mg sodium.

Tofu "Egg Salad"

PREP: 15 MINUTES

A real surprise! Looks and tastes just like egg salad but has no cholesterol. Enjoy on its own or make into a sandwich on whole-grain bread with sliced tomato and crisp lettuce.

1 package (16 ounces) firm or extrafirm tofu, drained
1 medium celery stalk, chopped
½ small red pepper, chopped
1 green onion, chopped
¼ cup light mayonnaise
½ teaspoon Dijon mustard
½ teaspoon salt
⅛ teaspoon turmeric

In medium bowl, with fork, mash tofu until it resembles the texture of scrambled eggs. Stir in remaining ingredients. Cover and refrigerate if not serving right away. Makes 4 main-dish servings.

Each serving: About 195 calories, 18 g protein, 10 g carbohydrate, 11 g total fat (1 g saturated), 2 g fiber, 0 mg cholesterol, 445 mg sodium.

Huevos Rancheros

PREP: 10 MINUTES • COOK: 15 MINUTES

Huevos rancheros is a Mexican fried-egg dish served with salsa and corn tortillas. For our fast supper, poach the eggs in a mixture of salsa and black beans and serve with toasted-cheese tortillas.

1 can (15 to 19 ounces) black beans, rinsed and
    drained
1 jar (11 ounces) mild or medium salsa
    (1¼ cups)
4 large eggs
6 (6-inch) corn tortillas, each cut into quarters
3 ounces shredded Mexican-cheese blend
    (¾ cup)
Coarsely ground black pepper

1 Preheat oven to 475°F. In small bowl, mash ½ cup black beans until almost smooth.

2 In 10-inch skillet, heat salsa, mashed and whole beans, and ¼ *cup water* to boiling over high heat. Reduce heat to medium-low. One at a time, break eggs into cup and slip into skillet on top of bean mixture. Cover and simmer 8 to 10 minutes, until eggs are set or cooked to desired firmness.

3 Meanwhile, arrange tortillas on large cookie sheet. Bake 7 minutes or until crisp and lightly browned. Sprinkle tortillas with cheese; bake 2 minutes longer or until cheese just melts.

4 Sprinkle eggs with pepper. Serve eggs and bean mixture with tortillas. Makes 4 main-dish servings.

Each serving: About 340 calories, 22 g protein, 38 g carbohydrate, 13 g total fat (6 g saturated), 6 g fiber, 234 mg cholesterol, 840 mg sodium.

BBQ Tofu Sandwich

PREP: 20 MINUTES • BROIL: 6 MINUTES

Here's a quick and easy way to flavor up tofu. Serve with our Creamy Broccoli Slaw (page 160).

1 package (16 ounces) extrafirm tofu
Nonstick cooking spray
¼ cup ketchup
2 tablespoons Dijon mustard
2 tablespoons reduced-sodium soy sauce
1 tablespoon molasses
1 tablespoon grated, peeled fresh ginger
⅛ teaspoon ground red pepper (cayenne)
2 garlic cloves, crushed with garlic press
2 teaspoons sesame seeds
8 slices whole-grain bread, toasted
Sliced tomatoes, sliced red onion, and lettuce
    leaves (optional)

1 Drain tofu; wrap in dish towel. Place wrapped tofu in pie plate; top with a dinner plate. Place 1 or 2 heavy cans on top of plate to weigh down tofu to extract excess water; set aside about 15 minutes.

2 Meanwhile, preheat broiler. Spray rack in broiling pan with nonstick cooking spray. In small bowl, stir ketchup, mustard, soy sauce, molasses, ginger, ground red pepper, and garlic until blended.

3 Remove plate and cans, and unwrap tofu. Place tofu on cutting board with shorter side facing you. Cut tofu lengthwise into 8 slices.

4 Place slices on rack in broiling pan; brush with half of ketchup mixture. Place pan in broiler about 5 inches from source of heat and broil tofu 3 minutes or until ketchup mixture looks dry. With metal spatula, turn tofu slices over; brush with remaining ketchup mixture and sprinkle with sesame seeds. Broil tofu 3 minutes longer.

5 To serve, place 2 tofu slices on 1 slice of whole-grain toast. If you like, top with tomato, onion, and lettuce. Top with another slice of toast. Repeat with remaining tofu and toast. Makes 4 sandwiches.

Each sandwich without tomato, onion, and lettuce: About 230 calories, 14 g protein, 35 g carbohydrate, 5 g total fat (0 g saturated), 2 g fiber, 0 mg cholesterol, 975 mg sodium.

◄ *Huevos Rancheros*

Spinach Risotto

PREP: 25 MINUTES • COOK: ABOUT 50 MINUTES

Rich in color and fresh in flavor, this unusual risotto is prepared with frozen spinach and handfuls of fragrant herbs. A sprinkling of crisp pancetta adds a nice salty touch.

1 package (10 ounces) frozen chopped spinach, thawed and squeezed dry
½ cup packed fresh parsley leaves
½ cup packed fresh basil leaves
1½ ounces pancetta, diced (⅓ cup), or 3 slices bacon, diced
1 can (14½ ounces) chicken broth
1 small onion, finely chopped
1 tablespoon olive oil
2 cups Arborio rice (Italian short-grain rice) or medium-grain rice
½ cup dry white wine
½ cup grated Parmesan cheese
½ teaspoon salt
Shaved Parmesan cheese for garnish

1 In blender, place spinach and 1½ cups water. Blend mixture until smooth, stopping blender occasionally and scraping down sides as necessary. Add parsley and basil, and blend until smooth; set aside.

2 Heat 12-inch skillet over medium heat until hot. Add pancetta or bacon, and cook 5 minutes or until browned, stirring occasionally. With slotted spoon, transfer pancetta to paper towels to drain; set aside. Discard all but 1 teaspoon fat from pan.

3 Meanwhile, in 2-quart saucepan, heat broth and 3¼ cups water to boiling over high heat. Reduce heat to low to maintain simmer; cover.

4 To same skillet, add onion and cook 5 minutes or until tender. Add olive oil and rice, and cook, stirring often, until grains turn opaque, 2 to 3 minutes. Add wine and cook, stirring, until wine is absorbed. Add ½ cup simmering broth mixture, stirring until liquid is absorbed.

5 Continue cooking, adding broth, ½ cup at a time, and stirring after each addition, until rice is tender but still firm and all liquid is absorbed, about 25 to 35 minutes (risotto should have a creamy consistency).

6 Into rice in skillet, stir pureed greens, Parmesan, and salt; heat through. Sprinkle with pancetta or bacon and shaved Parmesan to serve. Makes about 6 cups or 4 main-dish servings.

Each serving: About 600 calories, 20 g protein, 98 g carbohydrate, 11 g total fat (4 g saturated), 4 g fiber, 15 mg cholesterol, 970 mg sodium.

Mushroom-Fennel Risotto

PREP: 35 MINUTES • COOK: ABOUT 1 HOUR

A tantalizing trio of mushrooms plus sweet fennel makes this creamy rice dish a special treat.

1 package (0.35 to 0.5 ounce) dried porcini mushrooms
2 tablespoons margarine or butter
1 small fennel bulb, trimmed and cut into ¼-inch dice (2 cups)
1 small onion, finely chopped
1½ pounds assorted mushrooms (white, cremini, and shiitake), sliced
1 can (14½ ounces) chicken or vegetable broth
½ teaspoon salt
¼ teaspoon coarsely ground black pepper
⅛ teaspoon dried thyme
1 tablespoon olive oil
2 cups Arborio rice (Italian short-grain rice) or medium-grain rice
½ cup dry white wine
½ cup grated Parmesan cheese
2 tablespoons chopped fresh parsley leaves

1 In small glass measuring cup, combine porcini mushrooms with ¾ cup boiling water; let stand 20 minutes. Strain soaking liquid through sieve lined with paper towel; reserve liquid. Remove paper towel from sieve; return mushrooms to sieve and rinse to remove any grit.

2 Meanwhile, in 12-inch skillet, melt 1 tablespoon margarine or butter over medium heat. Add fennel and onion, and cook 10 minutes, stirring occasionally. Add remaining 1 tablespoon margarine or butter and increase heat to medium-high; add sliced assorted mushrooms (not porcini) and cook 10 minutes or until vegetables are tender, stirring occasionally.

3 While vegetables are cooking, in 3-quart saucepan, heat mushroom soaking liquid, broth, and 3½ *cups water* to boiling over high heat. Reduce heat to low to maintain simmer; cover.

4 Chop porcini mushrooms; stir into vegetable mixture with salt, pepper, and thyme, and cook 2 minutes longer.

5 Add ½ cup simmering broth mixture to vegetable mixture, stirring to loosen browned bits from pan, and cook 1 minute longer. Transfer mushroom mixture to medium bowl.

6 In same skillet, heat oil over medium heat until hot. Add rice and cook, stirring often, until grains turn opaque, 2 to 3 minutes. Add wine and cook, stirring, until wine is absorbed. Add ½ cup simmering broth mixture, stirring until liquid is absorbed.

7 Continue cooking, adding remaining broth, ½ cup at a time, and stirring after each addition, until rice is tender but still firm and all liquid is absorbed, about 30 minutes (risotto should have a creamy consistency). Stir in mushroom mixture and Parmesan; heat through. Sprinkle with parsley to serve. Makes about 8 cups or 6 main-dish servings.

Each serving: About 435 calories, 13 g protein, 71 g carbohydrate, 10 g total fat (3 g saturated), 3 g fiber, 7 mg cholesterol, 625 mg sodium.

RISOTTO COOK-OFF:
Can You Cut the Time but Keep the Texture? Yes.

If you've ever made risotto, you know what a commitment it is—you're hunched over a pot, eye on the clock, adding broth in increments and stirring constantly for about 30 minutes, all to achieve that creamy rich texture Italians pride themselves on. To find out if we could boil down the cooking time, we made basic risotto (with chicken broth, olive oil, Arborio rice, dry white wine, and grated Parmesan cheese) the standard way (in a saucepan) and in a glass baking dish in the microwave, in a 4-quart pressure cooker, and in a 12-inch skillet. (Our pros thought that using a wider pan might cause the liquid to be absorbed more quickly into the rice mixture.) Then 8 GH food experts compared them.

Grains of Truth: The old-fashioned way won out. The risotto made in a saucepan turned out creamiest, with rice grains that were separate and slightly firm, never gluey or dry. The skillet worked well too, but didn't save any time. The pressure cooker produced the most amazing results: It took just 13 minutes total, and the only downside was that the grains seemed a little less plump—not too high a price to pay to skip all that stirring (all the broth is added at once). The least risottolike dish came from the microwave. Although it took 22 minutes, with no stirring, our panelists panned it because it was so dry.

Pick of the Pack: Most pressure cookers hold 6 quarts, but a space-saving 4-quart model is just the right size for risotto. And it's still roomy enough to hold a batch of beef stew or chicken cacciatore.

Fastest Risotto

1 In 4- to 6-quart pressure cooker, heat *1 tablespoon olive oil* over medium heat until hot. Add *2 cups Arborio rice* (Italian short-grain rice) and *½ cup dry white wine*, and stir for 1 minute. Add *1 can (14½ ounces) chicken or vegetable broth, ½ teaspoon salt, ¼ teaspoon coarsely ground black pepper*, and *2½ cups water.*

2 Following manufacturer's directions, cover pressure cooker and bring up to high pressure. Cook 6 minutes. Remove cooker from heat and reduce pressure instantly by placing cooker in sink under cold running water. Stir in *½ cup grated Parmesan.* Makes about 4½ cups or 4 main-dish servings.

Each serving: About 530 calories, 15 g protein, 91 g carbohydrate, 8 g total fat (3 g saturated), 2 g fiber, 10 mg cholesterol, 830 mg sodium.

NOTE: You may have to experiment with your favorite risotto recipe to make it perfectly in a pressure cooker. We cooked the rice with wine in oil for 1 minute, then added all the cooking liquid, which we decreased to 4¾ cups to compensate for the lack of evaporation during cooking.

Rustic Tomato-Herb Risotto

PREP: 30 MINUTES • COOK: 45 MINUTES

We stirred in fresh mozzarella for a creamy finale to this irresistible Italian classic.

2 cups loosely packed fresh basil sprigs
1 cup loosely packed fresh parsley sprigs
½ cup loosely packed fresh mint sprigs
2 cans (14½ ounces each) chicken broth
2 tablespoons olive oil
1½ cups trimmed and finely chopped fresh
    fennel (8-ounce bulb)
1 cup minced shallots (about 6 medium)
3 garlic cloves, minced
1¼ cups Arborio rice (Italian short-grain rice)
    or medium-grain rice
½ teaspoon salt
¼ teaspoon coarsely ground black pepper
¼ cup dry white wine
3 ripe medium tomatoes, coarsely chopped
½ cup grated Parmesan cheese
¼ pound fresh mozzarella cheese, cut into
    ½-inch chunks (optional)

1 Mince enough basil leaves to equal 2 tablespoons. Mince enough parsley and mint leaves to equal 1 tablespoon each.

2 In 2-quart saucepan, combine remaining basil sprigs, parsley sprigs, and mint sprigs with chicken broth and *1 cup water*; heat to boiling over high heat. Reduce heat to low to maintain simmer; cover.

3 Meanwhile, in 4-quart saucepan, heat olive oil over medium heat until hot. Add fennel, shallots, and garlic, and cook until very soft but not browned, about 6 to 8 minutes, stirring frequently. Add rice, salt, and pepper, and cook, stirring constantly, until rice grains are opaque, about 5 minutes. Add wine; cook until wine is absorbed, about 1 minute.

4 Remove herb sprigs from broth; discard. Add ½ cup simmering broth to rice, stirring until liquid is absorbed. Continue cooking, adding remaining broth, ½ cup at a time, and stirring after each addition until liquid is absorbed and rice is tender but still firm, 25 to 30 minutes (risotto should have a creamy consistency).

5 Add tomatoes and cook 5 minutes, stirring. Remove saucepan from heat; stir in Parmesan, minced mint and parsley, 1 tablespoon minced basil, and mozzarella (if using). Spoon risotto into 6 shallow bowls; sprinkle with remaining minced basil. Serve immediately. Makes about 8 cups or 6 main-dish servings.

Each serving without mozzarella: About 320 calories, 11 g protein, 48 g carbohydrate, 8 g total fat (3 g saturated), 2 g fiber, 7 mg cholesterol, 790 mg sodium.

Caribbean Black Beans & Rice

PREP: 20 MINUTES • COOK: ABOUT 40 MINUTES

A hearty one-dish meal—rice simmered with black beans, spices, and a hint of sherry.

1 tablespoon olive oil
3 medium carrots, cut into ¼-inch dice
2 medium celery stalks, cut into ¼-inch dice
1 large onion, chopped
3 garlic cloves, minced
1 teaspoon salt
½ teaspoon ground allspice
¾ cup long-grain white rice
¼ cup dry sherry
1 tablespoon cayenne-pepper sauce*
2 cans (15 to 19 ounces each) black beans,
    rinsed and drained
1 cup packed fresh cilantro leaves, chopped

1 In 4-quart saucepan, heat oil over medium heat until hot. Add carrots, celery, and onion, and cook 15 minutes or until vegetables are tender, stirring often. Add garlic, salt, and allspice; cook 1 minute longer. Add rice, sherry, cayenne-pepper sauce, and *1¼ cups water*; heat to boiling over medium-high heat. Reduce heat to low; cover and simmer 15 to 18 minutes, until rice is tender and liquid is absorbed.

2 Stir in black beans and cook, covered, 5 minutes longer. Stir in cilantro just before serving. Serve with extra cayenne-pepper sauce if you like. Makes 4 main-dish servings.

*Cayenne-pepper sauce is a milder variety of hot pepper sauce that adds tang and flavor, not just heat. It can be found, near the ketchup, in the condiment section of the supermarket.

Each serving: About 400 calories, 23 g protein, 78 g carbohydrate, 5 g total fat (1 g saturated), 16 g fiber, 0 mg cholesterol, 1360 mg sodium.

Mushroom & Gruyère Rösti

PREP: 15 MINUTES • COOK: 40 MINUTES

This Swiss favorite is typically made with shredded potatoes that are formed into a pancake and cooked until golden and crisp on both sides. But we used 2 layers of white rice (short grain is best because it holds together so well), with a layer of melted cheese and mushrooms in between.

1⅓ cups short-grain white rice
1 teaspoon salt
4 teaspoons margarine or butter
1 large onion, finely chopped
2 ounces Gruyère cheese, shredded (½ cup)
8 ounces cremini and/or oyster mushrooms, thinly sliced
8 ounces shiitake mushrooms, stems removed and caps thinly sliced
1 garlic clove, minced
¼ teaspoon dried thyme
¼ teaspoon coarsely ground black pepper

Mushroom & Gruyère Rösti

½ cup loosely packed fresh parsley leaves, chopped
1 tablespoon vegetable oil
Thyme sprigs for garnish

1 In 2-quart saucepan, heat rice, ¾ teaspoon salt, and *2⅔ cups water* to boiling over high heat. Reduce heat to low; cover and simmer 15 minutes or until rice is just tender and liquid is absorbed.

2 Meanwhile, in nonstick 10-inch skillet, melt 2 teaspoons margarine or butter over medium heat. Add onion and cook 15 minutes or until tender, stirring occasionally. Stir half of cooked onion and ¼ cup cheese into cooked rice; set aside.

3 In same skillet, melt remaining 2 teaspoons margarine or butter over medium-high heat. Add mushrooms and cook 6 to 8 minutes, until tender and golden, stirring occasionally. Add garlic, thyme, pepper, remaining ¼ teaspoon salt, and remaining cooked onion, and cook 1 minute, stirring. Transfer mushroom mixture to medium bowl; stir in parsley. Reserve ¼ cup mushroom mixture for garnish. Stir remaining ¼ cup cheese into mushrooms in bowl.

4 In same skillet, heat 1½ teaspoons oil over medium-high heat until hot; remove skillet from heat. Add half of rice mixture to skillet and, with wide metal spatula, spread and press to form an even layer covering bottom of skillet (rice may be sticky). Top with mushroom mixture from bowl, leaving ½-inch border of rice. Spoon remaining rice mixture over mushroom layer; press to seal rice edges together.

5 Cook rösti over medium-high heat 5 minutes; invert onto large plate (if rösti cracks or sticks to pan, press pieces back together). Add remaining 1½ teaspoons oil to skillet; slide rösti back into skillet and cook 5 minutes longer or until golden and hot. To serve, slide rösti onto platter; top with reserved mushroom mixture and garnish with thyme sprigs. Cut into wedges. Makes 6 main-dish servings.

Each serving: About 270 calories, 7 g protein, 42 g carbohydrate, 8 g total fat (3 g saturated), 2 g fiber, 10 mg cholesterol, 430 mg sodium.

Caramelized Onion & Goat-Cheese Tart

PREP: 1 HOUR 15 MINUTES • BAKE: ABOUT 1 HOUR

A rich, golden pastry crust is the perfect foil for our cheese-topped filling. If you can't find mild goat cheese, use ⅓ cup freshly grated Parmesan instead. The companion salad of baby greens is tossed with an easy homemade vinaigrette.

CRUST:
1½ cups all-purpose flour
½ teaspoon salt
¼ cup vegetable shortening
4 tablespoons cold margarine or butter, cut up

ONION & GOAT-CHEESE FILLING:
1 tablespoon olive oil
1 tablespoon margarine or butter
2 jumbo onions (1 pound each), each cut lengthwise in half, then cut crosswise into thin slices
½ teaspoon salt
¼ teaspoon coarsely ground black pepper
3 large eggs
1 cup milk
⅔ cup half-and-half or light cream
1 package (3 to 4 ounces) mild goat cheese, such as Montrachet, crumbled
¼ cup loosely packed fresh parsley leaves, chopped

SALAD:
1 tablespoon olive oil
2 teaspoons seasoned rice vinegar
2 teaspoons balsamic vinegar
¼ teaspoon Dijon mustard
⅛ teaspoon salt
⅛ teaspoon coarsely ground black pepper
6 ounces mixed baby greens (about 10 cups)

1 Prepare Crust: In medium bowl, with wire whisk or fork, stir flour and salt. With pastry blender or 2 knives used scissor-fashion, cut in shortening with margarine or butter until mixture resembles coarse crumbs. Sprinkle about *4 tablespoons cold water*, 1 tablespoon at a time, into flour mixture, mixing lightly with fork after each addition until mixture is just moist enough to hold together. With hands, shape dough into a disk.

2 Preheat oven to 425°F. On lightly floured surface, with floured rolling pin, roll dough into a 14-inch round. Press dough onto bottom and up side of 11" by 1" tart pan with removable bottom. Fold overhang in and press against side of tart pan to form a rim ⅛ inch above edge of pan. With fork, prick dough at 1-inch intervals to prevent puffing and shrinking during baking.

3 Line tart shell with foil and fill with pie weights, dried beans, or uncooked rice. Bake 15 minutes; remove foil with weights and bake 15 minutes longer or until golden. If crust puffs up during baking, gently press it to tart pan with back of spoon. Remove tart shell from oven; cool on wire rack. Turn oven control to 400°F.

4 While tart shell is baking, prepare Onion & Goat-Cheese Filling: In nonstick 12-inch skillet, heat olive oil with margarine or butter over medium heat. Add onions, salt, and pepper, and cook 25 to 30 minutes, until onions are golden, stirring occasionally. Stir in *2 tablespoons water* during last minute of cooking time.

5 In medium bowl, with wire whisk or fork, mix eggs, milk, and half-and-half until blended.

6 Place onions in tart shell. Pour egg mixture over onions. Bake 25 to 30 minutes, until filling is set and lightly browned. Top tart with crumbled goat cheese and bake 3 minutes longer. Transfer tart to wire rack; let stand 10 minutes to serve hot. Or, cool tart on wire rack to serve at room temperature later.

7 While tart is baking, prepare Salad: In small bowl, with wire whisk or fork, mix olive oil, both vinegars, mustard, salt, and pepper until blended. Or, place vinaigrette ingredients in small jar and shake to blend.

8 To serve, in large bowl, toss greens with vinaigrette. Sprinkle tart with parsley; cut tart into 10 wedges. Serve each wedge with some salad. Makes 10 first-course servings.

Each serving: About 320 calories, 9 g protein, 26 g carbohydrate, 20 g total fat (7 g saturated), 2 g fiber, 78 mg cholesterol, 480 mg sodium.

Savory Rice & Ricotta Tart

PREP: 30 MINUTES • BAKE: 1 HOUR

An irresistible combination of rice and creamy ricotta cheese baked with spinach in a golden crust.

TART SHELL:
1½ cups all-purpose flour
½ teaspoon salt
4 tablespoons cold margarine or butter
¼ cup vegetable shortening

RICE FILLING:
½ cup long-grain white rice
¾ teaspoon salt
1 tablespoon margarine or butter
1 medium onion, finely chopped
1 package (10 ounces) frozen chopped spinach,
    thawed and squeezed dry
¼ teaspoon coarsely ground black pepper
⅛ teaspoon ground nutmeg
1 container (15 ounces) part-skim ricotta cheese
½ cup low-fat (1%) milk
3 large eggs
¾ cup grated Parmesan cheese

1 Prepare Tart Shell: Preheat oven to 425°F. In medium bowl, with fork, stir flour and salt. With pastry blender or 2 knives used scissor-fashion, cut in margarine or butter with shortening until mixture resembles coarse crumbs. Sprinkle about *4 tablespoons cold water*, 1 tablespoon at a time, into flour mixture, mixing lightly with fork after each addition until dough is just moist enough to hold together. Shape dough into a disk.

2 On lightly floured surface, with floured rolling pin, roll dough into 14-inch round. Press dough onto bottom and up side of 11" by 1" round tart pan with removable bottom. Fold overhang in and press against side of tart pan to form a rim ⅛ inch above edge of pan. With fork, prick dough at 1-inch intervals to prevent puffing and shrinking during baking.

3 Line Tart Shell with foil and fill with pie weights, dried beans, or uncooked rice. Bake Tart Shell 20 minutes; remove foil with weights, and bake 10 minutes longer or until golden. (If crust puffs up during baking, press it to pan with back of spoon.) Turn oven control to 350°F.

4 While Tart Shell is baking, prepare Rice Filling: In 1-quart saucepan, heat rice, ¼ teaspoon salt, and *1 cup water* to boiling over high heat. Reduce heat to low; cover and simmer 15 to 18 minutes, until rice is tender and liquid is absorbed.

5 Meanwhile, in 2-quart saucepan, melt margarine or butter over medium heat. Add onion and cook until tender, about 8 minutes. Stir in spinach, pepper, nutmeg, and remaining ½ teaspoon salt.

6 In large bowl, with wire whisk or fork, mix ricotta cheese, milk, eggs, and ½ cup Parmesan until well blended. Stir in rice and spinach mixture.

7 Spoon rice mixture into warm Tart Shell; spread evenly. Sprinkle remaining ¼ cup Parmesan over filling. Bake tart 30 minutes or until set. (To brown top after baking, turn oven control to broil. Place tart on rack in oven at closest position to source of heat; broil 3 to 5 minutes.) Remove side of pan and serve tart warm. Makes 8 main-dish servings.

Each serving: About 415 calories, 17 g protein, 34 g carbohydrate, 23 g total fat (8 g saturated), 2 g fiber, 104 mg cholesterol, 730 mg sodium.

Potato Pierogi with Cabbage & Dill

PREP: 15 MINUTES • COOK: ABOUT 25 MINUTES

Pierogi, the Polish-style dumplings, are available in many frozen varieties. The potato-filled kind is perfect with sweet pan-browned onions.

1 package (16 to 19 ounces) frozen potato
    pierogi
Salt
1 tablespoon margarine or butter
1 small head green cabbage (1½ pounds), thinly
    sliced, with tough ribs discarded
1 medium onion, thinly sliced
¼ teaspoon coarsely ground black pepper
2 tablespoons chopped fresh dill

1 In large saucepot, prepare pierogi in *boiling salted water* as label directs.

2 Meanwhile, in nonstick 12-inch skillet, melt margarine or butter over medium-high heat. Add cabbage, onion, ¾ teaspoon salt, and pepper, and cook 25 minutes or until vegetables are tender and lightly browned, stirring often.

3 Drain pierogi, reserving *1 cup pierogi cooking water*. Add pierogi and reserved cooking water to cabbage mixture; heat through, stirring often. Sprinkle with dill to serve. Makes 4 main-dish servings.

Each serving: About 320 calories, 9 g protein, 56 g carbohydrate, 6 g total fat (2 g saturated), 6 g fiber, 0 mg cholesterol, 1015 mg sodium.

Polenta with Garlicky Greens

PREP: 30 MINUTES • COOK: ABOUT 20 MINUTES

A nutritious vegetarian meal of soft cornmeal, with a tasty topping of sautéed Swiss chard, raisins, and pine nuts. We simplified and reduced the total prep time by microwaving the polenta. (Stir just once instead of constantly.)

2 bunches Swiss chard (about 3½ pounds)
1 tablespoon olive oil
3 garlic cloves, thinly sliced
¼ teaspoon crushed red pepper
1¼ teaspoons salt
¼ cup golden raisins
1½ cups yellow cornmeal
2 cups nonfat (skim) milk
2 tablespoons grated Parmesan or Romano cheese plus additional for serving
1 tablespoon pine nuts (pignoli), toasted and chopped

1 Cut off and discard bottom 3 inches of Swiss-chard stems. Cut remaining stems into ½-inch-thick slices; coarsely chop leaves. Rinse and dry stems and leaves separately; place in separate bowls.

2 In nonstick 12-inch skillet, heat olive oil, garlic, and crushed red pepper over medium heat about 2 minutes or until garlic is lightly golden, stirring occasionally.

3 Increase heat to medium-high; add sliced chard stems to skillet and cook 8 minutes, stirring occasionally. Gradually add chard leaves and ½ teaspoon salt, stirring until leaves wilt; stir in ⅓ *cup water*. Cover skillet and simmer 5 minutes or until stems and leaves are tender; stir in raisins and set aside.

4 Meanwhile, prepare polenta in micro-wave oven:* In 4-quart microwave-safe bowl or casserole, combine cornmeal, remaining ¾ teaspoon salt, milk, and 4½ *cups water*. Cover and cook on High 12 to 15 minutes, until thickened, stirring once.

5 To serve, stir Parmesan into polenta. Spoon polenta onto platter; top with Swiss-chard mixture and sprinkle with pine nuts. Serve with additional Parmesan to sprinkle over each serving if you like.

*If you like, polenta can be prepared on top of range: In 4-quart saucepan, stir 1 teaspoon salt with 2 cups cold milk. Gradually whisk in cornmeal until blended, then whisk in 4½ *cups boiling water*. Heat to boiling over high heat, stirring occasionally. Reduce heat to medium-low and cook, partially covered, 20 minutes, stirring frequently. Makes 4 main-dish servings.

Each serving: About 375 calories, 16 g protein, 66 g carbohydrate, 6 g total fat (1 g saturated), 9 g fiber, 5 mg cholesterol, 1265 mg sodium.

LEAFY GREENS: WHY YOU NEED THEM

Leafy greens are rich in beta-carotene—though its color is masked by chlorophyll—and supply lutein and zeaxanthin, carotenoids that may lower the risk of macular degeneration (retina deterioration), the leading cause of irreversible blindness among people over 65. Leafy greens also pack folic acid, a B vitamin that has been shown to decrease the risk of certain birth defects and may also help stave off heart disease. A serving (about ½ cup, cooked) of greens, such as Swiss chard, collard greens, or spinach, supplies about 10 to 50 percent of the Daily Value for magnesium, a mineral that fights high blood pressure. The lighter the shade of green, the fewer nutrients you're getting: Substitute romaine or fresh spinach for pale iceberg lettuce.

Stuffed Baby Eggplants

6 small or Italian eggplants (8 ounces each)
3 tablespoons olive oil
1 cup long-grain white rice
1¼ teaspoons salt
1 medium red onion, coarsely chopped
1 medium red pepper, cut into ¼-inch dice
1 garlic clove, minced
½ teaspoon dried mint
¼ teaspoon coarsely ground black pepper
1 tablespoon fresh lemon juice
2 ounces feta cheese, crumbled (½ cup)
6 large pitted green olives, coarsely chopped
Lemon wedges

1 Preheat oven to 450°F. Cut each eggplant lengthwise in half. Rub cut sides of eggplants with 2 tablespoons olive oil. Place eggplants, cut side down, in 15½" by 10½" jelly-roll pan and bake 20 to 25 minutes, until tender. Remove jelly-roll pan with eggplants from oven. Turn oven control to 400°F.

2 Meanwhile, in 2-quart saucepan, heat rice, ½ teaspoon salt, and 2 *cups water* to boiling over high heat. Reduce heat to low; cover and simmer 15 to 18 minutes, until rice is tender and liquid is absorbed.

3 With spoon, gently scoop out most of flesh from each eggplant half, leaving about ¼-inch-thick shell. Coarsely chop eggplant flesh and spoon into bowl. Sprinkle eggplant shells with ¼ teaspoon salt. Set eggplant flesh and shells aside.

4 In nonstick 12-inch skillet, heat remaining 1 tablespoon oil over medium heat until hot. Add onion and red pepper, and cook until vegetables are tender, about 10 minutes, stirring frequently. Add garlic, mint, black pepper, and remaining ½ teaspoon salt; cook 1 minute longer. Stir in eggplant flesh and cook 5 to 10 minutes, stirring often. Stir in lemon juice.

5 Spoon rice into eggplant shells; top with eggplant mixture. Return to same jelly-roll pan. Sprinkle feta cheese and chopped olives over filled eggplants. Bake 10 minutes or until heated through. Serve with lemon wedges. Makes 6 main-dish servings.

Each serving: About 275 calories, 6 g protein, 42 g carbohydrate, 10 g total fat (3 g saturated), 1 g fiber, 8 mg cholesterol, 575 mg sodium.

Eggplant Parmesan

Leftovers (and extra sauce) from this meatless classic make a splendid pasta sauce (see Pasta with Eggplant Sauce, page 104), for which you'll need 2 cups tomato sauce and one-fourth of the baked casserole.

TOMATO SAUCE:
1 tablespoon olive oil
1 medium onion, finely chopped
4 garlic cloves, minced
2 cans (28 ounces each) whole tomatoes in puree
¼ cup tomato paste
1 teaspoon salt
¼ teaspoon coarsely ground black pepper
¼ cup loosely packed fresh basil leaves, chopped (optional)

EGGPLANT:
3 medium eggplants (about 3¼ pounds), cut lengthwise into ½-inch-thick slices
2 tablespoons olive oil
½ teaspoon salt

BREAD-CRUMB TOPPING:
2 teaspoons margarine or butter
2 slices firm white bread, coarsely grated
1 garlic clove, minced
2 ounces part-skim mozzarella cheese, shredded (½ cup)
2 tablespoons grated Parmesan cheese

CHEESE FILLING:
1 container (15 ounces) part-skim ricotta cheese
2 ounces part-skim mozzarella cheese, shredded (½ cup)
2 tablespoons grated Parmesan cheese
¼ teaspoon coarsely ground black pepper

1 Prepare Tomato Sauce: In 4-quart saucepan, heat oil over medium heat until hot. Add onion and cook until tender, about 8 minutes, stirring occasionally. Add garlic and cook 1 minute, stirring frequently.

2 Stir in tomatoes with their puree, tomato paste, salt, and pepper, breaking up tomatoes with side of spoon; heat to boiling over high heat. Reduce heat to low and simmer, uncovered, 25 minutes or until sauce thickens slightly. Stir in basil. Makes about 6 cups. (Cover and refrigerate 2 cups sauce to make Pasta with Eggplant Sauce, page 104, or save for another use).

3 While sauce is simmering, prepare Eggplant: Preheat oven to 450°F. Grease 2 large cookie sheets. Arrange eggplant slices in single layer on cookie sheets. Brush top of eggplant slices with olive oil and sprinkle with salt.

4 Bake eggplant slices 25 to 30 minutes or until tender and golden, rotating sheets and turning slices over halfway through cooking. Remove eggplant from oven and turn oven control to 350°F.

5 Prepare Bread-Crumb Topping: In nonstick 10-inch skillet, melt margarine or butter over medium heat. Add grated bread and garlic, and cook about 7 minutes or until lightly browned, stirring occasionally. Transfer to small bowl. Add mozzarella and Parmesan; toss until evenly mixed.

6 Prepare Cheese Filling: In medium bowl, mix ricotta, mozzarella, Parmesan, and pepper until blended.

7 Assemble casserole: Into 13" by 9" glass baking dish, evenly spoon 1 cup Tomato Sauce. Arrange half of Eggplant, overlapping slightly, in baking dish; top with 1 cup Tomato Sauce then dollops of Cheese Filling. Top cheese with 1 cup Tomato Sauce, remaining Eggplant, and remaining Tomato Sauce (about 1 cup). Sprinkle with Bread-Crumb Topping.

8 Cover dish with foil and bake casserole 15 minutes. Uncover and bake 15 minutes longer or until hot and bubbly. Let Eggplant Parmesan stand 10 minutes for easier serving. Makes 6 main-dish servings.

Each serving: About 380 calories, 21 g protein, 35 g carbohydrate, 19 g total fat (8 g saturated), 5 g fiber, 39 mg cholesterol, 1385 mg sodium.

Eggplant Parmesan (opposite page) with Orange-Fennel Salad (page 156)

Stuffed Cabbage

PREP: 1 HOUR 10 MINUTES • BAKE: 40 MINUTES

We filled large cabbage leaves with a medley of veggies, flavorful seasonings, and textured vegetable protein (TVP), a soy product that can be used in place of ground meat in many recipes.

1 cup textured vegetable protein (TVP)
1 medium head savoy cabbage (about
    2¼ pounds)
1 tablespoon olive oil
2 medium carrots, chopped
2 medium celery stalks, chopped
1 medium red pepper, chopped
3 garlic cloves, minced
3 green onions, sliced
2 tablespoons minced, peeled fresh ginger
2 tablespoons plus 1 teaspoon reduced-sodium
    soy sauce
2 tablespoons seasoned rice vinegar
1 can (14½ ounces) diced tomatoes
1 tablespoon light brown sugar
2 tablespoons chopped fresh parsley leaves
    for garnish

1 Rehydrate TVP: In 1-quart saucepan, heat *1 cup water* to boiling over high heat. Remove saucepan from heat; stir in TVP and set aside.

2 Carefully remove 10 large outer leaves from cabbage (more, if leaves are small) and set aside; finely chop remaining cabbage.

3 In nonstick 5-quart saucepot, heat *12 cups water* to boiling over high heat. Add whole cabbage leaves and cook, pressing leaves under water with tongs, until leaves are pliable, 3 to 5 minutes. Drain leaves in colander; set aside. Discard water and wipe saucepot dry.

4 In same saucepot, heat oil over medium heat. Add carrots, celery, and red pepper, and cook 10 to 12 minutes, until vegetables are tender-crisp, stirring occasionally. Increase heat to medium-high; add chopped cabbage and cook 5 minutes, stirring, until cabbage wilts. Add garlic, green onions, and ginger, and cook 2 minutes longer, stirring.

5 Stir in *¼ cup water*. Reduce heat to low; cover and simmer 8 minutes or until vegetables are very tender. Remove from heat; stir in rehydrated TVP, 2 tablespoons soy sauce, and 1 tablespoon rice vinegar.

6 In small bowl, combine tomatoes with their juice, brown sugar, remaining 1 tablespoon rice vinegar, and remaining 1 teaspoon soy sauce.

7 Preheat oven to 350°F. With paper towel, pat cabbage leaves dry. With sharp knife, trim thick center ribs. With stem end toward you, place heaping ½ cup TVP mixture in center of bottom half of 1 leaf. Fold in sides of leaf and roll up. Place roll, seam side down, in shallow 2½-quart casserole or baking dish. Repeat with remaining cabbage leaves and TVP mixture, overlapping 2 smaller leaves to make 1 roll if necessary.

8 Spoon tomato mixture over cabbage rolls. Cover casserole and bake 40 minutes or until rolls are hot and sauce is bubbly. Sprinkle with parsley before serving. Makes 10 rolls or 5 main-dish servings.

Each serving: About 240 calories, 19 g protein, 41 g carbohydrate, 4 g total fat (1 g saturated), 7 g fiber, 0 mg cholesterol, 1115 mg sodium.

Stuffed Cabbage

Potato & Chutney Turnovers

PREP: 30 MINUTES • BAKE: 20 TO 25 MINUTES

Season a simple combination of veggies with cumin and mango chutney, and bake in pockets of store-bought pizza dough. Serve extra chutney on the side for dipping if you like.

1 pound all-purpose potatoes (about 3 medium), peeled and cut into ½-inch chunks
¾ teaspoon salt
¼ teaspoon coarsely ground black pepper
1 teaspoon ground cumin
¼ cup mango chutney, chopped
1 cup frozen peas and carrots, thawed
1 package (10 ounces) refrigerated pizza dough

1 Preheat oven to 425°F. In 3-quart saucepan, place potatoes and enough *water* to cover; heat to boiling over high heat. Reduce heat to low; cover and simmer 10 minutes or until potatoes are fork-tender; drain.

2 Return potatoes to saucepan. With fork, coarsely mash potatoes; stir in salt and pepper.

3 In 1-quart saucepan, toast cumin over medium heat 1 minute, stirring frequently; stir in chutney and *2 tablespoons water*. Stir chutney mixture into potatoes. Gently stir in peas and carrots.

4 On lightly floured surface, unroll package of pizza dough and cut into 4 squares. Place dough squares on large cookie sheet.

5 Spoon potato filling diagonally on half of each dough square. Fold unfilled side over filling. Press edges together; seal with tines of fork.

6 Bake turnovers 20 to 25 minutes, until dough is cooked through and lightly browned. Makes 4 main-dish servings.

Each serving: About 315 calories, 9 g protein, 62 g carbohydrate, 2 g total fat (0 g saturated), 4 g fiber, 0 mg cholesterol, 780 mg sodium.

Spicy Cheese Soufflé

PREP: 40 MINUTES • BAKE: 55 TO 60 MINUTES

For the lightest, most ethereal soufflé, be careful not to overmix the batter before pouring it into the baking dish. Serve with a crisp green salad to round out the meal.

4 tablespoons margarine or butter
¼ cup all-purpose flour
1¼ cups milk
8 ounces Monterey Jack cheese with jalapeño chiles, shredded (2 cups)
5 large eggs, separated, plus 1 large egg white

1 In 2-quart saucepan, melt margarine or butter over medium heat. Stir in flour until blended; cook 1 minute, stirring. Gradually add milk and cook, stirring frequently, until mixture boils; cook 2 minutes longer, stirring. Remove saucepan from heat; stir in cheese until melted.

2 In large bowl, with wire whisk, beat egg yolks slightly. While constantly beating with wire whisk to prevent lumping, gradually add cheese mixture to yolks and beat until smooth; set aside 10 minutes to cool slightly.

3 Meanwhile, preheat oven to 325°F.

4 In another large bowl, with mixer at high speed, beat egg whites until stiff peaks form. With rubber spatula, gently fold beaten whites into yolk mixture, one-third at a time, just until blended.

5 Pour mixture into soufflé dish. If desired, with back of spoon, make 1-inch-deep indentation all around in soufflé mixture about 1 inch from edge of dish (the center will rise higher than the edge, creating a top-hat effect when soufflé is done).

6 Bake soufflé 55 to 60 minutes, until knife inserted under "top hat" comes out wet but clean. Serve immediately. Makes 6 main-dish servings.

Each serving: About 330 calories, 18 g protein, 8 g carbohydrate, 26 g total fat (11 g saturated), 0 g fiber, 225 mg cholesterol, 445 mg sodium.

Scrambled Eggs Deluxe with 3 Toppings

PREP: 5 MINUTES NOT INCLUDING TOPPINGS
COOK: 10 MINUTES

Here's a twist on classic scrambled eggs—make 1 or all 3 of our toppings to serve with them as a savory brunch accompaniment. And put pan-browned store-bought sausage patties on the platter too.

Caribbean Black-Bean Topping (page 138)
French Pepper Topping (page 138)
Scandinavian Smoked-Salmon Topping
   (page 138)
18 large eggs
½ cup milk
½ teaspoon salt
2 tablespoons margarine or butter

1 Prepare toppings. Keep black-bean and pepper toppings warm if serving immediately or refrigerate to reheat later. (Salmon topping should be refrigerated.)

2 In large bowl, with wire whisk, beat eggs, milk, and salt until blended.

3 In deep nonstick 12-inch skillet, heat margarine or butter over medium-high heat until melted. Add egg mixture to skillet. As egg mixture begins to set around edge, stir lightly with heat-safe rubber spatula or wooden spoon to allow uncooked egg mixture to flow toward side of pan. Continue cooking 5 to 7 minutes, until eggs are set to desired doneness. Serve with toppings. Makes 8 main-dish servings.

Each serving eggs without topping: About 205 calories, 15 g protein, 2 g carbohydrate, 15 g total fat (4 g saturated), 0 g fiber, 480 mg cholesterol, 320 mg sodium.

Scandinavian Smoked-Salmon Topping

PREP: 10 MINUTES

4 ounces thinly sliced smoked salmon, chopped
¼ cup minced red onion
¼ cup loosely packed fresh dill, chopped
½ teaspoon freshly grated lemon peel
1 package (3 ounces) cream cheese, cut into
   small pieces

In small bowl, with fork, stir together all ingredients, except cream cheese, until mixed. Then, gently stir in cream-cheese pieces just to combine. Cover and refrigerate until ready to use. Makes about 1¼ cups.

Each tablespoon: About 25 calories, 1 g protein, 0 g carbohydrate, 2 g total fat (1 g saturated), 0 g fiber, 6 mg cholesterol, 60 mg sodium.

French Pepper Topping

PREP: 25 MINUTES • COOK: 40 MINUTES

Do-ahead: Cook pepper mixture with tomatoes the day before. When reheating to serve, add zucchini slices. Stir in parsley at the last minute.

1 tablespoon olive oil
1 large onion, thinly sliced
1 large red pepper, thinly sliced
1 large yellow pepper, thinly sliced
2 garlic cloves, crushed with garlic press
¾ teaspoon salt
⅛ teaspoon ground red pepper (cayenne)
1 can (14½ to 16 ounces) diced tomatoes in
   juice
1 medium zucchini, cut lengthwise in half then
   crosswise into ¼-inch-thick slices
½ cup loosely packed fresh parsley leaves,
   chopped

1 In nonstick 12-inch skillet, heat olive oil over medium-high heat until hot. Add onion and pepper slices, and cook 20 minutes or until vegetables are golden, stirring often. Add garlic, salt, and ground red pepper, and cook 1 minute longer, stirring.

2 Add tomatoes with their juice and ½ cup water, and cook 5 minutes longer, stirring occasionally. Add zucchini slices and cook until tender, 10 minutes longer, stirring gently. Keep warm or refrigerate until ready to use. Serve at room temperature or reheat. Stir in parsley to serve. Makes about 4 cups.

Each ¼ cup: About 25 calories, 1 g protein, 4 g carbohydrate, 1 g total fat (0 g saturated), 1 g fiber, 0 mg cholesterol, 195 mg sodium.

Caribbean Black-Bean Topping

PREP: 15 MINUTES • COOK: 20 MINUTES

Do-ahead: Make bean mixture the night before and refrigerate. Reheat and stir in cilantro and lime before serving.

1 tablespoon olive oil
1 large onion, chopped
2 garlic cloves, crushed with garlic press
2 teaspoons chili powder
½ teaspoon ground cumin
½ cup chicken broth
3 cans (15 to 19 ounces each) black beans, rinsed and drained
1 can (4 to 4½ ounces) chopped mild green chiles
½ cup loosely packed fresh cilantro leaves, chopped
1 tablespoon fresh lime juice

1 In nonstick 12-inch skillet, heat olive oil over medium heat until hot. Add onion and cook 10 minutes or until tender and golden, stirring occasionally.

2 Add garlic, chili powder, and cumin, and cook 2 minutes longer. Add chicken broth, beans, and green chiles with their liquid, and cook 8 minutes longer, stirring occasionally. Keep warm until ready to use, or refrigerate if not serving right away. Stir in cilantro and lime juice to serve. Makes about 6 cups.

Each ¼ cup: About 55 calories, 5 g protein, 11 g carbohydrate, 1 g total fat (0 g saturated), 4 g fiber, 0 mg cholesterol, 220 mg sodium.

Summer Squash & Potato Frittata with Sage

PREP: 50 MINUTES • BAKE: 15 MINUTES

It takes just a few teaspoons of minced sage to jazz up a humble egg entrée—we love it for brunch or supper.

1 large all-purpose potato (8 ounces), peeled and cut into ½-inch chunks
1½ teaspoons salt
2 tablespoons margarine or butter
1 medium red onion, thinly sliced
2 garlic cloves, minced
1 small yellow summer squash (about 4 ounces), cut into 2" by ¼" strips
1 small zucchini (about 4 ounces), cut into 2" by ¼" strips
2 teaspoons minced fresh sage leaves
¼ teaspoon coarsely ground black pepper
8 large eggs
2 teaspoons balsamic vinegar

1 Preheat oven to 350°F. In 2-quart saucepan, place potato, ½ teaspoon salt, and enough *water* to cover; heat to boiling over high heat. Reduce heat to low; cover and simmer 10 minutes or until tender. Drain.

2 Meanwhile, in nonstick 10-inch skillet with oven-safe handle (or cover handle with heavy-duty foil for baking in oven later), melt margarine or butter over medium heat. Add onion and cook 12 minutes or until very soft, stirring occasionally.

3 Stir in garlic; cook 1 minute. Add cooked potato, yellow squash, zucchini, sage, pepper, and remaining 1 teaspoon salt, and cook until zucchini is tender and liquid evaporates, about 12 minutes, stirring occasionally.

4 In medium bowl, with fork, beat eggs and vinegar. Pour egg mixture into vegetables in skillet and cook, covered, over medium heat 3 minutes or until mixture begins to set around edge. Remove cover and place skillet in oven; bake 15 minutes or until frittata is set. Cut into wedges to serve. Makes 6 main-dish servings.

Each serving: About 180 calories, 10 g protein, 11 g carbohydrate, 11 g total fat (3 g saturated), 1 g fiber, 284 mg cholesterol, 540 mg sodium.

Zucchini & Swiss Frittata

PREP: 15 MINUTES • BAKE: 10 TO 12 MINUTES

FRITTATA MIXTURE:
6 large eggs
¼ cup milk
¼ teaspoon coarsely ground black pepper

ZUCCHINI & SWISS FILLING:
1 teaspoon olive oil
2 small zucchini (about 8 ounces each), cut into
   ¼-inch-thick half moons
¼ teaspoon salt
1 small garlic clove, minced
2 ounces Swiss or Jarlsberg cheese, shredded
   (½ cup)

1 Preheat oven to 350°F. Use a nonstick 10-inch skillet with oven-safe handle or cover handle with heavy-duty foil for baking in oven later.

2 Prepare Frittata Mixture: In large bowl, with wire whisk or fork, beat eggs with milk and pepper until blended. Set Frittata Mixture aside.

3 Prepare Zucchini & Swiss Filling: In the skillet, heat oil over medium heat until hot. Add zucchini and salt, and cook until tender, about 8 minutes, stirring frequently. Stir in garlic, and cook 1 minute.

4 Reduce heat to medium-low. Pour Frittata Mixture over filling in skillet; sprinkle top evenly with cheese. Cook 3 minutes, without stirring, or until egg mixture begins to set around edge. Place skillet in oven and bake 10 to 12 minutes, until frittata is set.

5 To serve, gently slide frittata out of skillet and onto cutting board or platter. Cut into wedges. Makes 4 main-dish servings.

Each serving: About 200 calories, 15 g protein, 6 g carbohydrate, 13 g total fat (5 g saturated), 1 g fiber, 335 mg cholesterol, 275 mg sodium.

Tomato & Fontina Frittata

PREP: 15 MINUTES • BAKE: 10 TO 12 MINUTES

FRITTATA MIXTURE:
6 large eggs
¼ cup milk
¼ teaspoon coarsely ground black pepper

TOMATO & FONTINA FILLING:
1 teaspoon olive oil
1 small onion, sliced
1 medium tomato, cut into ¼-inch dice
¼ teaspoon salt
2 ounces Fontina cheese, shredded (½ cup)

1 Preheat oven to 350°F. Use a nonstick 10-inch skillet with oven-safe handle or cover handle with heavy-duty foil for baking in oven later.

2 Prepare Frittata Mixture: In large bowl, with wire whisk or fork, beat eggs with milk and pepper until blended. Set Frittata Mixture aside.

3 Prepare Tomato & Fontina Filling: In the skillet, heat oil over medium heat until hot. Add onion and cook until tender, about 8 minutes, stirring frequently. Stir in tomato and salt and cook 1 minute.

4 Reduce heat to medium-low. Pour Frittata Mixture over filling in skillet; sprinkle top evenly with cheese. Cook 3 minutes, without stirring, or until egg mixture begins to set around edge. Place skillet in oven and bake 10 to 12 minutes, until frittata is set.

5 To serve, gently slide frittata out of skillet and onto cutting board or platter. Cut into wedges. Makes 4 main-dish servings.

Each serving: About 200 calories, 14 g protein, 5 g carbohydrate, 14 g total fat (6 g saturated), 1 g fiber, 338 mg cholesterol, 350 mg sodium.

VEGETABLES & SALADS

Braised Red Cabbage

PREP: 20 MINUTES • COOK: 1 HOUR 15 MINUTES

Sliced cabbage is slow-cooked with onion, apple, cider vinegar, and brown sugar, then finished with a touch of butter for this traditional side dish. Do-ahead: Up to a day ahead, slice cabbage (don't dice onion early, because the flavor changes and odor intensifies). Store, in self-sealing plastic bag, in refrigerator. Or, prepare recipe through step 2; cover and refrigerate. When ready to serve, return to Dutch oven and heat through. Complete recipe.

3 tablespoons margarine or butter
1 medium onion, diced
2 medium heads red cabbage (about 2 pounds each), cored and cut into ¼-inch-thick slices
1 medium Granny Smith apple, peeled, cored, and coarsely shredded
3 tablespoons light brown sugar
1 teaspoon salt
¼ teaspoon coarsely ground black pepper
3 tablespoons cider vinegar

1 In 6-quart Dutch oven or saucepot, melt 2 tablespoons margarine or butter over medium heat. Add onion and cook, stirring often, until tender and golden, about 10 minutes.

2 Increase heat to medium-high; gradually add cabbage, stirring, until slightly wilted. Stir in apple, brown sugar, salt, pepper, 2 tablespoons vinegar, and ½ cup water. Reduce heat to medium; cover and simmer 55 minutes to 1 hour, until cabbage is tender, stirring occasionally.

3 To serve, stir in remaining 1 tablespoon margarine or butter and remaining 1 tablespoon vinegar. Makes about 8 cups or 10 accompaniment servings.

Each serving: About 100 calories, 2 g protein, 17 g carbohydrate, 4 g total fat (1 g saturated), 4 g fiber, 0 mg cholesterol, 280 mg sodium.

Green Beans with Fresh Orange Butter

PREP: 10 MINUTES • COOK: 10 TO 15 MINUTES

This recipe couldn't be simpler: You melt butter in a skillet with orange peel and other flavorings, then add cooked green beans and heat through. Do-ahead: Up to 1 day ahead, trim and cook the beans. After draining, be sure to cool them down rapidly by plunging them into a bowl of ice water. If you like, prepare orange-thyme butter and orange-peel slivers ahead; cover separately and refrigerate. The day of the dinner, just toss beans with orange butter in skillet and heat through.

1½ teaspoons salt
2½ pounds green beans, trimmed
2 tablespoons margarine or butter
½ teaspoon freshly grated orange peel
⅛ teaspoon dried thyme
2 tablespoons chopped fresh parsley leaves
1 strip orange peel (about 4" by 1"), cut into thin slivers for garnish

1 In 12-inch skillet, heat *1 inch water* and 1 teaspoon salt to boiling over high heat. Add green beans; heat to boiling. Reduce heat to low; simmer, uncovered, 5 to 10 minutes, until beans are tender-crisp; drain. Wipe skillet dry.

2 In same skillet, melt margarine or butter with grated orange peel, thyme, and remaining ½ teaspoon salt over medium heat. Add green beans and cook until beans are hot, about 5 minutes. Transfer to serving bowl. Sprinkle with parsley and orange-peel slivers. Makes 10 accompaniment servings.

Each serving: About 55 calories, 2 g protein, 8 g carbohydrate, 3 g total fat (1 g saturated), 2 g fiber, 0 mg cholesterol, 165 mg sodium.

Green Beans with Fresh Orange Butter ➤

Garden Beans with Sesame-Soy Sauce

PREP: 15 MINUTES • COOK: ABOUT 10 MINUTES

Coat cooked green beans with a soy-sauce dressing and sprinkle with toasted sesame seeds. Serve hot or cold—these are an instant crowd-pleaser!

2 teaspoons salt
4 pounds green beans, trimmed
¼ cup soy sauce
1 tablespoon grated, peeled fresh ginger
½ teaspoon Asian sesame oil
2 tablespoons sesame seeds, toasted

1 In 8-quart saucepot, heat salt and 5 *quarts water* to boiling over high heat. Add green beans and cook 10 minutes or until tender-crisp. Drain and place in large serving dish.

2 In small bowl, with fork, mix soy sauce, ginger, and sesame oil. Add soy-sauce mixture and sesame seeds to beans, and toss to coat. Serve beans warm, or cover and refrigerate until ready to serve. Makes about 16 cups or 20 accompaniment servings.

Each serving: About 40 calories, 2 g protein, 8 g carbohydrate, 1 g total fat (0 g saturated), 1 g fiber, 0 mg cholesterol, 260 mg sodium.

Baby Broccoli with Garlic

PREP: 10 MINUTES • COOK: ABOUT 7 MINUTES

Kids might like this gently flavored veggie, also called broccolini. If you can't find it at the market, use regular broccoli.

1 tablespoon plus 1 teaspoon olive oil
4 medium bunches broccolini (about 8 ounces each), ends trimmed, or 2 medium heads broccoli, stems peeled and sliced, flowerets separated into 1½-inch pieces
½ teaspoon salt
2 garlic cloves, crushed with garlic press

1 In deep 12-inch skillet, heat 1 tablespoon oil over medium-high heat. Add broccolini or broccoli and salt; cook 4 minutes, tossing to coat well.

2 Add garlic and remaining 1 teaspoon oil, and cook 1 minute longer, stirring.

3 Add 3 *tablespoons water*; cook broccoli 2 minutes longer or until tender-crisp. Makes 8 accompaniment servings.

Each serving: About 55 calories, 3 g protein, 6 g carbohydrate, 2 g total fat (0 g saturated), 1 g fiber, 0 mg cholesterol, 155 mg sodium

BABY BROCCOLI IS BORN

Have you seen broccolini, the newest veggie in the produce aisle? It looks like a skinnier version of broccoli, with tiny flowering buds atop pencil-thin stems. In fact, it's a hybrid of broccoli and Chinese kale, and it took 8 years to perfect before a Salinas, CA, farm rolled it out nationwide. Like broccoli, it's a cruciferous vegetable and a great source of cancer-fighting plant compounds, plus vitamin C, vitamin A, fiber, and potassium. But it's not as tough as broccoli; the slender stems are completely edible (they don't need to be peeled). We love the sweet, slightly peppery flavor raw or cooked (try Baby Broccoli with Garlic, at right). Price check: Baby broccoli is picked by hand, not mechanically, so it costs more ($2.99 per bunch, compared to $1.49 per bunch for regular broccoli)—but there's less waste.

Indian-Spiced Broccoli & Cauliflower Stir-Fry

Using 1 skillet makes cleanup a breeze.

1 cup chicken broth
1½ teaspoons cornstarch
4 cups broccoli flowerets (10 ounces), cut into
    ¾-inch pieces if large
2 tablespoons olive oil
3 cups cauliflower flowerets (10 ounces), cut into
    ¾-inch pieces if large
1 large onion, finely chopped
2 garlic cloves, minced
1 tablespoon minced, peeled fresh ginger
2 teaspoons fennel seeds, crushed
1½ teaspoons ground coriander
1 teaspoon ground cumin
½ teaspoon salt
⅛ to ¼ teaspoon ground red pepper (cayenne)
½ cup loosely packed fresh cilantro leaves,
    chopped

1 In cup, with fork, stir chicken broth and cornstarch; set aside.

2 Heat deep nonstick 12-inch skillet over medium-high heat until hot. Add broccoli flowerets and *2 tablespoons water*, and cook 2 minutes, stirring constantly. Add 1 teaspoon olive oil and cook broccoli 3 minutes longer, stirring, until lightly browned but still firm. Transfer broccoli to large bowl.

3 To same skillet, add cauliflower flowerets and *2 tablespoons water*, and cook 2 minutes, stirring constantly. Add 2 teaspoons olive oil and cook cauliflower 5 minutes longer, stirring, until lightly browned but still firm. Transfer cauliflower to bowl with broccoli.

4 Reduce heat to medium. Add remaining 1 tablespoon olive oil to skillet and cook onion 10 minutes or until tender, stirring occasionally. Add garlic, ginger, fennel, coriander, cumin, salt, and ground red pepper, and cook 2 minutes longer, stirring constantly.

5 Stir chicken-broth mixture, broccoli, and cauliflower into skillet; cover and cook 5 minutes or until vegetables are tender and broth thickens slightly. Sprinkle with cilantro leaves before serving. Makes about 5 cups or 8 accompaniment servings.

Each serving: About 70 calories, 3 g protein, 7 g carbohydrate, 4 g total fat (1 g saturated), 1 g fiber, 0 mg cholesterol, 250 mg sodium.

Roasted Cauliflower with Onions & Rosemary

This simple side dish can be made ahead through step 1, covered, and refrigerated up to 6 hours. When ready to serve, reheat in the microwave.

2 heads cauliflower (about 2 pounds each),
    separated into 1-inch flowerets
2 medium red onions, each cut into 12 wedges
4 garlic cloves, peeled and crushed with side of
    chef's knife
2 tablespoons olive oil
1 tablespoon fresh rosemary leaves, chopped
¾ teaspoon salt
¼ teaspoon coarsely ground black pepper
¼ cup fresh parsley leaves, chopped

1 Preheat oven to 450°F. In large bowl, toss all ingredients except parsley until evenly mixed. Divide mixture between two 15½" by 10½" jelly-roll pans. Roast vegetables on 2 oven racks 40 minutes or until tender and browned, stirring occasionally and rotating pans between upper and lower racks halfway through roasting time.

2 Transfer vegetables to platter. Sprinkle with parsley to serve. Makes about 8 cups or 12 accompaniment servings.

Each serving: About 55 calories, 2 g protein, 7 g carbohydrate, 3 g total fat (0 g saturated), 1 g fiber, 0 mg cholesterol, 160 mg sodium.

Summery Succotash

Native Americans taught the first English settlers how to prepare a simple dish of corn and lima beans, often flavored with bear fat. Our version is not quite as basic as the original (and certainly doesn't contain bear fat!), but makes a delicious family-style dish.

2 tablespoons margarine or butter
2 celery stalks including leaves, finely chopped
1 small red onion, thinly sliced
1 garlic clove, minced
2 cups fresh corn kernels (from 3 to 4 ears)
1 cup fresh or frozen baby lima beans, cooked
2 tablespoons minced fresh parsley
1 tablespoon seasoned rice vinegar
¼ teaspoon salt
⅛ teaspoon coarsely ground black pepper
1 medium tomato, coarsely chopped

1 In nonstick 12-inch skillet, heat margarine or butter over medium heat. Add celery and red onion, and cook, stirring, 10 minutes or until onion and celery are tender. Stir in garlic; cook 1 minute.

2 Add corn, lima beans, parsley, vinegar, salt, and pepper. Cook, stirring, 5 minutes or until heated through. Stir in chopped tomato. Serve hot or at room temperature. Makes about 4 cups or 6 accompaniment servings.

Each serving: About 130 calories, 4 g protein, 22 g carbohydrate, 5 g total fat (1 g saturated), 4 g fiber, 0 mg cholesterol, 295 mg sodium.

Savory Corn Custard

The ultimate comfort dish—creamy baked custard with tender corn kernels and a hint of spice.

1¼ teaspoons salt
2 cups fresh corn kernels (from 3 to 4 ears)
2 tablespoons all-purpose flour
2 tablespoons sugar
½ teaspoon ground coriander
⅛ teaspoon ground red pepper (cayenne)
1¾ cups milk
¼ cup heavy or whipping cream
2 tablespoons margarine or butter, melted
3 large eggs

1 Preheat oven to 325°F. Lightly grease 8" by 8" glass baking dish.

2 In 2-quart saucepan, heat *1½ cups water* and ½ teaspoon salt to boiling over high heat. Add corn kernels; heat to boiling, and boil 2 minutes. Drain corn well in colander; pat dry with paper towels.

3 In medium bowl, with wire whisk, combine flour, sugar, coriander, ground red pepper, and remaining ¾ teaspoon salt. Gradually whisk in milk, cream, margarine or butter, and eggs until smooth. Stir in corn. Pour mixture into baking dish.

4 Place baking dish in medium roasting pan (15" by 11"); place on oven rack. Pour *boiling water* into roasting pan to come halfway up side of baking dish. Bake custard 45 minutes or until top is lightly browned and knife inserted in center comes out clean. Makes 8 accompaniment servings.

CORN CUSTARD WITH BASIL: Prepare recipe as above, using basil-flavored milk in place of milk called for in step 3. To prepare basil-flavored milk, in 1-quart saucepan, heat *1¾ cups milk* and *1 cup loosely packed fresh basil sprigs* over medium-high heat until bubbles form around side of pan. Remove saucepan from heat; cover and let steep about 10 minutes. Discard basil.

Each serving: About 170 calories, 6 g protein, 16 g carbohydrate, 10 g total fat (4 g saturated), 1 g fiber, 97 mg cholesterol, 295 mg sodium.

Minty Snap Peas

We tossed sweet tender peas with mint gremolata—a mixture of citrus peel, herbs, and garlic that adds a burst of flavor to savory dishes.

1 tablespoon margarine or butter
¼ teaspoon salt
⅛ teaspoon coarsely ground black pepper
1 pound snap peas, strings removed
1 garlic clove, minced
⅓ cup loosely packed fresh mint leaves, minced
½ teaspoon freshly grated lemon peel
¼ teaspoon freshly grated lime peel

In nonstick 12-inch skillet, heat margarine or butter with salt and pepper over medium heat until melted. Add snap peas and cook, stirring, 5 minutes or until tender-crisp. Remove skillet from heat. Toss peas with garlic, mint, and peels. Makes about 4 cups or 4 accompaniment servings.

Each serving: About 75 calories, 3 g protein, 9 g carbohydrate, 3 g total fat (1 g saturated), 3 g fiber, 0 mg cholesterol, 175 mg sodium.

Collard Greens with Bacon & Cider Vinegar

Smoky bacon and tangy cider vinegar are perfect complements to hearty collard greens. Rinse the greens a couple of times to remove grit.

6 slices bacon (about 4 ounces), cut crosswise into ¼-inch-wide strips
1 medium onion, coarsely chopped
5 pounds collard greens, tough stems discarded, leaves coarsely chopped and rinsed, but not dried
3 tablespoons cider vinegar
¼ teaspoon salt
¼ teaspoon coarsely ground black pepper

1 In 8-quart saucepot, cook bacon and onion over medium heat until onion is tender and bacon is browned, about 15 minutes, stirring occasionally.

2 Increase heat to medium-high; gradually add collard greens to saucepot, stirring until wilted. Reduce heat to medium-low; cover and cook until tender, about 10 minutes. Increase heat to medium-high; uncover and cook, stirring, until most of liquid evaporates. Stir in vinegar, salt, and pepper. Makes about 8 cups or 12 accompaniment servings.

Each serving: About 110 calories, 3 g protein, 10 g carbohydrate, 7 g total fat (3 g saturated), 3 g fiber, 8 mg cholesterol, 145 mg sodium.

Southwest Creamed Corn

We cooked the corn quickly in a hot cream mixture, then accented it with fresh cilantro to serve. The best!

¼ cup heavy or whipping cream
½ teaspoon ground coriander
½ teaspoon salt
¼ teaspoon ground red pepper (cayenne)
¼ teaspoon ground cumin
4 cups fresh corn kernels (from 7 to 8 ears)
½ cup loosely packed fresh cilantro leaves, chopped

1 In 12-inch skillet, heat cream, coriander, salt, red pepper, and cumin to boiling over medium-high heat; cook 3 minutes, stirring occasionally.

2 Add corn and cook 5 minutes or until corn is tender and heated through, stirring occasionally. Sprinkle with cilantro to serve. Makes about 3 cups or 4 accompaniment servings.

Each serving: About 325 calories, 6 g protein, 40 g carbohydrate, 19 g total fat (11 g saturated), 6 g fiber, 61 mg cholesterol, 310 mg sodium.

COMPLETE GUIDE TO CORN

You can't always tell how corn will taste—or look—because it comes swaddled in a multilayered husk. In your quest for perfection, remember:

Golden Rules of Selection

Sweet corn has a higher ratio of sugar to starch than field corn, which is used primarily to make popcorn, livestock feed, cornstarch, and cornmeal. But even the sweet stuff, which we eat with 2 hands and our sleeves pushed up, comes in hundreds of varieties—some bred to be sweeter than others. Categories are based on sugar content:

Sweet: 5 to 10 percent (such as Silver Queen)
Sugar-Enhanced: 15 to 18 percent (such as Kandy Korn)
Supersweet: up to 30 percent (for example, Xtra-Sweet)

In all 3 categories, you can get yellow, white, or bicolored kernels; some are even red or blue. (Butter & Sugar and Sun & Stars are examples of corn that's yellow and white, and Ruby Queen has red kernels.)

Fresh local corn hits its stride from July through September in most regions. But Florida ships its Supersweets nationwide all year. These have a longer shelf life than other varieties and are better able to withstand travel because their sugar takes longer to turn to starch (approximately 10 days from harvest time, as long as ears are kept well chilled). The Southern Supersweet Corn Council recommends husking and rinsing ears, then storing them in an airtight container or plastic bag in the fridge. No matter which variety you buy, look for tightly wrapped, bright-green husks and plentiful, golden-brown tassels at the top that are not dried out.

It's not necessary to pull a husk all the way down to examine the kernels—you can feel for plumpness through the inner husk, or peek under it near the top to make sure there are full rows of kernels. They should be glossy, with no spaces in between.

Cook It Right

Corn on the cob is one of the easiest foods to master, and everyone has a favorite method. Whatever yours is, remember, the faster the better. Heat speeds the conversion of sugar into starch; if you leave corn over a flame longer than necessary, it will lose its sweetness. Remove fine silk strands by hand or with a soft vegetable brush, then:

Boil: In a large, deep saucepot, bring about *4 inches unsalted water* to boiling (salt toughens the kernels). Add husked corn; cover, and cook over high heat 3 to 7 minutes, depending on size and number of ears, until tender.

Microwave: Here's a job the microwave excels at—you don't even need to husk the ears first. Just rinse unhusked corn, then place 2 ears on oven floor, and cook on High 3 to 4 minutes (3 ears, 4 to 5 minutes), turning and rearranging halfway through cooking. Let stand 3 minutes, then husk (the silk will come off effortlessly at the same time).

Roast: Preheat oven to 500°F. Place husked ears in a shallow roasting pan, and brush with vegetable oil. Roast 15 minutes, turning every 5 minutes, until corn is tender and lightly browned.

Grill: Cook husked corn over medium heat 10 to 15 minutes, or until lightly browned. To grill corn in the husk, gently pull husk three-fourths of the way down and remove silk. Cut 8 inches of kitchen twine per ear of corn. Place unhusked corn, kitchen twine, and enough water to cover in a large saucepot or kettle, and let soak for at least 15 minutes. (Soaking in water helps keep husks and twine from burning on the grill.) Remove corn and kitchen twine from water; drain well. Pull husks back up, and tie ends together at tip of each ear with twine. Place corn on grill over medium heat, and cook 20 to 30 minutes, turning occasionally, until husks are brown and dry and kernels are tender.

Cook on Ice

You can also freeze corn kernels to use later in soups and side dishes. Blanch husked corn for 1 minute in boiling water. Cool quickly in ice water; drain. With sharp knife, cut kernels from cob. Spread on jelly-roll pan in single layer, and freeze until hard. Transfer to airtight containers or self-sealing, freezer-weight plastic bags, and return to freezer immediately. Frozen kernels will keep up to 3 months.

Caramelized Pearl Onions with Green Beans

PREP: 20 MINUTES • COOK: ABOUT 10 MINUTES

A trio of delicious vegetables all in one dish. You can precook them early and refrigerate until ready to glaze.

2 containers (10 ounces each) Brussels sprouts, trimmed and each cut in half
1 pound green beans, trimmed and each cut diagonally in half
1 container (10 ounces) pearl onions
4 tablespoons margarine or butter
2 tablespoons dark brown sugar
¾ teaspoon salt
¼ teaspoon coarsely ground black pepper

1 In 6-quart saucepot, place steamer basket in *1 inch water*. Add Brussels sprouts and green beans; heat to boiling over high heat. Reduce heat to medium and cook, covered, 5 to 8 minutes, until vegetables are tender-crisp. Drain and rinse vegetables under cold running water to stop cooking; set aside.

2 In 2-quart saucepan, place onions and enough *water* to cover; heat to boiling over high heat. Cook onions 3 minutes. Drain and rinse under cold running water. With paring knife, trim root end of each onion, then squeeze onion until skin slips off.

3 In 12-inch skillet, melt margarine or butter over medium-high heat. Add onions, brown sugar, salt, and pepper, and cook, stirring often, until onions are caramelized and tender, about 10 minutes. Add Brussels sprouts and green beans and cook 2 minutes longer, until vegetables are coated and heated through. Makes about 8 cups or 12 accompaniment servings.

Each serving: About 80 calories, 2 g protein, 10 g carbohydrate, 4 g total fat (1 g saturated), 3 g fiber, 0 mg cholesterol, 195 mg sodium.

Mashed Potatoes with Horseradish Cream

PREP: 25 MINUTES • BAKE: 20 MINUTES

We used buttery Yukon Golds for this addictive dish. You can make the potatoes a day ahead and refrigerate. When ready to serve, top with horseradish cream and bake until hot and golden.

4 pounds Yukon Gold potatoes (about 12 medium), peeled and cut into 1-inch chunks
1 container (8 ounces) reduced-fat sour cream
3 tablespoons snipped fresh chives
½ cup reduced-fat (2%) milk, warmed
1 teaspoon salt
¼ cup light mayonnaise
2 tablespoons prepared white horseradish
¼ teaspoon coarsely ground black pepper
Chives for garnish

1 Preheat oven to 450°F. In 6-quart saucepan, place potatoes and enough *water* to cover; heat to boiling over high heat. Reduce heat to low; cover and simmer 15 minutes or until potatoes are fork-tender; drain.

2 Meanwhile, reserve ¼ cup sour cream and 1 tablespoon snipped chives to use later in topping.

3 Return potatoes to saucepan. With potato masher, mash potatoes with milk, salt, remaining sour cream, and chives. Spoon potato mixture into shallow 2½-quart casserole.

4 In small bowl, stir mayonnaise with horseradish, pepper, reserved sour cream, and reserved snipped chives. Spread horseradish mixture over mashed potatoes.

5 Bake potatoes 20 minutes or until hot and bubbly and top is lightly browned. Garnish with whole chives. Makes 10 cups or 12 accompaniment servings.

Each serving: About 130 calories, 4 g protein, 25 g carbohydrate, 2 g total fat (0 g saturated), 2 g fiber, 7 mg cholesterol, 275 mg sodium.

Mashed Potatoes with Horseradish Cream ➤

Mashed-Potato Patties

PREP: 10 MINUTES • COOK: 10 MINUTES

If you don't get to make our special potatoes with horseradish cream, plain mashed spuds will work well too. These plump rounds are nice alongside roast meats or poultry.

2 cups cold leftover Mashed Potatoes with
   Horseradish Cream (page 150)
1 tablespoon all-purpose flour
1 large egg
¼ cup plain dried bread crumbs
¼ teaspoon salt
⅛ to ¼ teaspoon ground red pepper (cayenne)
2 tablespoons olive oil

1 Onto sheet of waxed paper, measure eight ¼-cup portions of mashed potatoes. With damp hands, shape each portion into 2½-inch round patty. With dry hands, lightly coat patties with flour.

2 Lightly beat egg in pie plate. On clean sheet of waxed paper, combine bread crumbs, salt, and ground red pepper. Dip each patty in egg, then in bread-crumb mixture to coat both sides.

3 In nonstick 12-inch skillet, heat 1 tablespoon olive oil over medium heat until hot. Add patties and cook 5 minutes. Turn patties over; add remaining 1 tablespoon olive oil and cook 5 minutes longer or until patties are lightly browned on both sides. Makes 8 patties.

Each patty: About 95 calories, 2 g protein, 11 g carbohydrate, 5 g total fat (1 g saturated), 1 g fiber, 29 mg cholesterol, 185 mg sodium.

Oven-Roasted Rosemary Potatoes

PREP: 20 MINUTES • ROAST: 50 MINUTES

This simple favorite will fill the house with the wonderful aroma of rosemary and thyme. Do-ahead: Up to 4 hours ahead, wash and cut potatoes and place in large self-sealing plastic bag. Press out excess air before sealing bag; refrigerate potatoes until ready to roast. If using fresh herbs, wash and chop them and wrap in damp paper towel; refrigerate until ready to use (up to 24 hours ahead).

2 tablespoons margarine or butter
4 pounds small red potatoes (about 24), each cut
   into quarters
1 tablespoon olive oil
1 tablespoon chopped fresh rosemary leaves or
   1 teaspoon dried rosemary, crumbled
1½ teaspoons chopped fresh thyme leaves or
   ½ teaspoon dried thyme
¾ teaspoon salt
¼ teaspoon coarsely ground black pepper
2 tablespoons chopped fresh parsley leaves

BEST-LOVED VEGGIES

We asked Gary Lucier, of the U.S. Department of Agriculture Economic Research Service, for a top-10 list of vegetables nationwide. It turns out we really are eating the good stuff—over the last decade, fresh-cut veggies like baby carrots and broccoli have gotten more popular because they're sold prepackaged. And last year alone, Americans each ate an average of 143 pounds of potassium-rich spuds (thanks partly to fast-food "supersizing"). While not all of these are nutritional powerhouses (iceberg lettuce and cucumbers don't pack a big nutrient punch), here's the overall ranking* of the most popular picks:

1. *Potatoes* **2.** *Tomatoes* **3.** *Corn* **4.** *Iceberg lettuce* **5.** *Onions* **6.** *Carrots* **7.** *Cabbage* **8.** *Cucumbers* **9.** *Dry beans* (including pinto, kidney, and black) **10.** *Broccoli*

*Rankings for vegetables (except dry beans) are based on fresh, frozen, and canned varieties where applicable.

1 Preheat oven to 450°F. Place margarine or butter in large roasting pan (17" by 11½"); place in oven until margarine or butter melts. Remove pan from oven; add potatoes and remaining ingredients except parsley, and toss until evenly mixed.

2 Roast potatoes 50 minutes or until tender and browned, stirring occasionally. Transfer potatoes to platter; sprinkle with parsley to serve. Makes 8 accompaniment servings.

Each serving: About 210 calories, 5 g protein, 38 g carbohydrate, 5 g total fat (1 g saturated), 4 g fiber, 0 mg cholesterol, 250 mg sodium.

Country-Style Creamed Spinach

PREP: 10 MINUTES • COOK: 20 MINUTES

4 packages (10 ounces each) frozen chopped spinach
2 tablespoons margarine or butter
1 medium shallot, minced (¼ cup)
1 teaspoon salt
⅛ teaspoon coarsely ground black pepper
Pinch nutmeg
1 cup heavy or whipping cream

1 Thaw spinach in microwave following manufacturer's directions. Drain spinach, reserving ½ cup spinach liquid.

2 Meanwhile, in nonstick 12-inch skillet, melt margarine or butter over medium-low heat. Add shallot and cook until tender, about 10 minutes, stirring frequently.

3 Increase heat to medium; add spinach, reserved spinach liquid, salt, pepper, and nutmeg, and cook, stirring occasionally, 5 minutes or until spinach is tender. Increase heat to medium-high. Stir in cream and heat to boiling; boil 3 to 5 minutes, until cream is slightly thickened. Makes about 5 cups or 10 accompaniment servings.

Each serving: About 135 calories, 4 g protein, 7 g carbohydrate, 11 g total fat (6 g saturated), 3 g fiber, 33 mg cholesterol, 350 mg sodium.

Squash with Winter Spices

PREP: 25 MINUTES • COOK: ABOUT 25 MINUTES

Fresh butternut squash is cooked with aromatic Indian flavors and finished with a touch of butter and brown sugar.

2 tablespoons olive oil
1 medium onion, chopped
2 garlic cloves, minced
2 teaspoons ground coriander
1½ teaspoons salt
1 teaspoon ground cumin
¼ teaspoon ground red pepper (cayenne)
¼ teaspoon ground cinnamon
2 medium butternut squashes (about 2½ pounds each), peeled and cut into ¾-inch chunks
¼ cup packed dark brown sugar
2 tablespoons margarine or butter
1 cup loosely packed fresh cilantro leaves, chopped

1 In 6-quart saucepot, heat oil over medium heat until hot. Add onion and cook until tender, about 5 minutes, stirring often. Add garlic and cook 30 seconds. Stir in coriander, salt, cumin, ground red pepper, and cinnamon; cook 1 minute.

2 Add squash and ½ *cup water* and cook, covered, 15 minutes or until squash is tender, gently stirring occasionally. (Use a heat-safe rubber spatula to help prevent squash from breaking up while stirring.) Stir in brown sugar, margarine or butter, and cilantro until squash is well coated. Makes about 8 cups or 12 accompaniment servings.

Each serving: About 105 calories, 1 g protein, 17 g carbohydrate, 4 g total fat (1 g saturated), 2 g fiber, 0 mg cholesterol, 300 mg sodium.

Candied Sweet Potatoes

PREP: 30 MINUTES • BAKE: 40 MINUTES

If there are marshmallow lovers in the family, top the already baked casserole with the soft, sweet candies and place in the oven for an extra 10 minutes. Do-ahead: This dish can be made through step 1, covered, and refrigerated overnight. When ready to serve, continue with steps 2 and 3.

4 pounds sweet potatoes (about 8 medium),
    peeled and sliced into 1-inch-thick rounds
½ cup packed dark brown sugar
4 tablespoons margarine or butter
¾ teaspoon salt
¼ teaspoon coarsely ground black pepper
Pinch nutmeg

1 In 6-quart saucepot, place potatoes and enough *water* to cover; heat to boiling over high heat. Reduce heat to low; cover and simmer 5 minutes or until potatoes are barely fork-tender (slightly underdone); drain. Place potatoes in shallow 2-quart casserole.

2 Preheat oven to 400°F. In 10-inch skillet, heat brown sugar, margarine or butter, salt, pepper, nutmeg, and ¼ *cup water* over medium heat until margarine melts, about 3 minutes, stirring frequently. Drizzle mixture evenly over potatoes.

3 Bake casserole, uncovered, 40 minutes, basting potatoes occasionally with sugar mixture and turning slices over halfway through cooking, until potatoes are tender and lightly browned and sugar mixture thickens slightly. Makes 12 accompaniment servings.

Each serving: About 205 calories, 2 g protein, 41 g carbohydrate, 4 g total fat (1 g saturated), 4 g fiber, 0 mg cholesterol, 205 mg sodium.

Crunchy Carrot Coleslaw

PREP: 10 MINUTES

⅓ cup fresh orange juice
¼ cup cider vinegar
2 tablespoons sugar
2 tablespoons Dijon mustard
1 tablespoon vegetable oil
1 teaspoon salt
¼ teaspoon dried mint
⅛ teaspoon ground red pepper (cayenne)
1 bag (16 ounces) shredded cabbage (for coleslaw)
1 bag (10 ounces) shredded carrots

In large bowl, with wire whisk, mix orange juice, vinegar, sugar, mustard, oil, salt, mint, and ground red pepper until blended. Add cabbage and carrots; toss well. Serve slaw at room temperature, or cover and refrigerate until ready to serve. Makes about 10 cups or 8 accompaniment servings.

Each serving: About 65 calories, 1 g protein, 12 g carbohydrate, 2 g total fat (0 g saturated), 2 g fiber, 0 mg cholesterol, 385 mg sodium.

Quick Carrot Salad with Cilantro

PREP: 10 MINUTES PLUS CHILLING

1 lime
1 bag (10 ounces) shredded carrots
⅓ cup loosely packed fresh cilantro leaves
2 tablespoons seasoned rice vinegar
1½ teaspoons Asian sesame oil
¼ teaspoon salt
⅛ teaspoon ground red pepper (cayenne)

1 From lime, grate ¼ teaspoon peel and squeeze 2 teaspoons juice.

2 In bowl, stir lime peel and lime juice with remaining ingredients. Cover and refrigerate. Makes about 4 cups or 6 accompaniment servings.

Each serving: About 40 calories, 1 g protein, 7 g carbohydrate, 1 g total fat (0 g saturated), 1 g fiber, 0 mg cholesterol, 240 mg sodium.

◄ *Candied Sweet Potatoes*

Simple Cucumber Salad for a Crowd

PREP: 20 MINUTES PLUS STANDING

5 pounds Kirby cucumbers (about 18)
1 tablespoon salt
¾ cup seasoned rice vinegar
2 tablespoons sugar
¼ teaspoon Asian sesame oil

1 With vegetable peeler, remove long, narrow, lengthwise strips of peel at ½-inch intervals around cucumbers. Thinly slice cucumbers crosswise.

2 In large colander set over large bowl, toss cucumbers with salt; let stand 30 minutes at room temperature, tossing cucumbers occasionally. With hands, press cucumbers to extract excess liquid. Discard liquid in bowl and pat cucumbers dry with paper towels. Transfer cucumbers to serving bowl. Cover and refrigerate cucumbers if not serving right away.

3 Meanwhile, in small bowl, with fork, mix vinegar, sugar, and sesame oil until blended; set aside.

4 Just before serving, drain cucumbers again if necessary. Toss cucumbers with vinegar mixture. Makes about 10 cups or 20 accompaniment servings.

Each serving: About 35 calories, 1 g protein, 9 g carbohydrate, 0 g total fat, 0 g fiber, 0 mg cholesterol, 430 mg sodium.

Citrus Salad

PREP: 40 MINUTES

Cool and festive, with orange and grapefruit segments at the height of their season—plus a touch of honey.

4 large navel oranges
4 large pink or red grapefruits
3 tablespoons olive oil
1 tablespoon honey
½ teaspoon salt
⅛ teaspoon coarsely ground black pepper
¼ cup cranberries, each cut in half, or pomegranate seeds

1 Cut peels and white pith from oranges and grapefruits, and discard. Holding oranges and grapefruits, one at a time, over medium bowl to catch juices, cut out segments between membranes. Drop segments into bowl.

2 Spoon 3 tablespoons juice from segments into small bowl. Drain remaining juice from bowl of segments; cover and refrigerate for another use. With wire whisk or fork, blend olive oil, honey, salt, and pepper into juice in small bowl.

3 Arrange citrus segments in deep platter; pour dressing on top. Sprinkle cranberries or pomegranate seeds over salad. Cover and refrigerate until ready to serve. Makes accompaniment 8 servings.

Each serving: About 140 calories, 2 g protein, 24 g carbohydrate, 5 g total fat (1 g saturated), 4 g fiber, 0 mg cholesterol, 135 mg sodium.

Orange-Fennel Salad

PREP: 20 MINUTES

Light and refreshing, this salad is a great complement to a hearty main dish.

3 large navel oranges
1 tablespoon extravirgin olive oil
½ teaspoon salt
⅛ teaspoon coarsely ground black pepper
1 large fennel bulb (about 1¼ pounds), trimmed and thinly sliced
1 tablespoon minced red onion
¼ cup loosely packed fresh flat-leaf parsley

1 Cut peel and white pith from oranges and discard. Holding oranges over medium bowl to catch juice, cut out segments between membranes; drop into bowl.

2 Spoon 2 tablespoons juice from segments into small bowl; cover and refrigerate remaining juice for another use. With wire whisk or fork, blend olive oil, salt, and pepper into juice in small bowl.

3 Add fennel, red onion, and dressing to orange segments and toss until mixed. Cover and refrigerate if not serving right away. Toss with parsley leaves before serving. Makes about 6 cups or 4 accompaniment servings.

Each serving: About 115 calories, 3 g protein, 20 g carbohydrate, 4 g total fat (1 g saturated), 2 g fiber, 0 mg cholesterol, 335 mg sodium.

Cherry-Tomato Salad with Chives & Lemon

••
PREP: 20 MINUTES

This refreshing salad doesn't hold well once combined; add tomatoes to lemon slices and dressing just before serving.

2 medium lemons
2 pints red cherry or grape tomatoes, each cut in half
1 pint yellow cherry tomatoes, each cut in half
1 tablespoon sugar
2 tablespoons snipped fresh chives
2 tablespoons extravirgin olive oil
¾ teaspoon salt
½ teaspoon coarsely ground black pepper

1 With knife, cut peel and white pith from lemons; discard. Cut each lemon crosswise into thin slices; remove seeds if necessary.

2 In medium bowl, toss lemon slices, tomatoes, and remaining ingredients. Makes 8 accompaniment servings.

Each serving: About 65 calories, 1 g protein, 9 g carbohydrate, 4 g total fat (1 g saturated), 2 g fiber, 0 mg cholesterol, 210 mg sodium.

FRESH OFF THE VINE: TEENY TOMATOES

Move over, big beefsteak! The newest red rival on the market is tiny but mighty—oval vine-ripened grape tomatoes make a healthy snack year-round. Coming to you from California, Florida, and Mexico, they're smaller, sweeter, and firmer than cherry tomatoes, and work well in all of your favorite recipes, including our Cherry-Tomato Salad with Chives & Lemon (above). Each garden gem is not much bigger than a gumball—and we've found that the littlest members of our families like them a lot.

Veggie Slaw with Thai Coconut Dressing

••
PREP: 35 MINUTES

This tasty new take on slaw is low-fat.

3 limes
¼ cup honey
½ cup well-stirred unsweetened light coconut milk (not cream of coconut)
1 teaspoon salt
½ teaspoon crushed red pepper
1 large head Napa cabbage (about 3½ pounds), thinly sliced (about 20 cups)
2 large red peppers, cut into thin strips
1 bag (10 ounces) shredded carrots
4 green onions, thinly sliced
1½ cups loosely packed fresh cilantro leaves, chopped

1 From limes, grate 1 teaspoon peel and squeeze ½ cup juice; place in small bowl. Add honey, coconut milk, salt, and crushed red pepper; whisk until blended. Set dressing aside.

2 In large bowl, toss cabbage, pepper strips, carrots, green onions, and cilantro. If not serving slaw right away, cover and refrigerate dressing and cabbage mixture separately until ready to serve.

3 To serve, add dressing to cabbage mixture, and toss until coated. Makes about 20 cups or 20 accompaniment servings.

Each serving: About 40 calories, 1 g protein, 7 g carbohydrate, 1 g total fat (0 g saturated), 1 g fiber, 0 mg cholesterol, 120 mg sodium.

Baby Greens with Herbed Croutons

PREP: 20 MINUTES • BAKE: ABOUT 15 MINUTES

Scatter some yummy homemade croutons over tender mixed greens, but set aside about 2 cupfuls for topping our Shortcut Cassoulet (page 97).

HERBED CROUTONS:
4 ounces French bread (half 8-ounce loaf), cut into ½-inch cubes
1 tablespoon olive oil
½ teaspoon dried fines herbes (store-bought French herb mixture)
¼ teaspoon salt
¼ teaspoon coarsely ground black pepper
3 tablespoons grated Parmesan cheese

MUSTARD VINAIGRETTE:
2 tablespoons olive oil
2 tablespoons raspberry vinegar
2 teaspoons sugar
2 teaspoons Dijon mustard with seeds
¼ teaspoon salt
¼ teaspoon coarsely ground black pepper

8 ounces mixed baby greens (about 16 cups)

1 Prepare Herbed Croutons: Preheat oven to 350°F. In 15½" by 10½" jelly-roll pan, toss bread cubes with oil, fines herbes, salt, and pepper until evenly coated. Toast bread in oven 10 minutes. Remove pan from oven; toss bread with cheese. Bake croutons 5 to 7 minutes longer, until lightly golden. Cool croutons completely in pan on wire rack. Makes about 4 cups. (Reserve 2 cups croutons to make Shortcut Cassoulet, page 97, or save for another use.)

2 Prepare Mustard Vinaigrette: In small bowl, with wire whisk or fork, mix oil, vinegar, sugar, mustard, salt, and pepper until blended. Cover and refrigerate if not using right away.

3 To assemble salad: In large bowl, toss baby greens with vinaigrette until well coated. Sprinkle salad with 2 cups croutons. Makes 6 accompaniment servings.

Each serving of salad with croutons: About 100 calories, 3 g protein, 9 g carbohydrate, 7 g total fat (2 g saturated), 1 g fiber, 1 mg cholesterol, 265 mg sodium.

Baby Greens with Fennel

PREP: 20 MINUTES

The cranberry vinaigrette turns an otherwise simple salad into a masterpiece. And the best news is that there's dressing left over for another day.

¾ cup dried cranberries
¾ cup extravirgin olive oil
⅓ cup balsamic vinegar
⅓ cup white wine vinegar
3 tablespoons Dijon mustard
1 teaspoon salt
1 teaspoon coarsely ground black pepper
1 pound mixed baby greens (about 30 cups)
2 medium fennel bulbs (about 1 pound each), trimmed and thinly sliced

1 In small bowl, place cranberries with enough *very hot water* just to cover; let stand 5 minutes to soften cranberries. Drain.

2 Prepare cranberry vinaigrette: In blender, combine olive oil, balsamic vinegar, white wine vinegar, mustard, salt, pepper, and ¼ cup cranberries, and blend until smooth. Makes about 1¾ cups.

3 To serve, in large salad bowl, toss baby greens, fennel, and remaining cranberries with ½ cup vinaigrette until well coated. (Cover and refrigerate remaining vinaigrette up to 3 days.) Makes 12 first-course servings.

Each serving of salad with dressing: About 85 calories, 2 g protein, 11 g carbohydrate, 4 g total fat (1 g saturated), 1 g fiber, 0 mg cholesterol, 115 mg sodium.

Each tablespoon dressing: About 60 calories, 0 g protein, 2 g carbohydrate, 6 g total fat (1 g saturated), 0 g fiber, 0 mg cholesterol, 115 mg sodium.

Baby Greens with Fennel ▶

Creamy Broccoli Slaw

PREP: 20 MINUTES

Combine fresh cilantro, seasonings, and silken tofu to create a new dressing for packaged broccoli slaw. Serve with our BBQ Tofu Sandwich (page 125).

8 ounces silken tofu, drained
1 cup loosely packed fresh cilantro leaves and stems
3 tablespoons seasoned rice vinegar
1 tablespoon olive oil
½ teaspoon ground cumin
½ teaspoon salt
¼ teaspoon coarsely ground black pepper
1 small garlic clove, peeled
1 package (16 ounces) broccoli slaw

1 In blender, combine all ingredients except broccoli slaw; blend until smooth. Makes about 1¼ cups.

2 Place broccoli slaw in large bowl, and toss with ¾ cup dressing until well coated. If not serving right away, cover and refrigerate broccoli slaw up to 6 hours. Store remaining dressing in small jar with tight-fitting lid in refrigerator up to 3 days. Makes 6 cups or 8 accompaniment servings.

Each serving dressed slaw: About 40 calories, 3 g protein, 5 g carbohydrate, 2 g total fat (0 g saturated), 2 g fiber, 0 mg cholesterol, 190 mg sodium.

Each tablespoon dressing: About 15 calories, 1 g protein, 1 g carbohydrate, 1 g total fat (0 g saturated), 0 g fiber, 0 mg cholesterol, 115 mg sodium.

FAST SALAD FIXINGS

Here, our favorite ingredients to toss with dressing and prewashed greens for a fast weeknight salad:

Canned Beans: kidney, garbanzo, black, pinto.

Canned Vegetables: sliced beets, baby corn, hearts of palm, water chestnuts.

Cheese: crumbled blue, goat, feta, ricotta salata; diced or shredded fresh mozzarella; grated or shaved Parmesan.

Crunchy Toppings: seasoned croutons; crumbled bacon; toasted walnuts, almonds, or seeds (sunflower or sesame).

Dried Fruit: cherries, cranberries, raisins, chopped figs, slivered apricots.

Fresh Fruit: chopped or sliced apple, pear, mango, or avocado; sliced or sectioned orange or tangerine.

Fresh Herbs: chopped chives, dill, parsley, tarragon, or oregano; snipped (or whole small leaves of) basil, chervil, cilantro, or mint.

Fresh Vegetables: uncooked corn kernels cut off the cob, shredded carrots, red cabbage, sliced tomato, daikon (Asian radish), red radishes, cucumber, sweet onion, bell peppers.

Jarred Condiments: drained roasted red-pepper slices, slivers of oil-packed sun-dried tomatoes, pickled beets, marinated artichoke hearts, marinated mushrooms, pepperoncini, pitted olives.

Protein Boosters: chopped or sliced hard-cooked eggs, strips of deli meat, flaked tuna, cut-up canned sardines, flaked smoked trout, surimi (imitation crabmeat), cooked shrimp.

Cool Rice Bowl with Radishes

PREP: 20 MINUTES PLUS COOLING
COOK: ABOUT 20 MINUTES

This test-kitchen favorite, a refreshing mixture of aromatic rice, sweet peas, crunchy radishes, and toasted almonds, is tossed in a light vinaigrette.

1 package (14 ounces) Texmati rice (2 cups)
⅓ cup seasoned rice vinegar
2 tablespoons vegetable oil
2 teaspoons grated, peeled fresh ginger
1½ teaspoons sugar
1 teaspoon salt
¼ teaspoon coarsely ground black pepper
¼ teaspoon Asian sesame oil
1 package (10 ounces) frozen peas
2 bunches radishes (about 15), each cut in half and thinly sliced
2 green onions, thinly sliced
½ cup slivered blanched almonds, toasted

1 In 3-quart saucepan, combine rice with 3½ *cups water*; heat to boiling over high heat. Reduce heat to low; cover and simmer 15 to 20 minutes, until rice is tender and water evaporates.

2 Meanwhile, in bowl, with wire whisk, mix vinegar, vegetable oil, ginger, sugar, salt, pepper, and sesame oil; set aside.

3 In large bowl, toss hot rice with vinegar mixture and frozen peas; set aside to cool slightly, about 10 minutes.

4 Serve salad at room temperature, or cover and refrigerate up to 4 hours, until ready to serve. Toss with radishes, green onions, and almonds just before serving. Makes about 12 cups or 16 accompaniment servings.

Each serving: About 155 calories, 4 g protein, 26 g carbohydrate, 4 g total fat (0 g saturated), 1 g fiber, 0 mg cholesterol, 285 mg sodium.

Peach & Arugula Salad

PREP: 25 MINUTES • COOK: 15 MINUTES

Peaches aren't just for snacking or making desserts—they're a nice fresh addition to a green salad, especially this one with arugula, smoky bacon, and mustard vinaigrette.

4 slices bacon (3 ounces), cut into ½-inch pieces
2 tablespoons chopped fresh parsley leaves
2 tablespoons olive oil
2 tablespoons seasoned rice vinegar
2 tablespoons minced shallots
1½ teaspoons Dijon mustard
¼ teaspoon salt
⅛ teaspoon coarsely ground black pepper
4 (3-ounce) bunches arugula, trimmed (about 8 cups)
3 ripe medium peaches (about 1 pound), peeled and sliced

1 In 10-inch skillet, cook bacon over medium-low heat until browned. With slotted spoon, transfer bacon to paper towels to drain.

2 In small bowl, with wire whisk, mix parsley, oil, vinegar, shallots, mustard, salt, and pepper until dressing is blended.

3 In large bowl, toss arugula and peaches with dressing until coated. Sprinkle with bacon. Makes 6 accompaniment servings.

Each serving: About 105 calories, 3 g protein, 10 g carbohydrate, 7 g total fat (1 g saturated), 2 g fiber, 4 mg cholesterol, 330 mg sodium.

3-Bean Salad with Sweet Onions

PREP: 20 MINUTES

For this 1-bowl wonder, toss a colorful mix of kidney, pinto, and pink beans, sweet onions, and parsley with a quick vinaigrette.

⅓ cup cider vinegar
2 tablespoons vegetable oil
1 teaspoon sugar
1 teaspoon Dijon mustard with seeds
½ teaspoon salt
¼ teaspoon coarsely ground black pepper
1 can (15 to 19 ounces) red kidney beans, rinsed and drained
1 can (15 to 16 ounces) pinto beans, rinsed and drained
1 can (15 to 16 ounces) pink beans, rinsed and drained
2 medium celery stalks, thinly sliced
½ cup finely chopped sweet onion, such as Vidalia or Walla Walla
½ cup loosely packed fresh parsley leaves, chopped

1 In large bowl, with wire whisk, mix vinegar, oil, sugar, mustard, salt, and pepper until blended. Add kidney beans and remaining ingredients; toss well.

2 Serve salad at room temperature, or cover and refrigerate until ready to serve. Makes about 6 cups or 8 accompaniment servings.

Each serving: About 185 calories, 9 g protein, 29 g carbohydrate, 4 g total fat (0 g saturated), 9 g fiber, 0 mg cholesterol, 560 mg sodium.

Parsley & Lentil Salad

2 orange and/or red peppers
1½ cups dry lentils (about 10 ounces)
1 bay leaf
1 small red onion, thinly sliced
2 medium lemons
6 ounces smoked mozzarella cheese, cut into
    ½-inch chunks
1½ cups loosely packed fresh parsley leaves,
    finely chopped
¼ cup olive oil
1 teaspoon salt
¼ teaspoon coarsely ground black pepper
Lemon wedges for serving (optional)

1 Roast peppers: Preheat broiler. Line broiling pan (without rack) with foil. Cut each pepper lengthwise in half; discard stems and seeds. Place peppers, cut side down, in broiling pan. With hand, flatten each pepper half. Place pan in broiler 5 to 6 inches from source of heat and broil peppers until charred and blistered, 10 to 15 minutes. Wrap foil around peppers and allow to steam at room temperature 15 minutes or until cool enough to handle.

2 Meanwhile, rinse lentils with cold running water; discard any stones or shriveled lentils. In 3-quart saucepan, place lentils, bay leaf, and enough *water* to cover lentils by 2 inches; heat to boiling over high heat. Reduce heat to medium-low; cover and simmer 20 minutes or until lentils are just tender.

3 When lentils are done, place sliced onion in colander; drain lentils over onion. Discard bay leaf. Transfer lentils and onion to large bowl.

4 Remove peppers from foil. Peel off skin and discard. Cut peppers into ½-inch pieces. From lemons, grate 2 teaspoons peel and squeeze ¼ cup juice.

5 To lentils, add peppers, lemon peel, lemon juice, mozzarella, parsley, olive oil, salt, and pepper. Serve warm, or cover and refrigerate until ready to serve. Squeeze juice from lemon wedges over each serving if you like. Makes about 6 cups or 8 accompaniment servings.

Each serving: About 255 calories, 12 g protein, 26 g carbohydrate, 11 g total fat (4 g saturated), 3 g fiber, 16 mg cholesterol, 390 mg sodium.

Roasted-Potato Salad with Buttermilk Dressing

Freshly grated lemon peel and creamy buttermilk add zing to everyone's favorite picnic food.

ROASTED POTATOES:
4 pounds medium red potatoes, cut into 1½-inch
    chunks
2 tablespoons olive oil
½ teaspoon salt
¼ teaspoon coarsely ground black pepper

BUTTERMILK DRESSING:
⅔ cup buttermilk*
¼ cup light mayonnaise
1½ teaspoons sugar
¼ teaspoon salt
¼ teaspoon coarsely ground black pepper
2 lemons
¼ cup snipped fresh chives

1 Prepare Roasted Potatoes: Preheat oven to 450°F. In large roasting pan (17" by 11½"), toss potatoes with oil, salt, and pepper. Roast potatoes 45 minutes or until golden and fork-tender, stirring halfway through roasting time.

2 Meanwhile, prepare Buttermilk Dressing: In small bowl, with wire whisk, mix buttermilk, mayonnaise, sugar, salt, and pepper; set aside.

3 From lemons, grate 1½ teaspoons peel and squeeze 2 tablespoons juice.

4 Transfer hot potatoes to large bowl and gently toss with lemon peel and juice; set aside to cool slightly, about 20 minutes. Add Buttermilk Dressing and chives; toss gently to coat. Serve salad warm or cover and refrigerate up to 2 hours. Makes about 8 cups or 12 accompaniment servings.

*To make your own buttermilk: In glass measuring cup, place *2 teaspoons fresh lemon juice* or distilled white vinegar, then pour in enough *milk* to equal ⅔ cup. Stir; let stand about 5 minutes to thicken slightly before using.

Each serving: About 150 calories, 4 g protein, 28 g carbohydrate, 3 g total fat (0 g saturated), 2 g fiber, 0 mg cholesterol, 205 mg sodium.

◀ *Parsley & Lentil Salad*

LEMONGRASS

This herb, which has a subtle lemon flavor, is sold by the stalk and looks something like green onions. It is very fibrous; for cooking, trim off the stalk top and use only five to seven inches from the stalk base. Some recipes pound the lemongrass to make the flavor more available. But for the Tabbouleh (at right), we have peeled away the outer layers and chopped the tender inner portion.

Other ways to incorporate lemongrass into your cooking: Use pounded or chopped lemongrass in homemade chicken broth or soup (if you do not chop the lemongrass, be sure to discard before eating). Use the chopped tender portion of lemongrass in your favorite stir-fries and rice pilaf.

Lemongrass Tabbouleh

PREP: 30 MINUTES PLUS STANDING

A blend of garden herbs and spices makes the popular cracked-wheat salad a welcome addition to any picnic table. Serve the traditional way, with small crisp romaine leaves to scoop up the tabbouleh.

1½ cups bulgur (cracked wheat)
3 stalks lemongrass or 1 tablespoon freshly
   grated lemon peel
2 cups loosely packed cilantro sprigs
½ cup loosely packed fresh mint leaves
1 garlic clove, cut in half
1 large ripe tomato, chopped
1 small red onion, finely chopped
¼ cup olive oil
¼ cup fresh lemon juice
¾ teaspoon salt
½ teaspoon ground coriander
⅛ teaspoon ground allspice
⅛ teaspoon ground red pepper (cayenne)

1 In large bowl, combine bulgur with *2 cups boiling water*, stirring to mix. Let stand until liquid is absorbed, about 45 minutes.

2 Meanwhile, trim lemongrass to 5-inch-long stalks, and peel away outer layers until tender inside parts remain. Coarsely chop lemongrass to equal ¼ cup.

3 In food processor with knife blade attached, process lemongrass, cilantro, mint, and garlic until finely chopped.

4 When bulgur is ready, stir in cilantro mixture, tomato, and remaining ingredients. Cover and refrigerate if not serving right away. Makes about 4 cups or 8 accompaniment servings.

Each serving: About 165 calories, 4 g protein, 23 g carbohydrate, 7 g total fat (1 g saturated), 7 g fiber, 0 mg cholesterol, 210 mg sodium.

BREADS & GRAINS

Featherlight Buttermilk Biscuits

PREP: 10 MINUTES • BAKE: 12 TO 15 MINUTES

These are extratender because they're made with cake flour!

3 cups cake flour (not self-rising)
2¼ teaspoons baking powder
¾ teaspoon baking soda
¾ teaspoon salt
6 tablespoons vegetable shortening
1 cup buttermilk*

1 Preheat oven to 450°F. Into large bowl, measure cake flour, baking powder, baking soda, and salt; stir until combined. With pastry blender, or 2 knives used scissor-fashion, cut in shortening until evenly combined.

2 Add buttermilk to flour mixture; mix together with hand just until dough forms. (Do not overmix; biscuits will be tough.)

3 On lightly floured surface, pat dough into 7-inch square. Cut dough into 4 strips, then cut each strip crosswise into 4 pieces to make 16 biscuits.

4 Place biscuits on ungreased large cookie sheet. Bake biscuits 12 to 15 minutes, until lightly golden. Serve warm, or cool on wire rack to serve later. Reheat before serving if you like. Makes 16 biscuits.

*To make your own buttermilk: In glass measuring cup, place *1 tablespoon fresh lemon juice* or distilled white vinegar, then pour in enough *milk* to equal 1 cup. Stir; let stand about 5 minutes to thicken slightly before using.

Each biscuit: About 125 calories, 2 g protein, 17 g carbohydrate, 5 g total fat (2 g saturated), 0 g fiber, 1 mg cholesterol, 225 mg sodium.

Banana-Soy Muffins

PREP: 20 MINUTES • BAKE: 20 TO 25 MINUTES

Bake a batch of tender muffins made with ground flax and soya powder—a great source of omega-3 and phytoestrogens. Muffins rise higher and look prettier when baked in fluted paper cups.

1 cup all-purpose flour
½ cup soya powder*
½ cup packed brown sugar
¼ cup whole flax seeds, ground (see page 172)
2 teaspoons baking powder
½ teaspoon baking soda
½ teaspoon salt
2 very ripe medium bananas, mashed (1 cup)
½ cup enriched plain light soy drink (soy milk)
3 tablespoons vegetable oil
2 teaspoons vanilla extract
1 large egg

1 Preheat oven to 400°F. Grease twelve 2½" by 1¼" muffin-pan cups or line muffin cups with fluted paper liners.

2 In large bowl, with whisk or fork, stir flour, soya powder, brown sugar, ground flax seeds, baking powder, baking soda, and salt. In small bowl, with wire whisk or fork, mix bananas, soy drink, oil, vanilla, and egg until blended. Stir banana mixture into flour mixture just until flour is moistened (batter will be lumpy).

3 Spoon batter into muffin-pan cups. Bake muffins 20 to 25 minutes, until toothpick inserted in center of muffin comes out clean. Immediately remove muffins from pans; serve warm. Or, cool on wire rack; reheat if desired. Makes 12 muffins.

*Soya powder is ground finer than soy flour and is more flavorful. It is available in health-food stores.

Each muffin: About 160 calories, 4 g protein, 25 g carbohydrate, 6 g total fat (1 g saturated), 2 g fiber, 18 mg cholesterol, 215 mg sodium.

*Banana-Soy Muffins (above)
and Multigrain Bread (page 172)* ➤

Corn &
Black-Pepper Scones

PREP: 10 MINUTES • BAKE: 20 TO 25 MINUTES

These are at their peak when warm, so serve straight from the oven or reheat.

2¼ cups all-purpose flour
2 tablespoons sugar
2 teaspoons baking powder
½ teaspoon coarsely ground black pepper
¼ teaspoon salt
4 tablespoons cold margarine or butter
1 can (8½ ounces) cream-style corn
1 large egg, beaten

1 Preheat oven to 400°F. In large bowl, mix flour, sugar, baking powder, black pepper, and salt. With pastry blender, or 2 knives used scissor-fashion, cut in margarine or butter until mixture resembles coarse crumbs. With fork, stir cream-style corn and egg into flour mixture just until blended.

2 Spoon dough onto ungreased large cookie sheet. With floured hands, pat dough into 9-inch round (dough will be sticky).

3 Bake scones 20 to 25 minutes, until golden. Transfer scones to wire rack to cool slightly, about 10 minutes. Cut into 12 wedges and serve warm. Makes 12 scones.

Each scone: About 150 calories, 3 g protein, 24 g carbohydrate, 5 g total fat (1 g saturated), 1 g fiber, 18 mg cholesterol, 220 mg sodium.

Sweet Corn Biscuits

PREP: 20 MINUTES • BAKE: 12 TO 15 MINUTES

If you don't have buttermilk on hand, you can make your own: Follow the instructions in the Featherlight Buttermilk Biscuits recipe (page 166), but use 2½ teaspoons lemon juice and enough milk to equal ¾ cup.

1¾ cups all-purpose flour
4 teaspoons baking powder
1 tablespoon sugar
½ teaspoon baking soda
½ teaspoon salt

¼ teaspoon coarsely ground black pepper
4 tablespoons cold margarine or butter, cut into pieces
1 cup fresh corn kernels (from 2 ears)
¾ cup buttermilk

1 Preheat oven to 450°F.

2 Into large bowl, measure flour, baking powder, sugar, baking soda, salt, and pepper. With pastry blender or 2 knives used scissor-fashion, cut in margarine or butter until mixture resembles coarse crumbs. Stir in corn kernels and buttermilk just until flour mixture is evenly moistened (do not overmix; dough should be crumbly and sticky).

3 Turn dough onto well-floured surface. With floured hands, knead 1 or 2 strokes until dough comes together. Pat dough to scant 1-inch thickness.

4 With floured 3-inch round biscuit cutter, cut out as many biscuits as possible. Press trimmings together; pat and cut as above.

5 Place biscuits on ungreased large cookie sheet. Bake 12 to 15 minutes, until golden. Serve warm. Makes about 8 biscuits.

Each biscuit: About 190 calories, 4 g protein, 29 g carbohydrate, 6 g total fat (1 g saturated), 2 g fiber, 1 mg cholesterol, 500 mg sodium.

Corn Bread
with Chives

PREP: 10 MINUTES • BAKE: 20 MINUTES

This moist, tender bread is best served warm. If you like, you can make it ahead and reheat it right in the baking pan, covered, at 400°F. for 10 minutes.

2¼ cups buttermilk
½ cup margarine or butter (1 stick), melted and cooled
3 large eggs
2 cups yellow cornmeal
1 cup all-purpose flour
2 tablespoons sugar
2½ teaspoons baking powder
¾ teaspoon salt
½ teaspoon baking soda
⅓ cup snipped fresh chives

1 Preheat oven to 400°F. Grease 13" by 9" metal baking pan.

2 In medium bowl, with fork, mix buttermilk, melted margarine or butter, and eggs until blended. Into large bowl, measure cornmeal, flour, sugar, baking powder, salt, and baking soda; stir until combined.

3 With fork, stir buttermilk mixture and chives into cornmeal mixture just until blended. Spoon batter into baking pan; spread evenly.

4 Bake corn bread 20 minutes or until toothpick inserted in center comes out clean. Cool in pan on wire rack 10 minutes to serve warm, or cool completely in pan to serve later. Reheat before serving if you like. Makes 20 servings.

Each serving: About 140 calories, 4 g protein, 18 g carbohydrate, 6 g total fat (1 g saturated), 1 g fiber, 33 mg cholesterol, 255 mg sodium.

Skillet Corn Bread

PREP: 10 MINUTES • BAKE: 15 TO 20 MINUTES

This delicious homemade corn bread is baked in an oven-safe skillet—preferably one that's heavyweight, such as cast iron.

1 cup all-purpose flour
1 cup yellow cornmeal
2 tablespoons sugar
2 teaspoons baking powder
¼ teaspoon salt
¼ teaspoon coarsely ground black pepper
4 tablespoons cold margarine or butter
1 can (8½ ounces) cream-style corn
1 large egg, beaten
2 ounces shredded Monterey Jack cheese with jalapeño chiles

1 Preheat oven to 400°F. Grease 10-inch skillet with oven-safe handle.

2 In large bowl, mix flour, cornmeal, sugar, baking powder, salt, and black pepper. With pastry blender or 2 knives used scissor-fashion, cut in margarine or butter until mixture resembles fine crumbs. With fork, stir corn, egg, and cheese into flour mixture just until blended (batter will be very stiff).

3 Place greased skillet in oven; preheat pan 5 minutes (to help brown bottom of corn bread). Remove

pan from oven; spoon batter into skillet and spread evenly with small metal spatula.

4 Bake corn bread 15 to 20 minutes, until toothpick inserted in center comes out clean and corn bread is just firm to the touch. Cut into 8 wedges and serve warm. Makes 8 servings.

Each serving: About 290 calories, 7 g protein, 44 g carbohydrate, 9 g total fat (3 g saturated), 1 g fiber, 34 mg cholesterol, 375 mg sodium.

Soda Bread

PREP: 20 MINUTES • BAKE: 1 HOUR

A rich and tender rustic Irish quick bread—the ideal dinner companion for corned beef.

¼ cup sugar
1 tablespoon baking powder
1 teaspoon salt
1 teaspoon baking soda
4 cups plus ½ teaspoon all-purpose flour
6 tablespoons cold margarine or butter
1 cup golden or dark seedless raisins
1½ cups buttermilk

1 Preheat oven to 350°F. Grease large cookie sheet.

2 In large bowl, combine sugar, baking powder, salt, baking soda, and 4 cups flour. With pastry blender or 2 knives used scissor-fashion, cut in margarine or butter until mixture resembles coarse crumbs. With spoon, stir in raisins, then buttermilk just until evenly moistened.

3 With floured hand, gently knead dough in bowl a few times until dough forms a ball (do not overmix, or bread will be tough). Place dough on cookie sheet; shape into a 7-inch round loaf (dough will not be smooth).

4 Sprinkle loaf with remaining ½ teaspoon flour. With sharp knife, cut 4-inch-long cross, about ¼ inch deep, on top of loaf. Bake loaf 1 hour or until toothpick inserted in center comes out clean. Cool on wire rack. Makes 1 loaf or 12 servings.

Each serving: About 275 calories, 6 g protein, 49 g carbohydrate, 6 g total fat (1 g saturated), 2 g fiber, 1 mg cholesterol, 485 mg sodium.

Zucchini & Cheese Bread

Great for brunch or alongside a soup or stew. Do-ahead: Mix the dry ingredients (store at room temperature), grate the cheeses, prep the vegetables, and whisk together the wet ingredients (store all separately in refrigerator) the night before. When ready, combine all the elements and bake.

4 ounces sharp Cheddar cheese, shredded
    (1 cup)
2 ounces grated Parmesan cheese (½ cup)
2½ cups all-purpose flour
4 teaspoons baking powder
1 tablespoon sugar
1½ teaspoons salt
½ teaspoon coarsely ground black pepper
1 small zucchini (about 5 ounces), coarsely
    shredded (1 cup)
1 medium red pepper, finely chopped (½ cup)
3 small green onions, finely chopped
2 large eggs
½ cup milk
3 tablespoons olive oil

1 Preheat oven to 350°F. Grease 9" by 9" metal baking pan.

2 In small bowl, mix ¼ cup Cheddar and 2 tablespoons Parmesan; set aside.

3 In large bowl, combine flour, baking powder, sugar, salt, and black pepper. Stir zucchini, red pepper, green onion, and remaining cheeses into flour mixture. In medium bowl, with wire whisk, beat eggs, milk, and oil until blended; add to flour mixture and stir just until evenly moistened.

4 Spoon batter into pan and spread evenly. Sprinkle top with reserved cheese mixture.

5 Bake bread 50 to 55 minutes, until toothpick inserted in center comes out clean. Cool bread in pan on wire rack 5 minutes. With small metal spatula, loosen bread from side of pan. Invert bread onto large plate and remove pan. Immediately invert bread onto wire rack to cool completely. Makes 16 servings.

Each serving: About 155 calories, 7 g protein, 17 g carbohydrate, 7 g total fat (3 g saturated), 1 g fiber, 38 mg cholesterol, 405 mg sodium.

Banana Bread

This recipe makes a beautiful loaf with a crackly top; if you like, fold 1 cup toasted, coarsely chopped walnuts or pecans into the batter before baking.

2½ cups all-purpose flour
2 teaspoons baking powder
¾ teaspoon salt
½ teaspoon baking soda
1½ cups mashed ripe bananas (about 3 large)
¼ cup milk
2 teaspoons vanilla extract
1 cup sugar
½ cup margarine or butter (1 stick), softened
2 large eggs

1 Preheat oven to 350°F. Grease 9" by 5" metal loaf pan.

2 On waxed paper, combine flour, baking powder, salt, and baking soda. In small bowl, mix bananas, milk, and vanilla until blended.

3 In large bowl, with mixer at low speed, beat sugar with margarine or butter until blended. Increase speed to high; beat 2 minutes, scraping sides occasionally. Reduce speed to low; add eggs, 1 at a time, beating well after each addition. Alternately beat in flour mixture and banana mixture, beginning and ending with flour mixture.

4 Spoon batter into loaf pan and spread evenly. Bake 1 hour 5 minutes to 1 hour 10 minutes, until toothpick inserted in center of loaf comes out clean. Cool loaf in pan on wire rack 10 minutes; remove from pan and cool completely on rack. Makes 1 loaf or 16 servings.

Each serving: About 210 calories, 3 g protein, 35 g carbohydrate, 7 g total fat (1 g saturated), 1 g fiber, 27 mg cholesterol, 270 mg sodium.

BANANA PICKING

More than 150 banana varieties are grown worldwide, but most Americans know only the common yellow Cavendish, the staple available year-round. Now exotic specialty bananas are getting more popular—check our list and experiment with some. (All but the plantain are interchangeable in recipes.)

Burro: This chunky one has creamy white flesh with a hint of lemony flavor. When ripe, heavy black spots form along the ribs of the skin. Orinoco, also the name of a river in Venezuela, is another term for this banana.

Manzano: Its label is derived from the Spanish word for apple, and this variety is firm with subtle apple and strawberry overtones. Short and stubby (no more than 4 inches long), the finger-length banana is ripe when its yellow skin turns completely black.

Niño: This diminutive banana (only 3 inches long) comes from Ecuador. You'll know it's ripe when the skin turns bright yellow with a few black spots. The flesh is soft and creamy with a rich, sweet flavor. The Mysore is a similar baby banana that hails from Western India.

Plantain: The large, firm "cooking banana" can be as long as 14 inches. Use at any stage of ripeness. When its skin is green, the fruit's starchy, squash-like taste is perfect boiled, steamed, fried, or baked. When ripe (the peel turns yellow, then black), the flesh has a sweeter, more traditional banana flavor; it's good thickly sliced and browned in butter.

Red: Also known as the Jamaican banana or Macabú, this is short and squat, with wine-red skin and a long shelf life. (When ripe, the skin is purplish with black patches.) The sweet light-pink flesh has a slight raspberry flavor.

Simple Stollen

PREP: 25 MINUTES PLUS COOLING • BAKE: 1 HOUR

Ricotta cheese adds a rich and moist texture to this fruit-and-nut-studded holiday quick bread. If there are any leftovers, try slicing and toasting. Do-ahead: Make ahead but do not glaze, and freeze for up to 2 months. After thawing, prepare glaze as in step 5.

2¼ cups all-purpose flour
½ cup sugar
1½ teaspoons baking powder
¼ teaspoon salt
6 tablespoons cold margarine or butter
1 cup ricotta cheese
1 large egg
1 large egg yolk
½ cup diced candied lemon peel
½ cup dark seedless raisins
⅓ cup slivered blanched almonds, toasted
1 teaspoon vanilla extract
½ teaspoon freshly grated lemon peel
2 cups confectioners' sugar

1 Preheat oven to 325°F. Grease large cookie sheet.

2 In large bowl, mix flour, sugar, baking powder, and salt. With pastry blender or 2 knives used scissor-fashion, cut in margarine or butter until mixture resembles fine crumbs. In small bowl, with spoon, mix ricotta with egg and egg yolk. Stir ricotta mixture into flour mixture until moistened. Stir in candied lemon peel and remaining ingredients except confectioners' sugar until well mixed.

3 On lightly floured surface, gently knead dough 2 or 3 times to thoroughly blend ingredients. With floured rolling pin, roll dough into 10" by 8" oval. Fold lengthwise almost in half, letting bottom half extend about 1 inch beyond edge of top half.

4 Place stollen on cookie sheet. Bake 1 hour or until toothpick inserted in center comes out clean. Remove stollen from cookie sheet to wire rack. Cool completely.

5 In medium bowl, with wire whisk, mix confectioners' sugar and 3 *tablespoons plus 1½ teaspoons water* until blended. Place waxed paper under wire rack to catch any drips. Pour glaze over stollen. Allow glaze to set about 20 minutes. Makes 12 servings.

Each serving: About 370 calories, 7 g protein, 60 g carbohydrate, 12 g total fat (3 g saturated), 2 g fiber, 46 mg cholesterol, 205 mg sodium.

Multigrain Bread

PREP: 40 MINUTES PLUS RISING AND COOLING
BAKE: 35 MINUTES

The trick to maintaining the light texture of these loaves is to keep the dough slightly sticky while kneading. Adding more flour than what's called for will make your bread too dense.

1 cup old-fashioned oats, uncooked
2 packages active dry yeast
1 tablespoon sugar
1 cup whole wheat flour
1 cup stone-ground rye flour
⅓ cup flax seeds, ground (see "Flax Facts," below)

¼ cup light (mild) molasses
3 tablespoons olive oil
2½ teaspoons salt
About 2¾ cups all-purpose flour
1 cup pitted prunes, coarsely chopped

1 Preheat oven to 350°F. Place oats in small baking pan; cook in oven 10 minutes or until lightly toasted, stirring occasionally.

2 Meanwhile, in cup, mix yeast, sugar, and ½ *cup warm water* (105° to 115°F.); let mixture stand until it foams, about 5 minutes.

3 In large bowl, with wooden spoon, stir oats, yeast mixture, whole wheat flour, rye flour, ground flax seeds, molasses, olive oil, salt, and *1½ cups warm water* (105° to 115°F.) until smooth. Gradually stir in 2½ cups all-purpose flour. With hand, knead in bowl until dough comes together.

4 Turn dough onto lightly floured surface and knead until elastic and almost smooth, about 8 minutes, working in more all-purpose flour (¼ cup) while kneading (dough will be sticky). Knead in prunes.

5 Shape dough into a ball; place in greased large bowl, turning dough over to grease top. Cover bowl with plastic wrap and let dough rise in warm place (80° to 85° F.) until doubled, about 1 hour.

6 Punch down dough. Turn dough onto floured surface; cut in half. Lightly sprinkle large cookie sheet (17" by 14") with flour. With hands, flatten half of dough on 1 end of cookie sheet to a 10" by 8" rectangle. Fold dough over lengthwise to make a 10" by 4" rectangle. Turn dough seam side down and pinch edges to seal; shape into 11" by 4" loaf. Repeat with remaining dough on other end of same cookie sheet.

7 Cover loaves loosely with greased plastic wrap, and let rise in warm place until doubled, about 45 minutes.

8 Preheat oven to 350°F. With sharp knife, cut 6 diagonal slashes about ¼ inch deep across top of each loaf. Sprinkle loaves with all-purpose flour if you like. Bake loaves 35 minutes or until loaves are lightly browned and sound hollow when lightly tapped with fingers. Transfer loaves to wire rack to cool. Makes 2 loaves, each 12 servings.

Each serving: About 160 calories, 4 g protein, 30 g carbohydrate, 3 g total fat (0 g saturated), 3 g fiber, 0 mg cholesterol, 225 mg sodium.

FLAX FACTS

Why You Need It: The tiny brown, nut-flavored seeds of the age-old grain called flax are the best source of plant substances called lignans—which are attracting attention as potential cancer fighters. Experts believe lignans (a type of plant estrogen) block some effects of the body's estrogen, thereby inhibiting the formation of certain types of breast and ovarian tumors. Flax is also the primary plant source of alpha-linolenic acid, the garden's version of the healthful omega-3 fatty acids found in fish oil. Flax seeds serve up cholesterol-reducing soluble fiber too. And although flax oil loses the lignans and fiber during processing, it too is a wellspring of omega-3s. (Don't use the oil for cooking; it doesn't deliver the good stuff when heated.)

Buying & Storing It: You can buy flax seeds already ground for recipes like our Multigrain Bread (above). Problem is, they may have been sitting at the health-food store for months, and be past their prime. The beneficial omega-3 fatty acids in flax can rapidly become rancid after the seeds are milled; you'll notice a strong paintlike smell if this happens. (In its other life, flax seeds are used to make linseed oil, a key ingredient in paint, varnish, and linoleum.)

Buy seeds whole, store in an airtight container in a cool area, and pulverize as needed in a coffee grinder. The seeds should keep well up to 1 year. If you have leftover ground flax seeds, refrigerate for up to 1 month or freeze for up to 6 months.

Sour-Cream Corn Pancakes

PREP: 15 MINUTES • COOK: ABOUT 10 MINUTES PER BATCH

Enjoy these hearty hotcakes for breakfast, lunch, or dinner with our homemade Corncob Syrup (below).

1¼ cups all-purpose flour
1 teaspoon baking powder
½ teaspoon salt
¾ cup milk
½ cup sour cream
2 large eggs
2 tablespoons margarine or butter, melted and cooled
2 cups fresh corn kernels (from 3 to 4 ears)
1 to 2 teaspoons vegetable oil

1 On waxed paper, combine flour, baking powder, and salt.

2 In medium bowl, with wire whisk, mix milk, sour cream, eggs, and melted margarine or butter until blended. Whisk in dry ingredients just until mixed. Stir in corn.

3 In nonstick 12-inch skillet, heat 1 teaspoon oil over medium heat. Drop batter by ⅓ cups into skillet, making a few pancakes at a time. Cook 5 to 7 minutes, until tops are bubbly and edges look dry. Turn pancakes over and cook 3 to 5 minutes, until undersides are golden. Transfer to platter; keep warm.

4 Repeat with remaining batter, using more oil if necessary. Makes about twelve 4-inch pancakes.

Each pancake: About 140 calories, 4 g protein, 17 g carbohydrate, 6 g total fat (2 g saturated), 1 g fiber, 42 mg cholesterol, 170 mg sodium.

CORNCOB SYRUP

We call for ears of corn to make this old-fashioned syrup, but all you really need are the cobs. So, save them when preparing any recipe that calls for fresh corn kernels.

With sharp knife, cut kernels from *8 medium ears corn* (husks and silks removed); reserve for use in another recipe. Cut each cob crosswise in half. In 5-quart Dutch oven, heat corncobs and *10 cups water* to boiling over high heat. Boil 1 hour or until liquid is reduced to 4 cups. Discard cobs. Strain liquid into 3-quart saucepan; stir in *1 cup packed light brown sugar* and *pinch of salt*, and boil mixture about 40 minutes longer or until reduced to a syrupy consistency. If not using syrup right away, pour into jars with tight-fitting lids, and refrigerate up to 1 month. Reheat to serve. Spoon over pancakes, waffles, corn fritters, or ice cream.

Each tablespoon: About 40 calories, 0 g protein, 11 g carbohydrate, 0 g total fat, 0 g fiber, 0 mg cholesterol, 10 mg sodium.

Farmhouse Pancakes

PREP: 15 MINUTES • COOK: 8 TO 12 MINUTES PER BATCH

2 ripe medium bananas
1 cup all-purpose flour
2 tablespoons sugar
2 teaspoons baking powder
½ teaspoon salt
¼ teaspoon baking soda
¾ cup low-fat (1%) milk
2 tablespoons margarine or butter, melted
1 large egg
Vegetable oil

1 In small bowl, with fork or potato masher, mash 1 banana. Cut remaining banana into ½-inch dice and set aside.

2 In large bowl, mix flour, sugar, baking powder, salt, and baking soda. Into mashed banana in bowl, with wire whisk or fork, beat milk, margarine or butter, and egg until blended. Add milk mixture to flour mixture and stir just until flour is moistened. (Do not overmix.) Fold in diced banana.

3 Heat griddle or skillet over medium heat until hot; brush lightly with vegetable oil. Drop batter by scant ⅓ cups onto hot griddle, making a few pancakes at a time. Cook 4 to 6 minutes, until tops are bubbly and edges look dry. With wide metal spatula, turn pancakes over and cook 4 to 6 minutes, until undersides are golden. Transfer pancakes to platter; keep warm.

4 Repeat with remaining batter, brushing griddle with more oil as necessary. Makes about eight 4-inch pancakes or 4 servings.

Each pancake: About 140 calories, 3 g protein, 23 g carbohydrate, 4 g total fat (1 g saturated), 1 g fiber, 28 mg cholesterol, 320 mg sodium.

Granola Breakfast Bars

PREP: 15 MINUTES PLUS COOLING
BAKE: 30 TO 35 MINUTES

Moist, delicious, and lower in fat than many store-bought snack bars—sure to be a winner with everyone in the family.

2 cups old-fashioned oats, uncooked
1 cup all-purpose flour
¾ cup packed light brown sugar
¾ cup dark seedless raisins
½ cup toasted wheat germ
¾ teaspoon salt
¾ teaspoon ground cinnamon
½ cup vegetable oil
½ cup honey
2 teaspoons vanilla extract
1 large egg

1 Preheat oven to 350°F. Grease 13" by 9" metal baking pan. Line pan with foil; grease foil.

2 In large bowl, with wooden spoon, mix oats, flour, brown sugar, raisins, wheat germ, salt, and cinnamon until combined. Stir in vegetable oil and remaining ingredients until blended. With wet hand, pat oat mixture into pan. Bake 30 to 35 minutes, until pale golden around edges. Cool completely in pan on wire rack.

3 When cool, transfer with foil to cutting board. Cut lengthwise into 4 strips, then cut each strip crosswise into 6 pieces. Makes 2 dozen bars.

Each bar: About 185 calories, 4 g protein, 30 g carbohydrate, 6 g total fat (1 g saturated), 2 g fiber, 9 mg cholesterol, 75 mg sodium.

Lower-Fat Granola

PREP: 10 MINUTES • BAKE: 35 TO 40 MINUTES

We baked oats, almonds, quinoa, wheat germ, and sesame seeds with apple juice instead of oil or butter. Perfect with a bowl of yogurt or a splash of milk!

4 cups old-fashioned oats, uncooked
½ cup honey
½ cup apple juice
1½ teaspoons vanilla extract
¾ teaspoon ground cinnamon
½ cup sliced natural almonds
½ cup quinoa
¼ cup toasted wheat germ
2 tablespoons sesame seeds
½ cup dried apricots, cut into ¼-inch dice
½ cup dark seedless raisins

1 Preheat oven to 350°F. Place oats in two 15½" by 10½" jelly-roll pans. Bake oats 15 minutes or until lightly toasted, stirring twice.

2 In large bowl, with wire whisk, mix honey, apple juice, vanilla, and cinnamon until blended. Add toasted oats, almonds, quinoa, wheat germ, and sesame seeds; stir to coat well.

3 Spread oat mixture evenly in same jelly-roll pans; bake until golden brown, 20 to 25 minutes, stirring frequently. Cool in pans on wire racks.

4 When cool, transfer granola to large bowl and stir in dried apricots and raisins. Store at room temperature in tightly covered container up to 1 month. Makes about 6 cups.

Each ¼ cup: About 175 calories, 6 g protein, 32 g carbohydrate, 4 g total fat (1 g saturated), 4 g fiber, 0 mg cholesterol, 5 mg sodium.

◄ *Granola Breakfast Bars*

Wild Rice with Mushrooms

PREP: 1 HOUR • BAKE: 20 MINUTES

This mixture of wild and white rices is simple but special. Do-ahead: The day ahead, prepare through step 3; cover and refrigerate. To serve, bake, covered, 40 minutes, or until hot.

1 cup wild rice (about 6 ounces)
1 cup regular long-grain rice
1 teaspoon salt
3 tablespoons margarine or butter
1 small onion, diced
1 medium celery stalk, diced
10 ounces white mushrooms, sliced
8 ounces shiitake mushrooms, stems discarded, caps sliced
¼ teaspoon coarsely ground black pepper
⅛ teaspoon dried thyme
1 cup chicken broth
½ cup loosely packed fresh parsley leaves, chopped

1 Prepare wild rice and white rice, separately, as labels direct, adding ¼ teaspoon salt to each rice, but omitting margarine or butter.

2 Meanwhile, preheat oven to 350°F. In 12-inch skillet, melt margarine or butter over medium heat. Add onion and celery, and cook until tender, about 10 minutes, stirring occasionally. Increase heat to medium-high; add mushrooms, pepper, thyme, and remaining ½ teaspoon salt, and cook 15 minutes longer, stirring occasionally, until mushrooms are tender and golden and liquid evaporates. Stir in chicken broth. Remove skillet from heat.

3 In shallow 2½-quart casserole or baking dish, stir both kinds of rice with mushroom mixture and parsley until blended.

4 Bake casserole, covered, 20 minutes or until hot. Makes about 9 cups or 10 accompaniment servings.

Each serving: About 180 calories, 5 g protein, 32 g carbohydrate, 4 g total fat (1 g saturated), 1 g fiber, 0 mg cholesterol, 345 mg sodium.

Crispy Middle-Eastern Polo

PREP: 5 MINUTES • COOK: ABOUT 35 MINUTES

For this traditional dish, rice is briefly boiled, drained, and then steamed in a pan, with additions like onion, dried fruit, and nuts, until a crunchy, buttery crust forms on the bottom. (*Polo* is called *chelo* when the rice is steamed without any additions.) We simplified the method to save time, and steamed the rice in a skillet to create more of the yummy crust.

1 cup basmati or Texmati rice
3 tablespoons margarine or butter
1 medium onion, minced
½ teaspoon salt
Green onions for garnish

1 In 3-quart saucepan, heat *6 cups water* to boiling over high heat. Add rice and cook, uncovered, 10 minutes, stirring occasionally. Drain rice; rinse with cold water. Drain well.

2 Meanwhile, in nonstick 10-inch skillet, melt 1 tablespoon margarine or butter over medium heat. Add onion and cook 10 minutes or until tender, stirring occasionally.

3 Add remaining 2 tablespoons margarine or butter to skillet and cook 1 minute or until melted. Add cool rice, salt, and ¼ *cup water*, and stir until rice is evenly coated. Spread mixture into even layer over bottom of skillet.

4 Cover skillet and cook 15 to 20 minutes, until rice is tender and golden crust forms on the bottom. With wide spatula, transfer rice to shallow serving bowl, crust side up. Garnish with green onions. Makes 4 accompaniment servings.

Each serving: About 255 calories, 4 g protein, 40 g carbohydrate, 9 g total fat (2 g saturated), 1 g fiber, 0 mg cholesterol, 385 mg sodium.

Crispy Middle-Eastern Polo ➤

Wheatberry Pilaf

PREP: 30 MINUTES • COOK: ABOUT 1 HOUR

You'll love this veggie-flecked combination of nutty wheatberries and brown rice.

1 cup wheatberries*
½ cup long-grain brown rice
3 teaspoons olive oil
4 medium carrots, cut into ¼-inch dice
2 medium celery stalks, cut into ¼-inch dice
1 large onion, cut into ¼-inch dice
1 can (14½ ounces) chicken broth
½ pound green beans, trimmed and cut into
    1½-inch pieces
¾ teaspoon salt
½ teaspoon freshly grated orange peel
¼ teaspoon coarsely ground black pepper
¼ teaspoon dried thyme
¾ cup dried cranberries

1 In 3-quart saucepan, heat wheatberries and *4 cups water* to boiling over high heat. Reduce heat to low; cover and simmer 50 minutes or until wheatberries are firm to the bite but tender enough to eat; drain and set aside.

2 Meanwhile, in 2-quart saucepan, prepare brown rice as label directs, but do not add butter or salt.

3 While wheatberries and brown rice are cooking, in deep 12-inch skillet, heat 2 teaspoons olive oil over medium heat until hot. Add carrots and celery, and cook 10 minutes or until almost tender, stirring occasionally. Add onion and 1 more teaspoon olive oil, and cook 12 to 15 minutes longer, until vegetables are lightly browned, stirring occasionally.

4 Increase heat to high; add chicken broth, green beans, salt, orange peel, pepper, and thyme, and heat to boiling. Reduce heat to medium-high; cook, uncovered, 5 minutes or until green beans are just tender, stirring often.

5 Add cranberries, wheatberries, and brown rice to skillet, and heat through, stirring to mix well. Makes about 8 cups or 8 accompaniment servings.

*Wheatberries are unmilled whole wheat kernels that have a delicious nutty, toasted flavor. Look for them in health-food stores and some supermarkets.

Each serving: About 210 calories, 7 g protein, 42 g carbohydrate, 3 g total fat (1 g saturated), 5 g fiber, 0 mg cholesterol, 395 mg sodium.

Persian Rice Pilaf

PREP: 15 MINUTES • COOK: 20 MINUTES

Sweet dates, garbanzo beans, and a touch of spice make delicious basmati rice even more aromatic—try it with roast chicken or lamb.

1 tablespoon margarine or butter
1 small onion, finely chopped
1 cup white basmati rice
1 can (14½ ounces) chicken broth
2 strips (3" by 1" each) fresh orange peel
⅛ teaspoon ground cinnamon
⅛ teaspoon coarsely ground black pepper
1 can (15 to 19 ounces) garbanzo beans, rinsed
    and drained
½ cup loosely packed fresh parsley leaves,
    chopped
⅓ cup pitted dates, chopped
¼ cup almonds, toasted and chopped

1 In 3-quart saucepan, melt margarine or butter over medium heat. Add onion and cook until tender, about 5 minutes, stirring occasionally. Stir in rice; cook 1 minute. Add chicken broth, orange peel, cinnamon, pepper, and *¼ cup water*; heat to boiling over high heat. Reduce heat to low; cover and simmer 15 to 18 minutes, until rice is tender and liquid is absorbed.

2 Stir in garbanzo beans; heat through. Remove saucepan from heat and gently stir in parsley, dates, and almonds. Makes about 7 cups or 8 accompaniment or 4 main-dish servings.

Each accompaniment serving: About 220 calories, 7 g protein, 37 g carbohydrate, 5 g total fat (1 g saturated), 5 g fiber, 0 mg cholesterol, 345 mg sodium.

PIES & CAKES

Deep-Dish Apple Pie

PREP: 40 MINUTES PLUS COOLING
BAKE: 1 HOUR 15 MINUTES

This is the easiest apple pie you'll ever make!

APPLE FILLING:
6 pounds Granny Smith apples (about 12 large apples), peeled, cored, and each cut into 16 wedges
¾ cup sugar
⅓ cup all-purpose flour
2 tablespoons fresh lemon juice
½ teaspoon ground cinnamon

CRUST:
2 cups all-purpose flour
2 teaspoons baking powder
½ teaspoon salt
¼ cup plus 1 tablespoon sugar
4 tablespoons margarine or butter
1 large egg, beaten
⅔ cup plus 2 tablespoons heavy cream

1 Prepare Apple Filling: In large bowl, combine apples, sugar, flour, lemon juice, and cinnamon; toss to coat well. Spoon apple mixture into 13" by 9" glass baking dish; set aside.

2 Preheat oven to 400°F. Prepare Crust: In medium bowl, mix flour, baking powder, salt, and ¼ cup sugar. With pastry blender or 2 knives used scissor-fashion, cut in margarine until mixture resembles coarse crumbs. Stir in egg and ⅔ cup cream until blended.

3 With floured hands, shape dough into a ball. Divide dough into 6 pieces; flatten each to about ½-inch thickness and arrange on top of apple mixture. (It is not necessary to completely cover top; as dough bakes, it will spread.) Brush dough with remaining cream, and sprinkle with remaining sugar.

4 Place sheet of foil underneath baking dish; crimp foil edges to form a rim to catch any drips during baking. To prevent overbrowning, cover pie loosely with a tent of foil halfway through baking time. Bake pie about 1 hour 15 minutes or until apples are tender when pierced with knife, filling is bubbly, and crust is golden. Cool pie on wire rack 1 hour to serve warm, or cool completely to serve later. Makes 12 servings.

Each serving: About 355 calories, 4 g protein, 64 g carbohydrate, 11 g total fat (5 g saturated), 3 g fiber, 39 mg cholesterol, 210 mg sodium.

Brown-Butter Peach Tart

PREP: 40 MINUTES PLUS COOLING • BAKE: 1 HOUR

This beautiful dessert is a nice change from the traditional pie—a thin layer of sliced peaches is baked in a buttery egg filling. Make sure to use real butter; margarine and substitutes don't do justice to the recipe.

CRUST:
7 tablespoons butter (no substitutions), melted and cooled to room temperature
⅓ cup sugar
¼ teaspoon vanilla extract
1 cup all-purpose flour
Pinch salt

BROWN-BUTTER FILLING:
½ cup sugar
2 large eggs
¼ cup all-purpose flour
½ cup butter (no substitutions)
3 medium peaches (about 1 pound), peeled and thinly sliced

1 Prepare Crust: Preheat oven to 375°F. In medium bowl, stir melted butter with sugar and vanilla until combined. Stir in flour and salt until dough just begins to come together. Press dough into 9-inch tart pan with removable bottom. Bake crust 15 minutes or until golden brown.

2 Meanwhile, prepare Brown-Butter Filling: In small bowl, with wire whisk, beat sugar and eggs until well mixed. Beat in flour until blended; set aside.

3 In 1-quart saucepan, heat butter over medium heat until melted and a dark, nutty brown but not burned, about 5 minutes, stirring occasionally. Whisking constantly, pour hot butter in steady steam into egg mixture until blended.

4 Arrange peach slices decoratively on warm tart shell; pour in brown-butter mixture. Bake 45 minutes or until puffed and golden. Cool completely on wire rack. Refrigerate any leftovers. Makes 12 servings.

Each serving: About 250 calories, 3 g protein, 27 g carbohydrate, 15 g total fat (9 g saturated), 1 g fiber, 74 mg cholesterol, 165 mg sodium.

Brown-Butter Peach Tart ▶

Pumpkin Pie with Pecan-Caramel Topping

PREP: 1 HOUR PLUS COOLING • BAKE: 1½ HOURS

Slice by slice, this will vanish quickly—toasted pecans in the crust give the pie extra appeal.

CRUST:
½ cup pecans, toasted
2 tablespoons sugar
1¼ cups all-purpose flour
¼ teaspoon salt
4 tablespoons cold margarine or butter
2 tablespoons vegetable shortening

PUMPKIN FILLING:
1 can (15 ounces) pure pumpkin (not pumpkin-pie mix)
¾ cup heavy or whipping cream
½ cup milk
½ cup packed light brown sugar
1½ teaspoons ground cinnamon
½ teaspoon salt
¼ teaspoon ground nutmeg
¼ teaspoon ground ginger
¼ teaspoon ground cloves
3 large eggs

PECAN-CARAMEL TOPPING:
1 cup packed light brown sugar
¼ cup heavy or whipping cream
2 tablespoons light corn syrup
2 tablespoons margarine or butter
1 teaspoon distilled white vinegar
1 cup pecans, toasted and broken
1 teaspoon vanilla extract

1 Prepare Crust: In food processor with knife blade attached, blend toasted pecans and sugar until finely ground. Add flour and salt to nut mixture and pulse to blend. Add margarine with shortening, and pulse just until mixture resembles very coarse crumbs. With processor running, add 3 *tablespoons ice water*, stopping just before dough forms a ball. Shape dough into a disk.

2 Preheat oven to 400°F. Between lightly floured sheets of waxed paper, with rolling pin, roll dough into a round 1½ inches larger in diameter than inverted 9-inch pie plate. Dough will be very tender; refrigerate if too soft to roll. Gently ease dough into pie plate; trim edge, leaving 1-inch overhang. Fold overhang under; bring up over pie-plate rim and pinch to form high decorative edge. With fork, prick bottom and side of pie shell at 1-inch intervals to prevent puffing and shrinking during baking. Refrigerate pie shell about 30 minutes.

3 Line pie shell with foil and fill with pie weights, dried beans, or uncooked rice. Bake pie shell 20 minutes; remove foil with weights and bake 10 minutes longer or until lightly browned. Cool pie shell on wire rack at least 15 minutes. Turn oven control to 350°F.

4 Prepare Pumpkin Filling: In large bowl, with wire whisk, beat pumpkin and cream, milk, brown sugar, cinnamon, salt, nutmeg, ginger, cloves, and eggs.

5 Pour filling into cooled pie shell. Bake pie 50 to 60 minutes, until knife inserted 1 inch from edge of pie comes out clean. Transfer pie to wire rack until it cools and becomes slightly firm, about 1 hour.

6 Prepare Pecan-Caramel Topping: In 2-quart saucepan, heat brown sugar, cream, corn syrup, margarine or butter, and vinegar to boiling over high heat, stirring occasionally. (Do not use smaller pan; mixture bubbles up during cooking.) Reduce heat to low; simmer, uncovered, 5 minutes, stirring frequently. Remove saucepan from heat; stir in pecans and vanilla. (Topping will be very thin when hot but will thicken as it cools.) Pour hot topping over cooled pie. Refrigerate pie at least 4 hours or overnight. Makes 12 servings.

Each serving: About 435 calories, 5 g protein, 49 g carbohydrate, 25 g total fat (7 g saturated), 2 g fiber, 80 mg cholesterol, 254 mg sodium.

Pumpkin Pie with Pecan-Caramel Topping and Spice Cake with Brown-Butter Frosting (page 186) ➤

Pear Custard Tart

PREP: 1 HOUR PLUS COOLING • BAKE: 55 TO 60 MINUTES

A sweet pastry crust holds creamy filling and juicy sliced fruit. The finishing touch: a light brushing of apricot preserves.

SWEET PASTRY:
1½ cups all-purpose flour
2 tablespoons sugar
½ teaspoon salt
4 tablespoons vegetable shortening
4 tablespoons cold margarine or butter

CUSTARD FILLING:
2 large eggs
8 ounces sour cream or crème fraîche
½ cup sugar
½ cup heavy or whipping cream
¼ teaspoon almond extract

PEARS & GLAZE:
3 firm but ripe Bosc pears (about 1¼ pounds), unpeeled
⅓ cup apricot preserves

1 Preheat oven to 425°F. Prepare Sweet Pastry: In medium bowl, with fork, stir flour, sugar, and salt. With pastry blender or 2 knives used scissor-fashion, cut in shortening with margarine or butter until mixture resembles coarse crumbs. Sprinkle about *4 tablespoons cold water*, 1 tablespoon at a time, into flour mixture, mixing lightly with fork after each addition until dough is just moist enough to hold together. Shape dough into a disk and wrap in plastic wrap; refrigerate until firm enough to roll.

2 Meanwhile, prepare Custard Filling: In large bowl, with wire whisk, beat eggs. Remove 2 tablespoons beaten eggs to cup; reserve and refrigerate to brush over crust later. Add sour cream, sugar, heavy cream, and almond extract to eggs in bowl; beat until well mixed. Cover and refrigerate custard.

3 On lightly floured surface, with floured rolling pin, roll dough into 13-inch round. Press dough onto bottom and up side of 11" by 1" round tart pan with removable bottom. Fold overhang in and press against side of tart pan to form a rim ⅛ inch above edge of pan. With fork, prick dough all over to prevent puffing and shrinking during baking.

4 Line tart shell with foil, and fill with pie weights, dried beans, or uncooked rice. Bake tart shell 15 minutes; remove foil with weights and bake 10 minutes

longer. Remove tart shell from oven; brush with reserved beaten egg. Bake 5 minutes longer. Cool on wire rack while preparing pears. Turn oven control to 375°F.

5 To prepare Pears: Cut each pear lengthwise in half and remove cores. Then, cut each half lengthwise into 10 slices. Arrange pear slices in concentric circle in tart shell, with narrow tops toward center of tart, reserving a few slices to cut to fit center of tart. Slowly pour custard over pears.

6 Bake tart 55 to 60 minutes, until custard is set and top is puffy and lightly browned around edge.

7 With back of spoon, press preserves through small strainer set over small bowl. With pastry brush, brush strained preserves over hot tart. Let tart cool at least 1 hour to serve warm, or refrigerate to serve later. Makes 12 servings.

Each serving: About 305 calories, 4 g protein, 36 g carbohydrate, 17 g total fat (7 g saturated), 2 g fiber, 58 mg cholesterol, 165 mg sodium.

Pear Custard Tart

Warm Banana-Cream Tart

PREP: 50 MINUTES PLUS CHILLING
BAKE/BROIL: ABOUT 40 MINUTES

This elegant dessert is slipped under the broiler at the last minute. The crust and filling can be made a day ahead and easily assembled when needed.

CRUST:
1 cup all-purpose flour
2 tablespoons sugar
¼ teaspoon salt
6 tablespoons cold margarine or butter
1 tablespoon vegetable shortening

PASTRY-CREAM FILLING:
1¼ cups half-and-half or light cream
2 large egg yolks
½ cup plus 2 tablespoons sugar
2 tablespoons cornstarch
2 tablespoons all-purpose flour
1 tablespoon vanilla extract
1 tablespoon dark rum (optional)
3 ripe medium bananas, sliced

1 Prepare Crust: In medium bowl, with fork, stir flour, sugar, and salt. With pastry blender or 2 knives used scissor-fashion, cut in margarine or butter with shortening until mixture resembles coarse crumbs. Sprinkle about *2 tablespoons cold water*, 1 tablespoon at a time, into flour mixture, mixing lightly with fork after each addition until dough is just moist enough to hold together. Shape dough into a disk; wrap with plastic wrap and refrigerate 30 minutes or until firm enough to roll.

2 Meanwhile, prepare Pastry-Cream Filling: In 2-quart saucepan, heat 1 cup half-and-half to boiling over high heat. In large bowl, with wire whisk, beat egg yolks, ½ cup sugar, and remaining ¼ cup half-and-half until smooth; whisk in cornstarch and flour. Gradually whisk hot half-and-half into yolk mixture.

3 Return mixture to saucepan and cook over medium-high heat, stirring constantly with wooden spoon (make sure to scrape bottom edge of pan), until mixture thickens and boils. Reduce heat to low and cook, stirring, 1 minute.

4 Remove saucepan from heat and stir in vanilla and rum. Pour filling into pie plate or shallow dish. Press plastic wrap onto surface of filling to keep skin from forming as it cools. Refrigerate 1 hour, or overnight if making day ahead.

5 While filling is chilling, preheat oven to 425°F. On lightly floured surface, with floured rolling pin, roll dough into an 11-inch round. Press dough onto bottom and up side of 9" by 1" round tart pan with removable bottom. Fold overhang in, and press against side of tart pan to form a rim ⅛ inch above edge of pan. With fork, prick dough at 1-inch intervals to prevent puffing and shrinking during baking.

6 Line tart shell with foil, and fill with pie weights, dried beans, or uncooked rice. Bake tart shell 20 minutes; remove foil with weights and bake 10 minutes longer or until golden. (If making day ahead, cool crust completely, wrap in foil, and refrigerate.)

7 When ready to serve, turn oven control to broil. Arrange banana slices, overlapping slightly, in tart shell. Whisk chilled filling until smooth; spoon evenly on top of bananas and sprinkle with remaining 2 tablespoons sugar. Cover edge of crust with foil to prevent overbrowning. Place tart on oven rack 6 inches from source of heat and broil 6 to 8 minutes, until top is lightly golden, watching carefully and rotating pan as necessary for even browning. Serve tart warm. Makes 10 servings.

Each serving: About 270 calories, 3 g protein, 37 g carbohydrate, 13 g total fat (4 g saturated), 1 g fiber, 52 mg cholesterol, 160 mg sodium

Caramelized Apple Crostata

PREP: 1 HOUR 20 MINUTES PLUS COOLING
BAKE: 1 HOUR

A crostata, a sweet Italian tart, is often filled with a thin layer of jam. But we made ours with a sautéed apple filling and topped it with a diamond lattice.

APPLE FILLING:
3 tablespoons butter
2½ pounds Granny Smith apples (about 5 large), peeled, cored, and cut into ¼-inch-thick slices
⅓ cup packed light brown sugar

COOKIE CRUST:
1 cup butter (2 sticks), softened (no substitutions)
½ cup sugar
1 large egg plus 1 large egg yolk
1 tablespoon vanilla extract
3 cups all-purpose flour
¼ teaspoon salt

1 Prepare Apple Filling: In nonstick 12-inch skillet, melt butter over medium heat. Add apples, brown sugar, and ¼ *cup water*, and cook 20 to 25 minutes, stirring occasionally, until apples are lightly browned and tender. Transfer apples to pie plate; refrigerate until chilled, about 30 minutes.

2 While apple mixture is chilling, prepare Cookie Crust: Preheat oven to 375°F. In large bowl, with mixer at low speed, beat butter and sugar until blended. Increase speed to high; beat until light and creamy, occasionally scraping bowl with rubber spatula. Reduce speed to medium; beat in whole egg and vanilla. With wooden spoon, stir in flour and salt until mixture is crumbly. Press mixture together in bowl and knead a few times until flour is evenly moistened. Divide dough into 2 pieces, 1 slightly larger than the other. Shape smaller piece of dough into a disk; wrap with plastic wrap and refrigerate.

3 Meanwhile, press larger piece of dough onto bottom and halfway up side of 11-inch round tart pan with removable bottom. Refrigerate lined tart pan.

4 Remove smaller piece of dough from refrigerator. On lightly floured waxed paper, roll dough into 12-inch round. With pastry wheel or knife, cut dough into twelve 1-inch-wide strips. Refrigerate 15 minutes.

5 Spread chilled Apple Filling over dough in tart pan to ½ inch from edge. Place 5 dough strips, 1 inch apart, across tart, trimming ends even with side of tart pan. Repeat with 5 more strips, placed diagonally across first ones to make a diamond-lattice pattern. Trim ends.

6 With hands, roll trimmings and remaining strips of dough into about ¼-inch-thick ropes. Press ropes around side of tart to create a finished edge. (If rope pieces break, just press them together.)

7 In cup, beat egg yolk with *1 tablespoon water*. Brush egg-yolk mixture over lattice and edge of tart.

8 Bake tart 1 hour or until crust is golden. To prevent overbrowning, cover tart loosely with a tent of foil during the last 15 minutes of baking time. Cool tart in pan on wire rack. Remove tart from pan to serve. Makes 12 servings.

Each serving: About 385 calories, 4 g protein, 50 g carbohydrate, 19 g total fat (12 g saturated), 2 g fiber, 84 mg cholesterol, 235 mg sodium.

Spice Cake with Brown-Butter Frosting

PREP: 1 HOUR PLUS COOLING • BAKE: 25 TO 30 MINUTES

CAKE:
2⅔ cups all-purpose flour
2½ teaspoons baking powder
2 teaspoons ground cinnamon
1 teaspoon ground ginger
½ teaspoon ground nutmeg
½ teaspoon salt
¼ teaspoon ground cloves
1 cup packed dark brown sugar
1 cup granulated sugar
1 cup margarine or butter (2 sticks), softened
5 large eggs
1 cup milk

BROWN-BUTTER FROSTING:
½ cup butter (1 stick), no substitutions
1 box (16 ounces) confectioners' sugar
¼ cup milk
1½ teaspoons vanilla extract
1 cup walnuts, toasted and finely chopped

1 Preheat oven to 350°F. Prepare Cake: Grease three 8-inch round cake pans. Line bottoms with waxed paper; grease paper. Dust pans with flour. In medium bowl, mix flour, baking powder, cinnamon, ginger, nutmeg, salt, and cloves.

2 In large bowl, combine both sugars, breaking up any lumps of brown sugar. Add margarine or butter and, with mixer at low speed, beat until blended, scraping bowl often with rubber spatula. Increase speed to medium; beat 4 minutes or until light and creamy, occasionally scraping bowl. Add eggs, 1 at a time, beating well after each addition. At low speed, alternately add flour mixture and milk, beginning and ending with flour mixture; beat until blended.

3 Pour batter into pans and spread evenly. Stagger pans on 2 oven racks, so layers are not directly above one another. Bake 25 to 30 minutes or until toothpick inserted in center of each layer comes out clean. Cool layers in pans on wire racks 10 minutes. Run small metal spatula or knife around edges of pans to loosen layers; invert onto wire racks and remove waxed paper. Cool layers completely.

4 Prepare Brown-Butter Frosting: In small skillet, melt butter over medium-low heat and cook until butter is golden-brown, about 10 minutes, stirring occasionally. Pour butter into large bowl; cool to room temperature, about 30 minutes.

5 To cooled butter, add confectioners' sugar, milk, and vanilla. With mixer at medium speed, beat ingredients until smooth. With mixer at high speed, beat frosting until light and fluffy, about 1 minute. Makes about 2⅓ cups.

6 Place 1 cake layer, rounded side down, on cake plate; spread with scant ½ cup frosting. Top with second cake layer; spread with another scant ½ cup frosting, then top with remaining cake layer. Frost top and side of cake with remaining frosting. With hand, press walnuts around side of cake. Refrigerate if not serving right away. Makes 16 servings.

Each serving: About 525 calories, 6 g protein, 73 g carbohydrate, 24 g total fat (7 g saturated), 1 g fiber, 85 mg cholesterol, 370 mg sodium.

CHOOSING THE BEST BAKING PAN

You've followed the recipe to a T. Nothing is wrong with your oven. Yet your cake bears no resemblance to the one pictured in the cookbook. What happened? The answer may be in the pan.

We baked basic butter cake layers in 31 different 9-inch round pans in the same oven at the same temperature for the same length of time—and the results looked like we had followed many different recipes. The cakes we liked best were a uniform golden brown on top and bottom, with a fluffy texture. They were baked in traditional light-colored metal pans. The pan that took the cake, the aluminum Wilton Professional, produced

level cakes with a thin, crisp crust. Other goodies: the aluminum-coated steel Chicago Metallic Commercial and the aluminum Mirro Comet.

Layers baked in nonstick pans were dark brown on the side and bottom and often had a thick crust. They were firm, and usually baked up about ¼ inch lower in height than our favorites. When we turned down the oven temperature by 25°F., we got the same results; and when we shortened the baking time, the centers were still uncooked. We did have 1 nonstick standout, from the Wearever Collections. Its light-colored finish didn't deliver an overbaked crust.

Wondering about insulated pans? Try Wearever's Air-Bake and nonstick CushionAire.

The Wilton Professional pan, top left, tops them all.

Lazy-Daisy Cake

PREP: 25 MINUTES PLUS COOLING
BAKE/BROIL: ABOUT 40 MINUTES

This old-fashioned pan cake earned its name because it's so easy to prepare.

1⅓ cups all-purpose flour
1½ teaspoons baking powder
½ teaspoon salt
¾ cup plus 2 tablespoons milk
6 tablespoons margarine or butter
3 large eggs
1 cup granulated sugar
1½ teaspoons vanilla extract
½ cup packed light brown sugar
½ teaspoon ground cinnamon
½ cup pecans, finely chopped
½ cup sweetened flaked coconut

1 Preheat oven to 350°F. Grease and flour 9" by 9" metal baking pan. On waxed paper, combine flour, baking powder, and salt.

2 In small saucepan, heat ¾ cup milk and 2 tablespoons margarine or butter over low heat until margarine melts and milk is hot.

3 Meanwhile, in small bowl, with mixer at medium-high speed, beat eggs and granulated sugar until slightly thickened and pale yellow, about 5 minutes, scraping bowl often with rubber spatula. Beat in vanilla.

4 Transfer egg mixture to large bowl. With mixer at low speed, alternately add flour mixture and hot milk mixture to egg mixture, beginning and ending with flour mixture, just until smooth, occasionally scraping bowl. Pour into pan.

5 Bake cake 35 to 40 minutes, until toothpick inserted in center comes out clean. Place pan with cake on wire rack while making topping. Preheat broiler.

6 In 2-quart saucepan, combine brown sugar, cinnamon, remaining 4 tablespoons margarine or butter, and remaining 2 tablespoons milk. Bring to a boil over medium heat, stirring occasionally. Remove saucepan from heat and stir in pecans and coconut. Spoon topping over hot cake and spread to cover top of cake.

7 Place pan with cake in broiler 5 to 7 inches from source of heat, and broil 1 to 2 minutes, until topping is bubbly and browned, watching carefully and rotating pan as necessary for even browning. Cool completely on wire rack. Makes 12 servings.

Each serving: About 275 calories, 4 g protein, 40 g carbohydrate, 12 g total fat (3 g saturated), 1 g fiber, 56 mg cholesterol, 240 mg sodium.

Banana Snack Cake with Brown-Butter Frosting

PREP: 30 MINUTES PLUS COOLING
BAKE: 25 TO 30 MINUTES

This moist, tender cake is baked and served right in the same pan for relaxed entertaining.

BANANA CAKE:
1⅓ cups mashed fully ripe bananas (about 4 medium)
1 tablespoon fresh lemon juice
2 teaspoons vanilla extract
2 cups all-purpose flour
1 teaspoon baking powder
½ teaspoon baking soda
½ teaspoon salt
⅛ teaspoon ground cinnamon
¾ cup packed brown sugar
½ cup granulated sugar
½ cup margarine or butter (1 stick), softened
2 large eggs

BROWN-BUTTER FROSTING:
6 tablespoons butter (no substitutions)
3 cups confectioners' sugar
5 tablespoons milk
2 teaspoons vanilla extract

1 Preheat oven to 350°F. Grease 13" by 9" metal baking pan; dust with flour.

2 In small bowl, mix bananas, lemon juice, and vanilla. On waxed paper, mix flour, baking powder, baking soda, salt, and cinnamon.

3 In large bowl, with mixer at medium speed, beat sugars with margarine or butter until light and

Banana Snack Cake with Brown-Butter Frosting

creamy, about 5 minutes, scraping bowl often with rubber spatula.

4 Add eggs, 1 at a time, beating well after each addition. At low speed, alternately add flour mixture and banana mixture, beginning and ending with flour mixture; beat just until smooth.

5 Spoon batter into pan and spread evenly. Bake cake 25 to 30 minutes, until toothpick inserted in center comes out clean. Cool cake in pan on wire rack.

6 Prepare Brown-Butter Frosting: In 1-quart saucepan, heat butter over medium heat until melted and dark nutty-brown in color but not burned, about 6 to

8 minutes, stirring occasionally. Immediately transfer butter to pie plate; refrigerate until firm, about 30 minutes.

7 In large bowl, with mixer at medium speed, beat chilled butter, confectioners' sugar, milk, and vanilla until creamy and smooth. Spread frosting evenly over cooled cake. Makes 24 servings.

Each serving: About 225 calories, 2 g protein, 39 g carbohydrate, 7 g total fat (3 g saturated), 1 g fiber, 26 mg cholesterol, 175 mg sodium.

Banana Cake with Fudge Frosting

PREP: 1 HOUR PLUS COOLING • BAKE: 25 TO 30 MINUTES

Bananas with chocolate is always a winning combination. This time, we've baked up 3 tender cake layers studded with mini chips and stacked them together with a doubly rich frosting.

CAKE:
1 cup mashed ripe bananas (2 to 3 medium)
¼ cup buttermilk or sour cream
1 teaspoon vanilla extract
2 cups cake flour (not self-rising)
1 teaspoon baking powder
½ teaspoon baking soda
¼ teaspoon salt
1¼ cups sugar
½ cup margarine or butter (1 stick), softened
2 large eggs
½ cup semisweet-chocolate mini chips (optional)

FUDGE FROSTING:
¾ cup sugar
¼ cup all-purpose flour
3 tablespoons unsweetened cocoa
1 cup milk
1 cup margarine or butter (2 sticks), softened
4 ounces semisweet chocolate, melted and cooled
1 tablespoon vanilla extract

1 Preheat oven to 350°F. Grease three 8-inch round cake pans. Line bottoms with waxed paper; grease paper. Dust pans with flour. In small bowl, mix bananas, buttermilk, and vanilla. On waxed paper, combine flour, baking powder, baking soda, and salt.

2 In large bowl, with mixer at medium speed, beat sugar with margarine or butter 5 minutes or until light and creamy, occasionally scraping bowl with rubber spatula. Add eggs, 1 at a time, beating well after each addition. At low speed, alternately add flour mixture and banana mixture, beginning and ending with flour mixture; beat just until blended, occasionally scraping bowl. With spoon, stir in chocolate chips.

3 Spoon batter into pans and spread evenly. Stagger pans on 2 oven racks, so layers are not directly above one another. Bake 25 to 30 minutes, until toothpick inserted in center of each layer comes out clean. Cool layers in pans on wire racks 10 minutes. Run small metal spatula or knife around edges of pans to loosen layers; invert onto wire racks and remove waxed paper. Cool layers completely.

4 Meanwhile, prepare Fudge Frosting: In 2-quart saucepan, with wire whisk, mix sugar, flour, and cocoa. Slowly whisk in milk until smooth.

5 Cook milk mixture over medium heat until mixture thickens and boils, stirring frequently. Reduce heat to low; cook 2 minutes, stirring constantly. Remove saucepan from heat; cool completely.

6 In large bowl, with mixer at medium speed, beat margarine or butter until creamy. Gradually beat in cooled milk mixture, melted chocolate, and vanilla until evenly blended and a creamy spreading consistency. Makes about 3 cups.

7 Assemble cake: Place 1 cake layer, rounded side down, on cake plate; spread with ½ cup frosting. Top with second cake layer; spread with another ½ cup frosting, then top with remaining cake layer. Frost top and side of cake with remaining frosting. Refrigerate if not serving right away. If cake is very cold, let stand at room temperature 20 minutes before serving to allow frosting to soften slightly. Makes 16 servings.

Each serving: About 385 calories, 4 g protein, 49 g carbohydrate, 20 g total fat (4 g saturated), 1 g fiber, 29 mg cholesterol, 350 mg sodium.

Banana Cake with Fudge Frosting ➤

Triple Chocolate-Cherry Cake

PREP: 40 MINUTES PLUS COOLING
BAKE: ABOUT 1 HOUR 10 MINUTES

For chocolate lovers only! You can even bake it ahead and stash in the freezer—wrapped well, it will keep up to 2 weeks.

1¾ cups all-purpose flour
¾ cup unsweetened cocoa
1½ teaspoons baking soda
½ teaspoon salt
1 cup dried tart cherries
1 tablespoon instant espresso-coffee powder
1½ cups buttermilk
2 teaspoons vanilla extract
1¾ cups sugar
1 cup butter (2 sticks), softened (no substitutions)
3 large eggs
2 ounces unsweetened chocolate, melted
1 package (6 ounces) semisweet-chocolate chips
  (1 cup)
Confectioners' sugar for dusting
Whipped cream (optional)

1 Preheat oven to 325°F. Grease and flour 10-inch Bundt pan. In medium bowl, combine flour, cocoa, baking soda, and salt; set aside.

2 In small bowl, place cherries with enough *very hot water* just to cover; let stand at least 5 minutes to soften cherries. In 2-cup glass measuring cup, dissolve espresso powder in *1 tablespoon very hot water*; stir in buttermilk and vanilla. Set aside.

3 In large bowl, with mixer at low speed, beat sugar with butter until blended, scraping bowl often with rubber spatula. Increase speed to medium; beat 2 minutes, occasionally scraping bowl. Reduce speed to low; add eggs, 1 at a time, beating well after each addition.

4 At low speed, alternately add flour mixture and buttermilk mixture, beginning and ending with flour mixture; beat until smooth, occasionally scraping bowl.

5 Drain cherries and pat with paper towels to remove excess water. With rubber spatula, fold melted unsweetened chocolate into batter. Then fold in chocolate chips and drained cherries.

6 Pour batter into pan. Bake cake 1 hour to 1 hour 10 minutes, until toothpick inserted in center of cake comes out clean. Cool cake in pan on wire rack 10 minutes. Invert cake onto rack to cool completely.

7 To serve, sift confectioners' sugar over cake. Pass whipped cream to spoon over each serving if you like. Makes 16 servings.

Each serving without whipped cream: About 365 calories, 5 g protein, 52 g carbohydrate, 17 g total fat (8 g saturated), 1 g fiber, 72 mg cholesterol, 345 mg sodium.

Black Forest Cake

PREP: 1 HOUR PLUS CHILLING OVERNIGHT
BAKE: 25 MINUTES

Do-ahead: The flavors blend best if you assemble this cake a day ahead. Cover and store in the refrigerator overnight. To really get a jump on prep, the cake layers can be made ahead and frozen up to 1 month.

CHOCOLATE CAKE:
2 cups all-purpose flour
1 cup unsweetened cocoa
2 teaspoons baking powder
1 teaspoon baking soda
½ teaspoon salt
2 cups sugar
1 cup margarine or butter (2 sticks), softened
4 large eggs
1⅓ cups milk
2 teaspoons vanilla extract

CHERRY FILLING:
2 cans (16½ ounces each) pitted dark sweet
  cherries (Bing) in heavy syrup
⅓ cup kirsch (cherry brandy)

CREAM FILLING:
1½ cups heavy or whipping cream
½ cup confectioners' sugar
2 tablespoons kirsch (cherry brandy)
1 teaspoon vanilla extract

Chocolate curls for garnish (opposite page)

1 Position 2 oven racks in center of oven. Preheat oven to 350°F. Grease three 9-inch round cake pans. Line bottoms with waxed paper; grease paper. Dust pans with flour.

2 Prepare Chocolate Cake: In medium bowl, combine flour, cocoa, baking powder, baking soda, and salt; set aside.

3 In large bowl, with mixer at low speed, beat sugar with margarine or butter until blended. Increase speed to high; beat until creamy, about 2 minutes. Reduce speed to medium-low; add eggs, 1 at a time, beating well after each addition.

4 Mix milk and vanilla. Alternately add flour mixture and milk mixture to margarine mixture, beginning and ending with flour mixture, until batter is smooth, occasionally scraping bowl with rubber spatula.

5 Divide batter among cake pans; spread evenly. Stagger cake pans on 2 oven racks, placing 2 on upper rack and 1 on lower rack, so that layers are not directly over one another. Bake layers 25 minutes or until toothpick inserted in centers of each comes out almost clean. Cool in pans on wire racks 10 minutes. Run small knife or metal spatula around edge of pans to loosen cake, then invert layers onto wire racks; peel off and discard waxed paper. Cool layers completely.

6 Meanwhile, prepare Cherry Filling: Drain cherries well in sieve set over bowl to catch syrup. Reserve ½ cup syrup; stir in kirsch. Set syrup mixture aside.

7 Prepare Cream Filling: In small bowl, with mixer at medium speed, beat cream, confectioners' sugar, kirsch, and vanilla until stiff peaks form.

8 Assemble cake: Place 1 cake layer on cake stand or serving plate; brush with one-third syrup mixture. Spread with one-third whipped-cream mixture, then top with half of cherries.

9 Place second cake layer on top of cherries. Brush with half of remaining syrup mixture, half of remaining cream mixture, and all of remaining cherries. Top with third cake layer; brush with remaining syrup mixture. Spoon remaining cream mixture onto center of top layer, leaving a border of cake around edge.

10 Pile chocolate curls on top of whipped cream in center of cake. Cover and refrigerate cake overnight. Makes 16 servings.

Each serving: About 450 calories, 6 g protein, 58 g carbohydrate, 22 g total fat (8 g saturated), 1 g fiber, 87 mg cholesterol, 380 mg sodium.

MASTER CLASS: CHOCOLATE CURLS

How do we make those gorgeous sweet scrolls piled on our Black Forest Cake (photo, at right)? It's no more challenging than cutting a piece of Jarlsberg or Cheddar with a cheese slicer. Use this easy technique to dress up anything, from a cake made from a mix to a cream-topped trifle.

The steps:

1. In small glass bowl, combine 6 ounces semisweet chocolate (squares or chips) and ½ teaspoon vegetable shortening. Place in microwave oven and cook, uncovered, on Medium (50 percent power) 2½ to 3 minutes, just until mixture is soft and shiny. Remove from microwave and stir until smooth. (Or, in heavy small saucepan, heat chocolate and shortening over low heat until melted and smooth, stirring frequently.)

2. Pour melted chocolate mixture into foil-lined or disposable 4½" by 2½" mini loaf pan. Refrigerate until firm, about 2 hours.

3. Remove chocolate block from pan; peel off foil. Let stand at room temperature about 30 minutes to soften slightly.

4. Using vegetable peeler, cheese slicer, or butter curler, draw blade evenly across the long narrow surface of chocolate block to make number of curls desired. (We made about 12.)

5. To avoid breaking curls, use a toothpick to transfer them to top of dessert. Or place curls on jelly-roll pan and refrigerate until ready to use. Wrap and refrigerate remaining chocolate block up to 1 month; use to make more garnishes as needed.

Lemon Angel Food Cake

This moist, fat-free cake is delicious on its own or with our light lemon sauce.

ANGEL FOOD CAKE:
2 large lemons
1 cup cake flour (not self-rising)
½ cup confectioners' sugar
1⅔ cups egg whites (12 to 14 large whites)
1½ teaspoons cream of tartar
½ teaspoon salt
1 teaspoon vanilla extract
1¼ cups granulated sugar

LEMON SAUCE:
1 large lemon
½ cup sugar
1 tablespoon cornstarch
1 tablespoon margarine or butter

1 Prepare Angel Food Cake: Preheat oven to 375° F. From lemons, grate 2 teaspoons peel and squeeze 1 tablespoon juice; set aside. On waxed paper, mix flour and confectioners' sugar; set aside.

2 In large bowl, with mixer at high speed, beat egg whites, cream of tartar, and salt until soft peaks form. Beat in vanilla and lemon juice. Beating at high speed, sprinkle in granulated sugar, 2 tablespoons at a time, beating until whites stand in stiff peaks.

3 Sift flour mixture over egg whites, one-third at a time, folding in with rubber spatula after each addition, just until flour mixture is completely incorporated. Fold in grated lemon peel.

4 Spoon batter into ungreased 10-inch tube pan with removable bottom; with metal spatula, gently spread evenly. Bake cake 35 to 40 minutes, until top springs back when lightly touched with finger. Invert cake in pan on funnel or bottle; cool completely in pan.

5 Meanwhile, prepare Lemon Sauce: From lemon, grate 1 teaspoon peel and squeeze ¼ cup juice. In 1-quart saucepan, mix sugar and cornstarch until blended. Add lemon peel, lemon juice, margarine or butter, and ⅔ *cup water*; heat to boiling over high heat, stirring frequently. Boil 1 minute, stirring. Transfer sauce to bowl; cover and refrigerate until ready to serve. Makes about 1¼ cups.

6 With metal spatula, carefully loosen cake from pan; place on cake plate. Serve cake with sauce. Makes 16 servings.

Each serving cake only: About 115 calories, 4 g protein, 25 g carbohydrate, 0 g total fat, 0 g fiber, 0 mg cholesterol, 115 mg sodium.

Each tablespoon sauce: About 25 calories, 0 g protein, 6 g carbohydrate, 1 g total fat (0 g saturated), 0 g fiber, 0 mg cholesterol, 10 mg sodium.

Golden Almond Cake with Peaches

Cut this glorious round cake into wedges and serve with peaches in their own syrup.

1 cup all-purpose flour
1 teaspoon baking powder
¼ teaspoon salt
¼ cup milk
1 teaspoon vanilla extract
⅓ cup packed almond paste
⅓ cup plus ¼ cup sugar
4 tablespoons margarine or butter, softened
2 large eggs
9 ripe medium peaches (about 3 pounds)

1 Preheat oven to 350°F. Grease 8-inch round cake pan. Line bottom with waxed paper; grease paper. Dust pan with flour.

2 On waxed paper, combine flour, baking powder, and salt. In 1-cup glass measuring cup, mix milk with vanilla. Set aside.

3 In small bowl, with heavy-duty mixer at low speed, beat almond paste and ⅓ cup sugar until mixture has a sandy consistency. (If heavy-duty mixer is unavailable, place almond paste and sugar in food processor with knife blade attached, and pulse until fine crumbs form. Transfer almond-paste mixture to small bowl and proceed as directed in step 4.)

4 At low speed, beat in margarine or butter. Increase speed to high; beat until well blended, about 5 minutes, scraping bowl often with rubber spatula. Reduce speed to low; add eggs, 1 at a time, beating well after each addition.

5 With mixer at low speed, alternately add flour mixture and milk mixture, beginning and ending with flour mixture, until batter is smooth, occasionally scraping bowl.

6 Spoon batter into pan. Bake cake 25 to 30 minutes, until golden brown and toothpick inserted in center comes out clean. Cool cake in pan on wire rack 10 minutes. Run small knife around side of pan to loosen cake, then invert cake onto wire rack to cool completely. Discard waxed paper.

7 Up to 20 minutes before serving, peel and thinly slice peaches. In medium bowl, stir peaches with remaining ¼ cup sugar; let stand 10 minutes until syrup forms.

8 Serve cake with peaches and their syrup. Makes 10 servings.

Each serving: About 245 calories, 5 g protein, 38 g carbohydrate, 9 g total fat (2 g saturated), 2 g fiber, 43 mg cholesterol, 170 mg sodium.

Lemon Pound Cake with Rosemary

PREP: 30 MINUTES PLUS COOLING • BAKE: 1 HOUR

The subtle texture of cornmeal and the infused notes of rosemary make this golden cake a treat.

1 cup milk
2 tablespoons minced fresh rosemary leaves
3 cups cake flour (not self-rising)
½ cup yellow cornmeal
½ teaspoon baking powder
¼ teaspoon salt
2 to 3 lemons
2 cups sugar
1 cup margarine or butter (2 sticks), softened
½ cup vegetable shortening
6 large eggs
1 teaspoon vanilla extract
1 teaspoon lemon extract

1 In 1-quart saucepan, heat milk with 1 tablespoon rosemary just to boiling over medium heat. Remove from heat; let stand, covered, 10 minutes to allow flavor to develop. Pour milk mixture through sieve into bowl; cool slightly.

2 Preheat oven to 350°F. Grease and flour 12-cup Bundt pan.

3 On waxed paper, combine flour, cornmeal, baking powder, and salt. From lemons, finely grate 1 tablespoon plus 1 teaspoon peel and squeeze ½ cup juice.

4 In large bowl, with mixer at low speed, beat 1¾ cups sugar with margarine or butter and shortening until blended. Increase speed to high and beat until light and creamy, about 5 minutes. At medium speed, add eggs, 1 at a time, beating well after each addition. Beat in vanilla and lemon extracts and 1 tablespoon lemon peel.

5 At low speed, alternately add flour mixture and milk mixture, beginning and ending with flour mixture; beat just until batter is smooth, occasionally scraping bowl with rubber spatula.

6 Spoon batter evenly into pan. Bake 1 hour or until toothpick inserted in center comes out clean. Cool cake in pan on wire rack 10 minutes. Run small knife around side of pan to loosen cake. Invert cake onto wire rack to cool completely.

7 While cake is cooling, in 1-quart saucepan, heat lemon juice, remaining ¼ cup sugar, 1 tablespoon rosemary, and 1 teaspoon lemon peel to boiling over medium heat. Remove saucepan from heat; let stand 5 minutes. Pour syrup through sieve into small bowl; brush over warm cake. Makes 20 servings.

Each serving: About 310 calories, 4 g protein, 37 g carbohydrate, 16 g total fat (4 g saturated), 0 g fiber, 66 mg cholesterol, 185 mg sodium.

Chocolate Pound Cake with Irish Whiskey-Cream Sauce

PREP: 30 MINUTES PLUS COOLING
BAKE: ABOUT 1 HOUR 15 MINUTES

Bake this dense, decadent chocolate cake in a Bundt pan and serve with a big dollop of flavored whipped cream.

CHOCOLATE CAKE:
3 cups all-purpose flour
1 cup unsweetened cocoa
½ teaspoon baking powder
1½ cups margarine or butter (3 sticks), softened
2¾ cups sugar
2 teaspoons vanilla extract
5 large eggs
1½ cups milk
2 ounces bittersweet or semisweet chocolate, grated

IRISH WHISKEY-CREAM SAUCE:
1 cup heavy or whipping cream
⅓ cup confectioners' sugar
¼ cup brewed coffee
2 tablespoons Irish whiskey or Bourbon
Confectioners' sugar for garnish

1 Prepare Chocolate Cake: Preheat oven to 350°F. Grease and flour 12-cup Bundt pan. In medium bowl, combine flour, cocoa, and baking powder.

2 In large bowl, with mixer at medium speed, beat margarine or butter until creamy. Gradually beat in sugar, scraping bowl often with rubber spatula. Beat 3 minutes, occasionally scraping bowl. Beat in vanilla. Reduce speed to low; add eggs, 1 at a time, beating well after each addition.

3 With mixer at low speed, alternately add flour mixture and milk, beginning and ending with flour mixture, until batter is blended, occasionally scraping bowl. Stir in grated chocolate. Spoon batter into Bundt pan, spreading evenly.

4 Bake cake about 1 hour 15 minutes, until toothpick inserted in center of cake comes out clean. Cool cake in pan on wire rack 10 minutes. Invert cake onto wire rack to cool completely.

5 Meanwhile, prepare Irish Whiskey-Cream Sauce: In small bowl, with mixer at low speed, beat cream until frothy. Add sugar; increase speed to medium, and beat until stiff peaks form. With rubber spatula or wire whisk, fold in coffee and whiskey until blended; cover and refrigerate up to 4 hours. Makes about 2 cups.

6 To serve, sprinkle cake with confectioners' sugar; cut into wedges and pass cream sauce to spoon over each serving. Makes 20 servings.

Each serving of cake only: About 350 calories, 5 g protein, 47 g carbohydrate, 17 g total fat (4 g saturated), 1 g fiber, 56 mg cholesterol, 220 mg sodium.

Each tablespoon sauce: About 35 calories, 0 g protein, 1 g carbohydrate, 3 g total fat (2 g saturated), 0 g fiber, 10 mg cholesterol, 5 mg sodium.

Skillet Pear Upside-Down Cake

PREP: 40 MINUTES PLUS COOLING
BAKE: 40 TO 45 MINUTES

Our recipe works well with sweet Bartletts, the most popular pears in America. Cake flour gives this a tender texture.

⅓ cup packed dark brown sugar
½ cup margarine or butter (1 stick), softened
5 firm but ripe Bartlett or Bosc pears (about 2 pounds), peeled, cored, and each cut into 8 wedges
1 cup cake flour (not self-rising)
1 teaspoon baking powder
¼ teaspoon salt
⅔ cup granulated sugar
1 large egg
1 teaspoon vanilla extract
⅓ cup milk

1 Preheat oven to 325°F. In nonstick 10-inch skillet with oven-safe handle (or wrap handle in double thickness of foil for baking in oven later), heat brown sugar and 2 tablespoons margarine or butter over medium-high heat until melted, stirring occasionally. Add pear wedges and cook until pears are golden and tender, and sugar mixture thickens slightly, about 10 minutes, stirring occasionally. Remove skillet from heat. With tongs, gently arrange pear wedges in concentric circles in skillet.

2 On sheet of waxed paper, combine flour, baking powder, and salt. In large bowl, with mixer at high speed, beat granulated sugar with remaining 6 tablespoons margarine or butter until smooth, scraping bowl often with rubber spatula. Reduce speed to low; beat in egg and vanilla until well blended. Mixture may look curdled. Alternately beat in flour mixture and milk, beginning and ending with flour mixture and beating just until blended. Spoon batter over pear mixture and spread evenly with small metal spatula (syrup may show through edge of batter).

3 Bake 40 to 45 minutes, until toothpick inserted in center of cake comes out clean. Immediately loosen edge of cake from skillet and invert cake onto serving plate. If any pears stick to skillet, place back on cake. Cool cake slightly to serve warm. Makes 8 servings.

Each serving: About 325 calories, 3 g protein, 52 g carbohydrate, 13 g total fat (3 g saturated), 2 g fiber, 28 mg cholesterol, 280 mg sodium.

Cook the pear wedges in brown sugar and butter until tender.

Spoon the cake batter over the pears in the skillet, then spread it evenly over the fruit with a spatula.

After baking, invert the skillet onto a serving platter. The cake should slip right out.

The finished product is a delectable marriage of pan-browned Bartlett wedges and golden-yellow cake.

Sour-Cream Pear Coffee Cake

. . . .

PREP: 25 MINUTES PLUS COOLING
BAKE: 40 TO 45 MINUTES

We used Boscs, the ultimate baking pears, for delicious results. Serve this for breakfast or teatime.

STREUSEL:
⅔ cup packed light brown sugar
½ cup all-purpose flour
1 teaspoon ground cinnamon
4 tablespoons margarine or butter, softened
⅔ cup walnuts, toasted and chopped

CAKE:
2½ cups all-purpose flour
1½ teaspoons baking powder
½ teaspoon baking soda
½ teaspoon salt
1¼ cups sugar

Sour-Cream Pear Coffee Cake

6 tablespoons margarine or butter, softened
2 large eggs
1½ teaspoons vanilla extract
1⅓ cups sour cream
3 firm but ripe Bosc pears (about 1¼ pounds), peeled, cored, and cut into 1-inch pieces

1 Preheat oven to 350°F. Grease 13" by 9" metal baking pan; dust with flour.

2 Prepare Streusel: In medium bowl, with fork, mix brown sugar, flour, and cinnamon until well blended. With fingertips, work in margarine or butter until evenly distributed. Add walnuts and toss to mix; set aside.

3 Prepare Cake: In another medium bowl, combine flour, baking powder, baking soda, and salt; set aside.

4 In large bowl, with mixer at low speed, beat sugar with margarine or butter until blended, scraping bowl often with rubber spatula. Increase speed to high; beat until creamy, about 2 minutes, occasionally scraping bowl. Reduce speed to low; add eggs, 1 at a time, beating well after each addition. Beat in vanilla.

5 With mixer at low speed, alternately add flour mixture and sour cream, beginning and ending with flour mixture, until batter is smooth, occasionally scraping bowl. With rubber spatula, fold in pears.

6 Spoon batter into pan; spread evenly. Sprinkle top with streusel mixture. Bake coffee cake 40 to 45 minutes, until toothpick inserted in center comes out clean. Cool cake in pan on wire rack 1 hour to serve warm, or cool completely in pan to serve later. Makes 16 servings.

Each serving: About 345 calories, 5 g protein, 49 g carbohydrate, 15 g total fat (4 g saturated), 1 g fiber, 35 mg cholesterol, 260 mg sodium.

COOKIES

Citrus Bars

PREP: 15 MINUTES PLUS COOLING
BAKE: ABOUT 35 MINUTES

CRUST:
1½ cups all-purpose flour
½ cup confectioners' sugar
¾ cup cold margarine or butter (1½ sticks)

CITRUS FILLING:
1 orange
1 lemon
1 lime
3 large eggs
1 cup granulated sugar
3 tablespoons all-purpose flour
½ teaspoon baking powder
½ teaspoon salt
1 tablespoon confectioners' sugar

1 Preheat oven to 350°F. Grease 13" by 9" metal baking pan. Line pan with foil; grease foil.

2 Prepare Crust: In medium bowl, combine flour and confectioners' sugar. With pastry blender or 2 knives used scissor-fashion, cut in margarine or butter until mixture resembles coarse crumbs. Sprinkle flour mixture evenly in pan; with hand, firmly pat onto bottom of pan to form a crust. Bake crust 20 to 22 minutes, until lightly browned.

3 Meanwhile, grate ½ teaspoon peel from orange, ½ teaspoon peel from lemon, and ½ teaspoon peel from lime; squeeze 2 tablespoons juice from each fruit. In large bowl, with mixer at high speed, beat eggs until thick and lemon-colored, about 2 minutes. Reduce speed to low; add citrus peel, citrus juice, granulated sugar, flour, baking powder, and salt, and beat just until blended, occasionally scraping bowl.

4 Pour citrus mixture over hot crust. Bake 15 minutes or until filling is just set and pale golden around edges. Transfer pan to wire rack. Place confectioners' sugar in fine sieve and sprinkle over warm filling. Cool completely in pan on wire rack.

5 When cool, transfer with foil to cutting board. Cut lengthwise into 3 strips, then cut each strip crosswise into 12 bars. If not serving right away, cover and refrigerate. Makes 3 dozen bars.

Each bar: About 90 calories, 1 g protein, 12 g carbohydrate, 4 g total fat (1 g saturated), 1 g fiber, 18 mg cholesterol, 90 mg sodium.

Cherry-Cheesecake Triangles

PREP: 20 MINUTES PLUS COOLING AND CHILLING
BAKE: 55 MINUTES

For bakery-quality results, swirl cherry-pie filling through cheesecake batter to create a marbled effect.

CRUMB CRUST:
1½ cups graham-cracker crumbs
6 tablespoons margarine or butter, melted
2 tablespoons sugar

CHERRY-CHEESE FILLING:
1½ packages (8 ounces each) light cream cheese (Neufchâtel), softened
½ cup sugar
1½ teaspoons vanilla extract
2 large eggs
1 cup canned cherry-pie filling

1 Preheat oven to 350°F. Grease 9" by 9" metal baking pan. Line pan with foil; grease foil.

2 Prepare Crumb Crust: In bowl, with fork, stir graham-cracker crumbs, melted margarine or butter, and sugar until blended. With hand, press mixture onto bottom of pan. Bake crust 10 minutes. Cool completely in pan on wire rack.

3 Prepare Cherry-Cheese Filling: In small bowl, with mixer at medium speed, beat cream cheese until smooth; gradually beat in sugar. Beat in vanilla and eggs just until blended.

4 Pour cream-cheese mixture evenly over cooled crust. Spoon dollops of cherry-pie filling over cheese mixture. With tip of knife, cut and twist through mixture to create marble design.

5 Bake 45 minutes or until toothpick inserted in center comes out almost clean. Cool completely in pan on wire rack; refrigerate until ready to serve.

6 When cold, transfer with foil to cutting board. Cut into 2 strips, then cut each strip crosswise into 2 squares. Cut each square diagonally into quarters. Makes 16 triangles.

Each triangle: About 210 calories, 4 g protein, 23 g carbohydrate, 11 g total fat (4 g saturated), 0 g fiber, 46 mg cholesterol, 220 mg sodium.

Cherry-Cheesecake Triangles ➤

Lemony Cheesecake Bites

PREP: 30 MINUTES PLUS CHILLING • BAKE: ABOUT 1 HOUR

Don't skip these! They're a cheesecake lover's dream, with a rich, creamy texture and a triple taste of citrus—there's lime in the crust, lemon in the filling, and an orange-flecked sour-cream layer on top. Do-ahead: Cheesecake always tastes better a day or so after it's baked, so make a panful of these up to 2 days ahead. Refrigerate in pan. Cut into bites when ready to serve.

CRUST:
5 tablespoons margarine or butter
¾ teaspoon freshly grated lime peel
1¾ cups vanilla-wafer cookie crumbs (about 48 cookies)

FILLING:
2 large lemons
1¼ cups sugar
2 tablespoons cornstarch
4 packages (8 ounces each) cream cheese, softened
½ cup heavy or whipping cream
5 large eggs

TOPPING:
1½ cups sour cream
3 tablespoons sugar
1 teaspoon freshly grated orange peel

1 Prepare Crust: Preheat oven to 350°F. Grease 13" by 9" metal baking pan. Line pan with foil. In 10-inch skillet, melt margarine or butter over low heat; stir in lime peel. With fork, stir crumbs into melted margarine mixture until crumbs are moistened. With hand, press crumb mixture firmly onto bottom of baking pan. Bake crust 10 minutes. Cool crust in pan on wire rack.

2 Prepare Filling: From lemons, grate 1 tablespoon peel and squeeze ¼ cup juice. In small bowl, combine sugar and cornstarch until blended. In large bowl, with mixer at medium speed, beat cream cheese until smooth, about 5 minutes, scraping bowl occasionally with rubber spatula. Slowly beat in sugar mixture, cream, lemon juice, and lemon peel until blended, scraping bowl often. At low speed, beat in eggs just until blended (do not overbeat).

3 Pour Filling onto Crust. Place medium roasting pan (15½" by 10-½") on rack in oven; fill with 1 inch boiling water. Carefully place cheesecake pan in roasting pan. (Water will come halfway up side of cheesecake pan.)

4 Bake cheesecake 55 to 60 minutes, until toothpick inserted 1 inch from center comes out almost clean and center of cheesecake is not completely set. Remove cheesecake from oven. Turn off oven.

5 While cheesecake is baking, prepare Topping: In small bowl, stir all Topping ingredients together; refrigerate until ready to use.

6 After removing cheesecake from oven, spread Topping over hot cake. Return cheesecake to oven for 5 minutes (oven is off but still hot) to heat Topping. Cool cheesecake completely in pan on wire rack. Cover and refrigerate at least 6 hours or overnight.

7 When cold, transfer cheesecake with foil to cutting board. Cut cheesecake lengthwise into 8 strips; cut each strip crosswise into 8 pieces. Refrigerate any leftovers. Makes 64 cheesecake bites.

Each bite: About 115 calories, 2 g protein, 8 g carbohydrate, 9 g total fat (5 g saturated), 0 g fiber, 39 mg cholesterol, 75 mg sodium.

Pecan Triangles

PREP: 30 MINUTES PLUS COOLING
BAKE: ABOUT 45 MINUTES

CRUST:
3 cups all-purpose flour
¼ cup granulated sugar
½ teaspoon salt
½ teaspoon baking powder
½ cup cold margarine or butter (1 stick)
½ cup vegetable shortening

FILLING:
1¼ cups packed brown sugar
1 cup margarine or butter (2 sticks)
¾ cup honey
½ cup granulated sugar
¼ cup heavy or whipping cream
1 pound pecans (4 cups), very coarsely chopped
1 tablespoon vanilla extract

1 Preheat oven to 400°F. Grease 15½" by 10½" jelly-roll pan; line with foil.

2 Prepare Crust: In large bowl, combine flour, granulated sugar, salt, and baking powder. With pastry blender or 2 knives used scissor-fashion, cut in margarine or butter with shortening until mixture resembles fine crumbs. With hands, firmly press crumbs on bottom and up sides of pan to form crust. Bake crust 12 to 15 minutes, until golden. Remove crust from oven. Turn oven control to 350°F.

3 While crust is baking, prepare Filling: In 3-quart saucepan, heat brown sugar, margarine or butter, honey, granulated sugar, and cream to boiling over high heat. Add pecans to sugar mixture and heat to boiling; stir in vanilla.

4 Carefully pour pecan mixture into warm crust. Bake 30 minutes or until edges of filling begin to set (filling will be bubbly and will become firm as tart cools). Cool in pan on wire rack until filling is firm to the touch.

5 When cool, invert onto rack and remove foil. Invert again immediately onto cutting board. Cut lengthwise into 4 strips, then cut each strip crosswise into 8 pieces. Cut each piece diagonally in half. Store cookies in tightly covered container up to 1 week. Makes 64 triangles.

Each triangle: About 160 calories, 1 g protein, 16 g carbohydrate, 11 g total fat (2 g saturated), 1 g fiber, 1 mg cholesterol, 80 mg sodium.

BAR EXAM
12 Tips for Never-Fail Results

Do:

• Let butter or margarine stand at room temperature if it must be softened. Leave stick(s) wrapped on counter or unwrapped in mixing bowl, cut into small pieces to speed up the process. Softening can take up to an hour. (Popping cold butter into the microwave is tempting, but our food editors caution that zapping can soften it unevenly, creating hot spots, or melt the butter in a blink. And if butter is melted or nearly melted, it will be too soft to cream properly and will affect a cookie's texture.)

• Prepare the pan before you start mixing the batter. Some rising occurs as soon as ingredients are moistened. If you line and grease the pan after making the batter, the mixture might start to swell and be harder to spread evenly.

• Dip knife or scissors in flour often when chopping sticky foods like figs or dates.

• Allow bars to cool completely before cutting with a chef's knife, to avoid jagged edges and broken pieces. Use a gentle sawing motion to avoid squashing squares.

• For fudgy, cheesecakelike, or topped bars, dip knife blade in hot water; quickly dry blade with a paper towel and redip between cuts.

• Keep soft bar cookies from getting stale by storing them in a cookie tin or jar with a slice of plain bread (replace the slice of bread every other day). The bars should keep for up to 3 days. Or, wrap and freeze the treats individually for up to 1 month to pop into a lunch box or briefcase.

Don't:

• Substitute light margarines, vegetable-oil spreads, or whipped butters for regular stick margarine or butter—they contain more water (or air) than standard sticks and are likely to throw off the recipe.

• Measure ingredients over the bowl. If you slip while measuring and add too much, you may have to start all over again.

• Use liquid measures for dry ingredients, or vice versa. Cup for cup, liquid measures have more volume.

• Choose a different pan size than the recipe calls for; the timing (and the doneness test for bar cookies) is based on specific bakeware dimensions.

• Open the oven door to check on bar cookies while they bake. The temperature can drop, and the cookies may not rise properly—wait until the minimum baking time is up before taking a peek.

• Wrap warm cookies or place them in any closed container. The heat will cause condensation and make the tops wet, so the bars stick together. Always let them cool completely first.

Whole-Grain Fig Bars

PREP: 15 MINUTES PLUS COOLING
BAKE: 20 TO 25 MINUTES

Made with whole wheat flour and dried figs (a healthful fiber-packed food), these soft, chewy goodies are good for you too! For an additional boost, sprinkle batter with 2 tablespoons honey-crunch wheat germ before baking.

4 ounces dried Calimyrna figs (about ¾ cup)
½ cup all-purpose flour
½ cup whole wheat flour
⅓ cup packed dark brown sugar
1 teaspoon ground cinnamon
½ teaspoon ground ginger
½ teaspoon baking powder
¼ teaspoon salt
⅓ cup light (mild) molasses
2 tablespoons margarine or butter, melted
1 teaspoon vanilla extract
1 large egg white

1 Preheat oven to 350°F. Grease 8" by 8" metal baking pan. Line pan with foil; grease foil.

2 With kitchen shears, cut stems from figs; cut figs into small pieces. In large bowl, with spoon, stir figs, all-purpose flour, whole wheat flour, brown sugar, cinnamon, ginger, baking powder, and salt until mixed.

3 Stir in molasses, melted margarine or butter, vanilla, and egg white just until blended and evenly moistened.

4 With metal spatula, spread batter in pan (batter will be sticky). Bake 20 to 25 minutes, until toothpick inserted in center comes out clean. Cool completely in pan on wire rack.

5 When cool, transfer with foil to cutting board. Cut into 3 strips, then cut each strip crosswise into 4 pieces. Makes 1 dozen bars.

Each bar: About 130 calories, 2 g protein, 26 g carbohydrate, 2 g total fat (0 g saturated), 2 g fiber, 0 mg cholesterol, 90 mg sodium.

Date Bars

PREP: 40 MINUTES PLUS COOLING
BAKE: 45 TO 50 MINUTES

These beloved triple-layer sweets have a simple streusel topping.

OAT CRUST & TOPPING:
1¼ cups all-purpose flour
1 cup old-fashioned or quick-cooking oats, uncooked
½ cup packed light brown sugar
½ cup butter (1 stick), softened
¼ teaspoon baking soda
¼ teaspoon salt
¼ teaspoon ground cinnamon

DATE FILLING:
1 container (10 ounces) pitted dates, chopped
2 tablespoons light brown sugar

1 Preheat oven to 375°F. Grease 9" by 9" metal baking pan. Line pan with foil; grease foil.

2 Prepare Oat Crust & Topping: In large bowl, with hand, mix flour, oats, brown sugar, butter, baking soda, salt, and cinnamon until mixture comes together. Transfer 2 cups mixture to baking pan; reserve remaining mixture for crumb topping. With hand, press mixture evenly onto bottom of pan to form a crust. Bake crust 10 minutes. Cool completely in pan on wire rack. Turn off oven.

3 While crust is cooling, prepare Date Filling: In 2-quart saucepan, cook dates, brown sugar, and ¾ *cup water* over medium heat until mixture thickens and all liquid is absorbed, about 6 to 8 minutes, stirring frequently. Spoon Date Filling into bowl; refrigerate until cool, about 30 minutes.

4 When filling is cool, preheat oven to 375°F. Spread filling over crust; top with reserved crumb mixture. Bake 35 to 40 minutes, until topping is golden. Cool completely in pan on wire rack.

5 When cool, transfer with foil to cutting board. Cut into 4 strips, then cut each strip crosswise into 3 pieces. Makes 1 dozen bars.

Each bar: About 275 calories, 4 g protein, 47 g carbohydrate, 9 g total fat (5 g saturated), 4 g fiber, 21 mg cholesterol, 155 mg sodium.

Hermit Bars

PREP: 10 MINUTES PLUS COOLING
BAKE: 18 TO 22 MINUTES

Chewy old-fashioned, raisin-and-spice hermits are said to have originated in Colonial New England. Some say they got their name because they taste better when hidden away like a hermit for a day or so. You don't need a mixer to make them—just a bowl and a spoon.

2 cups all-purpose flour
⅔ cup packed dark brown sugar
2 teaspoons ground cinnamon
1½ teaspoons ground ginger
½ teaspoon baking soda
½ teaspoon salt
⅔ cup mild molasses
6 tablespoons margarine or butter, melted
2 teaspoons vanilla extract
2 large eggs, lightly beaten
¾ cup dark seedless raisins

1 Preheat oven to 375°F. Grease 13" by 9" metal baking pan. Line pan with foil; grease foil.

2 In large bowl, with spoon, stir flour, brown sugar, cinnamon, ginger, baking soda, and salt until well combined.

3 Stir in molasses, melted margarine or butter, vanilla, and eggs just until blended. Stir in raisins.

4 Spread mixture evenly in pan. Bake 18 to 22 minutes, until golden around edges. Cool completely in pan on wire rack.

5 When cool, transfer with foil to cutting board. Cut lengthwise into 6 strips, then cut each strip crosswise into 4 pieces. Makes 2 dozen bars.

Each bar: About 130 calories, 2 g protein, 24 g carbohydrate, 3 g total fat (1 g saturated), 1 g fiber, 18 mg cholesterol, 120 mg sodium.

Turtle Bars

PREP: 35 MINUTES PLUS COOLING
BAKE: 15 TO 20 MINUTES

We mounded the scrumptious components of turtle-shaped candies—pecans, caramel, and chocolate—on a sweet, golden crust.

PASTRY CRUST:
1 cup all-purpose flour
¼ cup granulated sugar
⅛ teaspoon salt
6 tablespoons cold butter

CARAMEL:
1⅓ cups packed light brown sugar
½ cup heavy or whipping cream
⅓ cup light corn syrup
3 tablespoons butter
1 teaspoon distilled white vinegar
⅛ teaspoon salt
1 teaspoon vanilla extract

¾ cup pecans, toasted and chopped
3 ounces semisweet chocolate

1 Preheat oven to 425°F. Grease 9" by 9" metal baking pan. Line pan with foil; grease foil.

2 Prepare Pastry Crust: In medium bowl, combine flour, sugar, and salt. With pastry blender or 2 knives used scissor-fashion, cut in butter until mixture resembles coarse crumbs. Sprinkle about 3 *tablespoons cold water*, 1 tablespoon at a time, into flour mixture, mixing lightly with fork after each addition until dough is just moist enough to hold together.

3 With lightly floured hand, press dough evenly onto bottom of pan. With fork, prick dough at 1-inch intervals to prevent puffing and shrinking during baking. Bake crust 15 to 20 minutes, until golden (crust may crack slightly during baking). Cool completely in pan on wire rack.

4 When crust is cool, prepare Caramel: In 2-quart saucepan, heat brown sugar, cream, corn syrup, butter, vinegar, and salt to boiling over high heat, stirring occasionally. Reduce heat to medium-low and cook, uncovered, 5 minutes, stirring frequently. Remove saucepan from heat; stir in vanilla until blended and bubbling subsides, about 20 seconds.

5 Pour hot caramel evenly over crust; sprinkle with pecans. Set aside to allow caramel to cool, about 1 hour.

6 Place chocolate in 2-cup measuring cup or medium glass bowl. In microwave oven, cook, covered with waxed paper, on High 1 to 2 minutes, until almost melted; stir until smooth. (Or, in 1-quart saucepan, heat chocolate over low heat, stirring frequently, until melted and smooth.) Cool chocolate 5 minutes; drizzle over pecans. Place pan in refrigerator 30 minutes or until chocolate is set.

7 When set, transfer with foil to cutting board. Cut into 6 strips, then cut each strip crosswise into 6 pieces. Store bars in refrigerator. Makes 3 dozen bars.

Each bar: About 120 calories, 1 g protein, 16 g carbohydrate, 6 g total fat (3 g saturated), 0 g fiber, 12 mg cholesterol, 50 mg sodium.

Peanut-Butter Rocky-Road Bars

PREP: 15 MINUTES PLUS COOLING • BAKE: 25 MINUTES

These are every child's (and candy-lover's) dream come true—peanut-butter brownies topped with toasted marshmallows, peanuts, and chocolate.

¾ cup packed light brown sugar
⅔ cup creamy peanut butter
½ cup granulated sugar
4 tablespoons margarine or butter, softened
1¼ cups all-purpose flour
1 teaspoon baking powder
1 teaspoon vanilla extract
2 large eggs
1 cup miniature marshmallows
½ cup salted cocktail peanuts, chopped
½ cup semisweet-chocolate pieces

1 Preheat oven to 350°F. Grease 13" by 9" metal baking pan. Line pan with foil; grease foil.

2 In large bowl, with mixer at low speed, beat brown sugar, peanut butter, granulated sugar, and margarine or butter until blended. Increase speed to high; beat until creamy. At low speed, beat in flour, baking powder, vanilla, and eggs until well blended, constantly scraping bowl with rubber spatula.

3 With hand, press dough onto bottom of pan. Bake 20 minutes. Sprinkle marshmallows, peanuts, and chocolate pieces over top; bake 5 minutes longer or until golden. Cool completely in pan on wire rack.

4 When cool, transfer with foil to cutting board. Cut lengthwise into 4 strips, then cut each strip crosswise into 6 pieces. Makes 2 dozen bars.

Each bar: About 175 calories, 4 g protein, 22 g carbohydrate, 8 g total fat (1 g saturated), 1 g fiber, 18 mg cholesterol, 100 mg sodium.

Blondies

PREP: 10 MINUTES PLUS COOLING • BAKE: 30 MINUTES

These cakelike butterscotch/vanilla bars are the "light" alternative to dark brownies.

6 tablespoons margarine or butter
1¾ cups packed light brown sugar
2 teaspoons vanilla extract
2 large eggs
1 cup all-purpose flour
2 teaspoons baking powder
1 teaspoon salt
1½ cups pecans, coarsely chopped

1 Preheat oven to 350°F. Grease 13" by 9" metal baking pan. Line pan with foil; grease foil.

2 In heavy 3-quart saucepan, melt margarine or butter over low heat. Remove saucepan from heat. With wooden spoon, stir in brown sugar and vanilla, then stir in eggs until well blended. In small bowl, combine flour, baking powder, and salt; stir into sugar mixture just until blended. Stir in chopped pecans.

3 Spread batter evenly in pan. Bake 30 minutes or until toothpick inserted 2 inches from edge of pan comes out clean. Do not overbake; blondies will become firm as they cool. Cool completely in pan on wire rack.

4 When cool, transfer with foil to cutting board. Cut blondies lengthwise into 4 strips, then cut each strip crosswise into 6 pieces. Makes 2 dozen bars.

Each bar: About 155 calories, 2 g protein, 21 g carbohydrate, 8 g total fat (1 g saturated), 1 g fiber, 18 mg cholesterol, 170 mg sodium.

S'More Bars

PREP: 15 MINUTES PLUS COOLING • BAKE: 40 MINUTES

A panful of butterscotch-flavored blondies makes the perfect base for traditional s'mores ingredients.

8 graham crackers (5" by 2½" each)
¾ cup margarine or butter (1½ sticks), softened
1 cup packed light brown sugar
¾ cup granulated sugar
1 tablespoon vanilla extract
4 large eggs
1½ cups all-purpose flour
2¼ teaspoons baking powder
1 teaspoon salt
1 cup walnuts or pecans, coarsely chopped
1 bar (7 to 8 ounces) semisweet or milk
  chocolate bars, cut into small pieces
2 cups mini marshmallows

1 Preheat oven to 350°F. Grease 13" by 9" metal baking pan. Line pan with foil; grease and flour foil.

2 Coarsely crumble enough graham crackers to equal 1 cup pieces; set aside. With rolling pin, crush remaining graham crackers to equal ½ cup fine crumbs.

3 In heavy 3-quart saucepan, melt margarine or butter over low heat. Remove saucepan from heat. With spoon, stir in sugars and vanilla, then stir in eggs until well blended.

4 On waxed paper, combine flour, baking powder, salt, and finely crushed graham-cracker crumbs; stir into mixture in saucepan just until blended. Stir in chopped nuts.

5 Spread batter evenly in pan. Bake 30 minutes or until top is lightly golden. Remove pan from oven and sprinkle with graham-cracker pieces, chocolate pieces, and marshmallows. Bake 10 minutes longer or until marshmallows are puffed and golden. Cool completely in pan on wire rack. When cool, cut lengthwise into 4 strips, then cut each strip crosswise into 6 pieces. Makes 2 dozen bars.

Each bar: About 260 calories, 3 g protein, 36 g carbohydrate, 12 g total fat (2 g saturated), 0 g fiber, 36mg cholesterol, 250 mg sodium.

Chocolate-Chip Biscotti

PREP: 45 MINUTES PLUS COOLING • BAKE: 40 MINUTES

These crunchy dippers are like grown-up chocolate-chip cookies.

2 cups all-purpose flour
1 cup sugar
1 teaspoon baking powder
¼ teaspoon salt
Pinch ground cinnamon
4 tablespoons cold margarine or butter
3 large eggs, lightly beaten
6 ounces semisweet-chocolate mini chips (1 cup)
1 cup walnuts, toasted and coarsely chopped
1 teaspoon vanilla extract

1 Preheat oven to 350°F. In large bowl, mix flour, sugar, baking powder, salt, and cinnamon. With pastry blender or 2 knives used scissor-fashion, cut in margarine or butter until mixture resembles fine crumbs.

2 Spoon 1 tablespoon beaten eggs into cup; reserve. Add chocolate chips, walnuts, vanilla, and remaining beaten eggs to flour mixture; stir until evenly moistened. With hand, knead mixture a few times in bowl until dough forms.

3 On floured surface, with floured hands, divide dough into quarters. Shape each quarter into a 9" by 2" log. Place logs crosswise, 4 inches apart, on 2 large cookie sheets. With pastry brush, brush tops and sides of logs with reserved egg. Bake logs 25 minutes. Cool logs on cookie sheet on wire rack 10 minutes.

4 Place 1 log on cutting board. With serrated knife, cut warm log crosswise into ½-inch-thick diagonal slices. Place slices upright, ¼ inch apart, on cookie sheets. Repeat with remaining logs. Bake slices 15 minutes to allow biscotti to dry out. Cool completely on sheets on wire racks. (Biscotti will harden as they cool.) Store biscotti in tightly covered container. Makes about 5 dozen biscotti.

Each biscotti: About 65 calories, 1 g protein, 9 g carbohydrate, 3 g total fat (0 g saturated), 0 g fiber, 11 mg cholesterol, 30 mg sodium.

FORTUNE COOKIES

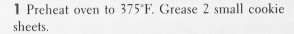

These better-than-storebought treats are made from a simple batter. Because the cookies must be shaped quickly while still hot, bake only 2 at a time. For the fortunes, use your favorite colored papers (cut into 3" by ½" strips) and write personalized messages for each family member.

PREP: 45 MINUTES
BAKE: ABOUT 4 MINUTES PER BATCH

2 tablespoons butter (no substitutions)
¼ cup confectioners' sugar
1 large egg white
1 teaspoon vanilla extract
Pinch salt
¼ cup all-purpose flour
14 strips paper (3" by ½" each) with fortunes

1 Preheat oven to 375°F. Grease 2 small cookie sheets.

2 In 1-quart saucepan, heat butter over low heat until melted. Remove saucepan from heat. With wire whisk, beat in confectioners' sugar, egg white, vanilla, and salt until blended. Beat in flour until batter is smooth.

3 Drop 1 heaping teaspoon batter onto cookie sheet. Repeat with another teaspoon batter, at least 4 inches away from first. With small metal spatula or back of spoon, spread batter evenly to form two 3-inch rounds.

4 Bake about 4 minutes or until cookies are lightly golden. Loosen both cookies with metal spatula. Working with 1 cookie at a time, place a fortune across center of hot cookie. Fold hot cookie in half, forming a semicircle, and press edges together (**A**). Quickly fold semicircle over edge of small bowl to create fortune-cookie shape (**B**). Repeat with other cookie. Let shaped cookies cool completely on wire rack.

5 Repeat with remaining batter and strips of fortune paper to make 14 cookies in all, cooling cookie sheets in between batches, and regreasing sheets as necessary. Store cookies in container up to 2 weeks. Makes about 14 cookies.

Each cookie: About 35 calories, 1 g protein, 4 g carbohydrate, 2 g total fat (1 g saturated), 0 g fiber, 4 mg cholesterol, 30 mg sodium.

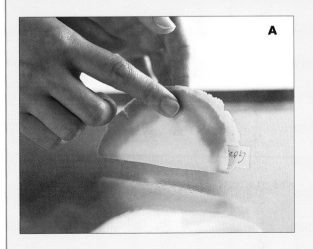

Peppermint Meringues

PREP: 15 MINUTES PLUS DRYING • BAKE: 2 HOURS

4 large egg whites
¼ teaspoon cream of tartar
1 cup confectioners' sugar
¼ teaspoon peppermint extract*
Red and green food coloring

1 Preheat oven to 225°F. Line 2 large cookie sheets with foil.

2 In small bowl, with mixer at high speed, beat egg whites and cream of tartar until soft peaks form; gradually sprinkle in sugar, beating until whites stand in stiff, glossy peaks. Beat in peppermint extract.

3 Transfer half of meringue mixture to another bowl. Add enough red food coloring to meringue in 1 bowl to tint it a pale red. Add enough green food coloring to remaining meringue to tint it a pale green.

4 Spoon red meringue into large self-sealing plastic bag; cut ¼-inch opening at corner. Repeat with green meringue in separate bag. Fit large decorating bag (we used a 14-inch bag) with basketweave or large round tip (½-inch- or ¾-inch-diameter opening). Place decorating bag in 2-cup glass measuring cup to stabilize bag; fold top third of bag over top of cup to keep top of bag clean. Simultaneously, squeeze meringues from both plastic bags into decorating bag, filling decorating bag no more than two-thirds full.

5 Pipe meringue onto cookie sheets, leaving 1 inch between each meringue. If using basketweave tip, pipe meringue into 3- to 4-inch long pleated ribbons; if using round tip, pipe meringue into 2-inch rounds. Bake meringues 2 hours. Turn oven off. Leave meringues in oven at least 30 minutes or overnight to dry.

6 Let meringues cool completely before removing from foil with wide metal spatula. Store meringues in tightly covered containers up to 3 weeks. Makes about 4½ dozen meringues.

*Do not use peppermint extract containing peppermint oil—the meringue mixture will quickly deflate. We had good results using imitation peppermint extract.

Each meringue: About 10 calories, 0 g protein, 2 g carbohydrate, 0 g total fat, 0 g fiber, 0 mg cholesterol, 5 mg sodium.

Pignoli Cookies

PREP: 45 MINUTES • BAKE: 10 TO 12 MINUTES PER BATCH

The secret to the success here are Mediterranean or Italian pine nuts, which are torpedo-shaped. They have a more delicate flavor than the flatter Chinese pine nuts.

1 tube or can (7 to 8 ounces) almond paste,
    crumbled into large pieces
¾ cup confectioners' sugar
1 large egg white
1 tablespoon plus 1 teaspoon honey
⅓ cup pine nuts (pignoli)

1 Preheat oven to 350°F. In food processor with knife blade attached, blend crumbled almond paste and confectioners' sugar until mixture resembles fine crumbs.

2 In large bowl, with mixer at low speed, beat almond-paste mixture, egg white, and honey until blended. Increase speed to high; beat 5 minutes or until very smooth, occasionally scraping bowl with rubber spatula (mixture will be thick).

3 Line large cookie sheet with kitchen parchment or greased foil. Spoon almond mixture into large decorating bag with large round tip (½-inch-diameter opening). Pipe mixture onto lined cookie sheet into 1¼-inch rounds, 2 inches apart. With moistened fingertip, gently smooth surface of each cookie. Sprinkle with pine nuts; lightly press to cover tops of cookies.

4 Bake cookies 10 to 12 minutes, until golden brown. Cool cookies completely on cookie sheet on wire rack. If you want to reuse cookie sheet right away, slide parchment or foil, with cookies attached, onto wire rack, and let cookies cool completely on parchment or foil. Repeat with remaining almond mixture.

5 When cool, carefully peel cookies off parchment or foil. Store cookies in tightly covered container up to 2 weeks. Makes about 2 dozen cookies.

Each cookie: About 70 calories, 2 g protein, 9 g carbohydrate, 3 g total fat (0 g saturated), 0 g fiber, 0 mg cholesterol, 5 mg sodium.

*Clockwise from lower lefthand corner:
Peppermint Meringues (above, left), Vanilla Kipferl
(page 215), Grandma's Rolled Crescents (page 218),
Cream Cheese-Walnut Cookies (page 219), Molasses
Lace Rolls (page 216), Palmiers (page 212)* ➤

Palmiers

PREP: 35 MINUTES PLUS RESTING
BAKE: 15 MINUTES PER BATCH

This version of palmiers starts with quick, or mock, puff pastry and turns out beautifully flaky in half the time that traditional puff pastry takes.

3 cups all-purpose flour
1½ cups butter (3 sticks), cut up (no substitutions)
¾ cup sour cream
1 cup sugar

1 Measure flour into large bowl. With pastry blender or 2 knives used scissor-fashion, cut butter into flour until mixture resembles coarse crumbs. Stir in sour cream. Transfer mixture to lightly floured work surface and knead until dough holds together. Flatten dough to 8" by 6" rectangle. Wrap in plastic wrap and refrigerate until firm enough to roll, at least 2½ hours or overnight.

2 Preheat oven to 400°F. Sprinkle ½ cup sugar onto work surface. Divide dough in half. Wrap half and return to refrigerator. Roll remaining half of dough on sugar to 14-inch square. Using side of hand, make an indentation down center of dough. Starting at 1 side, tightly roll dough until it reaches indentation. Repeat with other side, incorporating as much sugar as possible into dough. Refrigerate roll 2 hours or up to 3 days, or freeze up to 3 weeks.

3 Repeat with second half of dough and remaining ½ cup sugar.

4 With serrated knife, cut roll crosswise into ¼-inch-thick slices. (Return roll to refrigerator if it becomes too soft to slice.) Place slices, 2 inches apart, on ungreased large cookie sheet.

5 Bake 10 minutes; carefully turn cookies over and bake 5 minutes longer or until sugar has caramelized and cookies are deep golden. Let cookies remain on cookie sheet on wire rack 1 minute to cool slightly. Transfer cookies to wire rack to cool completely. Repeat with remaining dough. Store cookies in tightly covered container up to 1 week. Makes about 6 dozen cookies.

Each cookie: About 70 calories, 1 g protein, 7 g carbohydrate, 4 g total fat (3 g saturated), 0 g fiber, 11 mg cholesterol, 40 mg sodium.

Chocolate-Hazelnut Macaroons

PREP: 30 MINUTES PLUS COOLING
BAKE: 10 TO 12 MINUTES PER BATCH

GH Food Director Susan Westmoreland remembers that when she was 6, her great-uncle from Italy arrived bearing the largest box of chocolates that she'd ever seen. They were chocolate-hazelnut Baci, and she fell in love with the flavor combination. Although these chewy-crisp cookies are scrumptious on their own, you can make them even more elegant by sandwiching 2 together with some melted chocolate.

1 cup hazelnuts (filberts), toasted (opposite page)
1 cup sugar
¼ cup unsweetened cocoa
1 ounce unsweetened chocolate, chopped
⅛ teaspoon salt
2 large egg whites
1 teaspoon vanilla extract

1 Preheat oven to 350°F. Line large cookie sheet with kitchen parchment or foil.

2 In food processor with knife blade attached, blend toasted hazelnuts with sugar, cocoa, chocolate, and salt until finely ground. Add egg whites and vanilla, and process until blended.

3 Remove blade from processor. Drop batter by rounded teaspoons, 2 inches apart, on cookie sheet. If necessary, with moistened fingertip, push batter from teaspoon. Bake cookies 10 minutes or until tops feel firm when lightly pressed. Cool cookies completely on cookie sheet on wire rack. If you want to reuse cookie sheet right away, let cookies cool slightly, about 5 minutes, then slide parchment or foil, with cookies attached, onto wire rack and let cookies cool completely.

4 When cool, carefully peel cookies off parchment or foil. Store cookies in tightly covered container up to 2 weeks. Makes about 3 dozen cookies.

Each cookie: About 50 calories, 1 g protein, 7 g carbohydrate, 3 g total fat (1 g saturated), 1 g fiber, 0 mg cholesterol, 10 mg sodium.

Garden-Party Sugar Cookies

PREP: 30 MINUTES PLUS CHILLING AND COOLING
BAKE: 12 TO 14 MINUTES PER BATCH

These crisp, buttery treats are speckled with thyme and crystallized ginger. Make and freeze dough in logs, then slice and bake up to 1 month later.

2½ cups all-purpose flour
1 teaspoon baking soda
1 teaspoon cream of tartar
½ teaspoon salt
2 cups confectioners' sugar
1 cup margarine or butter (2 sticks), softened
1 large egg
1 tablespoon freshly grated lemon peel
1 tablespoon fresh thyme leaves (preferably
    lemon thyme), minced
1 tablespoon minced crystallized ginger

1 On waxed paper, combine flour, baking soda, cream of tartar, and salt.

2 In large bowl, with mixer at low speed, beat confectioners' sugar with margarine or butter until blended. Increase speed to high; beat until creamy. Reduce speed to low; beat in egg, lemon peel, thyme, and ginger, then beat in flour mixture just until blended.

3 Divide dough in half. Shape each half into 12" by 1½" squared-off log; wrap each log with plastic wrap. Freeze 2 hours or until firm enough to slice. (Or, logs can be frozen up to 1 month.)

4 Preheat oven to 350°F. Cut 1 log into ¼-inch-thick slices. Place slices, 1 inch apart, on ungreased large cookie sheets. Bake 12 to 14 minutes, until edges are golden brown. Transfer to wire rack to cool. Repeat with remaining log. Store cookies in tightly covered container up to 2 weeks. Makes about 8 dozen cookies.

Each cookie: About 40 calories, 0 g protein, 5 g carbohydrate, 2 g total fat (0 g saturated), 0 g fiber, 2 mg cholesterol, 50 mg sodium.

TOASTING NUTS

When cookie recipes call for nuts, we often specify that they be toasted (see Grandma's Rolled Crescents, page 218, and Chocolate-Hazelnut Macaroons, at left). That's because a few minutes of warmth and a quick shake in the pan bring out the deep, rich flavor of every nut from almonds to pecans.

Follow our toasting guidelines for best (no-burn) results. We even included a few ingredients that aren't quite nuts, but they taste so good browned that we couldn't resist! Toast nuts whole (without shells), then chop with a chef's knife. If you chop them before toasting, they burn quickly. For all of these edibles:

1 Preheat regular or toaster oven to 350°F.
2 Place nuts (or seeds) in single layer in metal baking pan (not cookie sheet).
3 Shake pan or stir nuts occasionally. Stir from edge (where they cook more quickly) to center and vice versa; watch carefully.

4 Immediately transfer to cool plate (otherwise, they'll continue to brown in the hot pan).

Almonds, macadamia nuts, pecans, raw cashews, raw shelled peanuts, walnuts, flaked coconut, and *sunflower seeds* or *pumpkin seeds*: Heat 10 to 15 minutes, until lightly browned.

Hazelnuts (with skins): Heat 15 minutes or until portions of nuts without skin are light brown. Wrap hot nuts in clean cloth towel. With hands, roll nuts back and forth to remove most of skin, which tastes bitter.

Shortcut for small amounts: (½ cup or less): Cook nuts in dry, ungreased skillet over low heat, until lightly browned (about 3 to 5 minutes), shaking or stirring often.

Expert tip: If you're making a basic drop-cookie batter (like oatmeal or chocolate-chip), fold in ½ cup toasted nuts—your choice—for irresistible flavor and texture.

Ginger Gems

PREP: 40 MINUTES PLUS COOLING
BAKE: 15 TO 16 MINUTES PER BATCH

GH's Associate Publisher Sean Sullivan fondly remembers these goodies from his childhood. The mother of one of his friends gave us this recipe from her grandmother, who grew up in the spice-trade town of Nuremberg, Germany. The recipe makes 7 dozen cookies; if you like, freeze half the dough for up to 2 months to use another time.

3¾ cups all-purpose flour
1 tablespoon ground ginger
1 tablespoon ground cinnamon
1 teaspoon baking soda
½ teaspoon salt
1 cup margarine or butter (2 sticks), softened
1 cup granulated sugar
1 cup packed brown sugar
1 cup unsweetened applesauce
1 large egg
1 tablespoon vanilla extract
1½ cups cornflakes
1 cup quick-cooking oats, uncooked
1 cup crystallized ginger, finely chopped
1 cup pecans, finely chopped
3 cups sweetened shredded coconut

1 Preheat oven to 350°F. In large bowl, combine flour, ground ginger, cinnamon, baking soda, and salt. In another large bowl, with mixer at low speed, beat margarine or butter with granulated and brown sugars until blended. Increase speed to high and beat until light and creamy, occasionally scraping bowl with rubber spatula. At low speed, beat in applesauce, egg, and vanilla until blended (mixture will look curdled).

2 At low speed, beat in cornflakes, oats, crystallized ginger, pecans, and 1 cup coconut just until blended. With spoon, stir in flour mixture (use hands if necessary to mix thoroughly).

3 Drop dough by heaping tablespoons, 2 inches apart, on ungreased large cookie sheet. Top each cookie with a scant ½ teaspoon remaining coconut. With floured flat-bottomed glass, gently press each dough mound to flatten to about ½ inch thick.

4 Bake 15 to 16 minutes, until cookies are lightly browned. Transfer cookies to wire rack to cool.

Repeat with remaining dough and coconut. Store cookies in tightly covered container up to 1 week. Makes about 7 dozen cookies.

Each cookie: About 105 calories, 1 g protein, 15 g carbohydrate, 5 g total fat (2 g saturated), 2 g fiber, 3 mg cholesterol, 80 mg sodium.

Scottish Shortbread

PREP: 15 MINUTES PLUS COOLING
BAKE: 1 HOUR 10 MINUTES

Harriet Sharrard (Executive Administrator at GH) was raised north of London and grew up enjoying her mother's traditional Edinburgh recipe. The semolina flour adds an interesting texture to these buttery wedges—"biscuits," as Harriet and her mum call them—and remind Harriet of afternoon tea at home in Britain.

¾ cup butter (1½ sticks), softened (no substitutions)
⅓ cup plus 1 tablespoon sugar

Scottish Shortbread and Pecan Triangles (page 202)

1½ cups all-purpose flour
½ cup finely ground semolina flour

1 Preheat oven to 300°F. In large bowl, with mixer at low speed, beat butter and ⅓ cup sugar until blended. Increase speed to high and beat until light and creamy, occasionally scraping bowl.

2 With hand, mix both kinds of flour into butter mixture just until crumbs form. (Do not overwork dough or shortbread will be tough.) Pat shortbread crumbs into ungreased 9-inch round tart pan with removable bottom or cake pan. With fork, prick dough all over in a decorative pattern. Sprinkle with remaining tablespoon of sugar.

3 Bake shortbread 1 hour 10 minutes or until lightly browned around the edge. Let cool in pan on wire rack 10 minutes.

4 Remove shortbread from pan to cutting board. While still warm, cut shortbread into 16 wedges. Cool wedges completely on wire rack. Store cookies in tightly covered container up to 1 week. Makes 16 cookies.

Each cookie: About 155 calories, 2 g protein, 18 g carbohydrate, 9 g total fat (5 g saturated), 0 g fiber, 23 mg cholesterol, 85 mg sodium.

Vanilla Kipferl

PREP: 1 HOUR 15 MINUTES PLUS COOLING
BAKE: 15 MINUTES PER BATCH

Test Kitchen Assistant Herta Guhl remembers her mother baking these tasty almond crescents when Herta was a child in Staschwitz, Germany. Herta still makes them every holiday even after living in the United States for 39 years.

1 cup blanched almonds, toasted
⅔ cup granulated sugar
1 cup butter (2 sticks), softened (no substitutions)
2½ cups all-purpose flour
3 large egg yolks
6 packages (0.32 ounces each) vanilla sugar (about ¾ cup)*
¾ cup confectioners' sugar

1 In food processor with knife blade attached, blend almonds and ⅓ cup granulated sugar until almonds are very finely ground.

2 In large bowl, with mixer at low speed, beat butter and remaining ⅓ cup sugar until blended, occasionally scraping bowl with rubber spatula. Increase speed to high; beat until light and creamy, about 2 minutes. At low speed, gradually beat in flour, almond mixture, and egg yolks until blended. With hand, press dough together and knead dough a few times. Divide dough in half.

3 Preheat oven to 325°F. Working with half of dough at a time, shape dough by level teaspoons into 1½-inch crescents (dough may be crumbly—heat of hands will help dough to stick together). Place crescents, 1½ inches apart, on 2 ungreased large cookie sheets.

4 Bake cookies on 2 oven racks 15 minutes or until lightly browned around the edges, rotating cookie sheets between upper and lower racks halfway through baking time. Cool cookies on cookie sheets on wire racks 3 minutes.

5 Meanwhile, in medium bowl, combine vanilla sugar with confectioners' sugar. While still warm, gently roll cookies, 1 at a time, in sugar mixture to coat. Place cookies on rack to cool completely. When cool, gently roll cookies in sugar mixture again.

6 Repeat with remaining dough and sugar mixture. Store cookies in tightly covered container up to 4 weeks. Makes about 9½ dozen cookies.

*Vanilla sugar is available in some supermarkets. To make your own vanilla sugar: With kitchen shears, cut a 3-inch-long piece of vanilla bean into small pieces. Place vanilla-bean pieces in blender with 1 cup granulated sugar and pulse blender on and off until very finely ground.

Each cookie: About 45 calories, 1g protein, 0 g carbohydrate, 2 g total fat (1 g saturated), 0 g fiber, 10 mg cholesterol, 15 mg sodium.

Molasses Lace Rolls

PREP: 30 MINUTES PLUS COOLING
BAKE: 8 MINUTES PER BATCH

GH Cookbook Editor Lisa Brainerd-Burge's family has been stocking the cookie jar with these lovely nibbles for 4 decades. The recipe came from a 1950's Illinois community cookbook called *Ladies of Lake Forest*.

½ cup light (mild) molasses
½ cup butter (1 stick), no substitutions
½ cup sugar
1 cup all-purpose flour
½ teaspoon baking powder
¼ teaspoon baking soda

1 Preheat oven to 350°F. Grease large cookie sheet.

2 In 2-quart saucepan, heat molasses, butter, and sugar to boiling over medium heat, stirring often. Boil 1 minute. Remove saucepan from heat; gradually stir in flour, baking powder, and baking soda until combined. Place saucepan in skillet of hot water to keep batter warm.

3 Drop batter by heaping teaspoons onto cookie sheet, 3 inches apart. (Do not place more than 6 on cookie sheet because, after baking, cookies must be shaped quickly before hardening.) Bake cookies 8 minutes or until lacy and lightly browned.

4 Remove cookie sheet from oven; cool about 1 minute to let cookies set slightly. Then, with wide metal spatula, quickly loosen and turn cookies over. One at a time, roll cookies around handle of wooden spoon. (If cookies get too hard to roll, reheat on cookie sheet in oven 1 minute to soften.) Remove cookies from spoon handle and cool on wire rack. Repeat with remaining batter. Store cookies in tightly covered container up to 2 weeks. Makes about 3½ dozen cookies.

Each cookie: About 50 calories, 0 g protein, 7 g carbohydrate, 2 g total fat (1 g saturated), 0 g fiber, 6 mg cholesterol, 35 mg sodium.

Molasses Cookies

PREP: 40 MINUTES PLUS CHILLING
BAKE: 10 TO 12 MINUTES PER BATCH

When she was a girl, Amy Callaway (Sales Planner at GH) used to love rolling this cookie dough into balls and coating them with sugar. Try them this year with your little helpers!

¾ cup margarine or butter (1½ sticks)
¼ cup light (mild) molasses
1¼ cups sugar
1 large egg
2 cups all-purpose flour
2 teaspoons baking soda
1 teaspoon ground cinnamon
½ teaspoon ground ginger
½ teaspoon salt
¼ teaspoon ground cloves

1 Preheat oven to 375°F. In 3-quart saucepan, melt margarine or butter over low heat. Remove saucepan from heat and, with wire whisk, beat in molasses and 1 cup sugar until blended; whisk in egg. With spoon, stir in flour and remaining ingredients until mixed.

2 Transfer dough to medium bowl and freeze 15 minutes or until firm enough to handle. Spread remaining ¼ cup sugar on waxed paper. Roll dough into 1-inch balls; roll balls in sugar to coat.

3 Place balls, 2½ inches apart, on ungreased large cookie sheet. Bake cookies 10 to 12 minutes, until cookies spread and darken. Let cookies remain on cookie sheet on wire rack 1 minute to cool slightly. Transfer cookies to wire rack to cool completely. Repeat with remaining dough. Store cookies in tightly covered container up to 2 weeks. Makes about 6 dozen cookies.

Each cookie: About 45 calories, 1 g protein, 7 g carbohydrate, 2 g total fat (0 g saturated), 0 g fiber, 3 mg cholesterol, 75 mg sodium.

Italian Angelette Cookies

PREP: 45 MINUTES PLUS COOLING
BAKE: 20 MINUTES PER BATCH

Steven Zara (Staff Engineer at GH) asked his wife, Olga, if she'd share one of her family's Christmas cookie recipes for this story. She didn't hesitate a moment to offer the Camoia family recipe for Italian egg cookies. Although Olga's family traditionally rolled pieces of dough into pencil-thin strips and then coiled the strips into a pyramid, we found that shaping the dough into balls was easier.

1 cup granulated sugar
4 tablespoons margarine or butter, softened
6 large eggs
½ teaspoon vanilla or lemon extract
4 cups all-purpose flour
1 tablespoon baking powder
½ teaspoon salt
2 cups confectioners' sugar
½ cup colored candy décors

1 Preheat oven to 325°F. Grease large cookie sheet.

2 In large bowl, with mixer at low speed, beat granulated sugar and margarine or butter until blended. Increase speed to high; beat 2 minutes, occasionally scraping bowl with rubber spatula. At low speed, beat in eggs, 1 at a time; beat in vanilla or lemon extract until mixed. Beat in flour, baking powder, and salt just until blended.

3 With heavily floured hands, shape dough into 1½-inch balls. Place balls, 2 inches apart, on cookie sheet. Bake cookies 20 minutes or until lightly browned. Transfer cookies to wire rack to cool. Repeat with remaining dough.

4 When cookies are cool, in small bowl, whisk confectioners' sugar and *3 tablespoons plus 1½ teaspoons water* until blended. Dip top of each cooled cookie into glaze. (Whisk more water into glaze if it becomes too thick.) Place cookies on wire rack set over waxed paper to catch any drips. Sprinkle with candy décors. Allow glaze to set, about 20 minutes. Store cookies in tightly covered container, with waxed paper between layers, up to 2 weeks. Makes about 4 dozen cookies.

Each cookie: About 95 calories, 2 g protein, 18 g carbohydrate, 2 g total fat (0 g saturated), 0 g fiber, 27 mg cholesterol, 65 mg sodium.

Gwen's Almond Slices

PREP: 25 MINUTES PLUS COOLING
BAKE: 10 MINUTES PER BATCH

GH Food Associate Lisa Troland's mother-in-law, Gwen Stebner, is famous in South St. Paul, MN, for these pretty nut-flecked cookies. She loves making a batch on the spur of the moment when her family asks for a treat. The dough can be refrigerated up to 1 week or frozen up to 3 months before slicing and baking.

1¾ cups sugar
1 cup margarine or butter (2 sticks), softened
¼ cup light (mild) molasses
1 tablespoon ground ginger
1 tablespoon vanilla extract
1 teaspoon baking soda
1 teaspoon salt
2 large eggs
4 cups all-purpose flour
2 cups sliced almonds

1 In large bowl, with mixer at medium speed, beat sugar, margarine or butter, molasses, ginger, vanilla, baking soda, salt, eggs, and 2 cups flour.

2 With wooden spoon, stir in almonds and remaining 2 cups flour; if necessary, use hands to mix thoroughly, as dough will be very stiff.

3 Divide dough in half. Shape each half into 10" by 3" by 1" brick; wrap each brick with plastic wrap. Refrigerate 4 hours or until firm enough to slice.

4 Preheat oven to 400°F. Grease large cookie sheet. With serrated knife, cut 1 brick into scant ¼-inch-thick slices. Place slices, 1 inch apart, on cookie sheet. Bake 10 minutes or until golden. Transfer cookies to wire rack to cool. Repeat with remaining brick. Store cookies in tightly covered container up to 2 weeks. Makes about 7 dozen cookies.

Each cookie: About 75 calories, 1 g protein, 10 g carbohydrate, 3 g total fat (1 g saturated), 0 g fiber, 5 mg cholesterol, 70 mg sodium.

Anna's Spice Thins

PREP: 45 MINUTES PLUS CHILLING AND COOLING
BAKE: 10 TO 12 MINUTES PER BATCH

Associate Food Director Debby Goldsmith's childhood nanny made these delicious Swedish cookies a Goldsmith family tradition. These fluted rounds are crisp and buttery and keep very, very well.

1 cup butter (2 sticks), softened (no substitutions)
1 cup sugar
½ cup dark corn syrup
½ cup heavy or whipping cream
2½ teaspoons baking soda
2 teaspoons ground cinnamon
2 teaspoons ground cloves
2 teaspoons ground ginger
4 cups all-purpose flour

1 In large bowl, with mixer at low speed, beat butter and sugar until blended. Increase speed to high; beat until light and creamy, occasionally scraping bowl with rubber spatula. At low speed, beat in corn syrup, cream, baking soda, cinnamon, cloves, and ginger until blended. Then gradually beat in flour until well mixed.

2 Divide dough into 8 pieces; wrap each piece with plastic wrap and refrigerate overnight.

3 Preheat oven to 350°F. On lightly floured surface, with floured rolling pin, roll 1 piece of dough at a time ⅛ inch thick. With floured 3-inch round fluted cookie cutter, cut dough into as many cookies as possible. Place cookies, 1 inch apart, on ungreased large cookie sheet. Reserve trimmings.

4 Bake cookies 10 to 12 minutes, until lightly browned. Transfer cookies to wire rack to cool. Repeat with remaining dough and trimmings to make more cookies. Makes about 7½ dozen cookies.

Each cookie: About 55 calories, 1 g protein, 8 g carbohydrate, 3 g total fat (2 g saturated), 0 g fiber, 7 mg cholesterol, 60 mg sodium.

Grandma's Rolled Crescents

PREP: 1 HOUR 15 MINUTES PLUS CHILLING AND COOLING
BAKE: 25 MINUTES PER BATCH

GH Fiction Editor Lee Quarfoot's grandmother, Mary Charney, made these when she was a young girl living at a parish in Ukraine. The priests she cooked for loved the flaky, not too sweet cookies. When she came to the United States in 1910, she brought this recipe with her. You can fill the dough with your favorite fruit preserves or almond paste instead of prune butter.

1 cup walnuts, toasted (see page 213)
½ cup plus 2 tablespoons granulated sugar
3¼ cups all-purpose flour
2½ teaspoons baking powder
½ teaspoon salt
1 cup cold butter (2 sticks), cut up (no substitutions)
2 large eggs
1 teaspoon almond extract
⅓ cup plus 2 tablespoons milk
1 jar (17 ounces) lekvar (prune butter), about 1½ cups
Confectioners' sugar

1 In food processor with knife blade attached, blend walnuts and ¼ cup granulated sugar until finely ground. Add flour, baking powder, and salt; pulse until blended. Add butter and pulse until coarse crumbs form. Add eggs, almond extract, and ⅓ cup milk, and pulse until dough just begins to form and comes away from side of work bowl. Gather dough together and pat into a ball. Divide dough into 6 equal pieces. Wrap each piece with plastic wrap and refrigerate until firm enough to roll, at least 2 hours or overnight.

2 In medium bowl, mix lekvar with ¼ cup granulated sugar. Grease 2 large cookie sheets.

3 On floured surface, with floured rolling pin, roll 1 piece of chilled dough into a 9-inch round, keeping remaining dough refrigerated. Spread dough with ¼ cup lekvar mixture. With pastry wheel or sharp knife, cut dough into 8 equal wedges. Starting at curved edge, roll up each wedge, jelly-roll fashion. Place cookies, pointed end down, 2 inches apart, on cookie sheet. Repeat with 2 more pieces of dough.

4 Preheat oven to 350°F. With pastry brush, brush crescents with 1 tablespoon milk, then sprinkle with 1 tablespoon granulated sugar.

5 Bake crescents on 2 oven racks 25 minutes or until golden, rotating cookie sheets between upper and lower racks halfway through baking time. Immediately remove crescents to wire rack to cool.

6 Repeat with remaining 3 pieces of dough. Store in tightly covered container up to 2 weeks. Sprinkle with confectioners' sugar before serving. Makes 4 dozen cookies.

Each cookie: About 110 calories, 2 g protein, 13 g carbohydrate, 6 g total fat (3 g saturated), 1 g fiber, 19 mg cholesterol, 105 mg sodium.

Cream Cheese-Walnut Cookies

PREP: 30 MINUTES • BAKE: 14 TO 18 MINUTES PER BATCH

1 cup sugar
½ cup margarine or butter (1 stick), softened
1 package (3 ounces) cream cheese
1 teaspoon vanilla extract
1 cup all-purpose flour
½ cup walnuts, finely chopped

1 Preheat oven to 350°F. In large bowl, with mixer at low speed, beat sugar with margarine or butter and cream cheese until blended. Increase speed to high; beat until creamy, about 2 minutes, occasionally scraping bowl with rubber spatula. Beat in vanilla. With spoon, stir in flour and nuts just until blended.

2 With lightly floured hands, roll dough into 1-inch balls. Place balls, 2 inches apart, on ungreased large cookie sheet. With floured fingertips, flatten balls into 1¼-inch rounds.

3 Bake cookies 14 to 18 minutes, until golden. Let cookies remain on cookie sheet on wire rack 2 minutes to cool slightly. Transfer cookies to wire rack to cool completely. Repeat with remaining dough. Store cookies in tightly covered container up to 2 weeks. Makes about 5 dozen cookies.

Each cookie: About 45 calories, 1 g protein, 5 g carbohydrate, 3 g total fat (1 g saturated), 0 g fiber, 2 mg cholesterol, 25 mg sodium.

Rich Chocolate-Cherry Cookies

PREP: 30 MINUTES PLUS COOLING
BAKE: 13 TO 15 MINUTES PER BATCH

GH Food Associate Lori Perlmutter has been enjoying these chewy brownielike cookies for years, thanks to her fiancé's mom. "Every holiday season my family anxiously awaits the delivery of these heavenly cookies," Lori says. "They've sort of become a Perlmutter tradition!"

1 package (8 ounces) semisweet-chocolate
    squares, coarsely chopped
6 tablespoons margarine or butter, cut up
¾ cup sugar
2 teaspoons vanilla extract
2 large eggs
¼ cup all-purpose flour
¼ cup unsweetened cocoa
½ teaspoon baking powder
¼ teaspoon salt
1 package (6 ounces) semisweet-chocolate
    chips (1 cup)
1 cup dried tart cherries

1 Preheat oven to 350°F. In 3-quart saucepan, melt chocolate with margarine or butter over low heat, stirring frequently. Remove saucepan from heat and, with wire whisk, stir in sugar and vanilla until blended. Whisk in eggs, 1 at a time. With spoon, stir in flour, cocoa, baking powder, and salt. Add chocolate chips and cherries; stir just until evenly mixed.

2 Drop dough by rounded tablespoons, 1½ inches apart, onto ungreased large cookie sheet. Bake 13 to 15 minutes, until tops of cookies are set. Let cookies remain on cookie sheet on wire rack 1 minute to cool slightly. With wide metal spatula, transfer cookies to wire rack to cool completely. Repeat with remaining dough. Store cookies in tightly covered container up to 2 weeks. Makes about 3 dozen cookies.

Each cookie: About 105 calories, 1 g protein, 16 g carbohydrate, 5 g total fat (1 g saturated), 0 g fiber, 12 mg cholesterol, 55 mg sodium.

Mama Arena's Cuccidati

PREP: 1 HOUR PLUS COOLING
BAKE: 18 TO 20 MINUTES PER BATCH

Tony Arena (GH Senior Staff Engineer) brought us his mom's recipe for these treats, traditional in Sicilian homes during the Christmas season. The almond filling is made from scratch and flavored with orange, lemon, and cinnamon.

ALMOND FILLING:

1½ cups blanched whole almonds (8 ounces)
1 cup sugar
2 strips (3" by 1" each) fresh orange peel
1 strip (3" by 1") fresh lemon peel
¼ teaspoon ground cinnamon

DOUGH:

2¼ cups all-purpose flour
½ cup sugar
2 teaspoons baking powder
4 tablespoons cold margarine or butter
¼ cup vegetable shortening
¼ cup milk
1 large egg
1½ teaspoons freshly grated orange peel
Confectioners' sugar for garnish

1 Prepare Almond Filling: In food processor with knife blade attached, pulse almonds and sugar until almonds are very finely ground. Pour mixture into 2-quart saucepan. Add orange and lemon peels, cinnamon, and *1 cup water*. Heat almond mixture to boiling over medium-high heat, stirring occasionally. Reduce heat to medium-low and simmer, uncovered, until mixture is thick and pastelike, about 45 minutes, stirring occasionally. Discard citrus peels. Set mixture aside to cool.

2 Meanwhile, prepare Dough: In large bowl, combine flour, sugar, and baking powder. With pastry blender or 2 knives used scissor-fashion, cut in margarine or butter with shortening until mixture resembles fine crumbs. With fork, stir in milk, egg, and grated orange peel. With hand, knead flour mixture in bowl until dough forms; shape into a ball. Divide dough into 4 equal pieces.

3 Preheat oven to 375°F. Grease large cookie sheet. On floured surface, with floured rolling pin, roll 1 piece of dough into 12" by 5" rectangle. With moist fingertips, gently spread one-fourth almond mixture into 2-inch-wide strip lengthwise down center of dough, leaving ½-inch border at each end. Fold long sides of dough over filling, slightly overlapping; press gently to seal. With floured wide metal spatula, transfer log, seam side down, to lightly floured cutting board; cut crosswise into 16 slices. Place slices, 2 inches apart, on cookie sheet.

4 Bake cookies 18 to 20 minutes or until lightly browned. Transfer cookies to wire rack to cool completely. Repeat with remaining dough and filling. Sprinkle with confectioners' sugar to serve. Store in tightly covered container up to 1 week. Makes 64 cookies.

Each cookie: About 75 calories, 2 g protein, 10 g carbohydrate, 4 g total fat (1 g saturated), 1 g fiber, 4 mg cholesterol, 25 mg sodium.

STORING A STASH OF COOKIES

• Cool cookies completely before packing in tins or other containers so they don't stick together, become misshapen, or get soggy.

• Tuck treats into self-sealing bags with air squeezed out, metal tins (coffee cans work well), or sturdy plastic containers. Bar cookies can be stored in their baking pan, cut or uncut, covered with a layer of plastic wrap and foil.

• Keep cookies at room temperature for 1 to 2 weeks, or freeze for up to 2 to 3 months, or as recipe directs. To defrost, just unwrap and thaw at room temperature.

• Store soft cookies (like our Ginger Gems, page 214) with a wedge of apple or a slice of white bread to keep them moist; replace the fruit or bread every couple of days.

• If you plan to keep cookies for an extended period, don't dust them with confectioners' sugar, or glaze or fill them. The sugar will be absorbed, stealing that pretty white finish; the glaze may dry and crystallize; and the jam will harden. For best results, dust, glaze, or fill right before serving—or giving away.

EXPERT TIP: Wash cookie sheets by hand and place in oven (turned off but still warm from baking) to dry. The same trick works for metal tins; put upside down in oven.

Thumbprint Cookies

PREP: 40 MINUTES • BAKE: 20 MINUTES PER BATCH

Senior Copy Writer Alice Garbarini Hurley got this recipe from her mother-in-law, who bakes an assortment of treats for her famous "cookie tray" each Christmas in Bangor, ME.

2 large eggs
¾ cup margarine or butter (1½ sticks), softened
¾ cup sugar
½ teaspoon vanilla extract
½ teaspoon almond extract
¼ teaspoon salt
2 cups all-purpose flour
1¼ cups walnuts, finely chopped
½ cup favorite jam

1 Preheat oven to 350°F. Grease large cookie sheet.

2 In large bowl, with fork, beat eggs lightly. Measure out 3 tablespoons beaten egg and transfer to small bowl to use later.

3 Add margarine or butter, sugar, vanilla and almond extracts, and salt to eggs in large bowl; with mixer at medium speed, beat until evenly mixed, occasionally scraping bowl with rubber spatula. Add flour and stir just until blended.

4 Divide dough into 4 equal pieces. Divide each piece into 14 balls. Spread walnuts on waxed paper. Dip balls in reserved egg, then roll in walnuts, gently pressing nuts onto dough.

5 Place balls, 2 inches apart, on cookie sheet. With thumb, make small indentation in center of each ball. Bake cookies 20 minutes or until golden. Transfer cookies to wire rack. Immediately, fill each indentation with a rounded ¼ teaspoon of jam. Cool cookies completely on wire rack. Repeat with remaining balls and jam. When jam has set, store cookies, with waxed paper between layers, in tightly covered container up to 1 week. Makes 56 cookies.

Each cookie: About 90 calories, 1 g protein, 10 g carbohydrate, 5 g total fat (1 g saturated), 0 g fiber, 9 mg cholesterol, 55 mg sodium.

Pecan Tassies

PREP: 45 MINUTES PLUS COOLING • BAKE: 30 MINUTES

Editorial Assistant Amy Sims's grandma lives in Savannah, GA, and will do whatever it takes to get these cookies to her granddaughter every Christmas. Amy loves to have them with a glass of cold milk or a bowl of her grandmother's Southern ambrosia.

1 package (3 ounces) cream cheese, softened
8 tablespoons margarine or butter, softened
1 cup all-purpose flour
¾ cup packed light brown sugar
1 teaspoon vanilla extract
Pinch salt
1 large egg
⅔ cup pecans, chopped

1 Preheat oven to 350°F. In small bowl, with mixer at high speed, beat cream cheese with 7 tablespoons margarine or butter until creamy. Reduce speed to low; add flour and beat until well mixed.

2 With floured hands, divide dough into 24 equal pieces (dough will be very soft). With floured fingertips, gently press dough pieces evenly onto bottoms and up sides of twenty-four 1¾" by ¾" ungreased miniature muffin-pan cups.

3 In medium bowl, with wire whisk or fork, mix brown sugar, vanilla, salt, egg, and remaining 1 tablespoon margarine or butter until filling is blended.

4 Place half of pecans in pastry-lined cups. Spoon filling by heaping teaspoons into each pastry cup; sprinkle tops with remaining pecans.

5 Bake 30 minutes or until filling is set and edges of crust are golden. With tip of knife, gently loosen tassies from muffin-pan cups and place on wire rack to cool completely. Store tassies in tightly covered container up to 1 week. Makes 2 dozen tassies.

Each tassie: About 115 calories, 1 g protein, 11 g carbohydrate, 7 g total fat (2 g saturated), 0 g fiber, 13 mg cholesterol, 75 mg sodium.

Florentines

PREP: 45 MINUTES PLUS COOLING
BAKE: 10 MINUTES PER BATCH

This heirloom recipe is from GH Chemistry Department Research Assistant Doria Lavagnino. Although Austrian bakers have been credited with inventing these crisp, lacy cookies coated with chocolate, Doria's recipe was passed down from her Italian grandmother. Doria warns us to be gentle while spreading the chocolate, because the cookies are very fragile.

1 cup slivered almonds
1 container (3½ ounces) candied orange peel (about ½ cup)
6 tablespoons butter (no substitutions)
½ cup sugar
¼ cup heavy or whipping cream
2 tablespoons all-purpose flour
1 tablespoon light corn syrup
8 ounces semisweet chocolate, melted and cooled

1 Preheat oven to 350°F. Line large cookie sheet with kitchen parchment. In food processor with knife blade attached, blend almonds and orange peel until finely chopped.

2 In 1-quart saucepan, combine butter, sugar, cream, flour, and corn syrup; heat to boiling over medium heat, stirring frequently. Remove saucepan from heat; stir in almond mixture.

3 Drop batter by rounded teaspoons onto cookie sheet, about 3 inches apart. (Do not place more than 6 on cookie sheet because, after baking, cookies must be removed quickly before hardening.) Bake cookies 10 minutes or until lacy and lightly browned.

4 Remove cookie sheet from oven. Let cookies remain on cookie sheet on wire rack about 2 minutes to set slightly. Then, with wide metal spatula, transfer cookies to wire rack to cool completely. (If cookies become too hard to remove, reheat on cookie sheet in oven 1 minute to soften.) Repeat with remaining batter.

5 With small metal spatula, gently spread flat side of each cookie with chocolate. Return cookies to wire rack, chocolate side up, and let stand at room temperature until chocolate has set. Store cookies, with waxed paper between layers, in tightly covered container up to 1 week. Makes about 4 dozen cookies.

Each cookie: About 70 calories, 1 g protein, 8 g carbohydrate, 4 g total fat (1 g saturated), 0 g fiber, 6 mg cholesterol, 20 mg sodium.

Nana's Spritz Cookies

PREP: 20 MINUTES PLUS COOLING
BAKE: 15 TO 17 MINUTES PER BATCH

Terry Salimbene (GH Media/Research Manager) gave us her grandmother's wonderful recipe for buttery spritz cookies. Every Christmas, Terry bakes these beauties by the trayful for relatives and coworkers.

1 cup butter (2 sticks), softened (no substitutions)
¾ cup sugar
1 large egg
1 teaspoon almond extract
2 cups all-purpose flour

1 Preheat oven to 375°F. In large bowl, with mixer at low speed, beat butter with sugar until blended. Increase speed to high and beat until light and creamy, occasionally scraping bowl with rubber spatula. At low speed, beat in egg and almond extract until mixed. Beat in flour just until blended.

2 Spoon dough into cookie press or large decorating bag fitted with large star tip (¾-inch-diameter opening). Onto ungreased large cookie sheet, pipe dough into S shapes, 2½ inches long and 2 inches apart.

3 Bake cookies 15 to 17 minutes, until lightly browned around the edges. Let cookies remain on cookie sheet on wire rack 2 minutes to cool slightly. Transfer cookies to wire rack to cool completely. Repeat with remaining dough. Store cookies in tightly covered container up to 1 week. Makes about 1½ dozen cookies.

Each cookie: About 175 calories, 2 g protein, 19 g carbohydrate, 11 g total fat (6 g saturated), 0 g fiber, 39 mg cholesterol, 105 mg sodium.

DESSERTS

Fall Fruit Compote

PREP: 10 MINUTES • COOK: 30 MINUTES

Tiny anise seeds give pears, sweet apricots, tart cherries, and golden raisins delicate licorice flavor; serve with crunchy biscotti for a refreshing finale.

⅔ cup sugar
1 tablespoon anise seeds
4 firm but ripe Bartlett or Anjou pears (about 1¾ pounds), peeled, cored, and cut into ¼-inch-thick wedges
⅔ cup dried apricot halves (about 3 ounces)
½ cup dried tart cherries
½ cup golden raisins
2 tablespoons fresh lemon juice

1 In 3-quart saucepan, heat sugar, anise seeds, and *4 cups water* over high heat until syrup boils and sugar dissolves, stirring frequently. Reduce heat to medium and cook 10 minutes, stirring occasionally. Pour syrup through sieve into bowl; discard seeds and return syrup to saucepan.

2 Add pears to syrup; heat to boiling over medium-high heat. Reduce heat to medium-low; cover and simmer 5 minutes or until pears are tender. Stir in apricots, cherries, and raisins, and cook, covered, 1 minute longer. Remove saucepan from heat; stir in lemon juice. Serve compote warm, or cover and refrigerate to serve cold later. Makes about 6½ cups or 6 servings.

Each serving: About 260 calories, 2 g protein, 67 g carbohydrate, 1 g total fat (0 g saturated), 3 g fiber, 0 mg cholesterol, 4 mg sodium.

Fresh Fruit Salad with Lime Syrup

PREP: 30 MINUTES PLUS CHILLING • COOK: 5 MINUTES

2 limes
1 cup sugar
1 piece (7 pounds) watermelon (preferably seedless), cut into 1-inch chunks
1 medium pineapple, cut into 1-inch chunks
2 mangoes, cut into ¾-inch chunks
3 medium kiwifruit, peeled and sliced
3 large bananas, sliced

1 With vegetable peeler, remove 1-inch-wide strips of peel from both limes. With knife, cut away white pith, if any.

2 In small saucepan, heat sugar and ½ *cup water* to boiling over high heat; boil 3 minutes or until mixture becomes a light syrup (mixture will thicken upon chilling). Remove saucepan from heat; stir in peel from 1 lime. Cover and refrigerate syrup until well chilled, at least 3 hours or overnight. (Cover remaining lime peel with plastic wrap and refrigerate until ready to assemble salad.)

3 In large bowl, place watermelon, pineapple, and mango; cover and refrigerate. Up to 2 hours before serving, add kiwifruit and banana to bowl with other fruit. Toss fruit with lime syrup and reserved lime peel; cover and refrigerate if not serving right away. Makes about 20 cups or 20 servings.

Each serving: About 120 calories, 1 g protein, 29 g carbohydrate, 1 g total fat (0 g saturated), 2 g fiber, 0 mg cholesterol, 3 mg sodium.

Rosy Peach Melba

PREP: 15 MINUTES PLUS CHILLING
COOK: ABOUT 5 MINUTES

Less is more! This combination of juicy peaches and berries in a sweet rosé syrup calls for only 5 basic ingredients.

¾ cup sugar
4 ripe large peaches (about 2 pounds), peeled and cut into ½-inch wedges
½ pint raspberries
1½ cups rosé or blush wine
3 tablespoons fresh lemon juice
Mint sprigs for garnish

1 In 1-quart saucepan, heat sugar and *1 cup water* to boiling over high heat; boil 1 minute. Pour syrup into large bowl; cool to room temperature.

2 To bowl with syrup, add peaches, raspberries, wine, and lemon juice; stir gently to combine. Cover and refrigerate at least 2 hours or overnight. Garnish with mint to serve. Makes about 6 cups or 8 servings.

Each serving: About 150 calories, 1 g protein, 31 g carbohydrate, 0 g total fat, 2 g fiber, 0 mg cholesterol, 3 mg sodium.

Rosy Peach Melba ➤

Roasted Vanilla Pears

··

PREP: 25 MINUTES PLUS COOLING
ROAST: 35 TO 40 MINUTE

The fragrant vanilla syrup has a hint of lemon and caramelizes slightly during roasting.

1 medium lemon
1 whole vanilla bean*
8 firm but ripe Bosc pears (about 3½ pounds),
    unpeeled
½ cup sugar
2 tablespoons butter, melted (no substitutions)

1 Preheat oven to 450°F. From lemon, with vegetable peeler or small knife, remove two 2" by 1" strips of peel. Squeeze 1 tablespoon juice from lemon. Cut vanilla bean crosswise in half, then cut each half lengthwise, without cutting all the way through to the other side. With knife, scrape out seeds. Reserve seeds and pod.

2 With melon baller or small knife, remove core and blossom end (bottom) of each pear, but do not remove stems. If necessary, cut thin slice from bottom of each pear so it will stand upright. Sprinkle ½ teaspoon sugar into cored area of each pear; swirl pears to coat insides with sugar. With pastry brush, brush pears with some melted butter; set aside.

3 In shallow 10-inch round ceramic or glass baking

VANILLA VERDICT:
IS PURE EXTRACT BETTER THAN IMITATION?

Vanilla extract is a key ingredient for dessert makers because it imparts a delicate flavor to cakes, custards, syrups, and frostings. But do you really need to buy pure vanilla extract (which we use in the *Good Housekeeping* kitchens), or will imitation work just as well?

In a blind test, our 6 food editors compared pure extracts (which are made by steeping chopped, dried vanilla beans in a solution of grain alcohol and water) to imitation vanilla, a synthetic flavoring that usually costs several dollars less.

We included brands made with beans from the island of Madagascar, considered to be the finest—and most expensive—in the world, and from Tahiti, known for its intensely aromatic beans, as well as blended extracts flavored with imported beans from Madagascar and Mexico.

What we sampled: Trader Joe's Tahitian Blend Pure Vanilla Extract (4 ounces), $2.39; Nielsen-Massey Madagascar Bourbon Pure Vanilla Extract (8 ounces), $11; McCormick Pure Vanilla Extract (4 ounces), $8.59; and Master Choice Pure Vanilla Extract (4 ounces), $5.19. For the imitation extract, we tried McCormick Premium Quality Imitation Vanilla Extract (4 ounces), $4.29.

Taste tests: First we diluted 2 teaspoons of each extract in ¼ cup whole milk to get a handle on true flavor and aroma. We could instantly detect the mock vanilla because of the murky brown color of

the mixture and the artificial smell. But when we used the vanillas in a basic butter cake recipe, we could barely discern a flavor difference. The layers made with imitation vanilla were darker than the others (the extract contains caramel coloring, cocoa, and tea), but all the cakes smelled sweet and buttery and tasted delicious.

For our final check, we made a custard sauce; the extract is stirred in at the end, so its flavor stands out. All of the sauces had a fragrant aroma, but the one made with the imitation extract had a brownish tint and left a bitter aftertaste.

Dollar for dollar, what really matters is how you're going to use the vanilla. Because its high concentration of alcohol evaporates during baking or cooking, it's not a big deal if you use the imitation kind in cakes and muffins. But for frostings, custard sauces, whipped cream, and ice cream, we say splurge!

Shopper's Notes:

• Don't buy vanilla extract in Mexico. It may contain coumarin, a potentially toxic extract (banned by the Food and Drug Administration) that has been linked to liver and kidney damage.

• Imitation vanillas contain synthetic vanillin, made from wood-pulp by-products that are treated with chemicals. Unless an ingredient list includes "natural vanillin," the flavor came from a tree, not a bean.

dish, mix lemon-peel strips, lemon juice, vanilla-bean pod, vanilla seeds, remaining sugar, any remaining melted butter, and ½ *cup water*. Place pears, cored ends down, in baking dish.

4 Roast pears 35 to 40 minutes, until fork-tender. With meat baster or large spoon, baste pears several times during roasting with syrup in dish.

5 Cool pears slightly to serve warm. Or, cover and refrigerate pears up to 1 day ahead; reheat to serve warm. Makes 8 servings.

*If not using vanilla bean, increase lemon peel to 3 strips and stir 2 teaspoons vanilla extract into syrup after pears have been roasted.

Each serving: About 160 calories, 1 g protein, 34 g carbohydrate, 3 g total fat (2 g saturated), 4 g fiber, 8 mg cholesterol, 30 mg sodium.

Tarragon Poached Pears

PREP: 5 MINUTES • COOK: 45 MINUTES

Serve this simple, aromatic dessert warm or chilled—it's your call.

2 large lemons
1 cup dry white wine
1 cup sugar
1 large bunch fresh tarragon
4 large firm but ripe pears, such as Bartlett or Bosc (about 2 pounds)

1 From lemons, with vegetable peeler, remove 8 strips peel, 3" by 1" each, and squeeze 1 tablespoon juice.

2 In 4-quart saucepan, heat lemon peel, lemon juice, wine, sugar, *4 cups water*, and all but 1 sprig tarragon to boiling over high heat; boil 10 minutes.

3 Meanwhile, peel pears; cut each in half lengthwise. With melon baller or spoon, remove cores.

4 Add pears to wine mixture; heat to boiling. Reduce heat to low; cover and simmer 10 to 20 minutes, until pears are tender. With slotted spoon, transfer pears to large shallow bowl.

5 Heat poaching liquid to boiling over high heat; boil, uncovered, 15 minutes or until syrup is reduced to about 2 cups. Pour hot syrup through sieve over pears. Return lemon peels to syrup.

6 Cool pears slightly to serve warm. Or, to serve cold, cover and refrigerate at least 4 hours or until well chilled, turning pears occasionally.

7 To serve, thinly slice leaves of remaining tarragon sprig; sprinkle over pears and syrup. Makes 8 servings.

Each serving: About 205 calories, 1 g protein, 51 g carbohydrate, 0 g total fat, 2 g fiber, 0 mg cholesterol, 5 mg sodium.

Poached Pears with Fresh Ginger

PREP: 20 MINUTES PLUS CHILLING
COOK: ABOUT 40 MINUTES

This do-ahead dessert—with only 5 ingredients—is fat-free. We love the sweet and slightly spicy taste of the poaching liquid.

8 firm but ripe Bartlett or Bosc pears (about 3½ pounds)
1 cup sugar
1 cinnamon stick (about 3 inches)
2 strips (3" by 1" each) fresh orange peel
2-inch piece fresh ginger, peeled and cut crosswise into 16 thin slices

1 Peel pears. With melon baller or small knife, remove core and blossom end (bottom) of each pear.

2 In 6- or 8-quart Dutch oven, place all ingredients and *6 cups water*; heat to boiling over high heat. Reduce heat to low; cover and simmer 10 to 20 minutes, until pears are tender. With slotted spoon, transfer pears to large bowl.

3 Heat pear poaching liquid to boiling over high heat; cook, uncovered, over high heat about 15 minutes or until syrup is reduced to about 3 cups.

4 Gently pour hot syrup through strainer over pears. To syrup around pears, return cinnamon stick, orange-peel strips, and 3 slices ginger. Cover and refrigerate at least 4 hours or until pears are well chilled, turning pears occasionally. Serve pears with syrup. Makes 8 servings.

Each serving: About 175 calories, 1 g protein, 45 g carbohydrate, 1 g total fat (0 g saturated), 2 g fiber, 0 mg cholesterol, 1 mg sodium.

Banana-Maple Sorbet

PREP: 5 MINUTES PLUS FREEZING

Here's what to do with very ripe bananas—just freeze them, then buzz in the food processor.

4 very ripe medium bananas
⅓ cup maple syrup
1 teaspoon vanilla extract
Pinch salt

1 Peel bananas and place in large self-sealing plastic bag; freeze overnight or until very firm.

2 Slice frozen bananas. In food processor with knife blade attached, blend bananas, syrup, vanilla, and salt until creamy, about 2 minutes. Serve immediately. Makes about 3 cups or 6 servings.

Each serving: About 115 calories, 1 g protein, 29 g carbohydrate, 0 g total fat, 1 g fiber, 0 mg cholesterol, 25 mg sodium.

Lemon-Thyme Sorbet

PREP: 20 MINUTES PLUS FREEZING • COOK: 20 MINUTES

You need lemon thyme for these lovely cool scoops.

1¼ cups sugar
¼ cup light corn syrup
¼ cup loosely packed fresh lemon-thyme sprigs
    plus 1 tablespoon chopped leaves
5 to 7 large lemons

1 In 2-quart saucepan, heat sugar, corn syrup, and *4 cups water* over high heat until sugar dissolves and mixture boils, stirring occasionally. Add lemon-thyme sprigs; cover and boil 2 minutes. Remove syrup from heat; let stand, covered, 10 minutes to allow flavor to develop.

2 Meanwhile, from lemons, finely grate 2 teaspoons peel and squeeze 1⅓ cups juice.

3 Pour syrup mixture through sieve into 8-cup glass measuring cup or large bowl; discard sprigs. Stir in chopped lemon thyme, lemon peel, and juice.

4 Pour juice mixture into 8" by 8" metal baking pan; cover with foil or plastic wrap. Freeze until partially frozen, about 4 hours, stirring occasionally.

5 In food processor with knife blade attached, blend juice mixture until smooth but still frozen. Return mixture to baking pan; cover and freeze until almost firm, at least 3 hours.

6 To serve, return frozen juice mixture to food processor and blend until smooth; serve immediately. Or, remove sorbet from freezer but do not blend; let stand at room temperature 10 minutes to soften slightly. Makes about 4 cups or 8 servings.

Each serving: About 155 calories, 0 g protein, 40 g carbohydrate, 0 g total fat, 0 g fiber, 0 mg cholesterol, 10 mg sodium.

Tropical Rice Pudding

PREP: 10 MINUTES PLUS CHILLING • COOK: 25 MINUTES

The ultimate rice pudding—made with light coconut milk and topped with sliced mango and toasted coconut. Don't pass this one up.

1 cup Japanese or other short-grain white rice
½ cup sugar
½ teaspoon salt
1 can (14 to 15 ounces) unsweetened light
    coconut milk (not cream of coconut)
1 large mango, sliced
½ cup shaved, peeled fresh coconut, toasted, or
    ¼ cup sweetened flaked coconut, toasted

1 In 3-quart saucepan, heat rice, sugar, salt, and 3 *cups water* to boiling over high heat. Reduce heat to low; cover and simmer 15 minutes.

2 Increase heat to medium; stir in coconut milk and cook, uncovered, until rice is tender, about 10 minutes, stirring occasionally.

3 Transfer rice pudding to serving bowl; cover and refrigerate at least 3 hours or overnight to serve cold. Top with mango slices and toasted coconut before serving. Makes about 5 cups or 8 servings.

Each serving: About 225 calories, 2 g protein, 40 g carbohydrate, 6 g total fat (3 g saturated), 1 g fiber, 0 mg cholesterol, 145 mg sodium.

◄ *Banana-Maple Sorbet*

Down-Home Peach Ice Cream

PREP: 20 MINUTES PLUS CHILLING • COOK: 5 MINUTES

An old-fashioned treat for the whole family—sweet homemade ice cream with swirls of crushed peaches.

1 medium lemon
6 ripe medium peaches (about 2 pounds)
¾ cup sugar
1 cup heavy or whipping cream
1 cup milk
1 piece vanilla bean (about 2 inches long), split in half
⅛ teaspoon salt

PEEL LIKE A PRO

1. Submerge peaches in boiling water for 20 to 30 seconds.

2. Plunge them into cold water (just long enough to stop any cooking).

3. Slip the skin off with your finger tips or the tip of a paring knife.

1 From lemon, finely grate ¼ teaspoon peel and squeeze 1 tablespoon juice. Peel and remove pits from peaches; reserve pits. Cut peaches into chunks.

2 In food processor with knife blade attached, combine peaches, sugar, and lemon juice; pulse just to a chunky consistency. Pour peach mixture into bowl; cover and refrigerate until well chilled.

3 Meanwhile, in 2-quart saucepan, combine cream, milk, vanilla bean, salt, lemon peel, and reserved peach pits; heat over medium-high heat just until bubbles form around edge of pan. Pour cream mixture into bowl; cover and refrigerate until well chilled, at least 2 hours.

4 Strain cream mixture through sieve into peach mixture; stir until blended. Pour mixture into ice-cream maker and freeze as manufacturer directs. Serve immediately or place in freezer to harden. Use within 2 weeks. Makes about 5½ cups or 10 servings.

Each serving: About 185 calories, 2 g protein, 25 g carbohydrate, 10 g total fat (6 g saturated), 1 g fiber, 36 mg cholesterol, 35 mg sodium.

Peach Clafouti

PREP: 20 MINUTES • BAKE: 35 TO 40 MINUTES

This country-French dessert pancake typically calls for cherries but is just as delicious with peaches and almonds. We love the puffy golden treat warm with whipped cream.

3 ripe medium peaches (about 1 pound), peeled and sliced
3 large eggs
1 cup half-and-half or light cream
¾ cup all-purpose flour
6 tablespoons margarine or butter, melted and cooled
2 tablespoons almond-flavor liqueur
½ teaspoon vanilla extract
⅛ teaspoon salt
⅓ cup plus 2 tablespoons sugar
¼ cup sliced natural almonds

1 Preheat oven to 400°F. Grease shallow 2-quart casserole or baking dish. Arrange peach slices evenly in casserole.

2 In blender, combine eggs, half-and-half, flour, melted margarine or butter, almond liqueur, vanilla, salt, and ⅓ cup sugar; blend until smooth.

3 Pour batter over peaches; sprinkle with almonds and remaining 2 tablespoons sugar.

4 Bake clafouti 35 to 40 minutes or until puffed and golden brown. Cool on wire rack 15 minutes (clafouti will deflate as it cools). Serve warm. Makes 8 servings.

Each serving: About 275 calories, 6 g protein, 29 g carbohydrate, 15 g total fat (4 g saturated), 1 g fiber, 89 mg cholesterol, 185 mg sodium.

Fruit Compote in Spiced Wine

PREP: 20 MINUTES PLUS CHILLING
COOK: ABOUT 25 MINUTES

This blend of pears, apples, and cranberries is simmered in red-wine syrup for a refreshing dessert.

1 lemon
2 cups dry red wine
1¼ cups sugar
1 tablespoon whole black peppercorns
6 whole cloves
1 cinnamon stick (3 inches long)
4 large Anjou or Bosc pears (about 2 pounds), peeled, cored, and each cut into 12 wedges
4 large Granny Smith apples (about 2 pounds), peeled, cored, and each cut into 16 wedges
2 cups cranberries

1 From lemon, with vegetable peeler, remove 1-inch-wide continuous strip of peel.

2 In 4-quart saucepan, place wine, sugar, peppercorns, cloves, cinnamon stick, lemon peel, and 2 *cups water*; heat to boiling over high heat, stirring frequently, until sugar dissolves. Reduce heat to medium-low; cover and simmer 10 minutes, stirring occasionally. Pour syrup through sieve set over bowl; discard peppercorns and cloves. Return syrup, lemon peel, and cinnamon to saucepan.

3 Add pears and apples to syrup, gently stirring to combine; heat to boiling over medium-high heat. Reduce heat to medium-low; cover and simmer 5 minutes or until apples and pears are tender. Stir in cranberries and cook, covered, 5 minutes longer.

4 Pour fruit mixture into heat-safe bowl and refrigerate at least 4 hours to blend flavors. Makes 12 cups or 16 servings.

Each serving: About 125 calories, 0 g protein, 30 g carbohydrate, 0 g total fat (0 g saturated), 2 g fiber, 0 mg cholesterol, 5 mg sodium.

Old-Time Bread Pudding

PREP: 20 MINUTES PLUS STANDING AND COOLING
BAKE: 45 TO 50 MINUTES

This luscious comfort food is a cinch to prepare and a great way to use day-old bread and ripe bananas.

2 cups half-and-half or light cream
½ cup milk
⅓ cup granulated sugar
2 teaspoons vanilla extract
⅛ teaspoon ground cinnamon
⅛ teaspoon ground nutmeg
3 large eggs
4 ounces day-old Italian bread, cut into ½-inch chunks (4 cups)
3 tablespoons light brown sugar
2 tablespoons margarine or butter
2 large bananas, sliced

1 In large bowl, with wire whisk, beat half-and-half, milk, granulated sugar, vanilla, cinnamon, nutmeg, and eggs until evenly blended. Add bread chunks; let stand 15 minutes, stirring occasionally.

2 Meanwhile, preheat oven to 325°F. Grease shallow 2-quart casserole or 8" by 8" glass baking dish.

3 In nonstick 10-inch skillet, heat brown sugar with margarine or butter over medium heat 5 minutes or until mixture boils and sugar dissolves, stirring frequently. Add banana slices and cook 1 minute, stirring gently to coat evenly. Remove skillet from heat.

4 Gently stir banana mixture into bread mixture; transfer to baking dish. Bake 45 to 50 minutes, until knife inserted near center of pudding comes out clean. Cool pudding on wire rack 30 minutes to serve warm. Makes 8 servings.

Each serving: About 260 calories, 6 g protein, 33 g carbohydrate, 12 g total fat (5 g saturated), 1 g fiber, 101 mg cholesterol, 180 mg sodium.

Cappuccino Cream with Warm Chocolate Sauce

You can make this silky dessert, including the sauce, up to 2 days ahead. Before serving, invert onto plates and drizzle with the semisweet topping. If you'd like, garnish the desserts with chocolate curls (see page 193).

CAPPUCCINO CREAM:
1 envelope unflavored gelatin
¼ cup milk
¾ cup finely ground espresso-coffee beans
   (about ¾ cup coffee beans)
1 cinnamon stick (3 inches long)
½ cup sugar
1¾ cups heavy or whipping cream

CHOCOLATE SAUCE:
2 ounces semisweet chocolate
¼ cup heavy or whipping cream

1 Prepare Cappuccino Cream: In 1-cup glass measuring cup, sprinkle gelatin over milk; set aside to allow gelatin to soften.

2 In 1-quart saucepan, heat ground coffee, cinnamon stick, and 1¼ cups water over high heat just until mixture begins to boil, stirring often. Remove saucepan from heat; cover and let steep 10 minutes.

3 Line sieve with coffee filter or paper towel and place over 2-cup glass measuring cup. Pour coffee mixture into sieve to drain; discard cinnamon stick. (You should have about ¾ cup liquid.)

4 Return liquid coffee to same saucepan. Add gelatin mixture and sugar, and heat over medium-low heat 1 minute or until gelatin and sugar dissolve completely, stirring frequently.

5 Pour coffee mixture and cream into medium bowl set in large bowl of ice water. Stir mixture until it just begins to set, about 20 minutes.

6 Immediately pour cream mixture into eight 4-ounce ramekins or custard cups. Place ramekins on jelly-roll pan for easier handling. Cover and refrigerate until well chilled, at least 4 hours or overnight.

7 Meanwhile, prepare Chocolate Sauce: In 1-quart saucepan, heat chocolate with cream over low heat until chocolate melts, stirring constantly. Remove saucepan from heat; cool 5 minutes.

8 To unmold each Cappuccino Cream, warm small knife under hot water; run along inside edge of ramekin. Then, firmly tap side of ramekin against palm of hand to break seal completely. Invert each ramekin onto a dessert plate. Spoon warm Chocolate Sauce over each dessert to serve. Makes 8 servings.

Each serving without chocolate curls: About 295 calories, 3 g protein, 20 g carbohydrate, 24 g total fat (14 g saturated), 0 g fiber, 83 mg cholesterol, 30 mg sodium.

Sweet Almond Cream

Make this silky, sweet dessert a day ahead and chill.

1 envelope unflavored gelatin
¾ cup heavy or whipping cream
¼ cup packed light brown sugar
1 strip (3" by 1") fresh lemon peel
Pinch salt
2 cups milk
3 tablespoons almond-flavor liqueur or
   ¼ teaspoon almond extract

1 In 1-cup glass measuring cup, evenly sprinkle gelatin over ¼ cup water; let stand 2 minutes to allow gelatin to soften slightly.

2 Meanwhile, in 2-quart saucepan, heat cream, brown sugar, lemon peel, and salt over medium-high heat just until mixture begins to boil, stirring occasionally. Remove saucepan from heat; discard lemon peel.

3 Stir softened gelatin into mixture in saucepan; heat over medium heat 2 minutes or until gelatin dissolves completely, stirring frequently. Remove saucepan from heat.

4 Add milk and liqueur to saucepan and stir until blended. Pour mixture into eight 4-ounce ramekins or custard cups. Place ramekins on jelly-roll pan for easier handling. Cover and refrigerate overnight. Makes 8 servings.

Each serving: About 160 calories, 3 g protein, 12 g carbohydrate, 10 g total fat (6 g saturated), 0 g fiber, 39 mg cholesterol, 60 mg sodium.

Cappuccino Cream with Warm Chocolate Sauce ➤

Pumpkin "Creams"

PREP: 20 MINUTES PLUS CHILLING • COOK: 3 TO 4 MINUTES

Here's a light and luscious dessert with a healthy helping of beta-carotene.

1 envelope unflavored gelatin
1 cup low-fat (1%) milk
1 can (15 ounces) pure pumpkin (not pumpkin-pie mix)
1 can (12 ounces) evaporated low-fat milk
⅔ cup packed light brown sugar
2 teaspoons vanilla extract
½ teaspoon freshly grated lemon peel
8 teaspoons pure maple syrup

1 In small saucepan, evenly sprinkle gelatin over ¼ cup low-fat milk; let stand 2 minutes to soften gelatin.

2 Meanwhile, in medium bowl, with wire whisk, stir pumpkin, evaporated milk, brown sugar, vanilla, lemon peel, and remaining ¾ cup low-fat milk until blended.

3 Heat gelatin mixture in saucepan over low heat just until gelatin dissolves, 3 to 4 minutes, stirring constantly. Pour gelatin mixture into pumpkin mixture in bowl, stirring to blend.

4 Pour pumpkin mixture into eight 8-ounce ramekins or custard cups. Place ramekins on jelly-roll pan for easier handling. Refrigerate until set and well chilled, at least 6 hours or overnight.

5 To serve, drizzle top of each pumpkin cream with 1 teaspoon maple syrup. Makes 8 servings.

Each serving: About 160 calories, 6 g protein, 33 g carbohydrate, 1 g total fat (1 g saturated), 2 g fiber, 5 mg cholesterol, 75 mg sodium.

No-Bake Peaches & Cream Cheesecake

PREP: 45 MINUTES PLUS CHILLING COOK: ABOUT 15 MINUTES

A luscious cheesecake with all the satisfaction of a baked one, without turning on the oven.

2 envelopes unflavored gelatin
2 cups peach nectar
½ cup sugar
4 large egg yolks
2 packages (8 ounces each) cream cheese, softened
1 container (8 ounces) sour cream
1 teaspoon vanilla extract
⅓ cup peach preserves
3 ripe medium peaches (about 1 pound), peeled and thinly sliced
2 tablespoons fresh lemon juice
½ cup pistachio nuts, shells removed (about ¼ cup)

No-Bake Peaches & Cream Cheesecake

1 In small bowl, evenly sprinkle gelatin over *1 cup cold water*. Let stand at room temperature 2 minutes to soften gelatin slightly.

2 In 3-quart saucepan, with wire whisk, mix 1 cup peach nectar with sugar and egg yolks until blended. Cook over medium heat 5 minutes or until slightly thickened and temperature on instant-read thermometer reaches 160°F., stirring constantly (do not boil). Reduce heat to low; whisk in softened gelatin and heat 3 minutes, just until dissolved.

3 Pour gelatin mixture into medium bowl; stir in remaining cup peach nectar. Set bowl with gelatin mixture in larger bowl filled halfway with ice water. With rubber spatula, stir gelatin mixture occasionally until it just begins to set, about 20 minutes. Remove gelatin mixture from bowl of ice water.

4 Meanwhile, in large bowl, with mixer at medium speed, beat cream cheese until very smooth, about 3 minutes. Add sour cream and vanilla, and beat 5 minutes or until blended, scraping bowl often.

5 Gradually beat gelatin mixture into cream-cheese mixture; beat until smooth.

6 Pour cream-cheese mixture into 9-inch springform pan; with spatula, smooth top. Cover with plastic wrap and refrigerate at least 3 hours or overnight, until set.

7 Up to 2 hours before serving, after cheesecake is set, heat preserves in small saucepan over low heat until melted. Press preserves through fine sieve into bowl; cool slightly.

8 When preserves are cool, toss peach slices with lemon juice. Arrange slices on top of cheesecake; brush with preserves. Cover and refrigerate cheesecake until ready to serve.

9 Meanwhile, set aside 1 tablespoon pistachios; finely chop remaining nuts.

10 To serve, loosen cheesecake from side of pan with knife; remove side. Place cheesecake on cake stand or dessert platter. Sprinkle whole pistachios over top of cheesecake. Using cupped hand or flat wide spatula, press remaining pistachios onto side of cake. Makes 16 servings.

Each serving: About 230 calories, 5 g protein, 20 g carbohydrate, 15 g total fat (9 g saturated), 1 g fiber, 90 mg cholesterol, 115 mg sodium.

Chocolate Cheesecake

PREP: 25 MINUTES PLUS CHILLING • BAKE: 50 MINUTES

Silken tofu adds a wonderful smooth texture to this lower-fat chocolate cheesecake. We dare you to stop at 1 forkful.

1 container (19 ounces) silken tofu
1 container (15 ounces) part-skim ricotta cheese
1 ounce unsweetened chocolate
1 package (8 ounces) light cream cheese (Neufchâtel), softened
1 cup packed dark brown sugar
½ cup unsweetened cocoa
2 teaspoons vanilla extract

1 Preheat oven to 325°F. Line large sieve with 2 layers paper towels and set over large bowl. Place tofu and ricotta in sieve and let stand 15 minutes to allow excess liquid to drain; discard liquid.

2 Transfer tofu mixture to food processor with knife blade attached; blend until smooth. Remove ½ cup tofu mixture; set aside.

3 In small saucepan, melt chocolate over low heat. Add reserved tofu mixture to warm chocolate; whisk until blended.

4 To tofu mixture remaining in food processor, add cream cheese, brown sugar, cocoa, vanilla, and chocolate mixture; process just until combined.

5 Pour mixture into 9-inch springform pan. Bake cheesecake 50 minutes or until edge is set and center jiggles slightly. Cool cheesecake in pan on wire rack 1 hour. Refrigerate until cold, at least 4 hours or overnight.

6 To serve, remove side of pan. Makes 12 servings.

Each serving: About 205 calories, 9 g protein, 25 g carbohydrate, 9 g total fat (5 g saturated), 0 g fiber, 18 mg cholesterol, 165 mg sodium.

Holiday
Baked Alaska with
Red-Raspberry Sauce

PREP: 1 HOUR 30 MINUTES PLUS FREEZING
BAKE: 2 TO 3 MINUTES

For this new take on an old favorite, line a dish with ladyfingers and fill with vanilla ice cream and ruby-red sorbet. Then spoon on a dome of meringue, and brown lightly in the oven right before serving. Do-ahead: Make and freeze cake without meringue up to 2 weeks before serving. The sauce can be made up to 3 days ahead. Baked meringue-topped cake can be frozen up to 4 hours before serving. Just remember to remove from freezer 20 minutes before serving for easier slicing.

ICE-CREAM CAKE:
2 pints vanilla ice cream
3 packages (3 to 4½ ounces each) sponge-type
   ladyfingers
2 pints raspberry sorbet

RED-RASPBERRY SAUCE:
1 package (10 ounces) frozen raspberries in
   quick-thaw pouch, thawed
2 tablespoons seedless raspberry jam
1 tablespoon orange-flavor liqueur

MERINGUE:
4 large egg whites
¾ cup sugar
¼ teaspoon salt
¼ teaspoon cream of tartar

Lemon leaves, roses, and berries for garnish

1 Prepare Ice-Cream Cake: Place vanilla ice cream in large bowl; let stand at room temperature to soften slightly, stirring occasionally, until spreadable.

2 Meanwhile, split each ladyfinger in half lengthwise. Line bottom and side of 10" by 1½" round baking dish, shallow 1½-quart round casserole, or 9½-inch deep-dish pie plate with about two-thirds of ladyfingers, placing ladyfingers with rounded side out

around side and allowing ladyfingers to extend above rim of baking dish.

3 Spoon vanilla ice cream into lined dish. Smooth with small metal spatula; place in freezer 30 minutes or until ice cream is firm.

4 Place raspberry sorbet in large bowl; let stand at room temperature to soften slightly, stirring occasionally, until spreadable. Spoon raspberry sorbet on top of ice cream, smoothing with spatula. Top sorbet with remaining ladyfingers. Cover cake with waxed paper and foil; freeze until firm, at least 6 hours.

5 Prepare Red-Raspberry Sauce: Blend all sauce ingredients in food processor until smooth. Pour sauce into small pitcher to serve. Refrigerate until ready to use. Makes about 1⅓ cups sauce.

6 About 30 minutes before serving, prepare Meringue: Preheat oven to 500°F. In large bowl set over simmering water or in top of double boiler, with handheld mixer at medium speed, beat egg whites, sugar, salt, cream of tartar, and *4 teaspoons water* for 12 to 14 minutes, until soft peaks form and temperature on thermometer reaches 160°F. Remove bowl with meringue to work surface. Beat meringue 8 to 10 minutes longer, until stiff peaks form.

7 Remove cake from freezer. Spoon Meringue over top of cake, swirling with spoon to make attractive top. Bake 2 to 3 minutes, until meringue top is lightly browned. Place Baked Alaska on heat-safe platter; garnish with lemon leaves, roses, and berries. Serve immediately, passing Red-Raspberry Sauce at table. Makes 16 servings.

Each serving: About 250 calories, 4 g protein, 40 g carbohydrate, 5 g total fat (3 g saturated), 1 g fiber, 73 mg cholesterol, 95 mg sodium.

◄ *Holiday Baked Alaska with Red-Raspberry Sauce*

Raspberry-Banana Trifle

This beautiful dessert is easier to make than you think—store-bought pound cake and jam are the secret ingredients. Do-ahead: To speed preparation, fill and slice cake day before assembling trifle; wrap and refrigerate until ready to use.

CAKE:
1 frozen pound cake (1 pound), thawed
6 tablespoons seedless red-raspberry jam

CUSTARD:
6 large eggs
¾ cup sugar
⅓ cup cornstarch
4 cups milk
4 tablespoons margarine or butter
2 tablespoons vanilla extract
3 large ripe bananas (1½ pounds), sliced

Raspberry-Banana Trifle

TOPPING:
1 cup heavy or whipping cream
2 tablespoons sugar
Fresh raspberries and fresh mint leaves for garnish

1 Prepare Cake: With serrated knife, cut crust from pound cake. Place cake on 1 long side; cut lengthwise into 4 equal slices. With small spatula, spread 2 tablespoons jam on top of 1 cake slice; top with another cake slice. Repeat with remaining jam and cake, ending with cake. Slice jam-layered cake crosswise into ¼-inch slices, keeping slices together, then cut cake lengthwise in half down center. (You should have about 26 slices jam-layered cake cut in half to make 52 half slices.)

2 Prepare Custard: In medium bowl, with wire whisk, beat eggs, sugar, and cornstarch; set aside. In 4-quart saucepan, heat milk just to boiling. While constantly beating with whisk, gradually pour about half of hot milk into egg mixture. Pour egg mixture back into milk in saucepan, and cook over medium-low heat, whisking constantly, until mixture thickens and begins to bubble around edge of pan; mixture will not boil vigorously. Simmer custard 1 minute, whisking constantly; it must reach at least 160°F. Remove saucepan from heat; stir in margarine or butter with vanilla.

3 Assemble trifle: In 4-quart glass trifle dish or deep glass bowl, place 2 rows of cake slices around side of bowl, alternating horizontal and vertical placement of cake slices to make a checkerboard design (see photo at left). Place some cake slices in a layer to cover bottom of bowl; top with one-third of sliced bananas. Spoon one-third of warm custard on top of bananas. Top with half of remaining bananas and half of remaining custard. Top with remaining cake, then bananas and custard. Cover surface of custard with plastic wrap to prevent skin from forming. Refrigerate trifle 6 hours or overnight.

4 Before serving, prepare Topping: In small bowl, with mixer at medium speed, beat cream with sugar until stiff peaks form. Remove plastic wrap from trifle; top trifle with whipped cream and garnish with raspberries and mint. Makes 24 servings.

Each serving: About 240 calories, 4 g protein, 28 g carbohydrate, 12 g total fat (5 g saturated), 1 g fiber, 72 mg cholesterol, 120 mg sodium.

Chocolate-Dipped Pops

PREP: 20 MINUTES PLUS FREEZING

A fun and easy treat for kids to make and enjoy. Use firm (not overripe) bananas.

12 wooden ice cream–bar sticks
4 large bananas, peeled and cut crosswise into thirds
1 package (6 ounces) semisweet-chocolate chips (1 cup)
2 tablespoons vegetable oil
Choice of toppings (1 cup total) such as: toasted sweetened flaked coconut, chopped salted peanuts, toffee bits, and colored candy décors

1 Insert a wooden stick, about 1 inch deep, into end of each banana piece; place on cookie sheet lined with waxed paper.

2 In heavy, small saucepan, heat chocolate chips with oil over low heat, until chocolate melts and becomes smooth, stirring occasionally. Place each topping on a separate sheet of waxed paper.

3 Holding 1 banana pop over saucepan, spoon some melted chocolate mixture over pop to coat, allowing chocolate to drip back into saucepan. Roll chocolate-coated banana in topping; return to cookie sheet. Repeat with remaining bananas, chocolate, and toppings. Freeze pops at least 1 hour or overnight.

4 To serve, remove chocolate-coated bananas from freezer and let stand at room temperature 5 minutes to soften slightly before eating. If not serving pops same day, place frozen pops in freezer-weight self-sealing plastic bag and freeze up to 1 week. Makes 12 pops.

Each pop: About 185 calories, 1 g protein, 27 g carbohydrate, 9 g total fat (3 g saturated), 1 g fiber, 7 mg cholesterol, 60 mg sodium.

10 LICKETY-SPLIT DESSERTS

Last-minute company? Grumpy kids who want an after-school treat? Try one of these superquick banana desserts:

Premium Pound Cake: Top sliced store-bought marble pound cake with banana slices, drizzle with honey, and sprinkle with toasted almonds.

Creamy Mocha Shake: Buzz frozen banana chunks, milk, coffee frozen yogurt, and chocolate syrup in blender until thickened.

Tropical Fruit Compote: Stir sliced bananas into canned fruit cocktail; sprinkle with freshly grated lime peel.

Pudding Parfait: Layer diced bananas, instant vanilla or chocolate pudding, and crushed cookies (vanilla or chocolate wafers, chocolate sandwich cookies, or shortbread) in a tall glass or goblet.

No-Bake Banana Crisp: Melt butter and brown sugar in skillet; add sliced bananas and orange juice, and cook until fruit is well coated. Spoon into serving dish or individual ramekins and sprinkle with crumbled oatmeal-raisin cookies.

Baked Banana Split: Peel fruit and halve lengthwise. Place in ungreased glass baking dish; sprinkle with chocolate chips; and bake at 350°F. for about 8 to 10 minutes, until chips soften. Serve in bowls topped with scoops of ice cream or frozen yogurt and jarred nuts in caramel syrup.

Waffle Sundae: Heat frozen waffle; warm a mixture of raisins and sliced bananas in maple syrup. Top waffle with a scoop of ice cream and spoon on the sauce.

Banana S'More: Top a graham cracker with sliced fruit, a thin piece of milk chocolate, a marshmallow, and another graham cracker; bake on cookie sheet at 350°F. until warm and gooey.

Frozen Banana Sandwich: Spread a layer of peanut butter on big, chewy store-bought molasses or chocolate-chip cookies; sandwich banana slices between cookies; wrap and freeze until firm.

Chocolate Fondue: Spear 1-inch banana chunks on cocktail picks; dunk into melted semisweet chocolate, then roll in toasted chopped walnuts.

Sweet Plum Cassata

PREP: 35 MINUTES PLUS CHILLING OVERNIGHT
COOK: ABOUT 15 MINUTES

Don't be put off by the timing of this recipe—you have to make it a day ahead so it can firm up enough to slice easily; but that frees up plenty of time to prepare the rest of the meal.

2 large navel oranges
1 tablespoon margarine or butter
1½ pounds ripe purple plums, coarsely chopped
⅓ cup packed light brown sugar
1 container (15 ounces) whole-milk ricotta
½ teaspoon vanilla extract
¼ teaspoon ground cinnamon
½ cup confectioners' sugar
4 teaspoons granulated sugar
1 frozen pound cake (10¾ ounces), cut into
   20 thin slices
Raspberries and mint sprig for garnish

1 From oranges, grate ½ teaspoon peel and squeeze ¾ cup juice. In 10-inch skillet, heat margarine or butter over medium heat. Add plums and brown sugar, and cook 5 minutes or until plums are tender, stir-ring frequently. Stir in ¼ cup orange juice; increase heat to high, and cook 7 to 8 minutes longer, until plums are very tender. Cool to room temperature.

2 Meanwhile, in food processor with knife blade attached, blend ricotta until smooth (or press ricotta through fine-meshed sieve over medium bowl). Stir in orange peel, vanilla, cinnamon, and confectioners' sugar. Cover and refrigerate until ready to use.

3 In 1-quart saucepan, heat granulated sugar and remaining ½ cup orange juice to boiling over medi-um heat; cook 1 minute. Cool orange syrup to room temperature.

4 Line 8½" by 4½' loaf pan with plastic wrap, leav-ing a 4-inch overhang around rim. Arrange 5 slices of pound cake, slightly overlapping, on bottom of loaf pan. Brush each slice with orange syrup before top-ping with next slice. Spread half the ricotta mixture over cake slices.

5 Top with 5 more slices pound cake, brushing with syrup and overlapping slightly; spread with plum mix-ture. Top with 5 slices pound cake, brushing with syrup and overlapping slightly; spread with remaining ricotta. Top with remaining pound cake slices, brush-ing with syrup and overlapping as before. Fold plastic wrap over to cover completely. Refrigerate overnight.

6 To serve, open plastic wrap. Invert cake onto long platter. Lift off loaf pan and plastic wrap. Garnish with raspberries and mint sprig. Makes 10 servings.

Each serving: About 300 calories, 6 g protein, 40 g carbohydrate, 14 g total fat (5 g saturated), 2 g fiber, 21 mg cholesterol, 145 mg sodium.

WHAT'S IN A NAME?

A cassata is an Italian dessert whose name liter-ally means "encased" or "in a case," which is probably a reference to a cassata's construction: creamy filling encased by layers of cake. The lav-ish confection originated in Sicily, where it is often prepared for special celebrations, such as weddings or Easter. Elaborate versions are lay-ered with candied fruit and chocolate and en-robed in marzipan. Our shortcut recipe (above) contains the required ricotta and orange-flavored syrup, but is made with store-bought pound cake to save time.

Mini Éclairs

PREP: 1 HOUR PLUS CHILLING • BAKE: 35 MINUTES

The traditional way of making these petite pastries is time-consuming. But we sped things up by baking long strips of cream-puff dough on a cookie sheet, then filling and icing strips before cutting them into small portions. Do-ahead: You can easily make all 3 components of this dessert the day before serving. Refrigerate pastry cream and glaze separately until ready to use. Wrap and store baked and split pastry strips at room temperature. When ready to glaze, warm chocolate glaze in saucepan over low heat and decorate éclair tops. Pastry strips also freeze well; make up to 1 month ahead and wrap in foil before freezing. Thaw unwrapped on wire rack to maintain their crispness.

PASTRY CREAM:
3 large egg yolks
⅓ cup sugar
3 tablespoons cornstarch
1½ cups milk
1 tablespoon margarine or butter
2 teaspoons vanilla extract

CREAM-PUFF DOUGH:
6 tablespoons margarine or butter
1 cup all-purpose flour
1 tablespoon sugar
¼ teaspoon salt
4 large eggs

CHOCOLATE GLAZE:
4 ounces semisweet chocolate
1 tablespoon margarine or butter
1 tablespoon milk
1 tablespoon light corn syrup

1 Prepare Pastry Cream: In medium bowl, with wire whisk, beat egg yolks, sugar, and cornstarch; set aside. In 2-quart saucepan, heat milk just to boiling. While constantly beating with whisk, gradually pour about half of hot milk into yolk mixture. Pour yolk mixture back into milk in saucepan and cook over medium-low heat, whisking constantly, until mixture thickens and begins to bubble around edge of pan; mixture will not boil vigorously. Simmer pastry cream 1 minute, whisking constantly; it must reach at least

160°F. Remove saucepan from heat; stir in margarine or butter with vanilla. Transfer mixture to bowl; cover surface with plastic wrap to prevent skin from forming, and refrigerate until cold, at least 2 hours.

2 Meanwhile, prepare Cream-Puff Dough: Preheat oven to 400°F. Grease and flour large cookie sheet (17" by 14"). In 2-quart saucepan, heat margarine or butter with *1 cup water* over high heat until mixture boils. Reduce heat to low; add flour with sugar and salt all at once, and stir vigorously with wooden spoon until mixture forms ball and leaves side of saucepan. Remove saucepan from heat. Add eggs, 1 at a time, beating well with wooden spoon after each addition, until mixture is smooth and shiny.

3 Spoon dough into decorating bag with large round tip (about ½ inch in diameter). Pipe dough in five 12-inch-long strips (about 1 inch wide) lengthwise down cookie sheet, leaving 1½ inches between strips.

4 Bake strips 30 minutes or until golden. Remove cookie sheet from oven; poke strips in several places with fork to let out steam. Bake 5 minutes longer. Remove strips from cookie sheet. While strips are warm, slice each strip horizontally in half to make top and bottom halves. Cool completely on wire rack. When cool, with fingertips, remove some of soft centers from top and bottom halves.

5 While strips are cooling, prepare Chocolate Glaze: In heavy small saucepan, melt all glaze ingredients over low heat, stirring frequently. Spoon warm glaze into sturdy plastic bag. Cut tip of bag to make small hole; use to drizzle glaze in crosshatch pattern over éclair-strip tops.

6 With clean decorating bag and tip, fill cooled éclair-strip bottoms with Pastry Cream (do not overfill—you may have a small amount of cream left over). Top with glazed tops and refrigerate until ready to serve, up to 1 hour.

7 To serve, cut strips crosswise with serrated knife into 2-inch-long pieces. Makes 30 éclairs.

Each éclair: About 100 calories, 2 g protein, 11 g carbohydrate, 6 g total fat (1 g saturated), 0 g fiber, 51 mg cholesterol, 75 mg sodium.

Dark Chocolate-Rum Truffles

PREP: 25 MINUTES PLUS CHILLING

We made these bittersweet confections with gutsy, dark Jamaican rum, but you can omit it or use your favorite liqueur instead. We like them with Grand Marnier, amaretto, or coffee-flavored liqueur too. Do-ahead: Make ahead and store in refrigerator for up to 2 weeks or freeze for up to 1 month. Remove from freezer 10 minutes before serving.

3 ounces bittersweet chocolate*
½ cup heavy or whipping cream
3 tablespoons unsalted butter, softened and
   cut up
2 tablespoons dark Jamaican rum
⅓ cup hazelnuts (filberts), toasted, with skins
   removed, and finely chopped (see page 213)
3 tablespoons unsweetened cocoa

Dark Chocolate-Rum Truffles

1 In food processor with knife blade attached, blend chocolate until finely ground.

2 In 1-quart saucepan, heat heavy cream to boiling over medium-high heat. With food processor running, add hot cream, butter, and rum to chocolate and blend until smooth.

3 Grease 9" by 5" metal loaf pan; line with plastic wrap. Pour chocolate mixture into pan; spread evenly. Refrigerate until cool and firm enough to cut, about 3 hours, or freeze 1 hour.

4 Remove chocolate mixture from pan by lifting edges of plastic wrap and inverting chocolate block onto cutting board; discard plastic wrap. Cut chocolate into 32 pieces. (To cut chocolate mixture easily, dip knife in hot water and wipe dry.)

5 Place chopped hazelnuts in a small bowl; place cocoa in another small bowl. One at a time, dip 16 chocolate pieces in hazelnuts to coat. Dip remaining chocolate pieces in cocoa. Store in tightly covered container, with waxed paper between layers, in refrigerator. Makes 32 truffles.

*Or, in place of bittersweet chocolate, use 7 ounces semisweet and 1 ounce unsweetened chocolate.

Each truffle: About 70 calories, 1 g protein, 5 g carbohydrate, 6 g total fat (3 g saturated), 0 g fiber, 8 mg cholesterol, 2 mg sodium.

INDEX

CREDITS

Cover: Mark Thomas. Page 8 (left): David Kelley. Page 8 (middle): Alexandra Grablewski. Page 8 (right): Michael Kraus. Page 9: James Worrell. Page 10: Michael Kraus. Page 11 (left): Michael Kraus. Page 11 (center): Michael Grimm. Pages 12-13: James Worrell. Page 14: Alexandra Grablewski. Page 15 (left): David Kelley. Page 15 (right): Michael Kraus. Pages 16-17: Devon Jarvis. Page 18: James Worrell. Page 19: David Kelley. Page 20: Michael Kraus. Page 23: Steven Mark Needham. Page 25: Alan Richardson. Page 26: Brian Hagiwara. Page 31: Ann Stratton. Page 32: Mark Thomas. Page 36: Ann Stratton. Page 40: Rita Maas. Pages 42 & 43: Ann Stratton. Page 44: Mark Thomas. Page 49: Rita Maas. Page 53: Ann Stratton. Page 55: Rita Maas. Pages 56, 59, 60, 62 & 65: Ann Stratton. Page 66: Michael Kraus. Pages 68, 72 & 76: Brian Hagiwara. Page 79: Steven Mark Needham. Page 82: Mark Thomas. Page 84: Ann Stratton. Page 88: Brian Hagiwara. Pages 92 & 94: Steven Mark Needham. Page 96: Brian Hagiwara. Pages 101 & 105: Mark Thomas. Page 107: Brian Hagiwara. Pages 108, 112 & 116: Mark Thomas. Page 121: Rita Maas. Page 124: Brian Hagiwara. Page 129: Ann Stratton. Page 131: Brian Hagiwara. Page 135: Mark Thomas. Page 136: Rita Maas. Page 143: Brian Hagiwara. Pages 144 & 146: Mark Thomas. Pages 151 & 154: Ann Stratton. Page 157: Mark Thomas. Page 159: Ann Stratton. Page 162: Mark Thomas. Page 164: Guy Kloppenburg. Page 167: Rita Maas. Page 175: Mary Ellen Bartley. Pages 177, 181, 183 & 184: Ann Stratton. Page 187: Alexandra Grablewski. Page 189: Ann Stratton. Page 191: Alison Miksch. Page 193: Brian Hagiwara. Pages 197 & 198: Ann Stratton. Page 201: Steven Mark Needham. Page 204: Mary Ellen Bartley. Pages 209, 211 & 214: Mark Thomas. Page 225: Ann Stratton. Page 228: Alison Miksch. Page 230: Alan Richardson. Pages 233 & 234: Ann Stratton. Pages 236 & 238: Brian Hagiwara. Page 241: Mark Thomas. Page 243: Brian Hagiwara.

METRIC CONVERSIONS

LENGTH

If you know:	Multiply by:	To find:
INCHES	25.0	MILLIMETERS
INCHES	2.5	CENTIMETERS
FEET	30.0	CENTIMETERS
YARDS	0.9	METERS
MILES	1.6	KILOMETERS
MILLIMETERS	0.04	INCHES
CENTIMETERS	0.4	INCHES
METERS	3.3	FEET
METERS	1.1	YARDS
KILOMETERS	0.6	MILES

VOLUME

If you know:	Multiply by:	To find:
TEASPOONS	5.0	MILLILITERS
TABLESPOONS	15.0	MILLILITERS
FLUID OUNCES	30.0	MILLILITERS
CUPS	0.24	LITERS
PINTS	0.47	LITERS
QUARTS	0.95	LITERS
GALLONS	3.8	LITERS
MILLILITERS	0.03	FLUID OUNCES
LITERS	4.2	CUPS
LITERS	2.1	PINTS
LITERS	1.06	QUARTS
LITERS	0.26	GALLONS

WEIGHT

If you know:	Multiply by:	To find:
OUNCES	28.0	GRAMS
POUNDS	0.45	KILOGRAMS
GRAMS	0.035	OUNCES
KILOGRAMS	2.2	POUNDS

TEMPERATURE

If you know:	Multiply by:	To find:
DEGREES FAHRENHEIT	0.56 (AFTER SUBTRACTING 32)	DEGREES CELSIUS
DEGREES CELSIUS	1.8 (THEN ADD 32)	DEGREES FAHRENHEIT